HOW TO REFORM THE GLOBAL DEBT AND FINANCIAL ARCHITECTURE

HOW TO REFORM THE GLOBAL DEBT AND FINANCIAL ARCHITECTURE

Edited by James Thuo Gathii

SHERIA
PUBLISHING
HOUSE

This book was published by Sheria Publishing House, an independent publishing house that publishes books that prioritize the development of affordable, accessible and high-quality legal materials.

Copyright by The Severlal Contributors (2023)

For more information, visit www.sheriapublishinghouse.com

ISBN: 979-8-9885111-0-6

Cover and interior page design and layout
by Stephen Tiano / stephen@stephentianobookdesign.com

Contents

Acknowledgments		vii
Contributors		ix
Introduction		xi
CHAPTER 1	*The Pressing Call for an International Debt Restructuring Framework and The Potential Gains Its Creation Will Have for African Countries*	
	Magalie Masamba	25
CHAPTER 2	*Designing an African Common Position and Strategy on Vulture Litigation*	
	Marie-Louise F. Aren	49
CHAPTER 3	*Deterring Debt Vultures from Distressed African Sovereign Debt*	
	Geoffrey Adonu	85
CHAPTER 4	*The Case Against International Arbitration in Sovereign Debt Contexts*	
	Geoffrey Adonu	109
CHAPTER 5	*Sovereign Debt as Investments: Dispute Resolution and Restructuring in Times of Crisis*	
	Ohio Omiunu and Titilayo Adebola	131
CHAPTER 6	*Debt Restructuring under the G20 Common Framework: Austerity Again? The Case of Zambia and Chad*	
	Nona Tamale	153

CHAPTER 7	*COVID-19 and Balance-of-Payments Crisis in Africa: A Critique of the IMF-WTO Convergence of Roles in the Balance-of-Payments Surveillance of Developing Countries* Akinyi J. Eurallyah	167
CHAPTER 8	*Supervising Sovereign Debt Restructuring Through the United Nations* Kelvin Mbithi	197
CHAPTER 9	*The African Sovereign Debt Crisis: Is the African Repo Market the Solution?* Horman Chitonge	217
CHAPTER 10	*The Challenge of Collateralization of Public Assets in Loan Contracts and Indentures: What is the Way Forward?* Ian Muriithi	253
CHAPTER 11	*China, Have Mercy: The Unacceptable Collateralised Sovereign Debt Burden that the Busanga Hydropower Plant Places in the DRC* Nciko wa Nciko	279
CHAPTER 12	*The Coloniality of Sovereign Debt* Bharath Gururagavendran	301
	Index	329

Acknowledgments

This book on Reforming the Global Debt and Financial Architecture featuring a new generation of thinkers was only possible because of the support of many people committed to this cause.

First, the African Sovereign Debt Justice Network, (AfSDJN), thanks the Open Society Institute for Southern Africa (OSISA) for the support that made this book and the workshops and seminars that preceded it possible. AfSDJN in particular thanks Lucia Makamure our Program Officer at OSISA for her guidance.

Second, the AfSDJN thanks the authors for their chapters and for participating in an authors' workshop and the 2022 AfSDJN Summer Debt Academy that was devoted to providing feedback for their chapters under the leadership of the Editors of Afronomicslaw.Org.

Third, the AfSDJN thanks the many research assistants who helped with organizational details and bluebook editing for all the chapters. These include Edward Cain, Kevin Cremoux, Visse Chantz, Rachel DeCaluwe, Geoffrey Adonu, and Walter Elochukwu Abah.

Last but not least, AfSDJN thanks Stephen Tiano for the cover and interior page design and layout.

Contributors

Editor

James Thuo Gathii is the Wing-Tat Lee Chair of International Law at Loyola University Chicago School of Law; the 2022–23 William H. Neukom Fellows Research Chair in Diversity and Law American Bar Foundation and Editor, Afronomicslaw.

Contributors

Titilayo Adebola is Lecturer, University of Aberdeen School of Law; Associate Director, Center for Commercial Law and Editor, Afronomicslaw.org

Geoffrey Adonu is an international lawyer and a sovereign debt consultant at Afronomicslaw. He received a J.D. from University at Buffalo School of Law in 2023, an LLM from New York University School of Law in 2020 and has an LLB from Babcock University.

Eurallyah J. Akinyi is PhD Candidate, (Sovereign Debt & International Financial Regulation) Schulich Law School, Dalhousie University. She holds LL.M. (International Trade and Investment Laws in Africa) from the University of Pretoria, 2019) and is an Advocate of the High Court of Kenya.

Marie-Louise Aren, Doctoral Candidate of International Tax Law at the University of Pretoria in South Africa. Before that she was Principal Law Researcher and Legislative Drafter of the Law Reform Commission of Nigeria. She holds a Masters Degree in International Trade and Investment Law from the University of Pretoria.

Horman Chitonge is a Professor of African Studies at the Centre for African Studies, University of Cape Town. He is a widely published author on economic development in Africa, agrarian political economy, poverty and inequality and alternatives for African economic growth.

Bharath Gururagavendran is an incoming student at NYU's Graduate School, pursuing a Master's in International Relations. Previously, he held the position of Assistant Professor at Jindal Global Law School.

Dr. Magalie L. Masamba is a Senior Fellow of the African Sovereign Debt Justice Network (AfSDJN) and a Post-Doctoral Law Fellow at the International Development Law Unit of the University of Pretoria's Centre for Human Rights.

Kelvin Mbithi is a lawyer and Certified Professional Mediator. He has published various works on human rights, elections, and campaign financing. He writes for his blog https://mbithiopinions.wordpress.com/

Ian Muriithi is an Advocate of the High Court of Kenya and Legal Assistant at CPF Financial Services Limited.

Nciko wa Nciko is an LL. M Candidate at the Geneva Graduate Institute of International and Development Studies. He is also an Amnesty International Regional Researcher on Climate Justice in Southern Africa and its lead adviser on human rights in Madagascar.

Ohio Omiunu, Reader/Associate Professor in Law Kent Law School and Editor Afronomicslaw.org

Introduction

James Thuo Gathii

This book brings together African voices on reforming the global debt and financial architecture convened by the African Sovereign Debt Justice Network (AfSDJN). The global debt and financial architecture is a colonial legacy established when the most debt vulnerable countries in Asia and Africa were not at the table. Africa's 55 countries are therefore under-represented in the governance structures of the International Monetary Fund (IMF) where they have a meagre 6.01% of the voting rights. The IMF sits at the helm of the global debt and financial architecture. Its governance system established by its Articles of Agreement is based on weighted voting. This means that the US with over 17% of the voting share at the IMF has an effective veto over any fundamental reforms of the system because 85% of the total voting power is required for any change in the voting structure. This in turn means the US Treasury and government have disproportionate influence over the affairs of the IMF including its role with regard to the sovereign debt crisis. Further, when the votes of the permanent members of the Paris Club are added to the weighted shares of the US at the IMF, it is quite clear the poorest economies of the world have no influence at the IMF. Since the approval of Paris Club members is necessary before the commencement of any renegotiation of sovereign debt, the subordination of indebted countries is etched into the architecture of the global debt and financial architecture.

From this perspective, the indebtedness of African countries is a systemic, structural and endemic feature of the global order. Sovereign indebtedness is not episodic and it requires fundamental or structural reform both at the global and national levels. At the global level, the kind of sustained reform required must include the tools the IMF uses to assess debt sustainability. The debt sustainability analysis the

IMF conducts to assess whether a country suffers from a temporary liquidity problem is heavily weighted in favor of continued borrowing. This imperative to repay debt means indebted governments have to prioritize debt repayments ahead of funding domestic priorities like education and food. It also means indebted countries are required to take stringent fiscal consolidation or austerity measures that offload the costs and risks of borrowing to them and their most vulnerable citizens who are the least culpable in contracting unsustainable debt. For these reasons, the practices of the IMF, the Paris Club and private creditors are opaque, inequitable and insensitive to the needs of borrower countries.

This book rejects minimalist reforms to the global debt architecture favored by the IMF such as the Common Framework and the new Global Sovereign Debt Roundtable bringing in China. The IMF and private creditors want minimalist reforms to the global financial system that are just enough to contain the pressure for more radical reform while they reap massive profits. Such minimalist reforms serve to kick the can down the road—they do not challenge the unequal governance of the IMF that is based on the assumption that the current international financial system is here to stay.

The menu of fundamental reforms should go beyond the minimalist reforms such as the Common Framework for Debt Treatments or the New Global Debt Roundtable. They could include past efforts led by the IMF like the Sovereign Debt Restructuring Mechanism, (SDRM) proposed in 2002, which would have provided a statutory framework with strengthened incentives for a sovereign and its creditors to reach a collaborative agreement on a restructuring. The SDRM would have allowed a stay on disruptive litigation by holdouts with the sovereign protecting creditor interests during the stay. Majority restructuring would have facilitated new money from private creditors during a stay. However, the SDRM was defeated by the United States at the behest of the private creditors. Civil society groups as well as the United Nations Conference on Trade and Development (UNCTAD) have long supported a sovereign debt restructuring mechanism that would be binding on all creditors, including commercial creditors, and that would make it difficult for hold-out creditors to prevent sovereign debt workouts.

In the United Nations, a 2014 Resolution adopted nine principles to guide establishment of a multinational legal framework sovereign debt restructuring. These principles, still relevant to the yet to be created framework are: sovereignty, good faith, transparency, equitable treatment of creditors, sovereign immunity, legitimacy, sustainability and majority restructuring. While these principles were agreeable to the United States and the United Kingdom, these two countries have favored resolution of sovereign debt issues outside the United Nations and instead preferred forums that they control with their voice and vote.

It is key to note that after the 2008 financial crisis, a UN Panel chaired by Joseph Stiglitz recommended UN oversight of the global financial system. The Stiglitz panel further argued in favor of a treaty regime to overcome the inefficiencies of multiple overlapping legal jurisdictions in which debt instruments had been taken out. The panel also proposed an oversight commission to mediate and supervise the restructuring process.

Without reforms like these that include indebted countries and the broad range of assorted creditors, it is not possible to produce legitimate and functional debt restructuring mechanisms. But there are even more far-reaching possible reforms like debt cancellation. This is not new. The London Debt Agreement of 1953, effectively canceled Germany's external debts. This cancellation has been one of the key factors accounting for Germany's post second world war economic success. Cancellation of sovereign debt was also pursued when in 2003 the Paris Club agreed to an 80% reduction of Iraq's external debt that included bilateral debt of over 42 billion, non-Paris club bilateral debt of over 67 billion, commercial debt of 20 billion and multilateral debt of half a billion dollars. This cancellation also came with shielding Iraq oil-related assets from creditor attachment, garnishment or execution under UN Security Council Resolution 1483 of May 22, 2003. An Executive Order of then US President George W. Bush immunized other Iraqi assets that very day. Para 16 of the foregoing UN Security Council Resolution may be of particular interest. It called "upon the international financial institutions to assist the people of Iraq in the reconstruction and development of their economy and to facilitate assistance by the broader donor community," as well as creditors.

The 1953 German and 2003 Iraq debt cancellations show that when the countries that control the global financial and security system want to achieve far reaching results on debt resolution, that it can be done. If Iraq reconstruction[1] could not

---

[1] Simon Hinrichsen, *The Iraq sovereign debt restructuring,* 16 Cap. Mkts. L.J. 95, 95–114 (2021).

happen without the debt overhung as the invading powers argued, then this is not possible especially for highly indebted economies following the COVID19 pandemic, the climate crisis and all the other crisis facing African countries.[2]

Another reality that African countries have to contend with now unlike when the current global financial architecture was set up, is that there are different kinds of lenders beyond the Bretton Woods institutions. For example, there are state owned banks like the China Development Bank. These public/private entities are raising questions about their governance within the current global debt architecture. In addition, today a much bigger share of Africa's debt is held by private creditors unlike a few decades ago.

One of the consequences of having more debt held by private creditors is the predominance of a contractual approach in debt restructuring processes. Under this approach, collective action and pari passu clauses have played a key role in coordinating restructurings. That has meant that the domestic law rules of the venues that govern private debt such as New York and London play a key role in restructurings. Under pressure from civil society groups, New York is considering multiple reform options including blocking taxes that fund US contributions to debt relief initiatives from funding bailouts of private creditors, and ensuring it supports spending on health (e.g. coronavirus vaccines and treatments), education, and other services for the most vulnerable in debtor countries.[3]

The chapters in this book advocate for overhauling the current ad hoc restructuring processes that are dominated by the former colonial powers and that only minimally represent the interests of African countries. The chapters expose how global capital is sheltered by the IMF and World Bank so that they evade and avoid confrontation with global publics who demand provisioning of basic needs such as affordable housing, medicines, food, healthcare in addition to democratizing the global

---

[2] International Panel of Experts on Sustainable Food Systems, Breaking the cycle of unsustainable food systems, hunger, and debt, Feb. 2023 (Relationship between debt and food prices—in other words austerity is the background condition on the ground that people have to suffer and live through without fundamental reforms).

[3] Rafael Bernal, *New York Democrats push bills to stop sovereign debt* "vulture funds," THE HILL, May 3, 2023.

financial and economic system. These legitimate demands of the global publics are key to providing the political momentum necessary to challenge the risk-averse and profit-oriented nature of global finance industry that has prevented more fundamental changes.

This book has 12 chapters that explore the foregoing themes in greater depth. Against the background of the long and checkered history of putting in place a global sovereign debt restructuring mechanism, in Chapter 1 Magalie Masamba[4] examines innovations for restructuring sovereign debt following the COVID19 pandemic. She discusses how Zambia became the first country to default on its debt in the COVID19 era and yet as of this writing has not managed to restructure its debt. As Zambia's experience shows, having a global sovereign debt restructuring mechanism is critical as many African countries continue to face high levels of debt distress following the COVID19 pandemic. Masamba examines the Debt of Vulnerable Economies (DOVE) Fund, the Debt Relief for a Green and Inclusive Recovery initiative and the now expired G20's Debt Service Suspension Initiative, (DSSI) and the Common Framework for Debt Treatments beyond the DSSI among others. Noting their ad hoc nature and related shortcomings, she argues in favor of a formal global debt restructuring mechanism informed by Africa's concerns and that is based on a human rights approach. She argues that as a starting point, consideration should be given to broad-based forgiveness such as was done under the Highly Indebted Poor Countries Initiative (HIPIC). In a key and important contribution, Masamba argues in favor of a parallel solution—an African regional solution through the establishment of an African Sovereign Debt Forum where African debtors and creditors can negotiate and discuss restructurings and other questions of debt sustainability. The value of such a forum she argues, would be that it would create a center of excellence that would also serve as a repository of African knowledge on contemporary sovereign debt restructuring. It would develop a model Sovereign debt restructuring statute and a model contractual approach. It would also provide resources and technical assistance to assist countries in debt distress."

---

[4] Magalie Masamba, *Chapter 1: "The Pressing Call for an International Debt Restructuring Framework and The Potential Gains its Creation will have for African Countries."*

Marie-Louise F. Aren's chapter[5] also takes up an African centered theme. It argues in favor of designing an African common position and strategy on vulture fund litigation. Vulture funds destabilize sovereign debt restructurings by purchasing distressed debts at discounted prices in the secondary markets and holding out to recover its full face value or for amounts far exceeding the face value through expensive and long-drawn out debt litigation. Marie-Louise argues that to prevent vulture funds sabotaging post-pandemic recovery efforts, African countries should act collectively. She argues that Africa should design a common position on vulture fund litigation. She shows that the Common African Position On The Post 2015 Development Agenda of the African Union only contains aspirational language seeking Africa's full and equitable representation in international financial and economic institutions. She outlines the key reasons for adopting a common African position on vulture funds. These include strengthening Africa's voice in negotiations on reform of the global financial architecture. A common position would also promote African solidarity and coordination which is necessary to counter the manipulative and exploitative tendencies of more powerful countries. Such united positions on a key question of shared vulnerability would also make it more difficult for powerful countries to divide African countries.

Geoffrey Adonu has two chapters in this volume. In Chapter 3 he discusses deterring debt vultures from distressed African debts.[6] This chapter complements Marie Louise's chapter very well. It does so by discussing in detail the business model that vulture funds pursue; the various international and domestic solutions devised to control them, including contractual mechanisms such as collective action clauses, redesignation and pacman techniques, exit consents and amendments, model pari passu clauses, trust structures as well as natural disaster clauses. Quite clearly the use of these mechanisms presupposes high levels of expertise and technical proficiency. Adonu therefore proposes the creation of a fund to finance countering the disruptive activities of vulture funds.

---

[5] Marie-Louise F. Aren, *Chapter 2: "Designing an African Common Position and Strategy on Vulture Fund Litigation."*

[6] Geoffrey Adonu, *Chapter 3: "Deterring Debt Vultures from Distressed African Sovereign Debt."*

INTRODUCTION xvii

In his second chapter in this book, Adonu discusses the case against international arbitration in sovereign debt contexts.[7] He shows how sovereign creditors have now resorted to pursuing enforcement of their claims through investor state dispute settlement or arbitration. This preference for arbitration, he shows, is favored by creditors because of the stronger enforcement regime for international arbitration awards as an alternative to domestic litigation in creditor friendly financial centers like New York and London. He argues that the stronger enforcement regime of international arbitration and other features of arbitration like confidentiality of arbitral proceedings can worsen holdout problems, prevent accountability in public debt transactions, exacerbate intercreditor asymmetry and threaten debt sustainability of debt-distressed countries which makes arbitration unsuitable in the sovereign debt context.

Ohio Omiunu and Titilayo Adebola's chapter also discusses investor state dispute settlement or use of arbitration in the context of sovereign debt.[8] Their chapter provides a very useful summary of the variety of arbitration provisions in the Financial Services Chapters of US and EU Bilateral Investment Treaties, (BITs). They recommend that BITS should carve out arbitration over sovereign debt cases because of the costs that are associated with arbitration over sovereign debt. Their overall argument is that developing countries contemplating FTAs with capital exporting countries should be vigilant in avoiding arbitration clauses over sovereign debt. Yet as they note some investors prefer to have the ability to invoke arbitration over their sovereign debt should any problems arise. On their part, developing countries they argue, have to consider the need to protect their policy space to deal with debt restructurings without the threat of expensive and destabilizing arbitration proceedings.

Nona Tamale's chapter discusses one of the consequences of Africa's indebtedness—the imposition of IMF austerity programs as a condition for debt restructurings using the case of Zambia and Chad.[9] These austerity programs impose cuts in public

---

[7] Geoffrey Adonu, *Chapter 4: "The Case Against International Arbitration in Sovereign Debt Contexts."*
[8] Ohio Omiunu & Titilayo Adebola, *Chapter 5: "Sovereign Debt as Investments: Dispute Resolution and Restructuring in Times of Crisis."*
[9] Nona Tamale, *Chapter 6: "Debt Restructuring under the G20 Common Framework: Austerity Again? The Case of Zambia and Chad."*

wage bills and in social programs which cripple critical social sectors like health and education. Countries in extreme debt distress like Zambia and Chad accept to implement these austerity measures, on the advice on the IMF, during the negotiations with their creditors, to prove to their willingness to meet their debt servicing obligations and hopefully to guarantee successful outcomes in the restructuring process. Unfortunately, austerity as Nona shows has devastating impacts that disproportionately affect the most vulnerable and marginalized groups in society who rely on public services. Nona therefore argues that taking the austerity path is counterproductive in achieving long term debt sustainability. Austerity, she argues, also contradicts the principle of shared responsibility between lenders and borrowers espoused in various sovereign debt soft law instruments, including in the G20 Operational Guidelines for Sustainable Finance and UNCTAD's Principles on Promoting Responsible Sovereign Lending and Borrowing.

Akinyi J. Eurallyah's chapter examines another economic reality for indebted African sovereigns—their Balance of Payments problems in the context of the challenges brought about by the COVID19 pandemic.[10] Balance of Payment difficulties for indebted sovereigns bring into the picture, the World Trade Organization, (WTO), alongside the IMF. Under the WTO's General Agreement on Tariffs and Trade, (GATT), countries that are members of both the WTO and the IMF can impose quantitative import restrictions to safeguard their external financing position. Since African economies are heavily dependent on foreign trade, their economic growth is highly sensitive and vulnerable to developments in external trade. Yet the coordination between the IMF and the WTO has discouraged developing countries from using quantitative restrictions to protect their balance of payments. In the WTO, Akinyi shows, litigation against developing countries that have used quantitative measures to enable them to balance their payments have suffered harsh defeats. It is not any better in the IMF where the opportunity to use quantitative measures is narrowly construed to deny developing countries the power to use it without violating the IMF's restrictions on interfering with trade liberalization. Unfortunately

---

[10] Akinyi J. Eurallyah, *Chapter 7: "COVID-19 and Balance-of-Payments Crisis in Africa: A Critique of the IMF-WTO Convergence of Roles in the Balance-of-Payments Surveillance of Developing Countries."*

for developing countries, the flexibility to use quantitative restrictions as one of their WTO privileges, referred to as special and differential treatment, has come to naught. Akinyi's chapter therefore shows how the convergence in the mandates of the IMF and the WTO over balance of payments works to systematically disadvantage indebted developing countries and to discourage them from even considering using quantitative restrictions as part of their policy tool kit.

Another major theme that runs through the book is the legacy of imperialism evident in the current global debt and financial architecture. Kelvin Mbithi's chapter examines this architecture using a Third World Approaches to International Law (TWAIL) lens.[11] In his view, the current architecture has roots in the imperial past though today this imperialism is maintained not through brute force in debt collection, but rather through more indirect means such as economic conditionalities or austerity. In addition, the former imperial powers still have the power to block and reduce access to credit to formerly colonized countries thereby raising the cost of living in those countries and slowing down their development. Ultimately, Mbithi proposes a binding debt restructuring mechanism under the auspices of the United Nations. He recalls that there are historical precedents calling for such an institutional solution in the various engagements over the last few decades in UNCTAD. For Mbithi such a solution would overcome the current ad hoc restructuring system that is dominated by creditors and that puts the human rights of African citizens and the sovereignty of African countries in jeopardy.

Horman Chitonge's chapter evaluates the establishment of the Liquidity Sustainability Facility, (LSF)—or the African Repo Market.[12] He argues that the LSF if implemented as proposed will reproduce a discriminatory development financing structure. For Chitonge, the African repo market will impose a penalty on poorer African countries, leaving only a few countries with stronger economic fundamentals to benefit from this facility. His chapter proceeds from the premise that the sovereign debt crisis in Africa is merely a symptom of a fundamental economic problem—the

---

[11] Kelvin Mbithi, *Chapter 8: "Supervising Sovereign Debt Restructuring Through the United Nations."*
[12] Horman Chitonge, *Chapter 9: "The African Sovereign Debt Crisis: Is the African Repo Market the Solution."*

lack of economic resilience as a result of specializing in the production and export of primary commodities in African economies. He argues that without addressing this structural problem, the sovereign debt crisis will keep recurring for a long time to come.

Ian Muriithi's chapter evaluates the collateralization of public assets in loan contracts and indentures.[13] Collateralization of State-owned assets such as commodities has become more frequent in the recent past. Muriithi shows that collateralized borrowing presents significant challenges. For example, it could potentially lead to the loss of collateral for the sovereign; it could lead to lack of transparency through hidden and contingent liabilities; and it could lead to protracted debt restructuring processes since the incentives driving the creditors in this context may diverge significantly with other types of creditors. He therefore shows that collateralized borrowing is not a panacea. For sovereigns, collateralization exposes them to commodity price volatility, foreign exchange risk and a reduction in fiscal flexibility. Yet, collateralized borrowing has historically been the only means through which some African countries can raise external finance to fund essential infrastructure development. In addition to recommending increased transparency in collateralization of State-owned assets, Muriithi argues in favor of collateralized borrowing only where it is the only mechanism to achieve particular goals—such as financing essential infrastructural development that would also offset borrowing costs.

Nciko wa Nciko's chapter on the resource for infrastructure contract between the Democratic Republic of Congo, (DRC), and a consortium of Chinese state-owned companies to construct the Busanga hydropower plant follows Muriithi's chapter very nicely.[14] Nciko argues that seeing the 2016 contract as one involving resources (in this case copper and cobalt) in exchange for infrastructure is mistaken. Instead, he shows that the contract has forced the DRC into an unsustainable collateralized sovereign debt position. Nciko advances several reasons for this. First, he

---

[13] Ian Muriithi, *Chapter 10: "The Challenge of Collateralization of Public Assets in Loan Contracts and Indentures: What is the Way Forward?"*

[14] Nciko wa Nciko, *Chapter 11: "China, Have Mercy: The Unacceptable Collateralised Sovereign Debt Burden that the Busanga Hydropower Plant Places on the DRC."*

shows that the $ 509. 43 million financing that the DRC now owes the consortium of Chinese state-owned companies was inflated by at least over $200 million. Corrupt DRC officials as well as Chinese officials involved in a complex web of entities were involved in procuring the deal. Second, Nciko shows that the electricity produced in the deal is only powering a Chinese entity's mining operations to the exclusion of the needs of the DRC and third, that the market value of the natural resources collateralized in the deal far exceed the infrastructure produced. Nciko concludes his chapter by urging a closer examination of the Busanga resources for infrastructure contracts for violating DRC and international anti-corruption rules.

Bharath Gururagavendran's chapter examines the relationship between economic, social and cultural rights, and the related work of United Nations human rights treaty bodies, on the one hand, with the role of international financial institutions, on the other, in the context of sovereign debt. He adopts a Third World Approaches to International Law (TWAIL) framework to examine this relationship.[15] He argues that the lending practices of international financial institutions are steeped in neo-colonial practices that have hobbled their ability to meaningfully realize the social and economic rights of their citizens. In addition, he argues that the practices of these international financial institutions have effectively created large-scale debt colonies in the Third World since most of the revenues these countries generate are used to service foreign debt ahead of paying for basic needs such as education and health for their citizens. One of the key recommendations that Bharath makes is that the richest countries with the largest voting shares in international financial institutions should undertake structural reforms of this system so that it can better guarantee the economic, social, and cultural rights of vulnerable populations in the Third World.

As I noted earlier, the chapters in this book are the product of the African Sovereign Debt Justice Network's, (AfSDJN), efforts to nurture and amplify African voices on the reforms of the global debt and financial architecture. This book represents the AfSDJN's efforts to make sure that fundamental reforms of this architecture do not get swept under the rug in the often episodic minimalist reforms that merely tinker with this architecture at the margins.

---

[15] Bharath Gururagavendran, *Chapter 12 "The Coloniality of Sovereign Debt."*

Some of the key demands of the AfSDJN over the last three years have included the following. First, a new comprehensive, fair and effective sovereign debt restructuring mechanism based in the United Nations that would be binding on all creditors, including private creditors. As the chapters in this book show, the G20 Common Framework has proved to be inadequate to address the systemic indebtedness of African countries. The initiative has not only been slow but has also failed to secure substantial debt relief for participating countries as demonstrated by the experience of Chad and Zambia. Ongoing efforts to revamp the Common Framework under the Global Sovereign Debt Roundtable are creditor led and shrouded in secrecy, reinforcing the unequal balance of power in sovereign debt relations.

Second, the AfSDJN has supported the incorporation of natural disaster and pandemic clauses across sovereign debt instruments, including during restructurings, allowing countries to defer principal and interest payments in the event of the occurrence of natural disasters and pandemics. The AfSDJN has also sought to discourage African countries from signing trade or investment agreements that come with financial services chapters that subject sovereign debt to arbitration.

Third, the AfSDJN has campaigned to ensure that ongoing debt restructurings undertaken under the aegis of the IMF are austerity free. Debt workouts should not prioritize payments to creditors while subjecting populations in Africa to debilitating austerity measures inconsistent with their human rights. Further, the AfSDJN has urged the IMF to review its debt sustainability assessments to ensure that they do not encourage the excessive accumulation of debt and that they take into consideration the required investment in sustainable development goals (SDGs), climate needs, and the human rights of populations in African countries.

These and similar recommendations are necessary for a just, equitable and sustainable global debt and financial architecture, one free from the colonial legacies that disenfranchise African countries from being able to have the policy space to meet their development objectives and the needs of their people without the stranglehold of sovereign debt literally hanging over their economies. For the authors in this book, it is not simply enough to rescue the current international financial and debt architecture. Rather, this architecture needs to be fundamentally reformed to de-prioritize and destabilize the predominance of the interests of creditors to the exclusion of the interests of the populations of many heavily indebted countries that experience the biggest downsides of sovereign indebtedness such as austerity. The fact that those who suffer austerity are majority poor, black and brown peoples make the case for fundamental reforms of the global debt and financial architecture all the more necessary and urgent. The resistance to this architecture, as this book tries to do, must begin with exposing how this architecture sediments and entrenches racialized legacies and hierarchies that came from the post-colonial order of the post-second world war era. But those legacies have a longer violent colonial past that many of today's post-colonial elite continue to embrace in alliance with other transnational capitalist elites and interests. It is these legacies that this book exposes and in doing so hopefully to serve as an inspiration for further research, resistance and far-reaching transformative reforms.

CHAPTER ONE

The Pressing Call for an International Debt Restructuring Framework and the Potential Gains Its Creation Will Have for African Countries

Dr. Magalie L. Masamba[*]

1 Introduction

The COVID-19 pandemic has not only triggered one of the most devastating health crises to date, but also has had an unprecedented social and economic impact in its scope and scale. The pandemic continues to restrict the economic flexibility of African countries due to sluggish economies and declining commodity prices. Additionally, the conflict between Russia and Ukraine is impacting commodity prices and is further weakening the already frail external debt landscape of African countries.[1] Currently, African governments are grappling not just with massively increasing debt levels, but also, frequently hidden foreign public debt that presents challenges of transparency and accountability.

After the debt cancellation programs for the official debt of developing countries in the late-1990s to mid-2000s, African countries are once again on the verge

---

[*] Dr. Magalie L. Masamba is a Senior Fellow of the African Sovereign Debt Justice Network (AfSDJN) and a Post-Doctoral Law Fellow at the International Development Law Unit of the University of Pretoria's Centre for Human Rights.

A version of this chapter was presented at the Inaugural Sovereign Debt Academy of the African Sovereign Debt Justice Network (AfSDJN) on 21 July 2022. The author wishes to thank Professor James T. Gathii (AfSDJN), Professor Daniel D. Bradlow (Centre for Human Rights, University of Pretoria), Harrison Mbori (Max Planck Institute) and participants in the Inaugural Sovereign Debt Academy of the AfSDJN, for their extremely insightful comments on this chapter.

[1] Christopher Tang & Alex Yang, "Global Supply Chains Face Disruption Following Russia's Invasion of Ukraine" (2022), available at https://www.forbes.com/sites/lbsbusinessstrategyreview/2022/03/24/global-supply-chains-face-disruption-following-russias-invasion-of-ukraine/?sh=6588610f2ce0.

of a debt crisis and still in need of broad-based restructuring.[2] The present debt crisis in Africa (which is in part COVID-19-induced) has refocused attention on national measures such as strengthening general debt management and parliamentary oversight of the accumulation of new debt, as well as the critical need for sovereign debt restructuring (SoDR) of current debt. Despite decades of debate on improving the SoDR legal landscape, it continues to produce complicated legal difficulties. Among these issues is the current absence of a mechanism to administer SoDR, which is now carried out in a fragmented environment, resulting in suboptimal and unjust outcomes.[3] Previous attempts to reform the sovereign debt restructuring architecture through a supranational body or mechanism were thwarted by resistance from the United States, European Union and other western creditor countries. In particular, the passing of UN General Assembly (UNGA) Resolution 68/304 (10 September 2014) *'Towards the establishment of a multilateral legal framework for sovereign debt restructuring processes'* which aspired to reform the debt restructuring architecture, was backed by 120 primarily developing debtor nations. However, it was opposed by 15 mostly developed creditor countries, while 35 countries abstained from voting. Despite this support by the majority, nothing substantive has come off it due to a lack of political will by creditor countries. However, it is becoming painfully clear that there is still a need to explore the development of a global sovereign debt restructuring arrangement despite what seems to be the lack of political will for a more comprehensive approach.[4] It is also clear that much-needed reform should not only seek to create procedural certainty but should also incorporate broad issues—environmental, social and governance.

---

[2] *See* Magalie L. Masamba, "Reflections on the Current Reality of Africa's Debt Landscape" (2021), AFRONOMICSLAW, available at https://www.afronomicslaw.org/category/african-sovereign-debt-justice-network-afsdjn/reflections-current-reality-africas-debt.

[3] *See* Magalie Masamba and Francesco De Bonis, Towards Building a Fair and Orderly International Framework for Sovereign Debt Restructuring: An African Perspective (2017), AFRODAD, available at https://www.africaportal.org/publications/towards-building-fair-and-orderly-international-framework-sovereign-debt-restructuring-african-perspective/.

[4] *See* Magalie L. Masamba, "Africa's Dance with Unsustainable Debt: Is It Time for a Comprehensive Mechanism for Debt Restructuring?" (2021), AFSDJN PAPER V AFRICAN SOVEREIGN DEBT JUSTICE PAPER SERIES, available at https://www.afronomicslaw.org/category/african-sovereign-debt-justice-network-afsdjn/africas-dance-unsustainable-debt-it-time-0.

In order to bridge the gap between the legal and policy discussions on SoDR, the purpose of this study is to analyze the reform of the sovereign debt restructuring landscape by tackling the following inquiries:

- What does the African debt landscape look like?
- What are the sovereign debt challenges African countries have faced in the past decade, and what are the global solutions proposed as countermeasures?
- Moving forward, what considerations should be made for a mechanism that could work for Africa?

This chapter is divided into four sections to address these inquiries. The first covers the existing issues in the restructuring landscape in an attempt to strengthen the case for more ambitious legal reform. The following section explores the current direction of the debate on solutions to the difficulties. It does so by analysing three recent approaches to address developing-country loans. The chapter then offers some suggestions towards an international debt restructuring framework before concluding.

2 Sovereign debt restructuring in the current landscape

2.1 Is Africa facing another debt crisis?

Africa is on the brink of debt distress and policymakers; civil society organisations and citizens of countries are, and should be concerned. Numerous African countries were part of the Heavily Indebted Poor Countries Initiative, (HIPC), and the Multilateral Debt Relief Initiative, (MDRI), which were implemented in 1996 and 2005, respectively.[5] These debt relief initiatives, which dealt with official debt owed to traditional creditors, sought to achieve 'more relief in exchange for more reform'.[6] The

---

[5] For a summary and update of the HIPC relief programs, *see* IMF, "Debt Relief Under the Heavily Indebted Poor Countries" (HIPC) INITIATIVE (2021), available at https://www.imf.org/en/About/Factsheets/Sheets/2016/08/01/16/11/Debt-Relief-Under-the-Heavily-Indebted-Poor-Countries-Initiative.

[6] Anna Gelpern, "Sovereign Debt: Now What?" (2016) 41–2 THE YALE JOURNAL OF INTERNATIONAL LAW 45, at 50.

HIPC program was implemented at a time when African nations were struggling with, among other things, the painful repercussions of the International Monetary Fund's (IMF) and the World Bank's Structural Adjustment Programs (SAPs).

It was hoped that these programs would result in a broad-based solution to the continent's unsustainable debt burden. Less than two decades after the HIPC initiatives intended to reduce unsustainable debt burdens, countries such as Zambia are once again in default of some of their financial obligations, suffering repayment issues and over-indebtedness. However, unlike the HIPC era, the debt landscape has changed. Today, the current debt stresses are also caused by debt owed largely to new private creditors such as bond holders and debts arising out of infrastructure projects, as well as newer official sources including but not limited to China.[7] The presence of private creditors (who may have divergent interests in renegotiation) and newer bilateral creditors, particularly China (which is Africa's largest bilateral lender and whose contracts have generated concerns on transparency), further complicates the situation.[8] If history is anything to go by, debt relief or debt forgiveness on its own may free up funds that would have otherwise been used for debt repayment in the short term, but such programs are usually once-off initiatives and are not the broad-based reform to the sovereign debt architecture needed.

After the previous debt relief programs and even prior to the Covid-19 pandemic, close to half of the continent already had unsustainable debt burdens or required debt restructuring.[9] For example, Ethiopia's external debt stock went up by a

---

[7] *See* Daniel D. Bradlow and Magalie L. Masamba, "Sovereign debt management and restructuring in SADC: Setting the scene and asking the right question," (2022) COVID-19 AND SOVEREIGN DEBT: THE CASE OF SADC, (PRETORIA UNIVERSITY LAW PRESS 2022) at 1–21, available at https://www.pulp.up.ac.za/edocman/edited_collections/sadc_book/2021%20SADC%20Debt%20Chapter%201.pdf.

[8] *See* Global Development Policy Center, Chinese Loans to Africa (CLA) Database, https://www.bu.edu/gdp/chinese-loans-to-africa-database/. Also, for an assessment of 100 Chinese loans to Africa, *see* Anna Gelpern, Sebastian Horn, Scott Morris, Brad Parks, Christoph Trebesch, "How China Lends: A Rare Look into 100 Debt Contracts with Foreign Governments" (2021), available at https://www.aiddata.org/publications/how-china-lends.

[9] UNCTAD, Sovereign debt crises more likely, new mechanisms needed (2016), available at https://unctad.org/en/pages/newsdetails.aspx?OriginalVersionID=1364.

staggering 885 percent between 2008 and 2018, in Ghana, it went up by 395 percent, in Uganda by 437 percent, and in Zambia by 521 percent.[10] Already in 2018, more than 40% of low-income nations in Sub-Saharan Africa were at high risk of debt distress, demonstrating that the issues of over-indebtedness predate the COVID-19 pandemic, which has only exacerbated matters and is one of the various triggers of the current debt crisis.[11] Naturally, African countries that were already seeing increased debt burdens, had even greater borrowing needs as a result of the inevitable obligation to finance the health response and efforts to mitigate the socioeconomic effects of the pandemic. In this respect, Park and Samples highlight the potential long-term impacts that the pandemic will have, and note that:

> ... countries are prone to borrow more than what is socially optimal and may be vulnerable to external shocks, such as a financial crisis, an economic recession, or a natural disaster. The COVID-19 pandemic underscores this point, as its economic effects are potentially devastating for vulnerable developing and emerging market countries. As a result, the possibility of sovereign debt gone bad casts a long shadow, affecting the government's ability to ensure the well-being of its citizens and the financial standing of the country's government and even its companies for generations.[12]

As at 29 August 2022, 16 African countries are at *moderate risk of debt distress* (Benin, Burkina Faso, Republic of Cabo Verde, Democratic Republic of Congo, Guinea, Ivory Coast, Lesotho, Liberia, Madagascar, Mali, Niger, Rwanda, Senegal, Tanzania, Togo and Uganda); 15 countries are at *high risk of distress* (Burundi, Cameroon, Central African Republic, Comoros, Djibouti, Ethiopia, The Gambia, Ghana, Guinea Bissau, Kenya, Malawi, Mauritania, Sierra Leone and South Sudan; Zambia) and 7 countries are in *debt distress* (Chad, Republic of Congo, Mozambique, São

---

[10] World Bank Group, International debt statistics (2020), available at https://openknowledge.worldbank.org/bitstream/handle/10986/32382/9781464814617.pdf?sequence=7&isAllowed=y.

[11] World Bank, Africa's Pulse 17: An Analysis of Issues Shaping Africa's Economic Future (2018) at 35, available at https://openknowledge.worldbank.org/handle/10986/29667.

[12] Stephen Kim Park & Tim R. Samples, "Distrust, Disorder, and the New Governance of Sovereign Debt," HARVARD INTERNATIONAL LAW JOURNAL, 62(1) (2021) at 180.

Tomé and Príncipe, Somalia, Sudan and Zimbabwe).[13] Of the countries with concerning debt burdens, Zambia was the first country in the COVID-19 era to require restructuring after defaulting on its US $42.5 million Eurobond payment in November 2020.[14] Zambia was not only the first African country to default on its debt in the COVID-19 era, but is also negotiating what could be a historical debt restructuring with both its bilateral and private creditors, including China which is the country's main bilateral lender and co-chair of the creditor committee.[15]

In light of the above, a vital question is what measures are required to tackle Africa's problem of over-indebtedness. In my view, a starting point in assessing the attempts to resolve the continents unsustainable debt in the COVID-19 era is consideration of whether debt forgiveness is an option. At the time of writing this chapter, broad-based debt forgiveness, such as was done under the HIPC, has not been as yet accepted by creditors as the appropriate or required reaction to growing debt levels. However there has been a call from civil society organisations for debt relief or even what has been described as "debt justice" that includes the "unconditional cancellation of public external debt payments by all lenders—bilateral, multilateral and private lenders—for all countries in need for at least the next four years as an immediate step and a clear program towards the unconditional cancellation of outstanding debt".[16]

Further, in the context of Zambia, in a 2022 open letter to Blackrock, Zambia's creditors and the G20, more than a hundred economists and professors have urged lenders to restructure Zambia's debt, and include significant haircuts as part of the restructuring.[17] Regarding the debt composition of Zambia's foreign debt repayments due between 2022 and 2028, the letter notes that 45% is owed to Western private

---

[13] IMF, List of LIC DSAs for PRGT-Eligible Countries as of June 30, 2021, available at https://www.imf.org/external/Pubs/ft/dsa/DSAlist.pdf.

[14] National Assembly of Zambia, "Recent Developments Regarding the Government's Engagement with Eurobond Holders," available at https://www.parliament.gov.zm/node/9923.

[15] Institute for Security Studies, 'Zambia on the Brink of Historic Debt Relief Deal' (2022), available at https://issafrica.org/iss-today/zambia-on-the-brink-of-historic-debt-relief-deal.

[16] *See* Global Action for Debt Cancellation, "Open Letter to All Governments, International Institutions and Lenders," available at https://debtgwa.net/.

[17] Open letter to BlackRock, Zambia's creditors and the G20, available at https://debtjustice.org.uk/wp-content/uploads/2022/09/Open-letter-from-experts_09.22.pdf.

lenders, 37% is owed to Chinese public and private lenders, 10% is owed to multilateral institutions, and 8% is owed to other countries.[18] The letter, which includes as one of it signatories the AfSDJN's James Thuo Gathii, observes that "at a time of global crisis, it is economically inefficient and morally wrong for high interest debts to be paid to private lenders, while governments cut back on support for their own people. The world urgently needs a strengthened scheme to deliver debt restructuring for countries and people in need."

Despite the numerous calls not just for restructuring, but debt relief through major haircuts, there is a reluctance for an HIPC-like arrangement. Among the reasons why there seems to be a reluctance from creditors for broad-based debt forgiveness could be that this is more complex to negotiate as the debt landscape has greatly changed since the HIPC/MDRI days. Today not only would such a proposal need the backing of newer bilateral creditors such as China, it would also need backing by private creditors such as bond-holders. A further complexity of the idea of debt forgiveness is that some of the challenges that have resulted in over indebtedness stem internally from weaknesses in public financial management and fiscal frameworks of countries and may relate to transparency, accountability and due processes of countries. While this chapter does not argue for universal debt forgiveness, it does argue that debt restructuring in the existing fragmented environment as a response to the rising debt burdens of low-income African countries is inadequate. The inadequacy is more so if some major haircuts are not applied. Finally, in spite of the proposal's seeming difficulty, a global framework for debt restructuring is more important than ever and the future of restructuring will continue to comprise a fragmented approach that faces weak co-ordination between different classes of creditors without a global rule of law.

2.2   *How difficult is it to restructure debt in the current environment?*

The Group of Twenty (G20) introduced the Debt Service Suspension Initiative (DSSI) which is a once-off program to suspend bilateral official debt payments up until the

---

[18] *Also see* Debt Justice (2022), "African governments owe three times more debt to private lenders than China" (2022), available at https://debtjustice.org.uk/press-release/african-governments-owe-three-times-more-debt-to-privatelenders-than-china.

end of 2021.[19] The DSSI was not aimed at reforming the debt landscape, but rather to temporarily help countries free up resources to focus on priority expenditures. It has been replaced by the 'Common Framework for Debt Treatments beyond the DSSI' (the Common Framework). The Common Framework aims at facilitating rapid and orderly debt treatment for DSSI-eligible countries with wide creditor participation, including private sector participation.[20] To date, only three African countries have requested debt relief through the Common Framework: Chad, Ethiopia, and Zambia. Notably, in each case, considerable delays have occurred. An important observation is that "in part, these delays reflect the problems that motivated the creation of the Common Framework in the first place. These include coordinating Paris Club and other creditors, as well as multiple government institutions and agencies within creditor countries, which can slow down decisions."[21] Delays have sometimes occurred due to factors unrelated to the Common Framework, such as decision-making being hampered by the heterogeneity of creditors on the part of debtors.[22] For instance, to restore debt sustainability, Chad must restructure a major collateralized obligation owned by a private enterprise and that is syndicated to banks and funds.[23] While the G20 Common Framework aims to mitigate the problems including protracted restructuring, it does not eliminate them.[24]

Despite the current criticisms of the Common Framework, the highly indebted case of Zambia, that has an official debt burden of approximately US$14.1 billion, is

---

[19] World Bank, "Debt Service Suspension Initiative" (2022), available at https://www.worldbank.org/en/topic/debt/brief/covid-19-debt-service-suspension-initiative; *Also see* Martin Kessler, "Debt Service Suspension in Southern African Development Community Countries," COVID-19 AND SOVEREIGN DEBT: THE CASE OF SADC, (PULP 2022) at 63–88, available at https://www.pulp.up.ac.za/edocman/edited_collections/sadc_book/2021%20SADC%20Debt%20Chapter%203.pdf.

[20] The Paris Club, "Common Framework For Debt Treatments Beyond the DSSI," available at https://openknowledge.worldbank.org/bitstream/handle/10986/36289/9781464818004.pdf.

[21] Kristalina Georgieva and Ceyla Pazarbasioglu, "The G20 Common Framework for Debt Treatments Must Be Stepped Up" (2021), IMF BLOG, available at https://blogs.imf.org/2021/12/02/the-g20-common-framework-for-debt-treatments-must-be-stepped-up/.

[22] *Supra* note 15.

[23] *Ibid.*

[24] Ibid.

the primary test case for how the Common Framework will work for other countries. It is not only an important test case for how African debt can be treated under the Common Framework but also important as it:

1. Raises broader challenges of debt transparency (potential secret debts);
2. Incorporates diverse lenders and an Official Creditor Committee that is co-chaired by China, France, with South Africa as vice-chair;
3. Brings to the fore the challenge of achieving comparable treatment for public and private creditors, as required under the Common Framework;
4. Reminds us of the challenge of the stigma of restructuring that may result in credit rating downgrades and losing access to capital markets; and also,
5. Will show what participants in negotiations will consider as important low-hanging fruit and more long-term considerations in contemporary restructuring.

Today it seems that the sovereign debt restructuring architecture, that has been previously described as the "modular debt restructuring regime" still faces challenges that echo those discussed in the policy debate on the debt restructuring architecture prior to the COVID-19 pandemic.[25] In 2015 for instance, the United Nations Conference on Trade and Development (UNCTAD) Roadmap noted three of the key issues affecting SoDR, all of which remain relevant today, and in some ways are amplified today:[26]

(i) The fragmentation and the lack of coordination
There is no institutional framework in place to manage SoDR, and the mechanisms that now govern restructuring operate under a variety of legal regimes.[27]

---

[25] Anna Gelpern, "Sovereign Debt: Now What?" (2016), 41: 2 THE YALE JOURNAL OF INTERNATIONAL LAW 45, at 69.
[26] UNCTAD, "Sovereign debt workouts: going forward—roadmap and guide" (2015) at 3, available at http://unctad.org/en/PublicationsLibrary/gdsddf2015misc1_en.pdf.
[27] Carlos Espósito, Yuefen Li, Juan PabloBohoslavsky, "Sovereign Financing and Law: The UNCTAD Principles on Responsible Sovereign Lending and Borrowing" (2013) at 360.

The absence of a unified SoDR governance system is the most pressing issue in the current SoDR ecosystem when it comes to coherence. The diversity of legal procedures and bodies dealing with SoDR demonstrates this incoherence. It has led to forum shopping and uncertainty in legal interpretations.[28]

(ii) The "too little too late" problem

A debtor should initiate a restructuring when it is evident that circumstances leave it unable to meet its debt obligations. This should be done in a timely manner, but a fragmented framework makes it difficult for debtors to freely use this option when necessary. It has become a recurrent theme in the literature on SoDR that when restructurings occur, often they are delayed, occur "too little too late," and are protracted. Sovereign debtors may be concerned that if a SoDR fails, their reputation will suffer, access to capital markets will be restricted, the local financial markets will suffer if local finance accounts for a significant portion of the sovereign debt, and the IMF could be unable to provide the additional funding they require.[29] Recent developments in the context of COVID-19 debt treatments demonstrate the immediate threat of credit rating downgrades if governments take steps to save their economies by restructuring their debt and participating in initiatives such as the Common Framework. Another reason that may deter prompt restructuring is the possibility that credit rating agencies could downgrade sovereign ratings, making access to international capital more difficult.[30]

---

[28] *Supra* note 19 at 3.
[29] IMF, "A New Approach To Sovereign Debt Restructuring: Preliminary Considerations" (2001) at 4, available at https://www.imf.org/external/NP/pdr/sdrm/2001/113001.pdf.
[30] For a discussion on credit rating agencies and access to international markets during the COVID-19 era *see* United Nations, Eurobonds, Debt Sustainability in Africa and Credit Rating Agencies (2022), available at https://www.un.org/osaa/sites/www.un.org.osaa/files/docs/2118580-osaa-eurobonds_policy_paper_web.pdf.

(iii) The lack of fairness

The current "non-system" of SoDR, according to the UNCTAD Roadmap, does not promote a fair workout. UNCTAD emphasizes four essential concerns in its assessment of fairness:

- There is a misalignment between the interests of creditors, and those of vulnerable debtors with commitments to citizens.
- Encouraging creditor engagement is difficult in the absence of an impartial organization to ensure "cram-down" in SoDR.
- Policy change is important to aid distressed countries to return to sustainable debt levels, and where a debtor requires interim finance, the issuing institutions naturally play a significant role in the debtor's internal policy space. As a result, there is a political dimension to fairness that occurs when creditors' structural adjustments and conditionality result in them interfering disproportionately in the internal economy of a debtor seeking interim finance. The challenge here is not only the notion of interference, but what may be perceived as the unfairness in the policies sought to be imposed. This necessitates the formulation of such policies in an objective and transparent manner.
- Furthermore, UNCTAD emphasizes the importance of striking a balance between much-needed international policy reform and the debtor's internal interests and objectives.

Looking at the challenges more broadly, it is clear that, as noted by Bradlow, "[t]he current sovereign debt architecture is failing African states in multiple ways".[31] One of these failures is the failure to incentivize private creditors to be sufficiently flexible in dealing with distressed sovereign debt, and what may be described as a presumption against providing adequate relief which is 'built in' SoDRs, even when the cause of the debtor's problems is beyond the debtor's control.[32] The notable impact of

---

[31] Daniel Bradlow, "A Proposal for a New Approach to African Debt" (2022), available at https://justmoney.org/daniel-bradlow-a-proposal-for-a-new-approach-to-african-debt/.

an inadequate restructuring is that it is causing human suffering and economic damage. Bradlow's solution to this challenge is however not debt forgiveness, it is tackling reform in a manner that could convince bondholders to participate in the development of a Debts of Vulnerable Economies (DOVE) fund, which is discussed in the coming section. The reality today is that while there are calls for the full cancellation of debt obligations, this may not be in the long-term interest of African countries and creativity is needed in formulating proposals. If history is anything to go by,

> previous experience with debt forgiveness programmes shows that creditor motivations are not purely altruistic and participation is typically conditional on accepting far-reaching economic reforms which could border on national sovereignty rights. A case in point is the Heavily Indebted Poor Countries (HIPC) Initiative of 1996 and the imposition of the popular Enhanced Structural Adjustment Facility (ESAF) on participatory countries with conditions ranging from implementing structural reforms such as reducing the size of government to having an influence over the use of budgetary savings from the interim debt service relief. Moreover, apart from the fact that creditors are generally not inclined to offer debt forgiveness as a first option, these programmes are typically led by international financial institutions and is unlikely to be welcomed by private lenders which would make such arrangements not as rewarding for the continent: 53% of Africa's debt is owed to private lenders.[33]

Again, the policy debate on the SoDR of foreign debt has been reopened, and the question of whether the current regime and procedures can sufficiently lead to better outcomes for participants in the restructuring process and those impacted by the process is relevant. Over the past few years, there have been various proposals beyond the DSSI and Common Framework, to deal with the challenges in the SoDR architecture. The difference today is that these proposals also seek to tackle

---

[32] *Supra* note 24.
[33] Mma Amara Ekeruche, "Africa and the Need for a New Debt Restructuring Architecture" (2020), available at https://www.ispionline.it/it/pubblicazione/africa-and-need-new-debt-restructuring-architecture-27026.

major social and economic challenges such as climate change, as well as the economic impacts of both the COVID-19 pandemic and Russia/Ukraine conflict. These are covered in the next section.

3 Innovations for Restructuring Sovereign Debt for Post-Pandemic Recovery

Recognizing the complexity of the challenges in SoDR points toward the need for creative solutions, but also viable options for sovereign debt restructuring. These proposals that have been seen as more viable in the short-term, have included amongst others, debt swap options like debt-equity, debt-for-nature, and debt for development swaps. Two proposals fall within these categories, (1) the use of climate-linked bond instruments through Debt Relief for a Green and Inclusive Recovery proposed by Ulrich Volz, Shamshad Akhtar, Kevin P. Gallagher, Stephany Griffith-Jones, Jörg Haas, and Moritz Kraemer; and (2) the proposal for the use of modern-day Brady Bond-like restructuring instruments proposed by Ying Qian. Another proposal, which originated from Africa, is the proposed establishment of a special purpose vehicle known as a "DOVE" Fund (Debts of Vulnerable Economies Fund) proposed by Daniel Bradlow. The common thread between these three initiatives is that they all aim to firstly promote private creditor participation in restructuring, while secondly promoting green recovery and sustainable development by addressing environmental, social, and governance issues to varied degrees. The latter in my view in effect incorporates human rights concerns into the discourse. However, the structural arrangements of each proposal differ, and are discussed below.

3.1 An African innovation to restructure African debt: Reforming the Sovereign Debt Architecture through a "Dove" (Debts of Vulnerable Economies) Fund

The DOVE Fund, as proposed by Daniel Bradlow, is an independent special-purpose investment vehicle that purchases African foreign currency debt bonds selling at the prevailing discount price on the open market.[34] It's main goal is to become a creditor

---

[34] Daniel Bradlow, "Africa Needs a DOVE Fund: Or Should We Starve So We Can Pay our Debts?" (2020), INTER PRESS SERVICES, available at https://www.ipsnews.net/2020/05/africa-needs-dove-fund-starve-can-pay-debts/.

and participant in creditor groups. In a presentation made by Bradlow, he notes that the DOVE Fund will (1) help African countries meet debt service obligations without undue hardship, while maintaining market access as much as possible, (2) require that due diligence and impact assessments form part of a restructuring processes, and (3) help maximize funding actually available and used for promoting sustainable and inclusive development in debtor countries.[35]

The DOVE Fund aspires to be linked to broader societal and environmental concerns through its use of international principles to govern debt restructuring under the Fund, such as those that for instance link restructuring to climatic and social implications. The DOVE Fund will encourage other private sector creditors to adhere to the guiding principles that the DOVE fund will develop. Already, many financial institutions are signatories to the Principles on Responsible Investment and have internal human rights, environmental and social policies. As such, for Bradlow, this creates a higher probability that these institutions could potentially agree to adopt principles that seek to strengthen the consideration of ESG issues.[36]

In terms of how the DOVE Fund will operate, it will purchase debt instruments from African countries who choose to participate in a restructuring program, and will then notify other bondholders that it intends to join in future negotiations on that country's bonds. To allow a country to recover from economic shocks or an ongoing crisis, the Fund will impose a debt repayment moratorium and will notify both debtors and markets of the moratorium. The DOVE Fund will urge other private sector creditors to participate in a similar suspension of debt payments and to subscribe to the guiding principles it will adopt.[37] In order to get the DOVE Fund to accept to participate in a debt restructuring, Bradlow notes that it must meet the following four criteria:

(i) The restructuring process must enable as many African debt stakeholders as practicable to participate;
(ii) The restructuring must conform to a set of guiding principles developed from a broad set of internationally recognized standards (the DOVE Fund Principles, and any other international standards);

---

[35] Daniel Bradlow, "Lessons from 'COVID 19 and Sovereign Debt: The Case of SADC" (2022).
[36] *Supra* note 35.
[37] *Supra* note 35.

(iii) The restructuring must free up resources that can be invested in social and environmental development efforts. The DOVE Fund provides for a monitoring framework to guarantee that investments are made in social and environmental activities; and

(iv) Despite the debt restructuring, the debtor should, to the maximum degree feasible, continue to have access to international financial markets.[38]

3.2 Linking debt relief in low- and middle-income countries to climate change: Debt Relief for a Green and Inclusive Recovery

The Debt Relief for a Green and Inclusive Recovery (DRGIR) proposal has been developed by Ulrich Volz, Shamshad Akhtar, Kevin P. Gallagher, Stephany Griffith-Jones, Jörg Haas, and Moritz Kraemer.[39] They acknowledge the past challenges of protracted restructuring and note that: *"past debt crises ought to have taught us that avoiding proactive and purposeful debt restructurings will delay recoveries and ultimately drive up the cost for debtors and creditors alike. The world is still at high risk of repeating the mistakes that resulted in two lost decades of development in the 1980s and 1990s."*[40] As such, this proposal like the others before it, is birthed out of the clear gap in the global governance on restructuring, that has been made even more evident from the effects of the Covid-19 pandemic.

The DRGIR, which is described as *"an ambitious, concerted, and comprehensive debt relief initiative that should be adopted on a global scale to free up resources to support recoveries in a sustainable way, boost economies' resilience, and foster a just transition to a low-carbon economy."*[41] The proposal's goals are twofold: to increase funding for climate resilience and to encourage private sector participation. In essence, the proposal seeks to help both low- and middle-income countries' free up resources through a

---

[38] Daniel Bradlow, "A Proposal for a New Approach to African Debt," available at https://justmoney.org/daniel-bradlow-a-proposal-for-a-new-approach-to-african-debt/.

[39] *See* Ulrich Volz, Shamshad Akhtar, Kevin P. Gallagher, Stephany Griffith-Jones, Jörg Haas, and Moritz Kraemer, "Debt Relief for a Green and Inclusive Recovery: Securing Private-Sector Participation and Creating Policy Space for Sustainable Development" (2021), available at https://www.bu.edu/gdp/files/2021/06/DRGR-Report-2021-FIN.pdf.

[40] *Supra* note 27 at 9.

[41] *Ibid.*

debt restructuring, that will in turn be used to meet climate and development goals.[42] This will be accomplished via a World Bank-managed Guarantee Facility for Green and Inclusive Recovery that will increase private engagement in restructurings. The guarantee facility would offer credit enhancements for new bonds that would be traded for existing debt, as well as debt relief tied to policy and budgetary adjustments (a Green and Inclusive Recovery Strategy developed by the debtor government in consultation with all the relevant stakeholders).[43] The value of this proposal is that it addresses the challenge of private participation in restructuring. Further, the proposal links debt relief to a green and inclusive recovery, which will necessitate participating governments strengthening debt management, transparency, and domestic resource mobilization. This proposal of a DRGIR does not however seek to replace the idea of an international framework for debt restructuring, which has been acknowledged as being needed, but instead seeks to develop a market-based solution that is more comprehensive and bolder in addressing debt crises, existential threats such as climate change and the development goals of countries:

> Although we emphatically support the calls for a Sovereign Debt Restructuring Mechanism, we recognise that many years of discussions have not yet resulted in a workable multilateral agreement. Time is of the essence in providing countries the fiscal space to stage green and inclusive recoveries. This proposal is designed to address the immediate challenges facing indebted developing and emerging economies to enable swift recoveries and address the most urgent needs in terms of financing Agenda 2030 and the Paris Agreement. But it could also provide a stepping stone towards a new global debt architecture that is fair, transparent and efficient, and cognisant of the needs of developing and emerging countries.[44]

3.3 *A new spin on Brady Bonds in the Post-Pandemic Era*

Ying Qian has investigated Brady Bond-style debt restructurings in the post-COVID period. Brady bond transactions were frequently employed in developing-country

---

[42] *Ibid.*
[43] *Ibid* at 32.
[44] *Supra* note 27 at 11.

distressed debt resolution in the 1980s and 1990s and proven to be effective, particularly in Latin America.[45] Brady Bonds are a debtor-initiated transaction structure facilitated by the IMF and World Bank that resulted in the exchange of distressed debt for secured and tradable bonds, generally after a haircut. The principal amount was often collateralized by specially issued 30-year zero-coupon US Treasury bonds acquired by the debtor nation using proceeds from IMF or World Bank loans and the country's own foreign currency reserves.[46] He emphasizes three fundamental aspects of Brady Bond restructuring: (i) bank creditors would offer debt relief in return for better guarantee of collectability of principle and interest collaterals; (ii) debt relief was connected to some sort of economic policy changes; and (iii) the new debt instruments would be tradable, allowing creditors to spread risk more broadly.[47] In this proposal, debtors could motivate creditor participation by creating more attractive instruments such as state-contingent debt instruments like commodity-linked bonds.[48] In light of this, it is proposed that this approach be modified to take climate change into account, perhaps using climate-linked instruments.[49] Climate initiatives are aggressively exploring green/climate-related finance options, and with all of these financial resources accessible, restructuring might take advantage of this.[50]

The three proposals discussed above are examples of recent innovations proposed to deal with immediate debt crisis. These proposals however fall short of an international framework for debt restructuring. It is therefore evident that an international framework or a more comprehensive approach to restructuring is needed.

However, in an effort to deal with the immediate needs of countries in distress, the proponents of these proposals have looked for solutions that would more or less be accepted by the markets, that also encourage private sector participation and that deals with broader issues of climate change and social concerns. The lesson that can

---

[45] Ying Qian, "Brady Bonds and the Potential for Debt Restructuring in the Post-Pandemic Era" (2021) at 1, GCI WORKING PAPER 018, available at https://www.bu.edu/gdp/files/2021/09/GCI_WP_018_FIN.pdf.
[46] *Supra* note 30 at 3.
[47] *Supra* note 45 at 2.
[48] *Ibid* at 1.
[49] *Ibid.*
[50] *Ibid.*

be drawn from all three is that innovation innovative approaches are needed. However, these market-based solutions cannot replace a more comprehensive approach for debt restructuring.

4 What Factors Must Be Considered in Order to Pave the Way for Broad-Based Reform?

In 2014, the United Nations General Assembly passed a resolution *"Towards the establishment of a multilateral legal framework for sovereign debt restructuring processes."*[51] The substantive contents and nature of the mechanism have not been agreed on. Nonetheless, among the points of contention among countries that voted in favour of the resolution is the question of what legal structure this mechanism should take—"a binding but not comprehensive framework" or "a comprehensive but non-binding framework."[52] The literature on SoDR raises many concerns with the statutory approach, yet close to a decade after the rejection of this approach within the IMF, and the lack of progress on an international framework for SoDR at the United Nations, the debate seems to have gone full circle since once again there is a call for institutional reform.[53] In the end, the challenge of correcting the SoDR framework could be corrected if all States could agree on one entity to which they could delegate responsibility for coordinating the development of international standards dealing with economics and finance issues as well as social, and human rights, and cultural issues.[54] Such coordination would guarantee that all of these issues are included in procedures such as

---

[51] UNGA Resolution, "Towards the Establishment of A Multilateral Legal Framework for Sovereign Debt Restructuring Processes" (2015), UNGA Resolution 68/304.

[52] Skylar Brooks and Domenico Lombardi, "Governing Sovereign Debt Restructuring Through Regulatory Standards" 2016 at 292, Journal of Globalization and Devcelopment 6:2 287.

[53] *See* Federico Sturzenegger and Jeromin Zettelmeyer, "Debt Defaults and Lessons from a Decade of Crises" (2006) at 277. (With the failure of the IMF's SDRM, Sturzenegger and Zettelmeyer noted that "it is doubtful that a mechanism of this kind will ever see the light of day." With the efforts at the UNGA, this may no longer be the case as statutory mechanisms are being reconsidered, although the form will probably differ from the IMF's SDRM).

[54] Daniel Bradlow, "Can Parallel Lines Ever Meet? The Strange Case of the International Standards on Sovereign Debt and Business and Human Rights" (2016) Vol. 41: 2, The Yale Journal of International Law 236. *Also see* Anna Gelpern, "Sovereign Debt: Now What?" (2016) 41: 2 at 86, The Yale Journal of International Law 45.

SoDRs, which are ultimately holistic in nature and are seen as such by their stakeholders.[55] What is needed for broad-based reform includes:

- An independent third party that can intervene in SoDR;
- Resolution of procedural inefficiencies that are resulting in protracted restructurings, which I believe requires the development of an independent SoDR mechanism that can adequately deliver SoDR in a timely and efficient manner;
- More significant development of concrete tools to resolve substantive shortcomings in the present regime through better treatment of human rights and development concerns. These human rights and developmental challenges can arise when debtors use limited resources for debt repayment at the expenses of human rights, as well as the austerity measures by governments; and
- Development of measures that emphasise more equitable burden-sharing.

4.1 *The rationale for a formal and global approach/mechanism from an African perspective*

A formal and global approach to restructuring is appealing from an African perspective in that it will not only facilitate a fresh start but also ensure that debtors have a fair start. The threats arising from default or even debt distress is even more evident in countries that lack checks and balances such as effective stakeholder engagement and participation, transparency in the law-making processes and institutional mechanisms that hold people accountable. There is indeed appeal in a more informal structure that may be perceived as promoting more flexibility. Nonetheless, legal uncertainty should not be mistaken for flexibility, although there is a thin line separating the two. Neither should legal certainty presuppose undesired inflexibility. The rationale for the creation for a formal SoDR framework is to create predictability and stability, through the legal certainty of norms; promote fairer outcomes for all parties; and reinforce legitimacy through its very adoption and ensure accountability of all parties. It might also be utilized to address not just ex-ante procedural concerns

---

[55] *Supra* note 44.

in restructuring, but also wider challenges such as human rights and climate change, among others. This may be accomplished by ensuring that the normative framework upon which a new approach should be established is founded on good principles, includes procedures to promote and defend human rights, and takes into consideration vulnerable nations' developmental concerns. An alternative argument that may be made, that what is needed instead is to strengthen the Common Framework. Notably, so far, only Chad, Ethiopia, Ghana, and Zambia have requested debt treatment under the Common Framework, and none of them have progressed much in the process. Further, the program faces the criticism of being a long-drawn process, being vague and facing the challenge of not translating principles into tangible outcomes, all of which have weakened its credibility.[56] Notably, the challenges in the debt landscape predate the COVID-19 Pandemic, which required a broad-based challenge. The Common Framework was a response to the shocks of the Pandemic. Despite the name, the Common Framework has been designed as more of a case-by-case approach. The notion of strengthening this framework does not negate the need for a broad-based mechanism for debt restructuring.

4.2 *African solutions should be sought in parallel to global solutions*

The case for reform is compelling enough to merit looking at African solutions in parallel to a global approach. As a result, in addition to global approaches, African solutions should be investigated concurrently. A key motivation for this approach in part stems from what may be seen as political limitations of a global statute. Specifically, among the critical motivations of an incremental approach to SoDR architectural reform and the various proposals to date is the view that there are political limitations to the acceptance of an international treaty by critical global financial centres. In this respect, Bradlow correctly notes that:

> Given the general complexities of SODRs and the lack of agreement on the need for an independent third-party mechanism capable of enforcing a SODR outcome, and the range of considerations that should be taken into account in a SODR, it is

---

[56] Masood Ahmed and Hannah Brown, "Fix the Common Framework for Debt Before It Is Too Late" (2022), CDG, available at https://www.cgdev.org/blog/fix-common-framework-debt-it-too-late.

unlikely that agreement could be reached on establishing a coordinating mechanism that has anything more than advisory powers. Nevertheless, such an advisory mechanism if it had sufficient expertise and credibility and a sufficiently high profile, could play a useful informational role and could shift the burden of justifying exclusion of either the procedural or the substantive standards from an SODR onto those parties that are resistant to including both sets of standards.[57]

African countries ought to be afforded the opportunity to determine and contribute to the approaches that respond to debt-related issues and to design a future for the continent. In line with this view, I propose the development of African regional solutions to SoDR. In this respect, I propose the establishment of an 'African Sovereign Debt Forum' (ASDF) specifically aimed at creating a 'centre of excellence' on SoDR as well as a forum where debtors and creditors may negotiate and discuss critical issues on SoDR and other debt sustainability-related issues. This not only presents the opportunity to create a repository of African knowledge on contemporary SoDR but among the main responsibilities that this institution may be tasked with is the development of a model SoDR statute and model contractual approach. The value of this is that countries that are currently facing debt distress may not only have the benefit of a neutral venue for the deliberation of debt-related issues but the 'centre of excellence' will provide resources and technical assistance that may assist countries. Additionally, it will act as a platform for the dissemination of information between parties in the SoDR process and as a platform for consultations. It may also be a venue for supervised negotiations between SoDR stakeholders. This is distinct from the African Legal Support Facility, which offers technical assistance to African Development Bank member states on SoDR and other legal matters. The question that this proposal raises is why there should be an African institutional arrangement. This proposal offers the potential to create an environment in which Africa-specific SoDR challenges may be addressed, as well as the ability to analyse SoDR and other debt-related issues from an African perspective. The core features of this proposal requires further development.

---

[57] Daniel D. Bradlow, "A Parallel Lines Ever Meet? The Strange Case of the International Standards on Sovereign Debt and Business and Human rights" (2016) Vol. 41: 2 at 237, THE YALE JOURNAL OF INTERNATIONAL LAW.

Notably, as economies become more interconnected, there will be an increase in systemic concerns surrounding debt crises, which may be international or even regional in scope. In this regard, although African regional integration differs from that of the European Union, there is an important lesson to be learned from the European regional experience and approach to SoDR. Regional integration in Africa brings with it the risk of integrated spill over effects of debt crisis and restructuring, necessitating a regional approach. In the case of African nations, regional integration is at the point of an African Continental Free Trade Area (AfCFTA), that has already been established. It remains to be seen what effect African regional integration may have on individual African nations in times of financial difficulty.

4.3 SoDR Reform Requires a Human Rights-Based Approach

There is a case for creating greater links between human rights and sovereign debt and the process of restructuring more specifically. There is however a gap in the human rights treatment of SoDR.[58] A significant component of a "successful" SoDR is the process that preserves 'at the outset creditors' rights while promoting sustained and inclusive economic growth and sustainable development, minimizing economic and social costs, warranting the stability of the international financial system and respecting human rights. As such, the question, therefore, is how to reform SoDR in a manner that both leads to efficiency gains, and stabilised debt while also taking into account the human cost and development concerns. In this respect, transforming SoDR as we know it, requires developing, amongst other things, a Human Rights-Based Approach (HRBA) to SoDR.

A human rights approach requires the consideration of human rights concerns from the onset. In this respect, a key feature is the incorporation of human rights in the definition and shared understanding of "debt sustainability." Taking human rights into account in SoDR necessitates the following:

(i) Promoting the enjoyment of fundamental human rights by invoking existing human rights obligations in current human rights instruments

---

[58] *See* Magalie L. Masamba, "Sovereign Debt Restructuring and Human Rights: Overcoming A False Binary" (2022) at 176-211, COVID-19 AND SOVEREIGN DEBT: THE CASE OF SADC.

and their enforcement in SoDR. A rights-based approach to SoDR is one that will result in normatively basing SoDR on international human rights standards. In particular, the HRBA 'integrates the norms, standards and principles of the international human rights system into the plans, policies and processes of development. The norms and standards are those contained in the wealth of international instruments.'[59]

(ii) Developing human rights impact assessment tools and their incorporation in the SoDR process. There is a need for consistent use of Human Rights Impact Assessment tools throughout the lending lifecycle. In fact, in 2019, the UN Independent Expert developed the Guiding Principles on Human Rights Impact Assessments of Economic Reforms. Among these, Principle 12 on 'Debt sustainability, debt relief and restructuring' sets out that: *"Independent debt sustainability analysis should incorporate human rights impact assessments. Findings of human rights impact assessments should be used to inform debt strategies, debt relief programmes and restructuring negotiations, potentially triggering the latter where actual or potential adverse impacts are identified."* [60] There is a need for further research on the use of human rights-based impact assessments in debt management and debt restructuring. While these are only high-level principles they are important as they stress the need for an impact assessment that tackles human rights.

From the world of trade and investment law, a Human Rights Impact Assessment of the AfCFTA, can be very instructive on the substance of human rights

---

[59] S Gruskin, MA Grodin, CJ Annas & SP Marks (eds) Perspectives on health and human rights, (2005), at 102.

[60] Guiding Principles On Human Rights Impact Assessments Of Economic Reforms, Report of the Independent Expert on the effects of foreign debt and other related international financial obligations of States on the full enjoyment of human rights, particularly economic, social and cultural rights, Human Rights Council Fortieth session, (25 February–22 March 2019) at 13, available at https://undocs.org/A/HRC/40/57.

impact assessments, especially in the African context.[61] However, the complexity will be adapting an assessment tool to the restructuring context.[61] Developing a human rights impact assessment linked to a restructuring is complex as it requires determining the nature of the rights to be assessed, the timing of that assessment, who and how will conduct is and how will it be conducted during the very stressful and time sensitive context of a restructuring.

5 Conclusion

The purpose of this chapter was to contribute to the policy debate on SoDR, offer a new point of view of a post-COVID 19 pandemic world, as well as stimulate discussion on SoDR and its relationship to and treatment of broader problems such as climate change. What is evident is that the debt situation of African countries is very concerning and the continent is at the brink of a debt crisis. The debate on solutions to debt restructuring has sought to do two things, stimulate private sector participation in restructuring, and secondly deal with the broad issues of climate change, and to a lesser extent social justice and human rights. This chapter has highlighted some of the key challenges in the landscape. The chapter presented three very valuable innovations to these challenges, the proposal of Debt Relief for a Green and Inclusive Recovery, the use of Brady bond-like restructuring and the possibility of the use of climate-related instruments, and finally the development of a DOVE Fund to buy and restructure African distressed debt and possibly link restructuring with broader issues such as environmental, social and governance concerns. These proposals are very valuable and should be further developed through case studies of how they could apply in the African context. Nevertheless, they cannot replace the need for a broad-based mechanism or global rule of law for debt restructuring, which this chapter has shared thoughts on.

---

[61] James Thuo Gathii, Kimberly Burnett, Chris Changwe Nshimbi and Caroline Domme, "The Continental Free Trade Area (CFTA) in Africa—A Human Rights Perspective," available at https://www.ohchr.org/sites/default/files/Documents/Issues/Globalization/TheCFTA_A_HR_ImpactAssessment.pdf

CHAPTER TWO

Designing an African Common Position and Strategy on Vulture Fund Litigation

Marie-Louise F. Arena*

1 Introduction

In today's global financial architecture, vulture fund litigation appears to be weaponised against sovereignty of indebted states. The predatory investment practices of vulture funds threaten the development opportunities of many highly indebted poor countries (HIPC), especially in Africa.[1] Vulture funds take advantage of distressed economies' hardship by profiting at the expense of other creditors who participate in debt restructurings. The world's attention had turned to the practices of vulture funds after The United States' Supreme Court decision in the case of *Republic of Argentina v. NML Capital, Ltd. (Equal Treatment Case III)*.[2] Since then, the heat has been on the regulation of vulture fund leading to series of foreign legislations aiming to curb the lawlessness around vulture fund investments.[3] The fundamental strategy of

---

* Doctoral Candidate of International Tax Law at the University of Pretoria in South Africa. Before that she was Principal Law Researcher and Legislative Drafter of the Law Reform Commission of Nigeria. She holds a Masters Degree in International Trade and Investment Law from the University of Pretoria.

[1] AFRICAN DEVELOPMENT BANK GROUP, *Vulture Funds in the Sovereign Debt Context*, https://www.afdb.org/en/topics-and-sectors/initiatives-partnerships/african-legal-support-facility/vulture-funds-in-the-sovereign-debt-context (last visited 12 May 2022).

[2] *Republic of Arg. v. NML Capital, Ltd.*, 573 U.S. 134 (2014).(The Court ordered Argentina to pay the holdout creditor who rejected the debt restructuring debt swap. NML bought Argentinian bonds in 2008 at US$48 million and six years later Argentina was ordered to pay US$832 million.)

[3] For example, the [AntiVulture Funds Law] of July 12, 2015, MONITEUR BELGE [M.B.] [Official Gazette of Belgium] Sept. 11, 2015, 57357; the United Kingdom Debt Relief (Developing Countries) Act 2010, and others.

vulture funds is to apply pressure on sovereign debtors to honour their debts, especially when the debtors are in financial distress. Through the unbridled use of litigation, vulture fund investors attempt to obtain attachment on the sovereign debtor's overseas assets to recover their bond principal and interest.

Recently, Puerto Rico, an island territory of the United States has felt the callousness of vulture funds.[4] Taking advantage of the fall in prices because of Covid-19 pandemic, these vulture investors bought over US$ 400 million worth of Puerto Rican bonds, aided by insider trading.[5] In 2007 Zambia experienced the brunt of vulture funds when Donegal was sued for over US$ 50 million after acquiring a debt owed by Zambia to Romania for its credit purchase of agricultural machinery from Romania in 1979.[6] Since 2020, Zambia has been struggling with external debt owed mainly to China and Chinese Creditors, valued at about US$ three billion.[7] Similarly, the current international investor-state dispute settlement (ISDS) mechanism has also contributed to the reckless "litigation-thirst" of holdout creditors.[8] Pahis notes that the current spate of investment-state decisions show that sovereign debt will continue to be governed by bilateral investment treaties (BITs). Given the fact that several uncoordinated institutions have governed previous debt crises and the ISDS system is plagued with the preferential treatment of investors at the expense of states, the governance of sovereign debt under BITs would eventually subvert the

---

[4] Public Accountability Initiative, *The 21 Vulture Funds Stalking Puerto Rico's Central Government*, 1–13 (2020), https://public-accountability.org/wp-content/uploads/2020/08/PAI-VultureDebtReport_English.pdf; HEDGEPAPER, *Pain And Profit In Sovereign Debt: How New York Can Stop Vulture Funds From Preying On Countries*, (December, 15 2021), https://hedgeclippers.org/pain-and-profit-in-sovereign-debt-how-new-york-can-stop-vulture-funds-from-preying-on-countries/.

[5] Public Accountability Initiative, supra note 4. See also Not a Game Its People, The Gamification of Puerto Rico, *Op ed* https://notagameitspeople.org/oped accessed 4 June 2022

[6] *Donegal Int'l Ltd. v. Zambia & Anor*, [2007] EWHC (Comm) 197 (Donegal bought the debt from Romania in 1999 and held the debt until the IMF HIPC debt relief in 2005); *See also* ACW Kariuki, *The State, the Vulture and the Debt*, 5 INT'L CORP. RESCUE 1, 1–3 (2008).

[7] Chris Mfula & Karin Strohecker, *Zambia heads toward Africa's first post-COVID default as debt deadlines loom* REUTERS FINANCIALS, (Nov. 13, 2020).https://www.reuters.com/article/zambia-debt-idUSL8N2HY84L

[8] Stratos Pahis, *BITs & Bonds: The International Law and Economics of Sovereign Debt* 115 AM. J. OF INT'L L. 242, 244–280 (2021).

economic purpose of BITs by encouraging unproductive State and creditor conduct.[9] Investors take advantage of the protective provisions of BITs, enforced by the International Centre for the Settlement of Investment Disputes (ICSID) to refuse participation in sovereign restructuring efforts with the intention of using ICSID proceedings and decisions to receive larger payments from defaulted bonds.[10] Vulture funds have been successful in bringing recovery actions against sovereign governments and making profits from their struggling economies. As a lot of African countries have entered the debt twilight zone, a common position on vulture funds become essential.

Several global north protagonists of vulture funds (from a creditor right perspective) have supported the practices of vulture funds.[11] So far, vulture investors/creditors do not perceive a problem with the investment practices of vulture funds. Instead, creditors have commended vulture funds for providing relief to desperate primary creditors reluctant to sue sovereign states for recovery.[12] Some scholars have argued that vulture funds have some benefits. For example, for their higher returns on low investments; their ability to influence the international bond market; for resolving the financial problems of the banks; and for forestalling short-term debt crisis by sovereigns. Vulture investors insist that the pressure from vulture fund litigation might encourage transparency and due diligence in the sovereign debtors by exercising caution and fiscally prudent strategies in future bond transactions.[13] Fisch and Gentile

---

[9] *Id. See also,* Marie-Louise Aren, *The Brazilian Cooperation and Facilitation Investment Agreement in the International Investment System: Crucial Lessons for Global South Countries in Triangular Cooperation* IFP RESEARCH COHORT PAPERS 87–105 (2021)(on the unfavourable treatment of sovereign states vis-a-viz the foreign investor in the ISDS system).

[10] Alison Wirtz, *Bilateral Investment Treaties, Holdout Investors, and Their Impact on Grenada's Sovereign Debt Crisis* 16 CHI. J. INT'L L. 249 (2015).

[11] William W. Bratton & G Mitu Gulati, *Sovereign Debt Restructuring and the Best Interest of Creditors*, 57 VAND. L. REV. 1 (2004).

[12] Devi Sookun STOP VULTURE FUNDS LAWSUIT: A HANDBOOK 10 (2010).

[13] Andrei Shleifer, *Will The Sovereign Debt Market Survive?* 93 AM. ECON. REV. –85–90 (2003). *See* Lucas Wonzy, *National Anti-Vulture Funds Legislation: Belgium's Turn,* 2017 COLUM. BUS. L. REV. 697, 705–709 (2017) (who espouses from a corporate law perspective the benefits of vulture funds in promoting efficient capital structures and sovereign responsible financial behaviour). *See also* Colby Smith, *The Utility of Vulture Funds*, FINANCIAL TIMES, (Apr. 16, 2019), https://www.ft.com/content/ccc417fa-e2b8-37d2-b017-3852ef8dd6d2.

argue that holdout creditors also put a safety check on unscrupulous defaults and excessive restructuring terms.[14] This is indeed coupled with the legal recognition of vulture fund investing and debt recovery arrangements under the sanctity of contracts doctrine, where granting debt restructuring protection and opportunity is regarded as a unilateral annulment of the sovereign lenders contractual right to debt repayment.[15]

Vulture funds have been condemned for profiting from countries that are in financial distress and lacking the resources to engage in lengthy judicial processes.[16] Vulture funds have also been criticized for their immoral debt recovery mechanisms. This is because vulture funds buy sovereign debts at deep discounts, for the purpose of suing debtors for recovery of the full face value of outstanding interest and principal.[17] Vulture fund litigation pose a huge hazard to countries in debt distress and the global debt restructuring regime.[18] The holdout tactics of vulture funds delay debt restructuring processes and thus prolong debt crises and the suffering of their populations through high litigation costs and buy-out costs for the sovereign debtor country. The judicial system has preserved this hegemonic brutality of vulture funds by endorsing the legality of vulture activities under private contractual law, thereby enabling a lack of responsibility for the debt distress of the country in question.[19] This is particularly worrisome because vulture funds are able to operate effectively because of the absence

---

[14] Jill E. Fisch & Caroline M. Gentile, *Vultures or Vanguards? The Role of Litigation in Sovereign Debt Restructuring*, PENN L. FACULTY SCHOLARSHIP (2004); *See also* Daniel J. Brutti, *Sovereign Debt Crises and Vulture Hedge Funds: Issues and Policy Solutions* 61 B.C. L. REV. 1819, 1836–1837 (2020) (mentions that vulture funds provide a deterrent effect against sovereign moral hazard and provide much required liquidity).

[15] James Gathii, *The Sanctity of Sovereign Loan Contracts and its Origins in Enforcement Litigation*, 38 GEO. WASH. INTL. L REV. 251 (2009).

[16] Hancen Yu, *"Official" Bondholder: A New Holdout Creature in Sovereign Debt Restructuring After Vulture Funds?*, 16 WASH. U. GLOB. STUD. L. REV. 535 (2017).

[17] Daniel Bradlow, *Op-Ed: Vultures, Doves and African Debt: Here's a Way Out*, CTR. FOR HUM. RTS (Jan. 12, 2021). https://www.chr.up.ac.za/opinion-pieces/2075-op-ed-vultures-doves-and-african-debt-here-s-a-way-out; *See also* Mine Doyran, *The Argentine Dilemma: "Vulture Funds" and the Risks Posed to Developing Economies*, 2 CLASS, RACE AND CORPORATE POWER 13–20 (2014).

[18] Michael Waibel, *Opening Pandora's Box: Sovereign Bonds in International Arbitration*, 101 AM. J. INT'L L. 711, 711–759 (2007).

[19] See the following successful cases backing holdout strategies—*CIBC Bank & Trust Co (Cayman) Ltd v Banco Central do Brasil*, 886 F. Supp. 1105 (SDNY 1995); *Elliott Associates LP v Peru*, General Docketno 2000/QR/92 (Court of Appeals of Brussels, 8th Chamber, 26.9.2000).

of a binding legal bankruptcy and debt restructuring framework and an overdependence on the foreign domestic laws to regulate debt activities.

For Africa, the Covid-19 pandemic and the frantic economic recovery efforts being made create a perfect investment prospect for vulture fund to enlarge their business.[20] Vulture funds are circling to acquire the distressed and exposed debt of endangered African economies. The non-existence of clear global rules on sovereign lending and debt restructuring is disastrous for vulnerable African economies.[21] In arriving at a common African position, this chapter seeks to address the following main questions: are the current national and regulations sufficient and soft international laws sufficient to protect the vulnerable debt situations of African countries from the onslaught of vulture litigation? It is the purview of this chapter, thus, to analyse the vulture fund litigation and the present legal framework both at domestic and legal level protecting African sovereigns with the aim of coming up with a common position on debt.

2 Overview of Vulture Fund and Litigation

Sovereign nations like many other corporate organisations, require steady flow of income to finance their budgets.[22] Traditionally, taxation and multilateral bank loans have been the main channels of raising sovereign finance. However, in recent times, sovereign nations have sought to raise finance by issuing fixed-income debt securities that pay regular interest payments.[23] This has led to the emergence of a secondary

---

[20] Makhtar Diop, *Africa's Economic Recovery: Financing Post-Pandemic Growth in* Brooking Foresight Africa 8 (2022); *See also* Rabah Arezki & Aitor Erce, *How to reignite Africa's growth and avoid the need for future debt jubilee* Brookings Future Development (Dec. 8 2020). https://www.brookings.edu/blog/future-development/2020/12/08/how-to-reignite-africas-growth-and-avoid-the-need-for-future-debt-jubilee/.

[21] *See* IMF, *Heavily Indebted Poor Countries Initiative and Multilateral Debt Relief Initiative Statistical Update*, Staff Report on Heavily Indebted Poor Countries Initiative, 46 (Mar. 2016) (the IMF reported in 2013 there were 17 commercial creditor lawsuits against eight HIPCs with six in Africa (Democratic Republic of the Congo, Ethiopia, Republic of the Congo, Sudan, Togo and Uganda), seeking about $775 million against $477 million in original claims).

[22] Solabomi Omobola Ajibolade & Collins Sankay Oboh, *A Critical Examination of Government Budgeting and Public Funds Management in Nigeria*, Int'l J. Pub. Leadership (Dec. 1, 2017)

[23] Michael Olabisi & Howard Stein, *Sovereign Bond Issues: Do African Countries Pay More to Borrow?*, 2 J. Afr. Trade 87, 87–109 (2015).

market for sovereign bonds, and in particular a demand for distressed debt bonds, thereby affording opportunities for vulture fund investing and attendant arbitrage.[24] Vulture funds are a sub-set of hedge funds that invest in distressed sovereign securities (with a high chance of default), often at highly discounted prices in the secondary market.[25] A distinguishing feature of vulture fund investing from other hedge funds is the intentionality of the purchase by vulture funds from the original creditors, who prefer to unload the bad debt risk from their books.[26] As a main strategy, vulture fund investors calculatedly seek out risky and highly discounted debt instruments of almost bankrupt sovereign states, with the aim of suing the defaulting sovereign state for the full nominal amount of the debt, including interest.[27] Doyran describes them as a particular type of holdout creditors who through the secondary market buy distressed assets at a discount and then abstain from sovereign debt restructurings.[28]

Distressed securities are very attractive to vulture funds. Due to the sovereign issuer's high default risk and the failure to service the debt, the debt instruments consequently drop in value and carry a credit rating of CCC or below from the popular rating agencies like S&P, Moody's and Fitch Group Investors, sending a signal to the vultures to swoop in with the promise for high investment yields.[29] Sovereign debt credit ratings do indirectly contribute to the explosion of vulture fund activities as a result of their evaluative impact on investors' decision. Credit rating agencies provide a summary appraisal of the capability and willingness of sovereign governments to repay their public debt as an indicator of their default probability without a full consideration of the fundamentals and nuances.[30] Debt ratings encourage the swarming of vulture funds on distressed bonds and deepen the debt distress of the

---

[24] Sookun, *supra* note 12, at 7–8.

[25] AFRICAN DEVELOPMENT BANK GROUP, *supra* note 1.

[26] *Id.*

[27] *Id.*

[28] Mine Doyran, *The Argentine Dilemma: "Vulture Funds" and the Risks Posed to Developing Economies*, 2 (3) CLASS, RACE AND CORPORATE POWER 13–20 (2014).

[29] CORPORATE FINANCE INSTITUTE, *Vulture Funds* https://corporatefinanceinstitute.com/resources/knowledge/trading-investing/vulture-funds/.

[30] Peter Yeoh, *Sovereign default restructuring options and challenges in the European Monetary Union*, 53 INT'L J. L. & MGMT. 182, 182–198 (2011) (on the role of credit agencies); *See*, RESEARCH HANDBOOK ON HEDGE FUNDS, PRIVATE EQUITY AND ALTERNATIVE INVESTMENTS 343-345 (Phoebus Athanassiou ed., 2012) (the role of vulture funds in eds).

sovereign state as was seen in the European debt crisis, which has been controversially attributed to the activities of vulture funds.[31] Against this backdrop, the emergence of predatory funds targeted at sovereign guarantees of emerging economies for discounted investment opportunities and its modus operandi becomes vital.

The stage for present vulture fund investing began around the early 1970s. Prior to the 1970s, the sovereign debt was prudently restricted to bilateral and multilateral loan agreements from the Bretton Woods Institutions. However, the Yom-Kippur War of 1973 led to the imposition of oil embargo by Arab delegation of OPEC against major Western nations who relied on foreign oil, resulting in oil supply disruptions and price increase.[32] The rise in oil prices produced huge surpluses of petro-dollars for exporting countries which were deposited in international commercial banks. The bank deposits glut positioned these commercial banks over time to nearly oust the Bretton Wood institutions as major sovereign financiers by becoming the new leading credit intermediaries for sovereigns. Subsequently, the banks organised themselves into syndicates to provide syndicated commercial loans to developing countries, especially the least developing countries required development finance.[33] There were three main factors why syndicated loans were not aggressively enforced as vulture funds now do with bonds. Sovereign immunity was absolute, strict banking regulations/monitoring mechanisms estopped sovereign debt litigation, and the syndicated nature of the loans made enforcement of debt contracts against sovereigns' asset attachment almost impractical.[34] Despite these risks, bank lending to sovereigns continued despite a high risk of sovereign payment default.

---

[31] *Id.* at 340.

[32] *See* Roy L. Nersesian, ENERGY FOR THE 21ST CENTURY 147 (2006) (OPEC was supplying 56% of the world's oil at the time of the War in 1973). *See also* Felix Kruse, OIL POLITICS: THE WEST AND ITS DESIRE FOR ENERGY SECURITY SINCE 1950, 33 (2014).

[33] Craig N. Murphy & Enrico Augelli, *International Institutions, Decolonization, and Development*, 14 INT'L POL. SCI. REV. 71 (1993).

[34] Gathii, *supra* note 15 (states could rely easily on sovereign immunity defence because it was before the enactment of the FSIA and UK State Immunity Act and the narrow interpretation of the Courts on sovereign immunity under the sanctity of contract principle. *See* Michael P. Dooley, *A Retrospective on the Debt Crisis in* UNDERSTANDING INTERDEPENDENCE: THE MACROECONOMICS OF THE OPEN ECONOMY (1995) (also, the syndication of debt among banks made recovery impractical, as a fund intending to litigate had to buy out the entire syndicate of holders or risk having the proceeds of litigation attached pursuant to sharing clauses in the loan agreements).

In the late 1970s, the United States and United Kingdom remedied the sovereign default redress risk by enacting laws that relaxed litigation against sovereign states by securing the right of foreign creditors to seize assets abroad and also allowed governments to borrow under the domestic legal systems of developed countries.[35] Perhaps, it was becoming apparent that the increasingly unsustainable borrowing by developing countries would eventually result to a default, hence the laws prepared the way for developed country creditors to sue. Whatever the reason for these laws, the implication was that it set the enabling environment for sovereign debt litigation to occur in the 80s and upwards from Latin American debt payment defaults.[36] Regardless of the new laws, the demand for capital drove an upsurge in interest rates. Around 1982, things began to fall apart from the global recession resulting in a series of debt repayment defaults in Latin America beginning with Mexico.[37] In response, the Baker Plan was instituted where the Bretton Wood Institutions increased their lending to developing countries in exchange for market-oriented reforms.[38]

These reforms provided a hedge of sorts for commercial banks to re-finance the debt of these heavily indebted countries. However, the plan failed mainly because increased private capital inflow did not result in economic growth as envisaged. In its place, the Brady plan emerged in 1986 to restructure the debt mechanism through the IMF. The Brady plan proposed the exchange of IMF dollar loans for dollar bonds issued by heavily indebted developing countries. The Brady Bond provided some respite to Mexico but not without severe implications on the sovereign debt market. First, the Brady bonds reconfigured the debt market by bringing new non-traditional players consisting of private investment/hedge funds with different agenda and playing rules. Also, the Brady plan paved the way for the initial creditors (syndicated bank lenders) to sell their debt into the secondary market with little restraint. In this

---

[35] Foreign Sovereign Immunities Act of 1976 (FSIA), 28 U.S.C. §§ 1602–1611; State Immunity Act of 1978, 1978 c. 33.

[36] David Felix, *Alternative Outcomes of the Latin American Debt Crisis: Lessons from the Past*, 2 LAT. AM. RSCH. REV. 3 (1987).

[37] Rabobank, *The Mexican 1982 debt crisis* Economic Report 1-6 (2013).

[38] *See* LA Sulaiman, SO Migiro, & OA Aluko, *The structural adjustment program in developing economies: pain or gain? Evidence from Nigeria*, 3 PUB. & MUN. FIN., 41–50 (2014) (like the Structural Adjustment Programme).

process, a lot of sovereign debts were repurchased and converted into local currency.[39] By the 1990s sovereign debt had changed from syndicated bank loans into sovereign bonds that could be traded in the secondary market and become cheap up for a new set of speculative investors known as vulture investors. Since then, the participation of vulture investors steadily increased culminating in the very public Argentine debt crisis of 2001 and ensuing aggressive vulture fund litigation for recovery in the US and other developed countries.[40]

2.1 Vulture Fund Litigation

Vulture funds centre around its foundational purpose and strategy- the use of litigation to enforce payments. To this end, vulture funds employ various legal and non-legal strategies in undermining the economic sovereignty of its victims. They include the successful use of litigation, model parri-passu clauses and instrumentality of foreign domestic laws.[41] Litigation remains the favourite weapon of vulture funders in enforce their debt contracts. Initially, vulture funders were not very certain about their ability to successfully claim against sovereign debtors due to the principle of sovereign immunity and the non-commercial purpose of lending. However, vulture fund investors ensure sovereigns waived their immunity via loan agreement terms, emboldened by the provision of section 1605(1) of the FSIA.[42] The direct waiver of immunity by many sovereigns created the effect of bringing the loan agreement under the realms of private law. The impact is that it tied the hands of sovereign states in ceasing from honouring the debt contract using public policy.

The courts also contributed to the current barrage of vulture fund litigation. Previously, for a sovereign debt default claim to be successful, the sovereign immunity

---

[39] ANTHONY SANDERS & MARCIA CORNETT, FINANCIAL INSTITUTIONS MANAGEMENT 443 (2008)

[40] *Donegal Int'l Ltd. v. Zambia & Anor*, *supra* note 6 (from global bond issuance in the 1990s and the commercial loan conversion to bonds from the political upheaval in the Democratic republic of Congo and most recently the Zambia crisis).). *See also* L Farry, *When Globalisation Fails: Vulture Funds and Sub-Saharan Africa's Debt Crisis*, UCLA CENTRE FOR AMERICAN POLITICS AND PUBLIC POLICY POLITICAL SCIENCE 16 (2007).

[41] Charles G. Berry, *Pari Passu Means What Now?* N.Y. L. J. (Mar. 6, 2006).

[42] FSIA *supra* note 35 (an express waiver under § 1605(a)(1) must give a clear, complete, unambiguous, and unmistakable manifestation of the sovereign's intent to waive its immunity).

waiver by the sovereign state had to be direct, for example by way of an agreement, because sovereign states enjoyed absolute immunity.[43] However, in the case in the case of *Republic of Argentina v. Weltover*, the Courts began to change the trend of absolute sovereign immunity and its direct waiver by interpreting specific provisions of the FSIA to enforce a restrictive theory of sovereign immunity.[44] In the *Weltover* case, the Supreme Court affirmed the decision of a US District Court that it had jurisdiction under the FSIA to determine the sovereign bond payment default suit filed against Argentina for unilaterally changing the terms of a bond agreement to reschedule debt payment.[45] It was also held that foreign states are subject to lawsuit in American courts for, inter alia, acts taken "in connection with a commercial activity" that have "a direct effect in the United States".[46] Granted, the evolving structure of the international law includes the recognition that individuals and other non-sovereign persons have rights under international law and by implication necessitates a change in the approach to sovereign immunity.[47] However, vulture creditors appear to be

---

[43] Renana B. Abrams, *The Foreign Sovereign Immunities Act: Inconsistencies in Application of the Commercial Activity Direct Effect Exception*, 5 EMORY INT'L REV. 211 (1991).

[44] *Republic of Arg. v. Weltover, Inc.,* 504 U.S. 607, 609-620 (1992).(the FSIA provides the sole basis for US courts exercising jurisdiction over a foreign sovereign); *See Argentine Republic v. Amerada Hess Shipping Corp.,* 488 U. S. 428, 434–439 (1989) (the FSIA thus serves as an instrument to enforce restrictive immunity in foreign sovereign commercial activities in the marketplace).

[45] *Id.* (the Court arrived at this decision because the actions of Argentina, regardless of the motive behind them were regarded by the courts as the type of actions done by private parties in commerce. Also, the Bonods (Argentine Bonds) were regarded as "garden-variety debt instruments". Therefore, by issuing the Bonods in the marketplace, Argentina had indirectly waived its immunity (by engaging in "commercial activities")—which is an exception to foreign sovereign immunity under the FSIA).

[46] FSIA supra note 35 (similarly, the "commercial activity exception" is also recognised by Article 10 of the UN General Assembly, *United Nations Convention on Jurisdictional Immunities of States and Their Property,* 2 December 2004, A/RES/59/38 (not yet in force), which provides that "If a State engages in a commercial transaction with a foreign natural or juridical person and, by virtue of the applicable rules of private international law, differences relating to the commercial transaction fall within the jurisdiction of a court of another State, the State cannot invoke immunity from that jurisdiction in a proceeding arising out of that commercial transaction." This UN position appears to "internationalise" "commercial activities exception," created by the US courts where State immunity cannot be invoked for commercial transactions).

[47] *See* Adam C Belsky et al., *Implied Waiver under the FSIA: A Proposed Exception to Immunity for Violations of Peremptory Norms of International Law,* 77 CAL. L. REV. 365–415 (1989) (a change from the principle of comity, then to an absolute legal principle, and presently to a restrictive principle).

abusing these rights and its enforcement. Likewise, the use of champerty and its subsequent legalisation encourages vulture fund lawsuits.[48]

Vulture fund have been able to officially legalize their right to litigate via shrewd exploitation of specific clauses embedded in the debt contract like the pari-passu clause, which ordinarily lacks interpretative clarity.[49] The problem with the clause is that it protects the vulture fund from their proportionate share in debt restructuring by forbidding governments to pay majority creditors that participated and accepted a restructuring process without also paying the holdout creditors. Vulture funds use the pari-passu clause to guarantee face value recoveries on debt contracts that have been restructured. For instance, in *Re: Elliott Associates, L.P. v. Republic of Peru*, Elliot Associates owned by the kingpin of Vulture funders Paul Singer purchased defaulted Peruvian sovereign debt with a nominal value of $20 million.[50] During debt restructuring, while other creditors accepted a haircut Elliott held out its debt, stalling the debt restructuring process. Elliott sued and argued that the pari-passu clause in the loan agreement forbade the prioritisation of the majority creditors to the detriment of the holdout minority creditors. The lower court accepted Peru's champerty defence. However, the appeal court reversed the decision in Elliott Associate favour, enabling Elliot to enforce its right to collect the total value of the debt plus interest by petitioning to seize Peruvian overseas assets and even before debt payments to Peru's Brady Bond holders.

Vulture funds also prefer to secure their holdout tactics by buying sovereign bonds governed by UK or US law. The reason for this is not far-fetched. Foreign law bonds provide more security than domestic law bonds because the bond terms cannot be easily changed by the sovereign debtor governments without changing the foreign law protecting the bond, unlike domestic bonds that can be easily changed by

---

[48] *See* S.J. Brooks, *Champerty and Maintenance in the United States*, 3 VA. L. REV. 421 (1916) (champerty is an agreement between the party suing (plaintiff) and another person, usually an attorney, who agrees to finance and carry the lawsuit in return for a percentage of the recovery (money won and paid)).

[49] *See* Lee Buchheit & Jeremiah S. Pam, *The Pari Passu Clause in Sovereign Debt Instruments*, 53 EMORY L.J. 869 (2003) (the pari passu clause requires the equal treatment in bankruptcy for holders of unsecured and unsubordinated debt and assumes that the debt must be repaid pro rata among all creditors.); Jonathan Blackman & Rahul Mukhi, *The Evolution Of Modern Sovereign Debt Litigation: Vultures, Alter Egos, And Other Legal Fauna in* A Modern Legal History of Sovereign Debt, 47–55 (Anna Gelpern & G. Mitu Gulati eds., 2010).

[50] Elliott Associates, L.P. v. Republic of Peru, 948 F.Supp. 1203 (S.D.N.Y. 1996).

parliament with a retrospective impact. Foreign laws thus serve a stabilisation purpose. For example, in 2004, shortly after *Re: Elliot*, the New York state legislature amended the law on champerty by restricting its usage.[51] Vulture funds like private equity funds thrive under an obscure regulatory structure both domestically and abroad through beneficial ownership structures created to avoid securities and other regulatory and reporting requirements, like tax havens. Indeed, it is no surprise that a good number of vulture funds are beneficially formed and owned in offshore jurisdictions such as the British Virgin Islands (BVI), the Channel Islands and similar others.[52] The domestic laws of foreign jurisdictions encourage these vulture funds not to disclose the amount or extent of their ownership structures.[53] Another problem with vulture fund litigation mechanism is that it leaves sovereign debtors in a dilemma. Refusal to submit to litigation exposes the sovereign nation to its inability to raise capital in the future from the international markets from the lobbying influence of vulture fund.

The increasing participation of private creditors has exposed the market to new risks and has allowed vulture funds and rogue creditors to take advantage of the system. Their growing number has also undermined the efforts to manage holdouts and has eliminated regulatory pressures on the legal tactics and strategies that hedge funds use to sue sovereign countries. Presently, the unchecked activities of vulture funders undermine the World Bank/International Monetary Fund Heavily Indebted Poor Country Initiative (HIPC). This is because debt disbursement made under the HIPC initiative gets swopped by vulture waiting by the side-lines without remedy for indebted sovereign states, despite sovereign states undergoing series of neo-liberal reforms to qualify for the initiative.[54]

---

[51] N.Y. Judiciary Law §489 (McKinney 2004) (to effectively eliminate the defence of champerty as to any debt purchases or assignments having a value of more than $500,000).

[52] Olufunmilayo B. Arewa, *Vultures, Hyenas, and African Debt: Private Equity and Zambia*, 29 N.W. J. INT'L L. & BUS. 643, 643–648 (2009).

[53] *Id.* at 650.

[54] Matthew S. Williams, *The Bush Administration, Debt Relief, and the War on Terror: Reforming the International Development System as Part of the Neoconservative Project* 35 SOC. JUST. 49 (2008); *See* INT'L FIN., *Vulture Funds Threat to HIPC*, (Aug. 26, 2013) https://internationalfinance.com/vulture-funds-threat-to-hipc/.

It is also not very surprising that vulture funds undermine the little relief received under the HIPC, since the HIPC has been critiqued as a tool used to shape the economic policies of recipient countries in a way that reproduces and maintains power asymmetry between donors and aid recipients. The HIPC initiative has also been condemned as an initiative aimed at ensuring countries continue to remain under cyclical debt burden by using inhumane and flawed debt sustainability standards (ability to pay off loans), without truly addressing the social cost of high debt burden despite many HIPC reforms.[55] Vulture fund litigation is a threat that widens the growing economic inequality by denying indebted countries a promising new start, and the chance to reinvest in its own infrastructure, healthcare, and education.

The African Development Bank 2007 report on Vulture Funds showed that 11 out of 24 poor countries said they were involved in legal cases with Vulture Funds and other creditors not participating in debt relief worth a total of $1.8 billion.[56] According to a Mckinsey report, private Equity and Hedge funds are the new power brokers in the international financial markets.[57] Like all originations, the near absolute power wielded by these funds with little or no global regulation over their activities make them a threat to the emerging economies of the world including Africa. Under-regulated vulture fund activity under the guise of free-market economy supports an insidious economic/political recolonisation of African sovereigns, and at large an ominous hazard to world peace. An unchecked vulture fund in this era of widening social and economic inequality may well provide an enabling environment towards global financial chaos.

3 Global Position on Vulture Fund Litigation Control

There are no legally binding bankruptcy mechanisms for sovereign states under international or domestic law. Under current global practices, sovereign debt default pressures a sovereign debtor to negotiate a voluntary restructuring agreement with

---

[55] *Id.*
[56] Lee C. Buchheit & G. Mitu Gulati, *Exit Consents in Sovereign Bond Exchanges*, 48 UCLA L. Rev. 59 (2000).
[57] Diane Farrell, Susan Lund, Eva Gerlemann & Peter Seeburger, *The New Power Brokers: How Oil, Asia, Hedge Funds and Private Equity Are Shaping Global Capital Markets*, McKinsey Glob. Ins. 19 (2007).

its creditors.[58] This pressure-packed approach to debt restructuring has facilitated a vicious business model where vulture fund investors have unbridled access to purchase distressed debt on the secondary market and hold out with little repercussions. International responses to vulture fund litigation have taken two major forms. The contractual reform approach supported by the IFIs, notably the IMF and other international groups like the ICMA and the soft law or norm setting approach supported by the United Nations. Another example is the Debt Suspension Legislative Proposal aimed at providing legislative effect to the Debt Service Suspension Initiative (DSSI) with respect to private creditors.[59]

3.1 *Contractual Reform Approach*

The IMF conducts surveillance over its Member States' economic, financial, exchange policies and its balance of payment lending policies and conditionalities attached to these.[60] This empowers the IMF to assess the level indebtedness of its Member States, especially through the Debt Sustainability Analysis (DSA).[61] Due to the absence of stronger global mechanisms, the IMF also proposed the Sovereign Debt Restructuring Mechanism (SDRM), a regulatory mechanism of an international bankruptcy procedure elements derived from the United States corporate bankruptcy legal framework and re-adjusted to the peculiarities of the global sovereign debt market, aimed at guaranteeing a predictable process for sovereign debt deals.[62] The SDRM

---

[58] SOOKUN, *supra* note 12 at 51–55.

[59] Stephen Connelly, Karina Patricio Ferreira Lima & Celine Tan, *Proposal for Debt Service Suspension Initiative*, IEL LAW AND FINANCE WORKING GROUP (Jun. 3, 2020), https://papers.ssrn.com/sol3/papers.cfm?abstract_id=3935371 (the DSSI Legislation would grant a statutory standstill to all DSSI eligible countries on qualifying debt that are governed by English law. The proposal covers sovereign bonds, with an ultimate effect of providing breathing space for sovereign debtors by diminishing private creditor litigation threats).

[60] Articles of Agreement of the IMF, Art. 4 §1, 3, 60 Stat. 1401, 2 U.N.T.S. 39.

[61] Francois Gianviti, *Evolving Role and Challenges for the International Monetary Fund, in*, INTERNATIONAL MONETARY AND FINANCIAL LAW UPON ENTERING THE NEW MILLENIUM: TRIBUTE TO SIR JOSEPH AND RUTH GOLD 46–47 (2002); IMF POL'Y PAPERS, *The Fund's Lending Framework and Sovereign Debt—Further Considerations—Supplementary Information and Proposed Decision*, 6, (Apr. 9, 2015).

[62] Anne O. Krueger & Sean Hagan, *Sovereign Workouts: An IMF Perspective*, 6 CHI. J. INT'L L. 203 (2005) (elements of the SDRM include mandatory collective action clauses, creditor enforcement stay clause, negotiation capital inflow mechanisms and creditor protection mechanism).

proposal did not work out. In about 2003, the IMF adopted collective action clauses into sovereign debt contracts that some economists had advocated in favor of since the 1990.[63] Several other contractual clauses have been included in sovereign debt restructuring, offering some protection to sovereign debts. In no order, these include exit consent amendment terms (ECAT), trusteeship and collective action clauses. ECAT works by aiding majority bondholders taking part in bond exchanges to use the amendment clauses in their existing bonds to modify important non-payment clauses of the original bonds. While they are useful, exit consents do not completely rule out holdout litigation, especially when the changes to the payment and non-payment terms of the original bonds is too wide.[64]

Under the trusteeship terms, a trustee, usually a financial institution is appointed with fiduciary responsibilities to enforce bond issuance matters by ensuring issuer meets all the terms and conditions of the issuance. A trustee ensures that bond interest payments and principal repayments are made as scheduled, and fairly protects the interests of the bondholders if the issuer defaults in a way that balances the sovereign's interest. The trusteeship clause inclusion discourages litigation hungry creditors because, bond payments received by a trustee will be less vulnerable to third party creditor attachment because only the trustee can sue. In addition, when the need arises, the trustee may act as a mediator between creditor and debtors' conflict of interests and the modification of the trust instrument is made a bit easier.[65]

The IMF also introduced a series of contractual terms like the enhanced Collective Action Clauses (CACs) in sovereign debt contracts.[66] Further, the International Capital Market Association (ICMA), endorsed by the IMF have proposed a change to sovereign debt contractual terms.[67] CACs are provisions in debt contracts

---

[63] *See* IMF, *Fourth Progress Report on Inclusion of Enhanced Contractual Provisions in International Sovereign Bond Contract* (2019) (clauses like Enhanced CAC and modified pari-passu clauses).

[64] Kenneth Daniels, & Gabriel Ramirez, *Debt Restructurings, Holdouts, and Exit Consents*, 3 J. FIN. STABILITY 1 (2007).

[65] Lee C. Buchheit, *Trustees Versus Fiscal Agents for Sovereign Bonds*, 13 CAP. MARKETS L.J. 410 (2017).

[66] Anna Gelpern & Mitu Gulati, *Public Symbol in Private Contract: A Case Study*, 84 WASH. U. L.R. 1627, 1641.

[67] To prevent situations like the one Argentina experienced with the vultures. The suggested new terms include a formula for aggregating collective action clauses. *See* MARTÍN GUZMAN, JOSÉ A OCAMPO AND JOSEPH STIGLITZ, TOO LITTLE, TOO LATE: THE QUEST TO RESOLVE SOVEREIGN DEBT CRISES 17–18 (2016).

stipulating that the terms of the contract regarding principal, interest, and maturity can change if there is consent of a predetermined supermajority of bondholders.[68] CACs benefits sovereign debtors by providing flexibility in financial distress and facilitating renegotiation. In their absence, bondholders have no incentives to enter the renegotiation process since, individually, they are unable to affect the probability of repayment. CACs deter free riding among creditors within a legal jurisdiction because a supermajority of bondholders can make the outcome of the renegotiation mandatory for all. The problem with CACs is that different versions of improved CAC have shown up in restructuring processes and disrupt the process by providing too many options with an attendant disagreement on the best version to adopt.[69] These varieties include Collective representation clauses, Majority action clauses, Sharing clauses, Non-acceleration clauses.[70] Bonds issued under New York law typically do not contain CACs, while those issued under UK law do include the provision.[71] Collective action clauses also are not designed to limit post-default litigation but before a restructuring becomes effective.[72]

Conditions precedent are pre-conditions in the loan agreement which activates the validity of contract after being met.[73] Aptly put, they are the private sector prior actions. Conditions precedent are extremely important but could easily be overlooked. An overlooked condition precedent is the negative pledge clause, designed to prioritise certain creditor claims over others. Sookun acknowledges that sovereign states should seek legal advice for a proper understanding of their implications before acquiescing to them.[74] In the same vein, African sovereign states are encouraged to create similar

---

[68] F Weinschelbaum & Jose Wynne, *Renegotiation, Collective Action Clauses and Sovereign Debt Markets* Soc'y Econ. Dynamics (2005).

67 *See* Mitu Gulati & Lee C. Buchheit, *Drafting a Model Collective Action Clause for Eurozone Sovereign Bonds*, 6 Cap. Markets L.J. 1 (2011).

[69] IMF, *The International Architecture for Resolving Sovereign Debt Involving Private-Sector Creditors— Recent Developments, Challenges, And Reform Options*, 30 (Oct. 1, 2020).

[70] Liz Dixon & David Wall, *Collective Action Problems and Collective Action Clauses*, Fin. Stability Rev. 142–145 (2000).

[71] *Id.*

[72] Elizabeth Broomfield, *Subduing the Vultures: Assessing Government Caps on Recovery in Sovereign Debt Litigation*, 2010 Colum. Bus. L. Rev. 490–495.

[73] Sookun, *supra* note 12, at 26–40.

[74] *Id.*

conditions precedent that serve to protect their interests because unlike the creditors, they have more to lose. One of such pre-conditions could be beneficial ownership disclosures. Sovereign nations can also use pre-existing conditions precedent to negotiate better terms like lower interest rates, repayment reschedules and so on.

3.2 Soft International Law Vulture Litigation Response

Since no legal means are available to persuade non-member cooperation, international institutions attempt to make soft law provisions to regulate sovereign debt restructuring and vulture fund litigation. Regrettably, efforts to encourage those outside the Paris Club to cooperate have been mostly unproductive. Aside from the Brady bond restructuring process, the HIPC Initiative was a far-reaching global initiative instituted by the World Bank and IMF used to revamp the financial situations of distressed countries, especially where traditional rescheduling and concessional financing had proved insufficient.[75] The HIPC debt relief is largely based on a country-by- country common reduction factor (CFR), which is a calculated level of debt relief necessary for an HIPC country to reach debt sustainability to qualify for refinancing. The problem with the CFR is that it assumes creditors' have the same agenda for amicable debt workouts and ultimately desire to support the restructuring process to reach debt sustainability. As the Zambian restructuring of the early 2000s proved, vulture funds are not on board with the cooperative debt workouts of the HIPC Initiative. This is because under the HIPC, creditors including vulture funds retained their legal rights to sue sovereign debtors.[76] The HIPC thus may be fittingly described as an elusive resolution.

Most recently, due to the crushing economic impact of Covid-19 on sovereign finance, the Debt Service Suspension Imitative (DSSI) emerged, providing provisional relief funding. Essentially, the DSSI operated solely as a mid-term debt deferment with a maturity period of about 5 years. It was only used for G-20 bilateral creditors and Paris Club Creditors. The IMF's Catastrophe Containment and Relief Trust supported the DSSI. The problem with the DSSI was that private sector participation, unlike the bilateral creditors was made voluntary, undermining the

---

[75] *Id.* at 93.
[76] Broomfield, *supra* note 72, at 493.

efficacy of the Initiative and signalling an unwillingness to recognise the relevance of private creditors in sustainable debt crisis resolution. The DSSI expired in 2021, and the Common Framework for post-DSSI debt restructuring (CF) replaced the DSSI. The CF is a wide-ranging DSSI intended for post-crisis debt relief. The CF has the same eligibility criteria for the beneficiary nations. Substantively, the CF offers semi-structured approach to debt restructuring which has appeared to be its shortcoming. The absence of a debt restructuring process and forum creates uncertainty and a lack of urgency in the restructurings processes, leading to a general distrust and lack of resolution commitment among sovereign creditors.

Outside of the IMF debt relief structure, other debt relief mechanisms have been created. In 2012, the United Nations Conference on Trade and Development (UNCTAD), adopted the Principles on Promoting Responsible Sovereign Lending and Borrowing, Principles of Responsible Financing, Roadmap Guide on Sovereign Debt Workouts. The UNCTAD principles encourage creditors should act in good faith and cooperation towards a swift and orderly resolution of a debt restructuring.[77] The UNCTAD principles remain a soft law mechanism for debt restructuring, for the purpose of identifying rules and best practices for the restructuring process.[78] The UNCTAD Roadmap Guide contains five principles to guide debt restructuring and provides that a restructuring process should be initiated as soon as debt service becomes unsustainable.[79]

Specific soft law on vulture funds is addressed in the United Nations Human Rights Council (HRC) Guiding Principles on Foreign Debt and Human Rights 2012. The HRC Principles focuses on the relevance and consideration importance of human, economic, social and cultural rights to sovereign debt resolutions.[80] Likewise, the

---

[77] United Nations Conference on Trade and Development, *Principles of Responsible Financing, Roadmap Guide on Sovereign Debt Workouts* (2012).

[78] Mauro Megliani, *For the Orphan, the Widow, the Poor: How to Curb Enforcing by Vulture Funds against the Highly Indebted Poor Countries*, 31 LEIDEN J. INT'L L. 11 (2018).

[79] United Nations Conference on Trade and Development, *Sovereign Debt Workouts: Going Forward Roadmap and Guide*, 16–22 (2015).

[80] *See* Marie-Louise Masamba *Sovereign debt restructuring and human rights: Overcoming a false binary in* COVID-19 AND SOVEREIGN DEBT THE CASE OF SADC 176–208 (2022) (on the link between Human Rights and Sovereign Debt).

UNGA Resolution 68/304 passed in September 2014, culminated in the UN Basic Principles on Sovereign Debt Restructuring Processes adopted by the UN General Assembly (UNGA) in September 2015.[81] The UNGA resolution approved a set of nine principles that should serve as the starting point for restructuring processes. These include sovereignty, good faith, transparency, impartiality, equitable treatment of creditors, sovereign immunity, legitimacy, sustainability. Principle 8 provides that debt restructuring process should foster inclusive growth and sustainable development and minimizing the social and economic costs. For vulture fund creditors, the resolution provides that minority creditors should not impair the outcome of restructuring processes and affirms the insertion of CACs into loan agreements to prevent disruptive ligation associated with these band of creditors.[82] Masamba & de Bonis argue that while the UN soft law provisions for debt restructuring are a step in the right direction, their effectiveness could be undermined by the lack of consensus between developing and developed countries, due to the apprehension of private contractual law interference the principles appear to support.[83] While these standards are welcome, they still stay as best practices with an influential sway, not a binding one. Similarly, Guzman & Stiglitz maintain that for now the creation of a multinational statutory framework for debt crises resolution is not practical, however the UN principles are a starting point for the form and substance of a future international debt resolution framework.[84]

3.3 Review of Anti-Hold Out Legislation

The scantiness of binding international initiatives for abusive vulture fund litigation has incited the drive for control through various domestic anti-holdout legislations. This indeed has been sparked by public outrage at the audacity of vulture fund ligation since the Argentine debt crisis and intensified by the Eurozone debt crisis of

---

[81] G.A. Res. 69/319, Basic Principles on Sovereign Debt Restructuring Processes (Sept. 29, 2015).
[82] G.A. Res. 69/319, supra note 81.
[83] Marie-Louise Masamba & Francesco de Bonis, *Towards Building A Fair And Orderly International Framework For Sovereign Debt Restructuring An African Perspective,* AFRODAD ISSUE PAPERS 9–10 (Dec. 29, 2017) (there is also a lack of clarity concerning the interpretation and application of the Principles).
[84] Martin Guzman & Joseph Stiglitz, *Creating a Framework for Sovereign Debt Restructuring That Works in* TOO, LITTLE, TOO LATE: THE QUEST TO RESOLVE SOVEREIGN DEBT CRISES (2016).

2012. This section examines the anti-vulture fund laws of United Kingdom, United States, and Belgium. Australian and France also have Anti-Vulture Law Funds.

3.3.1 UNITED KINGDOM DEBT RELIEF (DEVELOPING COUNTRIES) ACT 2010

The vulture fund recovery litigation by creditors against Zambia and Liberia after it had received the HIPC debt relief package, public support and parliamentary go-ahead.[85] The DRA aims to outlaw profiteering by putting a cap on the amount that vulture funds can ask in repayment; require more accountability for the secret activities of vulture funds through disclosure to be made to the UK courts before bringing a lawsuit; and create transparency to disclosure of investors and beneficiaries and to ban corrupt payments.[86] A defining feature of the DRA is its limitation to 33 per cent of the amount HIPC eligible but unapproved commercial creditors could recover on their sovereign debt. The DRA also provides for limited recovery of small proportion of the sovereign debt in accordance with the reduction factor set by the HIPC initiative. The DRA augments and promotes a binding enforcement of the HIPC initiative by introducing a mandatory debt reduction which ends up giving commercial creditors including vulture funds no special advantages and forces them to accept deals agreed under the HIPC Initiative. It also dissuades vulture litigation in the United Kingdom's courts. The DRA waives HIPCs' a portion of sovereign debts issued by HIPCs before the commencement of the DRA and prior to the HIPC decision point, which provides the sovereign state much need fiscal breathing space.

Regarding enforcement, the DRA applies to foreign judgments or arbitration awards on qualifying debt which discourages the vulture fund litigation shopping and its associated arbitrage exploitation. The DRA also protects the interest of the creditor against the sovereign debtor by binding it to the HIPC's terms and achieves this through excluding all sovereign debt settlement offer on comparable HIPC terms from its scope. The DRA in effect forces the Sovereign debtor to actively participate in the HIPC initiated debt recovery process by actively making offers to the creditor and prevents irresponsible debt resolutions.

3.3.2 THE UNITED STATES STOP VULTURE FUNDS PROPOSED LEGISLATIONS

In 2008, the first national anti-vulture funds legislation in the United States was

---

[85] Ufuoma Akpotaire, *Vulture Funds and Sovereign Debts*, 1–11 (2011).
[86] Debt Relief (Developing Countries) Act, 2010 c.22.

introduced by Maxine Waters as "Stop Very Unscrupulous Loan Transfers from Underprivileged Countries to Rich, Exploitative Funds Act."[87] The 2009 Bill proposed to prevent speculation and profiteering in the defaulted debt of HIPC Initiative countries. The Act does this by imposing a punitive fine on holdout creditors equal to the total amount sought through the sovereign debt profiteering and establishes mandatory disclosure requirements that expose vulture creditors to judicial scrutiny. The Bill also prohibits any US person from engaging in sovereign debt profiteering, any person from engaging in such profiteering in the USA, and any US court from issuing a summons, subpoena, writ, judgment, attachment, or execution in aid of a claim which would further sovereign debt profiteering. The bill also requires court disclosures in actions involving the collection of sovereign debt. There is also a proposed New York State Senate Bill S6627 that seeks to block hedge funds from purchasing sovereign debt for the purpose of litigating on it. It would also enact bankruptcy-like protectors for sovereign debtors.[88] Currently, the legislative stage of the bill is at the Committee level.

3.3.3 BELGIUM'S ANTI-VULTURE ACT 2015 Belgium's Federal Parliament approved its first legislation to "safeguard Belgian funds disbursed towards development cooperation and debt relief from the actions taken by vulture funds." The law forbade the seizure or transfer of development assistance between parties and prohibited creditors from recovering interest owed to vulture creditors. The Act also

---

[87] Stop Very Unscrupulous Loan Transfers from Underprivileged countries to Rich, Exploitive Funds Act, H.R. 2932, 111th Cong. (2009) (the House of Representatives shelved the bill for committee review. US Congress under H.R. 6796. On June 18, 2009, Ms. Waters re-introduced the same bill, "Stop Vulture Funds Act." Bill (H.R. 2932)).

[88] N.Y. S.6627, 2021 https://www.nysenate.gov/legislation/bills/2021/S6627&gt (last visited Jun. 29, 2022) (the Bill is sponsored by Gustavo Rivera. The Bill proposes an amendment to Art. 7 of the New York Banking law to address some of the concerns that have been raised surrounding vulture funds and provide effective restructuring of sovereign debt unsustainable sovereign debt, "reduce the need for bailouts, negative social costs, systemic risk to the economy and creditor uncertainty." Once enacted, the bill will automatically apply to all debts governed by New York law and will enjoy supremacy over any contractual clause to the contrary); *See also* Rafael Bernal, *New York Democrats Push Bill to Stop Sovereign Debt 'Vulture Funds,'* THE HILL (May 3, 2023 5:27 PM), https://thehill.com/home-news/3986681-new-york-democrats-push-bills-to-stop-sovereign-debt-vulture-funds/.

provides that no monies granted by the Belgian authorities can be seized by or transferred to vulture funds or any other creditor. This legislation has automatically barred vulture fund from pursuing any Belgian money or companies investing in the sovereign debtor country to obtain repayment.

On July 12, 2015, the Belgian Federal Parliament passed its second national legislation against vulture funds, known as the Anti-Vulture Funds Law. The Act applies to creditors who pursue an "improper advantage" by purchasing distressed sovereign debts. Two conditions must be met for a debt purchase to qualify as an improper advantage. First, there must be an undisputed imbalance between the original bond price and the discounted/nominal bond value. Second, one of the following criteria must be met. The debtor was in proven or imminent insolvency or cessation of payments at the moment of the acquisition of the loan or debt; the creditor's registered office is in a low tax jurisdiction or tax haven; the creditor systematically uses court proceedings to claim payment of the (debts or) loans it has acquired; the creditor has refused to contribute to other restructuring mechanisms; the creditor has abused the weakened position of the debtor State to obtain, through negotiations, a clearly unbalanced repayment agreement; and finally the full repayment of the amounts claimed by the creditor would have a provable adverse public financial effect on the sovereign debtor and harms its citizen's socio-economic development. The Act restricts enforcement measures in Belgium in these circumstances. Since the creditor's rights are limited to the price actually paid for the loan or debt, it discourages vulture fund lawsuits in the long run. Simultaneously, there is certainty for the debtors on the actual amount owed.

The Belgian laws have been severely criticised for having broad and imprecise terms and scope. Critics fault it for failing to provide a standard for defining an apparent imbalance, leaving it open to legal uncertainty, especially for the creditors.[89]

---

[89] Alexander Hansebout, *Anti-Vulture Legislation: the Belgian Attempt—or How Not to Do It*, LEXGO (Mar. 12, 2020), https://www.lexgo.be/en/papers/commercial-company-law/financial-law/anti-vulture-legislation-the-belgian-attempt-ai-or-how-not-to-do-it,140536.html#:~:text=The%20Act%20applies%20to%20%E2%80%9Ccreditors,result%20in%20an%20improper%20advantage.

4 Does Africa need a Common Position on Public Finance and Debt: Benefits and Challenges

Common positions on African issues are not new. African countries have congregated together to discuss many issues affecting them and common to their interests. Often, these have culminated in documents such as The African Common Position on Migration.[90] While there is no globally formal definition of a common position, a common position can nonetheless be described from its content and objectives. A common position occurs when a group of persons with similar interests, challenges and priorities reach a consensus on actively working together to alleviate their common challenges, while fostering their common goals, priorities, and aspirations. Zondi defines a Common African Position (CAP) as follows:

> Common positions are decisions that Africa takes after a protracted negotiation processes within the AU processes to constitute a common stance on a matter. They are outcomes of lengthy consensus decisionmaking, the usual manner in which Africa takes critical decisions. These take the form of AU resolutions, declarations and common positions that serve as concrete negotiation mandatesfor African negotiators on specific issues.[91]

The intensity of Africa's need for more common positions has been heightened after the setting of the sustainable development goals (SDGs) by the United Nations in 2015. One of the most prominent CAPs emerged from the 2012 Decision of the African Union Summit (Assembly/AU/Dec. 423 (XIX)), which mandated the African Union Commission in close consultation with Members States and

---

[90] OAU, African Charter on Human and Peoples Rights, O.A.U. Doc. CAB/LEG/67/3 (1982); *See also* African Common Position On Migration And Development 2006, Executive Council, Ninth Ordinary Session, EX.CL/277 (IX) (Jun. 25–29, 2006) (the OAU was unsuccessful however due to policy of non-intervention and inability to influence the policies of its members; *See* TIMOTHY MURITHI, THE AFRICAN UNION: PAN-AFRICANISM, PEACEBUILDING AND DEVELOPMENT 5 (2005).

[91] Siphamandla Zondi, *Africa in International Negotiations: A Critique of African Common Positions*, CHATHAM HOUSE SEMINAR 1-21 (2011), https://www.open.ac.uk/socialsciences/bisa-africa/files/africanagency-seminar1-zondi.pdf.

Regional Economic Communities, to identify Africa's priorities for the post-2015 Development Agenda. Furthermore, the African Union Summit Decision of 2013 established a High-Level Committee (HLC) of Heads of State and Government to sensitize and organise the activities of African leaders, while building regional and inter-continental alliances on the Common African Position (CAP) on the post-2015 Development Agenda (Assembly/AU/Dec.475(XXI).[92]

The Common African Position post-2015 Development Agenda as an ultimate expression of Africa's unity, articulates Africa's consensus on several substantive issues, concern, and goals that impact its development such as migration and brain drain, climate change, socio-economic inequalities, and suchlike. The consensus on African development interests were to be reflected in the outcomes of the post-2015 negotiation process, that is member-state and stakeholder driven in furtherance of the global SDGs.[93] The CAP adopts a development-centred approach using development pillars, adequate policy space, and productive capacities that foster Africa's development.

Africa's development priorities in the CAP are grouped into six pillars namely- structural economic transformation and inclusive growth; science, technology and innovation; people-centred development; environmental sustainability natural resources management, and disaster risk management; peace and security; and finance and partnerships.[94] Similarly, Africa's common stance on development aid effectiveness at the Busan High-Level Forum in 2011 recognized the unsustainability of development aid in financing Africa's development, and pushed for the need to mobilize domestic resources and the private sector in sustainably financing its development.[95] Eleven years after, the common position on development aid has contributed fairly to African efforts to increase efficiency and volume in domestic resource mobilisation

---

[92] AFRICAN UNION [AU], COMMON AFRICA POSITION (CAP) ON THE POST-2015 DEVELOPMENT AGENDA, 4 (2014).

[93] This was achieved by considering the wealth of information collected and collated from national and regional stakeholders.

[94] AU, *supra* note 92, at 7–24 (this also included implementation strategies of the CAPs).

[95] Organisation for Economic Co-operation and Development, *Busan Partnership for Effective Development Co-operation: Fourth High Level Forum on Aid Effectiveness, Busan, Republic of Korea, 29 November–1 December 2011*, OECD PUBLISHING, (2011).

through taxation and the creation of the African Continental Free Trade Area to foster intra-African trade and investment.[96]

The African Union has other common position documents. These include the Common African Position on Humanitarian Effectiveness 2016,[97] Draft Africa Common Position to the UN Food Systems Summit.[98] Due to rising unsustainable sovereign debt levels prior to and since the outset of COVID-19 pandemic, it has become imperative for Africa to adopt a common position on public finance and sovereign debt. Debt in Africa and the impending underdevelopment accompanying it, makes it a substantive challenge and priority for its 2030 and AU 2063 development agenda. Presently, documents relating African sovereign finance include commitments made by developed countries in financing development such as the Johannesburg Plan of Implementation, the Monterrey Consensus of the International Conference on Financing for Development, and the Doha Declaration on Financing for Development, and others have some content on Africa's finance through economic and social development.

These documents are quite vital in ensuring a stable global financial architecture that guard against systemic economic risk.[99] Yet, these commitments do not represent a specific African position on finance, sovereign debt, and allied development problems. As it stands, the CAP deals very inadequately with an African position on its rising debt level because it only provides an aspirational leaning of promoting responsive and accountable global governance architecture.[100] This aspirational

---

[96] *See* AFRICAN UNION, *Revenue Statistics In Africa: Latest Findings And Developments*, (Mar. 4–8, 2019), https://au.int/sites/default/files/newsevents/workingdocuments/35970-wd-revenue_statistics_in_africa_-_3rd_stc_cameroon-en.pdf (tax to GDP ratio has risen from 11 % of GDP in the early 2000s to about 20 % in recent times).

[97] AU, COMMON FRICAN POSITION (CAP) ON HUMANITARIAN EFFECTIVENESS (2016) (the CAP lays emphasis on humanitarian effectiveness in Africa).

[98] *See* International Conference on Financing for Development, *Monterrey Consensus of the International Conference on Financing for Development*, ¶ 56–72, U.N. Doc. A/CONF.198/11 (Mar. 18-22, 2002) (where Leading Action 6 addresses systemic issues on enhancing the coherence and consistency of the international monetary, financial, and trading systems in support of development).

[99] *Id.*

[100] CAP, *supra* note 92, at ¶ 69–71.

leaning includes African countries' full and equitable representation in international financial and economic institutions debt, while urging for an expeditious transition to a development-friendly, international financial architecture.[101] In essence, the substantively detrimental concern of Africa's rising sovereign debt is not accorded high priority.

There are strong reasons supporting the use of common positions to address challenges, whilst realising development goals and targets. Common positions especially when used by the African Union support collective African interests on development which makes achieving common goals and interests feasible. A common position on pressing issues under the auspices of the AU as a regional organisation may also enable greater co-operation aimed at strengthening the voice of the African continent, pertaining to negotiations and contributions to the reform of the global financial architecture. In the same vein, common position contributes to the development of guiding principles or model laws, which has the potential to build self-reliant capacity. Common positions may also provide reference point for future national, continental, and global discourses and cooperation on issues, provide continuity, and encourage responsiveness to change. Common positions also concretise pan African solidarity while promoting agency in its own fate.[102]

Sholtz alludes to the importance of common position for key issues in the African continent owing to the deficiency of capacity and bargaining power of individual African states to pursue their interests at larger global negotiations.[103] Usually, the more powerful parties (states) are influentially enough to control the negotiating process while obtaining negotiation outcomes that are more beneficial to their interest and priorities. In the same vein, Zartman and Rubin argue that the reason for these dynamics is that negotiators with high relative power tend to act manipulatively and exploitatively, while negotiators with perceived lesser power tend to act submissively,

---

[101] CAP, *supra* note 92, at ¶ 76.

[102] Siphamandla Zondi, *Common positions as African agency in International Negotiations: An Appraisal in* AFRICAN AGENCY IN INTERNATIONAL POLITICS 19–33 (2013).

[103] Werner Scholtz, *The promotion of regional environmental security and Africa's common position on climate change* 10 AFR. HUM. RTS. L. J. 1, 5 (2010).

leading to the negotiating outcome confirming to a given power distribution.[104] By using common positions African states can be strategically positioned for adaptive capacity through international negotiations with developed states.

Additionally, common position helps African states to co-operate and increase their collective bargaining power through deeper regional integration that accords respect that translates to increase global voting power to African states. As Scholtz concludes, common positions provide a golden opportunity to challenge the "rule-taking marginalised" narrative concerning of African states.[105] This is because the solidarity that comes from undermining African states creates an advantage based on shared vulnerability that positions Africa in a more powerful position to counter marginalisation by laying its demands and meting out consequences for global disregard of its legitimate concerns. To garner respect and effective dialogue at global forum, African countries require common strategies and positions. A more coordinated and united response to pressing development issues like sovereign debt reduces the "divide and kill" tactics of stronger negotiating powers.

As advantageous as CAPs are, there are challenges associated with the use of CAPs. One of the problems with common positions is the heterogeneity of African countries and the process in arriving at common positions. Many African countries are at different stages of development, colonial history, financial systems, and other differences which influence priorities and challenges at the national level and end up creating complex interests. As Zondi observes, many African countries due to their colonial antecedents are grouped into three major groups—the Anglophones, Francophones, and Lusophones with little commonalities among them in terms of language, outlook, financial regulation, culture, and other indices necessary to having lasting shared interests.[106] Similarly, there are no systems in place to integrate differences and incorporate the interest of Africa's Island Countries and Low Income Countries where many common positions work against their national interests. In

---

[104] WILLIAM ZARTMAN & JEFFREY Z. RUBIN, POWER AND NEGOTIATION, 4-16 (2002).

[105] Scholtz, *supra* note 103.

[106] Zondi, *supra* note 102.

response, these countries prefer to pay passing interest to common position while pursuing myopic national interests.

For example, in arriving at a global corporate tax rate and taxing the digital economy as tool for revenue mobilisation, many African LDCs signed the OECD inclusive framework despite developing countries unofficial common stance that the OECD New Pillar 1 and 2 of 2021 did not work in their long-term best interest.[107] These countries chose to acquiesce to the short-term benefits of OECD pillars because their national interest required more revenue than many middle-income Africa countries like Kenya and Nigeria who rejected the deal. Further, discussions at the African Union are inclusive in form and are geared towards getting countries to rely on regional interests, than country level interests which make these countries to eventually deviate from common positions reached. This frustrates the progress that should have been made with a substantive developmental challenge.

Another challenge with CAP is the lack of political will which affects implementation of a position reached. According to Scholtz, the most important aspect of common positions is the implementation of CAPs at the sub-regional level, which requires capacity. Since African states have in the past made a show of making grand positions without ensuring implementation, newer common positions may not be prioritised by the countries involved.[108] Closely mirroring the dearth of political will is a leadership culture which creates power distances between governing and governed, and the strata of leadership (at the regional, state, and provincial level). According to GLOBE studies conducted on organizations and middle-level managers around the world, it was discovered sub-Saharan Africa scored high in power distance and in-group collectivism, but low in performance orientation.[109] Sustained political commitment is necessary to procuring the necessary resources and coordination efforts.

---

[107] Carmel Peters, *Developing Countries' Reactions to the G20/OECD Action Plan on Base Erosion and Profit Shifting,* 69 BULL. FOR INT'L TAX'N 375 (2015); *See also* Yara Rizk, *Why some African countries reject the global agreement to tax multinationals,* THE AFR. REP. (Oct. 21, 2021), https://www.theafricareport.com/138469/why-some-african-countries-are-rejecting-the-global-agreement-to-tax-multinationals/.
[108] Scholtz, *supra* note 102.
[109] ROBERT J. HOUSE ET AL., CULTURE, LEADERSHIP, AND ORGANIZATIONS: THE GLOBAL STUDY OF 62 SOCIETIES, 1–30 (2004).

However, due to the AU's disinclination to act swiftly while showing reluctance to address governance issues like life-long presidencies in some African countries or human right abuses, states may justifiably hesitate to join the CAP bandwagon.[110] Despite these challenges, it is necessary for African countries to unite and coordinate pro-active responses to the rising plague of vulture funds and unsustainable sovereign debt with its negative ripple effect on the African economy.

5 Designing a Common African Position on Vulture Fund Litigation

Given the ominous debt prognosis for Africa, some African institutional and civil societies endeavours have been made to attend to the debt issues and vulture fund problem. The African Legal Support Facility established in 2008 offers advisory and active support to African sovereigns in managing debt issues negotiation of contractual arrangements between governments and investors.[111] In 2019 & 2020, it published a handbook that discusses the fundamentals of sovereign debt and serves as a primer for technical, financial, and legal aspects of debt instruments, the markets, and the methods for managing or avoiding large sovereign indebtedness.[112]

The handbook provides detailed knowledge without indicating a position on vulture fund related issues.[113] It is possible to infer an African position from civil society groups actively involved in debt sustainability and justice like the African Forum and Network on Debt and Development (AFRODAD), created to influence

---

[110] Remofiloe Lobakeng, *African Solutions to African Problems: A Viable Solution towards a United, Prosperous and Peaceful Africa?*, 71 INST. GLOB. DIALOGUE OCCASIONAL PAPER 1 (2017); Alhaji Ahmadu Ibrahim, *African Union and the Challenges of Underdevelopment in Contemporary Africa* 14 BRITISH J. ED. SOC'Y & BEHAVORAL SCI. 1(2016); Githy Muigai, *From the African Court on Human and Peoples' Rights to the African Court of Justice and Human Rights in* THE AFRICAN REGIONAL HUMAN RIGHTS SYSTEM, 265–282 (Manisuli Ssenyonjo ed., 2012).

[111] AFRICAN DEVELOPMENT BANK GROUP, *African Legal Support Facility,* https://www.afdb.org/en/topics-and-sectors/initiatives-partnerships/african-legal-support-facility (last vistited May 23, 2023).

[112] ALSF, *Handbook on Sovereign Debt Level 1* (2019); ALSF, *Handbook on Sovereign Debt Level 2* (2020).

[113] *See* ALSF, *supra* note 112, at 97 (discussing sovereign immunity waiver).

policy on debt management and development finance in Africa based on rights approaches.[114] In 2021, AFRODAD sponsored the change agenda/policy titled of "Africa the Rule Maker not the Rule Taker," inspired by the 2018 AFRODAD Borrowing Charter.[115] The Charter aims at contributing to improvements in the transparency of the political, institutional and administrative processes in procuring external debt, while ensuring the accountability of the State actors involved in the contraction and management of public debt. Other civil societies include Pan African Lawyers Forum, and The African Sovereign Debt Justice Network (AfSDJN).

As Arewa affirms, corruption, colonialism, neo colonialism and mismanagement of resources cannot be divorced from the Africa's deteriorated public debt circumstances.[116] In the light of these initiatives, an African position would include a position that augments the current global solutions and creates new rules and policies to manage and discourage vulture fund opportunistic litigation. An anti-vulture fund litigation strategy should involve the following:

A. *A Club of Sovereign Debtors and a Designated Forum for Sovereign Debt Restructuring and Management*

Presently, sovereign debt matters are managed at the national level, despite increasing awareness for a more coordinated and collective approach to the issue. A collective approach provides the opportunity for sovereign debt to be restructured where there is a pooling of collective bargaining powers and an opportunity for a speaking with a stronger voice. The creditor side of the divide has several clubs like the Paris and

---

[114] AFRICAN FORUM AND NETWORK ON DEBT AND DEVELOPMENT, *About Page-Vision and Mission,* https://afrodad.org/about-page/ (last vistied May 23, 2023).

[115] Ismail Musa Ladu, *Debt Crunch: Africa is a Net Creditor to the Rest of the World,* MONITOR BUSINESS (May 17, 2022), https://www.monitor.co.ug/uganda/business/prosper/debt-crunch-africa-is-a-net-creditor-to-the-rest-of-the-world-3818248; AFRICAN FORUM AND NETWORK ON DEBT AND DEVELOPMENT, *The Harare Declaration 2021,* (Aug. 27, 2021 https://afrodad.org/wp-content/uploads/2021/12/The-Harare-Declaration-2021.docx-5.pdf.

[116] Arewa, *supra* note 52, at 650; *See also* Marie-F Aren, *Adopting proactive debt management policy strategies to forestall a debt crisis in South Africa in* COVID-19 AND SOVEREIGN DEBT: THE CASE OF SADC 211–224 (Daniel Bradlow & Magalie L. Masamba eds., 2022) (on the role of corruption and fiscal wastage in exacerbating sovereign debt crisis).

London Club that articulate the common interest while protecting the large exposure of sovereign creditors to States in an organised manner.[117] The issue however with this collective creditor club arrangement for indebted countries is that most of the debt-rescheduling negotiations are systematized from the perspective of the creditors, not the sovereign debtor.[118] African countries are encouraged to replicate a similar system where the interests and challenges faced by African countries plagued by debt distress are consolidated/negotiated from a sovereign debtor perspective and from a position of strength. An African club of sovereign debtors should have a set of procedures for re-negotiating payment obligation while facilitating sovereigns to access short-term financing from the capital markets or from official credit sources in a fiscally responsible manner.

In addition, a proper African forum where the management of debt arising from vulture funds and their impact from an African-interest paradigm should be created using existing or a combination of existing institutions. For example, the African Support Legal Facility, (ASLF), and the African Union. The best African Union Body for this task would be The African Monetary Fund (AMF) whose key objectives include acting as a clearing house, undertaking macro-economic surveillance within the continent, coordinating the monetary policies of Member States, and promoting cooperation between their monetary authorities. The creation of a Vulture Fund Management Unit would provide a perfect opportunity for the AMF to play the "IMF role" for Africa.

It is believed that an active and responsible AMF would provide an institutional/regulatory platform for sovereign debt restructuring and development of stronger contractual standards, while monitoring sovereign debt legislative developments. Further, an African forum will be well-placed to use existing soft law and international norms to develop protective African Anti-Vulture Fund standards,

---

[117] A Reinisch, *Debt Restructuring and State Responsibility Issues, in* LA DETTE EXTÉRIEURE/THE EXTERNAL DEBT 544–546 (Dominique Carreau & Malcolm N. Shaw eds., 1995); *See also* Annamaria Viterbo, *The Role of the Paris, and London Clubs: Is It Under Threat?*, THE HAGUE CTR. STUD. & RSCH. (2017) (forthcoming).

[118] Alexis Rieffel, *The Role Of The Paris Club In Managing Debt Problems* 161 ESSAYS IN INTL' FIN. 2–10 (1985).

guides, and best practices aimed at protecting African sovereigns from the onslaught of vulture litigation. It would also provide guidance and standards such as the OECD Principles of Corporate Standards, the International Financial Reporting Standards, and so on. Countries may then have the option of enacting or including these standards into their public finance domestic laws or strengthen existing public finance domestic laws.

B. *African Sovereign Debt Restructuring Regime with Improved Core Contractual Terms*

A common position that Africa can take in tackling rising and unstainable sovereign debt is through the creation of a vulture-fund debt restructuring mechanism that dissuades Vulture-fund investors from buying its distress debts. This can be achieved through a mechanism like using an agreement that stays litigation by all creditors irrespective of their class or amount of debt provided. In the same vein, assets and revenues of African countries should be stayed from execution until the restructuring process is completed. This would dis-incentivise vultures swarming around distressed African debts while ensuring that sovereign states are not arm-twisted by the dubious tactics of vulture investors into harmful concessions or to face litigation in foreign jurisdictions.

The use of an Archetypal African Bond Agreement containing well-defined protective sovereign debtor terms and clauses is encouraged. One of such clause is the *"reverse champerty"* protective clauses where new debt agreements should contain contractual clauses that would bind third-party debt buyers (including vulture fund investors), agents, and assignees to the original debt terms in cases of debt instrument resale from the original holder, renegotiations, and restructuring. This is because vulture-fund investing involves a person with no previous interest in a lawsuit buying the distressed debt with a view to benefiting from a successful lawsuit against the debtor suit. It should follow that if previously uninterested third parties like vulture fund investors are allowed in the interest of facilitating commerce to lay claims to proceeds of lawsuits, then the original and main party to the debt agreement (the debtor), should be able to protect its national and development interests from preempting parties with harmful agendas.

Another common position under this heading should be an outright removal of the pari passu clause (meaning-in equal step) in foreign-law bonds contracts which presently frustrates the ability to bind all creditors to the decisions of the supermajority. The reason for this is not far-fetched. First, the pari-passu clause is not a fundamental part of any sovereign debt contract because it has no meaning within the context of sovereign debt.[119] Gulati and Scott describe the irrelevant nature of the clause as follows:

> ... in essence, pari passu was a boilerplate contract provision that most parties treated as ornamentation. All that changed, however, when the local commercial court in Brussels issued a preliminary injunction based on Elliot's interpretation of the clause as an inter-creditor agreement to share equally in any payment ...[120]

Another problem with the pari-passu clause is its lack of clear meaning and propensity for ambiguity. So far, it is unclear whether the pari-passu clause is an interpretation of an intrinsic component of the debt where the bonds will rank in equal step with each other or an extrinsic component where bonds are ranked in equal step with other unsecured sovereign debt.[121] Going forward, African debt instrument should explicitly remove the ornamental pari-passu clause because like many other boilerplate clauses, it has clearly outlasted its origins and purpose while carrying with it a huge litigation risk and error of interpretation at the expense of African sovereign states.

From a public international law perspective, Africa has a right to development acknowledged by the United Nations Declaration on the Right to Development and the African Charter, where states are at the centre of formulating and implementing initiatives that facilitate their right to development. States are also encouraged to work with other states (by implication their people) to foster development. Vulture

---

[119] Mitu Gulati & Robert E. Scott, *The Three and a Half Minute Transaction: Boilerplate and the Limits of Contract Design* 40 HOFSTRA L. REV. 1, 1–12 (2012).
[120] *Id.* at 4.
[121] Rodrigo Olivares-Caminal, *The Pari Passu Clause in Sovereign Debt Instruments: Developments in Recent Litigation,* 72 BANK INT'L SETTLEMENT PAPERS 121–128 (2013).

fund litigation hampers the ability of states to actualise their development goals and associated rights by diverting resources into a few foreign private hands, thereby contributing to global inequality. While one might argue that the right to development through the UN Declaration is not binding, the African Charter is a legally binding treaty that covers civil, political, economic, social- cultural rights, and has been ratified by every member state of the African Union. Therefore, African States can adopt the right to development covered by the treaty and redesign them into public policy terms that should be a fundamental term of debt agreements and instruments. This would be helpful where in case of default, debt restructuring mechanisms and processes will consider the development and public policy of the sovereign state, in a manner that is similar to the preferences accorded to Low-Income Developing Countries (LDCs) by the World Trade Organisation to increase their global trade volume and aid their development. Likewise, sovereign debtcontracts should contain such preferences for African emerging market bonds, upholding African development interests.

Finally, African debt agreements should include emergency circumstance clauses as fundamental terms to ward of vulture-fund interests and litigation. The unplanned nature of the COVID-19 pandemic and other global diseases like the Monkey Pox in 2022 indicate that more of these unforeseen health disasters may become regular in the future. Equally, the current climate change issues like rising temperature plaguing the planet brings with them increased propensity for natural disasters. No country is spared from the consequence of climate change. Climate change related impact thus changes the balance and equality of circumstances vital to fulfilling a contractual obligation. The war between Ukraine and Russia and the ever present threat of the invasion of Taiwan by China show that the normal contractual premise of 'all things being equal' is fast becoming uncertain. African states for these reasons should ensure that debt agreements and renegotiation agreements contain emergency circumstance clauses that protect their fiscal resources from predatory creditors, like the Hurricane clause adopted by the Caribbean countries.[122] Hurricane clauses are clauses inserted into contracts in hurricane prone regions like the Caribbean because they allow deferral of contractual obligations in event of natural disasters without liability.

---

[122] Enrico Mallucci, *Natural Disasters, Climate Change, and Sovereign Risk*, BD. GOVERNORS OF THE FED. RESERVE SS. (2020) https://www.federalreserve.gov/econres/ifdp/files/ifdp1291.pdf

C. Revisiting Sovereign Immunity Waiver from Capital Market Borrowing

Recently, it was reported that some vaccine companies like Pfizer resorted to pressuring sovereign states to waive their immunity on subsequent litigation from the use of vaccine. This shows a new norm of uber powerful corporations disregarding and stripping off the protective immunity/independence status of Global South Countries including Africa. This weakens how law (including agreements) could be used as a tool for the redistributing wealth or promoting social/economic justice. Arising from this perspective, waiver of sovereign immunity in international loan agreements appears to favour the economic interests of a few over the socio-economic interest of majority people (represented by their sovereign state).

Furthermore, most international organisations like the Bretton Woods institutions enjoy immunities. If these institutions were created for the purpose of serving the economic and social interests of their member countries, and therefore that the protective shield of immunity is relevant to discharging their functions, the same protective standard should also apply to sovereign states. African Governments, therefore, should cooperatively adopt a position that reinstates the sovereign immunity protective clause into all state agreements and guard their immunity clauses jealously. The need for sovereign immunity protection becomes pertinent, especially under the current global debt architecture that still covertly enables the swarming of sovereign vulture fund investors on the hunt to make a killing at the expense of Africa's developmental interests. Similarly, it is difficult to imagine any of the developed countries fully waiving their sovereign immunities to raise public finances.

Ultimately, an African position should include all mechanisms that limit the use litigation used by a few legally approved profiteers to effect financial neo-colonialism against African sovereign while balancing the responsibly of African states to manage their public finances wisely.

6 Recommendation and Conclusion

The debt problem aggravated by the absence of strong global mechanisms in checking the excesses of vulture fund litigation harms all stakeholders especially the sovereign debtors. Strict opposition to the binding global framework using the excuse of protecting and advancing private contractual rights has the potential to disrupt capital flows for development and a possible threat to global prosperity and world peace.

This is a reversal of functional legal order where private rights are unjustifiably exalted above public benefit for private corporate profit. In the absence of firmer and more effective global solutions for now, it is up to African sovereigns to adopt a common position, dealing with the vulture litigation menace. It is hoped that this may just act as a catalyst to expedite an effective global legal framework.

CHAPTER THREE

Deterring Debt Vultures from Distressed African Sovereign Debt

Geoffrey Adonu*

1 Introduction

Developing countries, especially those in Africa, face precarious financial, economic, and debt situations partly due to the Coronavirus pandemic and the ongoing war in Ukraine. On the debt front, most developing countries are confronted by rising debt levels and higher borrowing costs.[1] In Africa, the situation is very dire, with African governments owing an estimated $493.6 billion to their external official and commercial creditors[2] and debt service consuming a large chunk of public revenue in the continent (many African governments spend more on debt service than on healthcare, education and social protection investments combined).[3]

---

* Geoffrey Adonu is an international lawyer and a sovereign debt consultant at Afronomicslaw. He received a J.D. from University at Buffalo School of Law in 2023, an LLM from New York University School of Law in 2020 and has an LLB from Babcock University. The author would like to thank the editors of Afronomicslaw, in particular James Thuo Gathii and Olabisi D. Akinkugbe, for their useful suggestions, comments and mentorship.

[1] Marcello Estavao, "Are we ready for the coming spate of debt crises?" (2022), available at https://blogs.worldbank.org/voices/are-we-ready-coming-spate-debt-crises (warning that over the next 12 months, as many as a dozen developing countries may not be able to service their debt. Sri Lanka has since defaulted, and many more countries are expected to follow).

[2] The World Bank, "2022 International Debt Statistics," available at https://datatopics.worldbank.org/debt/ids/region/SSA; Danny Bradlow "Vultures, doves and African Debt: here's a way out" (2020), available at https://theconversation.com/vultures-doves-and-african-debt-heres-a-way-out-137643 (*hereinafter* Bradlow, Vultures, Doves and African Debt).

[3] Debt Justice, "Sixty-four countries spend more on debt payment than health" (2020), available at https://debtjustice.org.uk/press-release/sixty-four-countries-spend-more-on-debt-payments-than-health; Bradlow, *Vultures, Doves and African Debt, supra* note 2; Cephas Lumina & Nona Tamale, "Sovereign

As of 2021, more than 20 Africa countries were in debt distress (either in default or facing high risk of default).[4] For instance, Mali and Zambia defaulted in early 2022 and 2020 respectively and are at various stages of debt workouts with their respective creditors[5] while Eritrea, Sudan, and Zimbabwe have all fallen into arrears on their interest payments. On the other hand, Benin, Chad, Ghana, Ethiopia, and Kenya among others are at the brink of debt distress and have approached the IMF for financial assistance in recent months.[6] Ghana fell into default by the end of 2022 and is presently restructuring its domestic and external debts as a condition for receiving IMF bailout.[7] With over $21.5 billion in Eurobond debt service due in the next five years amidst the current spate of interest hikes by central banks in the Global North and low foreign reserves, more African countries are unlikely to cope with their debt service and may slide into debt distress and even default in the next few years.[8] Given this situation, a spate of sovereign debt workouts is expected across the continent over

---

Debt and Human Rights: A Focus on Sub-Saharan Africa" (2021), PAPER 1 OF THE AFRICAN SOVEREIGN DEBT JUSTICE PAPER SERIES, available at https://www.afronomicslaw.org/sites/default/files/pdf/Lumina%20and%20Nona%20AfSDJN%20Paper%20on%20Sovereign%20Debt%20and%20Human%20Rights%20(times%20new%20roman).pdf (noting that in 2019, 16 African countries spent more on debt repayment than on education, health and social protection combined).

[4] Alex Vines, Creon Butler and Yu Jie, "Addressing Debt Distress in Africa," available at https://www.chathamhouse.org/2022/01/addressing-debt-distress-africa.

[5] Joseph Cotterill, "Zambia's $1.3bn IMF bailout to test how China handles defaults" (2022), FINANCIAL TIMES, available at https://www.ft.com/content/d15d6c2b-5208-4173-b3e3-49aacb9ffeb5; African Sovereign Debt Justice Network, "Fiftieth Sovereign Debt News Update: IMF Executive Board Approves $1.3 Billion Extended Credit Facility for Zambia," available at https://www.afronomicslaw.org/category/african-sovereign-debt-justice-network-afsdjn/fiftieth-sovereign-debt-news-update-imf.

[6] African Sovereign Debt Justice Network, "Forty Ninth Sovereign Debt News Update: IMF Programs and Events in Africa in Context" (2022), available at https://www.afronomicslaw.org/category/african-sovereign-debt-justice-network-afsdjn/forty-ninth-sovereign-debt-news-update-imf.

[7] Christian Akorlie et al., "Ghana to Defualt on most External Debts as Economic Crisis worsen" (2022), REUTERS, available at https://www.reuters.com/world/africa/ghana-announces-external-debt-payment-suspension-slipping-into-default-2022-12-19/.

[8] Pangea-Risk, "Special Report: Which African Sovereigns are most likely to default?" available at https://www.pangea-risk.com/special-report-which-african-sovereigns-are-most-likely-to-default/#:~:text=In%20the%20five-year%20outlook%20%28May%202022%20to%20May,as%20more%20African%20sovereigns%20fall%20into%20debt%20distress.

the next few years as governments seek to reduce their debt burden and return to the path of debt sustainability.[9]

The foregoing circumstances make African countries susceptible to exploitation by vulture funds in their quest for profit maximization. Vulture funds are speculative investors that specialize in buying deeply discounted sovereign debts from secondary markets and exploiting loopholes in the sovereign debt architecture—particularly, the absence of a sovereign bankruptcy procedure—to extract the full face value from their debtor countries.[10] In addition to "holding out" and undermining restructurings in order to extract preferential payments from debt-stricken countries (which deters other creditors from participating in restructurings and granting debt relief to distressed countries), vulture funds also use aggressive and expensive foreign court litigations to capture debt reliefs granted by other creditors and even development aids received by poor countries in some cases. Furthermore, through their tactics, vulture funds force vulnerable countries to prioritize debt service over public services and the basic needs of their most population. In effect, vulture funds maximize enormous profits by exploiting the precarious financial situation of indebted countries and inflicting enormous pain on debt-distressed countries and their citizens.

Despite the enormous pain vulture funds inflict on poor countries, warding them off is an uphill task for the affected countries given extant lacunas in the global debt architecture such as the absence of mandatory sovereign debt restructuring mechanism. The situation is compounded by the fact that reforming the global debt architecture requires the concurrence of the Global North where these funds are domiciled which have no significant incentive to endorse holistic reforms given that the system, as presently constituted, favors advanced countries and their

---

[9] Oxford Economics, "Pre-emptive debt Restructuring: a Viable Scenario for Africa?" (2022), RESEARCH BRIEFING, available at https://www.oxfordeconomics.com/resource/pre-emptive-debt-restructuring-a-viable-scenario-for-africa/ (noting that in recent weeks, many African sovereigns have openly or discreetly mulled public debt reorganization, called for debt relief, or suffered credit rating downgrades owing to rising debt default odds); *See also* Carlos Lopez, "Is Sovereign Debt Impending Africa's Covid-19 Recovery?", available at https://www.chathamhouse.org/2021/11/sovereign-debt-impeding-africas-covid-19-recovery.

[10] Alison Wirtz, *Bilateral Investment Treaties, Holdout Investors, and Their Impact on Grenada's Sovereign Debt Crisis* 16 CHI. J. INT'L L. 249 (2015).

institutions.[11] In contrast, developing countries that are most affected by the activities of vulture funds are rule-takers in the global financial system with no meaningful power to enact the reforms needed to protect their interests, a status quo which the Third World Approach to International Law (TWAIL), an insurgent scholarly movement in the Global South, is working to change.[12] It is however noteworthy that while some developed countries have passed laws to deter vulture funds (the so-called anti-vulture statutes), these simply amount to papering over cracks.[13]

Against the foregoing background, this chapter examines the activities of vulture funds in the sovereign debt context, their tactics, and the way their activities harm countries in debt distress. The chapter also examines policy and contractual measures that can be used to protect poor countries from their scourge. The chapter commences with this introduction as Section I and examines the activities of vulture funds in sovereign debt markets in Section II. Section III focuses on the tactics used by vulture funds while Section IV examines the adverse effects of their activities on poor countries and their populations. Section V examines the statutory and contractual mechanism can be used to deter vulture funds and minimize their activities in sovereign debt markets while Section VI concludes the chapter and provides the way forward for African countries.

2 Vulture Funds in Sovereign Debt Context

In general, vulture funds are mostly equity or hedge funds based in the Global North.[14] Their business model involves purchasing the debts of financially distressed countries in the secondary markets at steep discounts and exploiting loopholes in the global

---

[11] *See generally*, James Thuo Gathii, "The Agenda of Third World Approaches to International Law (TWAIL)" (2019), INTERNATIONAL LEGAL THEORY: FOUNDATIONS AND FRONTIERS (CAMBRIDGE UNIVERSITY PRESS 2019); Makau Mutua, *"What Is TWAIL?"* (2000), 94 PROCEEDINGS OF THE ASIL MEETING 31, available at https://digitalcommons.law.buffalo.edu/journal_articles/560/.

[12] *Supra* note 11.

[13] Daniel Bradlow, "Deterring the Debt Vultures in Africa" (2020), available at https://www.project-syndicate.org/commentary/new-fund-can-deter-africa-sovereign-debt-vultures-by-daniel-d-bradlow-2020-05.

[14] *See* Michael Sheehan, "Vulture funds—the key players" (2011), THE GUARDIAN, available at https://www.theguardian.com/global-development/2011/nov/15/vulture-funds-key-players.

financial architecture and domestic legal systems of jurisdictions like New York and London to demand payment of the contractual face value of the debts.[15]

Vulture funds became active in the sovereign debt markets in the 1980s and in African sovereign debt markets in the 1990s.[16] Initially, vulture funds operated in corporate debt markets mostly in the United States and Europe but ventured into sovereign debt markets during the Latin American debt crisis.[17] In the 1980s, many Latin American countries became overwhelmed with unsustainable debt, with Mexico the first to default. During this time (known as the lost decade in Latin America), sovereign debts were mostly in the form of syndicated bank loans held by international commercial banks from the Global North. As a result, the region-wide debt-distress threatened in financial stability in the United States and other advanced countries whose banks held these debts.

To protect their banks and financial systems and to provide debt relief to Latin American countries, the United States and its allies came up with the Brady Plan—named after the then US Treasury Secretary.[18] The Brady Plan involved cancelling some of the syndicated bank loans of Latin American countries and converting the outstanding loans thereafter into tradable securities (known as the Brady Bonds).[19] These securities were then offered to the public in the secondary markets mostly at steep discounts which made them attractive to speculative investors.[20] Given this opportunity for arbitrage and high returns, vulture funds swooped in, acquired a

---

[15] Cephas Lumina & Nona Tamale, "Sovereign Debt and Human Rights: A Focus on Sub-Saharan Africa" (2021) at 4, PAPER 1 OF THE AFRICAN SOVEREIGN DEBT JUSTICE PAPER SERIES, available at https://www.afronomicslaw.org/sites/default/files/pdf/Lumina%20and%20Nona%20AfSDJN%20Paper%20on%20Sovereign%20Debt%20and%20Human%20Rights%20(times%20new%20roman).pdf; African Development Bank, "Vulture Funds in the Sovereign Debt Context," available at https://www.afdb.org/en/topics-and-sectors/initiatives-partnerships/african-legal-support-facility/vulture-funds-in-the-sovereign-debt-context.

[16] Hector Timerman, "Africa and Latin America Still Fight Vulture Funds" (2013), HUFFPOST, available at https://www.huffpost.com/entry/africa-latin-america-vulture-funds_b_2100827.

[17] Ibid.

[18] James Gathii, "The Sanctity of Sovereign Loan Contracts and its Origins in Enforcement Litigations" (2006), 38 THE GEO. WASH. INT'L L L. REV. 260; For a judicial discussion of the Brady Plan, see Elliot Assoc., L.P. v. Banco De La Nacion, 194 F.3d 363, 366–367 (2d Cir. 1999).

[19] Ibid at 260–61.

[20] Ibid.; Elliot Assoc., L.P. v. Banco De La Nacion, 194 F.3d 363, 366–367 (2d Cir. 1999).

significant chunk of the Brady Bonds, and started suing the debtor countries for the full-face value of the debt before American and European courts.[21] Thus, although the Brady Plan was designed to provide debt relief to the affected countries, it became the entry point for vulture funds into sovereign debt and was subject of the earliest vulture fund lawsuits against sovereign debtors which set the tone for vulture funds' intervention in sovereign debt markets.[22]

With their successful outing in the Latin American crisis, the vulture funds struck again in the 1990s when low income countries were plagued by debt distress[23] and the World Bank and the IMF launched the Highly Indebted Poor Countries (HIPC) initiative to provide them with debt relief.[24] The HIPC Initiative was followed by the Multilateral Debt Relief Initiative (MDRI) which expanded the countries eligible for debt relief under the HIPC Initiative.[25] Under the HIPC and MDRI initiatives, thirty-seven low- and middle-income countries—thirty-one of which are in Africa—had all or some of their official and bilateral debts cancelled.[26] With their official and bilateral debts cancelled, these poor countries were confronted by vulture funds who bought up their commercial loans at steep discounts. Like the Brady Bonds era, these funds sued these HIPCs for the face value of the debts and captured some of the debt relief received by them.[27]

According to the African Development Bank, vulture funds have targeted more than a dozen African countries—Zambia, Cote d'Ivoire, Burkina Faso, Angola, Cameroun, Congo, Democratic Republic of Congo, Ethiopia, Liberia, Madagascar, Mozambique, Niger, Sao Tome and Principe, Tanzania, and Uganda—since 1990s.[28]

---

[21] *Supra* note 16.

[22] *Supra* note 18, 20.

[23] *Supra* note 16.

[24] International Monetary Fund, "Debt Relief Under the Heavily Indebted Poor Country" (2021), (HIPC) Initiative, available at https://www.imf.org/en/About/Factsheets/Sheets/2016/08/01/16/11/Debt-Relief-Under-the-Heavily-Indebted-Poor-Countries-Initiative.

[25] The World Bank, "Heavily Indebted Poor Countries" (2018), (HIPC) Initiative, available at https://www.worldbank.org/en/topic/debt/brief/hipc.

[26] *Ibid.*

[27] *Id.*

[28] African Development Bank Group, "Vulture Funds in the Sovereign Debt Context," available at https://www.afdb.org/en/topics-and-sectors/initiatives-partnerships/african-legal-support-facility/vulture-funds-in-the-sovereign-debt-context.

3 The Playbook of Vulture Funds

Typically, when low-and-middle income countries are in financial distress—often due to external shocks like the ongoing Covid-19 pandemic and the war in Ukraine—their credit ratings are typically downgraded by international credit rating agencies. For instance, during the global economic crisis triggered by COVID-19, many African countries—more than 60 percent—suffered credit rating downgrades.[29] Depending on the degree of credit rating downgrades, the bonds of the affected sovereign may become ineligible for investment by some institutional investors leading to a rapid sell-off which results in massive price decline.[30] The price decline creates an arbitrage opportunity and, at this juncture, vulture funds come in to buy up these debts at discounted prices in the hope that they will ultimately default.[31] Once their target countries default or start restructuring negotiations with creditors, vulture funds employ two main tactics to coerce the debtor countries to pay them off.[32]

First, vulture funds holdout and (where possible) outrightly block any attempts by the sovereign to engineer a restructuring of its debts—even if the restructuring package is in the interest of and approved by majority of the creditors—with a view to maximizing their own returns.[33] Describing this tactic of vulture funds, Gill and Buchheit explained that vulture funds typically "hold out until other creditors make concessions—in the expectation that concessions from others will free up cash that enables [i.e., the vulture funds] to collect the biggest possible payoff."[34] This opportunistic behavior by vulture funds is made possible by the absence of an international

---

[29] Hippolyte Fofack, "Downgrading Africa's Development" (2021), available at https://www.project-syndicate.org/commentary/africa-credit-rating-downgrades-hurt-economic-development-by-hippolyte-fofack-2021-08.

[30] Gene Frieda, "Sovereign Debt Markets" (2014) at 307, in Rosa Lastra and Lee Buchheit, eds., Sovereign Debt Management, Oxford University Press.

[31] Hedgeclippers, "Pain and Profit in Sovereign Debt: How New York Can Stop Vulture Funds from preying on countries" (2021), available at https://hedgeclippers.org/pain-and-profit-in-sovereign-debt-how-new-york-can-stop-vulture-funds-from-preying-on-countries/.

[32] *Ibid.*

[33] *Ibid.*

[34] Indermit Gill and Lee C. Buchheit, "Targeted Legislative Tweaks can help contain the harm of debt crisis" (2022), Brookings, available at https://www.brookings.edu/blog/future-development/2022/06/27/targeted-legislative-tweaks-can-help-contain-the-harm-of-debt-crises/.

framework for sovereign debt restructurings to make workouts approved majority of the creditors effective and binding on holdouts like vulture funds.[35]

Second, in addition to holding out and blocking restructurings, vulture funds initiate expensive litigation in foreign courts (usually in New York and London) against debtor countries in order to frustrate their restructuring efforts and extract a preferential pay-off from these vulnerable countries.[36] Since these suits are typically commenced in creditor-friendly jurisdictions, they often result in judgments in favor vulture funds (forcing most target countries to settle most of the time).[37] According to the African Development Bank, vulture funds typically recoup profits in the region of three to twenty times their investment net legal fees.[38]

4 The Case against Vulture Funds

Proponents and advocates of vulture funds and their business model and tactics cite the role played by these funds in supporting active secondary markets trading in sovereign debts—a liquid secondary market in these bonds benefits the issuers in the form of lower cost of financing.[39] In other words, by being readily available to buy sovereign debt instruments from the initial holders, they create demand and obviate the need for other creditors to hold their instruments till maturity which reduces the interest rate premium the investors would have demanded to lend to these debtor countries.[40] Despite the foregoing benefit, critics argue that the harm inflicted by tactics deployed by vulture funds on debt-distressed countries (as discussed below) outweigh the secondary market liquidity gains.[41]

---

[35] Michael Sean Winters, "Vulture Funds" (2013), NATIONAL CATHOLIC REPORTER, available at https://www.ncronline.org/blogs/distinctly-catholic/vulture-funds; *Supra* note 31.

[36] *Supra* note 29; AfDB, Vulture Funds in the Sovereign Debt Context, https://www.afdb.org/en/topics-and-sectors/initiatives-partnerships/african-legal-support-facility/vulture-funds-in-the-sovereign-debt-context.

[37] *Supra* note 31.

[38] AfDB, "Vulture Funds in the Sovereign Debt Context," available at https://www.afdb.org/en/topics-and-sectors/initiatives-partnerships/african-legal-support-facility/vulture-funds-in-the-sovereign-debt-context.

[39] *Ibid.*

[40] *Ibid.*

[41] *Ibid.*

First, vulture funds use their tactics to prolong the unsustainable debt situation of poor countries which shuts them out of the capitals and denies them access to much-needed funding.[42] In the absence of a sovereign debt restructuring framework to compel sovereign creditors to participate in restructuring negotiations or to do so in good faith,[43] vulture funds refuse to participate in restructurings and use their voting power to block restructurings irrespective of the benefits to their debtor countries and its citizens as well as the creditors as a whole.[44] Of course, the longer restructuring negotiations drags out, the longer a distressed country is shut out of the markets, with limited or no access to crucial funding for public services and critical imports (like food, medicine, and energy) needed for the survival of its population.[45]

Second and relatedly, when vulture funds fail to outrightly block a restructuring or in addition to doing so, they proceed to initiate expensive foreign court litigations against the indebted country and claim the full contractual value of their instruments.[46] Given that the claims of creditors are interdependent and any preferential recovery by vulture funds comes at the expense of creditors that made concessions during a restructuring,[47] the threat posed by vulture funds discourage other creditors refrain from participating in restructurings and providing debt relief to poor countries for fear that any relief they provide will be captured by opportunistic creditors i.e., vulture funds.[48] The infamous Argentina restructuring in 2001 aptly illustrates this ugly situation.

After rejecting Argentina's restructuring proposal that was backed and approved by ninety three percent of the creditors, vulture funds led by Elliot Management

---

[42] *Supra* note 31.

[43] Magalie Masamba, "Towards Building a Fair and Orderly International Framework for Sovereign Debt Restructuringm An African Perspective" at 3, available at https://www.afronomicslaw.org/sites/default/files/pdf/AFRICA'S%20DANCE%20WITH%20UNSUSTAINABLE%20DEBT%20IS%20IT%20TIME%20FOR%20A%20COMPREHENSIVE%20MECHANISM%20FOR%20DEBT%20RESTRUCTURING.pdf; *Supra* note 31.

[44] *Supra* note 37.

[45] *Supra* note 31.

[46] *Ibid.*

[47] *Supra* note 37.

[48] Lee Buchheit & Elena Daly, "Minimizing Holdout Creditors" (2014) at 15, in Rosa Lastra and Lee Buchheit, eds., SOVEREIGN DEBT MANAGEMENT, OXFORD UNIVERSITY PRESS.

sued Argentina in New York.[49] After over a decade of expensive court battles, the vulture funds prevailed following a controversial New York court decision that prohibited Argentina from making payments on the new bonds issued to creditors in the restructuring unless it makes ratable payments to the vulture funds.[50] Argentina unsuccessfully appealed the decision up to the Supreme Court of the United States and was forced to pay more than $2 billion to vulture funds after fifteen years of bitter litigation.[51]

In Africa, Zambia is an example of how the tactics of vulture funds can negatively affect poor countries plagued by financial problems.[52] Zambia purchased equipment of $30 million from Romania on credit.[53] When Zambia ran into financial problems and was unable to service the debt, it agreed with Romania to settle the debt for about $3 million.[54] However, before the settlement was finalized, Romania sold the debt to a vulture fund for $4 million; the vulture fund then sued Zambia claiming $55 million in the United Kingdom.[55] After almost a decade of controversy, Zambia settled the case for $15 million in 2007 (the venture fund made a gross profit of $11 million).[56]

Third, many poor countries are compelled to divert funds that could have gone into public services like education and health care into defending law suits and settling judgment awards in favor of vulture funds.[57] Sovereign debt lawsuits are very expensive and last between three to ten years on average—in fact the Argentina case last about fifteen years.[58] Thus, apart from settling the judgment awards (twenty six of

---

[49] *Supra* note 31.

[50] *Ibid.*

[51] *Ibid.*

[52] African Development Bank Group, "Vulture Funds in the Sovereign Debt Context," available at https://www.afdb.org/en/topics-and-sectors/initiatives-partnerships/african-legal-support-facility/vulture-funds-in-the-sovereign-debt-context.

[53] J.C. Watts, "Africa easy prey for vulture funds" (2007), LAS VEGAS REVIEW-JOURNAL, available at https://www.reviewjournal.com/opinion/africa-easy-prey-for-vulture-funds/0.

[54] *Ibid.*

[55] *Ibid.*; *Supra* note 52; *See also* https://www.theguardian.com/global-development/2011/nov/15/vulture-funds-key-players (for more details on the case and profile of the Donegal International, the vulture fund involved in the Zambian case, and its founder).

[56] *Ibid.*

[57] *Supra* note 31.

[58] *Ibid.*; *Supra* note 52.

which have been more than $1 billion in judgment awards in favor of vulture funds), defendant countries channel enormous amount of funds that could have gone into public services towards litigation costs.[59] For example, it is estimated that countries targeted by vulture funds spend about 18% of their healthcare and education budgets in defending these suits.[60]

5 Deterring Vultures Funds from African Sovereign Debts

There is no single solution that would end the menace of vulture fund. However, certain governance reforms in the global financial architecture as well as contractual mechanisms can be used to deter and neutralize them. For example, international and domestic law mechanisms like the establishment of a mandatory international sovereign debt restructuring framework, enactment of sovereign debt restructuring statutes in key sovereign debt jurisdictions like New York and London as well as strengthening the champerty statutes of key sovereign debt jurisdictions can provide significant protections to vulnerable countries targeted by vulture funds. These public law and domestic statutory solutions are however difficult to attain given that the balance of power in the global financial system is in favor of the Global North—and by extension vulture funds—rather than the poor countries most affected by vulture fund activities. For instance, the sovereign debt restructuring mechanism (SDRM) that was proposed by the IMF failed due to lack of support primarily from the United States which exercises veto power over IMF governance matters like amending the articles of agreement to adopt the SDRM. As a result, these solutions are at best long-term solutions. In the meantime, vulnerable countries can resort to contractual mechanisms such as collective action clauses, exit consent clauses, reformed *pari passu* clauses and natural disaster clauses to deter vulture funds from their sovereign debts.

(a) International law and domestic statutory Solutions
    (i) Creating an International sovereign debt mechanism

The predatory practices of vulture funds are to a large extent enabled by the lack of a mandatory sovereign debt restructuring framework. In fact, their entire business

---

[59] *Ibid.*
[60] *Supra* note 31.

model is built around exploiting lacunas in the sovereign debt governance architecture. A formal sovereign debt restructuring mechanism that will permit indebted countries to restructure their liabilities in the same way as corporate debtors will close the loophole and deter the vultures by "imposing the will of the majority of similarly situated creditors on any naysaying minority."[61] This kind of cramdown mechanism will provide much-needed protections for debt countries.[62]

The closest we have come to a formal restructuring framework is the SDRM proposed by the IMF in 2002. As proposed by the then deputy managing director of the IMF, Anne Krueger, the SDRM would have replicated the key features of Chapter 11 of the US Bankruptcy Code—supermajority creditor approval of restructurings, an automatic stay on creditor enforcement actions, and a quasi-judicial oversight body to process creditor claims.[63] The SDRM would have also enabled debtor countries to obtain new financing during restructurings and confer priority on such new lenders just like the debtor-in-possession financing mechanism in US Chapter 11.[64]

The SDRM was vigorously opposed by creditor countries, i.e., the Global North, especially the United States which has the decisive vote that was required to amend the IMF's Articles of Agreement to effect the SDRM. It was ultimately defeated.[65] Subsequent attempts by developing countries to resuscitate the SDRM via the United Nations General Assembly (UNGA) equally failed due to opposition from the United States and its allies.[66] The UNGA however succeeded in establishing the Principles for Fair Sovereign Debt Restructuring which sets out nine principles—sovereignty, good faith, transparency, impartiality, equitable treatment, sovereign immunity, legitimacy, sustainability and majority restructuring, that would guide sovereign debt restructurings.[67] Nevertheless, being a non-binding soft-law instrument, these principles are toothless and ineffective against vulture funds but constitute a step in the right direction.[68]

---

[61] *Supra* note 31.
[62] *Ibid* at 15.
[63] *Ibid* at 21.
[64] *Ibid*.
[65] *Supra* note 52.
[66] *Supra* note 9.
[67] *Ibid*.
[68] *Ibid*.

The debt crisis occasioned by Covid-19 pandemic resulted in renewed calls for the establishment of an SDRM but there has been no significant progress in this regard.[69] Developing countries, including African countries, that are most affected by the activities of vulture funds must continue to push for an SDRM or a similar framework to give them some protection against predatory tactics of vulture funds.[70]

(ii) Domestic Restructuring statutes in key jurisdictions

Nearly all sovereign debt contracts are governed by New York and English law and enforcement actions by vulture funds predominantly happen in these two jurisdictions.[71] Thus, the enactment of statutes that will facilitate sovereign debt restructurings in these jurisdictions can effectively protect poor countries.[72] To this end, these key sovereign debt jurisdictions have been urged to enact SDRM-like statutes to protect vulnerable countries against vulture funds. In New York, there is a bill pending before the legislature for this purpose.[73] When passed, the bill will enable financially distressed sovereigns with New York law governed debt instruments to petition the New York State Senate Finance Committee for debt relief.[74] The petition will be supported by a restructuring plan that would be submitted for creditors' approval.[75] And if approved by at least two-thirds majority by number of debts and more than one-half in number of each class of creditors designated in the restructuring plan, the plan will become effective and binding on the sovereign and its creditors (including vulture funds).[76] The bill also states that a debtor country can raise fresh

---

[69] *See* Magalie Masamba, "Africa's Dance with Unsustainable Debt: is it Time for a Comprehensive Mechanism for Debt Restructuring?", available at https://www.afronomicslaw.org/sites/default/files/pdf/AFRICA%E2%80%99S%20DANCE%20WITH%20UNSUSTAINABLE%20DEBT%20IS%20IT%20TIME%20FOR%20A%20COMPREHENSIVE%20MECHANISM%20FOR%20DEBT%20RESTRUCTURING.pdf; *Supra* note 34.

[70] *See* Devi Sookun, "Stop Vulture Fund Lawsuits, *A Handbook* 100" (2010), COMMONWEALTH SECRETARIAT, available at https://production-new-commonwealth-files.s3.eu-west-2.amazonaws.com/migrated/key_reform_pdfs/Stop%20Vulture%20Fund%20Lawsuits%20EB.pdf.

[71] *Supra* note 34.

[72] *Ibid.*

[73] New York State Senate Bill S6627 and New Assembly Bill A7562. Available at https://www.nysenate.gov/legislation/bills/2021/S6627 and https://www.nysenate.gov/legislation/bills/2021/a7562 respectively.

[74] § 302, Bill S6627.

[75] § 305, Bill S6627.

[76] *Ibid.*

capital to finance its restructuring and the new lenders will be accorded priority over existing creditors.[77]

(iii) Anti-Vulture Statutes

Some jurisdictions, including Belgium, France, and United Kingdom, have enacted legislations that limit the profits that vulture funds can amass from their predatory activities.[78] These so-called anti-vulture statutes seek to prevent vulture funds from using the judicial system to exploit poor countries and profit from development aid and debt relief received by them by donors and other creditors.

In the United Kingdom, the Debt Relief Act (DRA) was enacted in 2010 and states that vulture funds suing to enforce pre-2004 debts of highly indebted poor countries (HIPCs) cannot recover on terms that are more favorable than the debt relief provided to these countries under the HIPC Initiative.[79] The DRA is very limited in scope as its application is restricted to countries that received HIPC debt relief and excludes debts incurred by HIPCs after 2004 i.e., only debts that are subject to the HIPC Initiative.[80] In contrast to the DRA, the Belgian statute is broader and bars holdout creditors from seeking and obtaining relief in Belgian courts if their claim is disproportionate to the secondary market price at which their debts were purchased.[81] The French law on the other hand prevents creditors from seizing the foreign assets of countries that receive overseas development aid.[82] Civil society activists are still lobbying the legislature to enact an anti-vulture law in New York.[83]

---

[77] § 306, Bill S6627.
[78] IMF 2020 Paper at 27 ¶ 23.
[79] § 3 & 4. See IMF 2020 Paper at 28 ¶ 23.
[80] § 1, DRA.
[81] IMF 2020 Paper at 28 ¶ 23; Allen & Overy, "New Belgian Law targets 'Vulture Funds' buying up distressed Sovereign debt," available at https://www.allenovery.com/en-gb/global/news-and-insights/european-finance-litigation-review/northern-europe/law-targets-vulture-funds-buying-up-sovereign-debt.
[82] Tim Jones, "France passes law to clip vulture funds" wings' (2017), DEBT JUSTICE, available at https://debtjustice.org.uk/blog/france-passes-law-clip-vulture-funds-wings.
[83] *Supra* note 27; James Baratta, "Activists are Challenging Laws that Enasble Vulture Funds to Exploit Global South," available at https://truthout.org/articles/activists-are-challenging-laws-that-enable-vulture-funds-to-exploit-global-south/.

While the effectiveness of anti-vulture statutes is yet to be tested in court, anti-vulture statutes make it unattractive for vulture funds to holdout during restructurings by diminishing their chances of recovering more than their counterparts that make concessions during restructurings.[84] Anti-vulture statues also protect development aids received by poor countries from being captured by vulture funds.[85]

(iv) Strengthening Champerty Statutes

Champerty is a common law doctrine that protects debtors from predatory creditors that buy their debts with the intent of recovering them using litigation.[86] In New York, for example, the doctrine of champerty is codified in § 489 of the New York Judicial Law which prohibits acquisition of "a thing in action or claim with the intent and for the purpose of bring an action or proceeding thereon."[87]

Since vulture funds acquire the debts of poor countries with the intent of using litigation to enforce the debt instruments, construing champerty statutes to include their playbook will prevent them from using the judicial system to extort poor countries and their citizens.[88] However, it is noteworthy New York courts and indeed the courts of other jurisdictions where vulture lawsuits are adjudicated are creditor-friendly and presently construe their champerty statutes to exclude the business model of vulture funds.[89]

For instance, in *Turkmani v. Republic of Bolivia* and by *Elliot Assocs., v. Banco De La Nacion* respectively, New York courts dismissed the champerty defense raised by the debtor countries' (Bolivia and Peru) and held that the business model of vulture funds does not violate New York champerty law. The *Tukmani* and *Elliot* decisions have been criticized by debt advocates for prioritizing and entrenching the private

---

[84] IMF 2020 Paper at 28 ¶ 23.
[85] *Ibid.*
[86] Petit & Daniel Jacobs, "Champerty and Maintenance: An end to Historic Rules preventing third-party funding?" (2016) at 9, in NORTON ROSE FULBRIGHT, INTERNATIONAL ARBITRATION REPORT.
[87] IMF 2020 Paper at 28. *See Elliot Assocs., LP v. Banco de la Nacion,* 194 F.3d 363 (2d Cir. 1999); *Turkmani v. Republic of Bolivia,* 193 F. Supp.2d 165 (D.D.C.2002).
[88] *Supra* note 32; James Gathii, "The Sanctity of Sovereign Loan Contracts and its Origins in Enforcement Litigations" (2006) at 38, THE GEO. WASH. INT'L L. REV. 311.
[89] *Ibid.*

contractual rights of vulture funds at the expense of debtor countries.[90] Gathii, for example, submitted that by drawing an artificial distinction between champerty and ordinary debt collection, the *Turkmani* and *Elliot* courts failed to give the doctrine of champerty its intended meaning.[91] Gathii further argued that by construing the champerty doctrine as they did, the *Turkmani* and *Elliot* courts prioritized sanctity of contracts and entrenched creditor rights at the expense of the debt-distressed countries and their residents.[92]

(b) Contractual Mechanisms

In the short to medium term, vulnerable countries can utilize certain contractual devices like collective action clauses, exit amendments, and natural disaster clauses to reduce the scourge of vulture funds. These contractual measures will not only facilitate orderly restructurings but will limit the ability of vulture funds to holdout and hound poor countries with aggressive lawsuits in foreign courts.

(i) Collective Action Clauses

Collective action clauses (CACs) are designed to neutralize holdout creditors by empowering a pre-agreed majority of creditors to change the payment terms of their debt instruments either by reducing the interest and principal or by extending their maturities.[93] By dispensing with unanimous consent of creditors in restructurings, CACs reduce incidences of holdout behavior by binding minority creditors to any agreement reached by the majority.[94] The prospect of being bound by the restructuring package if approved by the majority serves as a coercive mechanism that can be

---

[90] *See* James Gathii, "The Sanctity of Sovereign Loan Contracts and its Origins in Enforcement Litigations" (2006) at 38, The Geo. Wash. Int'l L. Rev. 311.

[91] *Ibid* at 311–12.

[92] *Ibid* at 313.

[93] African Legal Support Facility, "Understanding Sovereign Debt, Options and Opportunities for Africa" (2004) at 68; Steven L. Schwarcz, "Idiot's Guide to Sovereign Debt Restructuring" (2004) at 53, Emory L.J. 1189, 1190; *See* International Monetary Fund, "Strengthening the Contractual Framework to Address Collective Action Problems in Sovereign Debt Restructuring" (2014).

[94] Steven L. Schwarcz, "Idiot's Guide to Sovereign Debt Restructuring" (2004) at 53, Emory L.J. 1189, 1190.

used to force holdouts, including vulture funds, to the negotiating table in a restructuring and to ultimately participate in the restructuring thereby reducing free riding among creditors and facilitating orderly restructurings.

The most recent iteration of CACs (the third generation or single-limb CACs) was introduced in 2014 and allows sovereigns to restructure multiple bond series in one transaction with a single supermajority vote of the bondholders across all the series being restructured.[95] In other words, rather than doing multiple transactions (series-by-series restructurings), debtor countries can restructure all their outstanding bonds containing single-limb CACs in one transaction. In addition to being cost effective compared to its predecessors, these new CACs make it more difficult for vulture funds to block restructurings by significantly increasing the amount of stake they would need to block a multi-series restructuring transaction.[96]

Although single-limb CACs have been widely adopted since their introduction (ninety one percent of the 690 international sovereign bonds (worth about US$870 billion in total principal nominal value) issued between October 1, 2014, and June 30, 2020 contain the third-generation CACs),[97] many bond instruments do not contain these improved CACs.[98] Also, many outstanding bond instruments, especially those issued before 2003,[99] as well as subordinated loans, arbitral awards, resource for infrastructure loans and other secured and contingent liabilities that constitute a significant chunk of sovereign debt stock have no CACs.[100] Thus, despite the effectiveness of CACs in reducing the scourge of vulture funds, there is enough room for them to operate.[101]

---

[95] International Monetary Fund, "The International Architecture for Resolving Sovereign Debt Involving Private-Sector Creditors—Recent Developments, Challenges, and Reform Options" (2020) at 22; African Legal Support Facility, "Understanding Sovereign Debt, Options and Opportunities for Africa" at 68–69.
[96] *Supra* note 95 at 22.
[97] *Ibid* at 21 ¶ 14.
[98] *Ibid* at 23 ¶ 15.
[99] *Ibid*.
[100] *Ibid* at 23, 29–34.
[101] *Ibid*.

(ii) Redesignation and Pacman Techniques

In restructuring restructurings, countries that are vulnerable to vulture funds attack might explore the redesignation and pacman strategies that emerged in Argentina and Ecuador 2020 restructurings. Redesignation and Pacman strategies are used to gerrymander the voting pools in order to satisfy the voting threshold required to approve a restructuring that would otherwise be hampered or blocked by holdout creditors.[102]

With respect to redesignation, Argentina and Ecuador reserved the right to determine the bonds series that will be restructured after the close of their exchange offers which then allows the sovereign to aggregate only the bond series that received sufficient votes needed to approve the restructuring to be included in the restructuring.[103] For instance, if a sovereign makes an exchange offer to creditors across ten bond series, the sovereign can ex post exclude any of the ten series subject to the offer from its restructuring if it did not secure enough votes from that series for restructuring. By so doing, redesignation can be used by sovereigns to neutralize vulture funds by excluding bond series in which vulture funds successfully take blocking positions from the restructuring even after the voting has closed.

The Pacman strategy on the other hand involves launching subsequent exchange offers or restructurings immediately following the close of an earlier one and including the new bonds issued to participants in the immediately preceding transactions for voting purposes in the present restructuring.[104] In other words, holders of the newly issued bonds will be aggregated with holdouts from the prior restructuring rounds and offered slightly better terms to entice them to vote in favor of the subsequent restructuring.[105]

Redesignation and pacman can be used complementarily—once redesignation has been used to push through the first restructuring, Pacman can be used to engineer the restructuring of the outstanding series—to cramdown on vulture funds seeking to disrupt a restructuring. It is however noteworthy that creditors strongly opposed

---

[102] *Ibid* at 24–25.
[103] *Ibid* at 25.
[104] *Ibid*.
[105] *Ibid*.

these techniques in the Argentina and Ecuador restructurings on the ground that they undermine the procedural fairness and integrity of restructurings and may abused by sovereigns.[106] New clauses were wired into the new bonds issued in those restructurings to protect creditors from these strategies in future restructurings involving the bonds being restructured.[107]

(iii) Exit Consents and Amendments

Exit consents allow a pre-determined majority of bondholders to amend the non-payment terms of their instruments (exit amendments) and contemporaneously exchange them for new bonds. The exit amendments and the vote approving the restructuring are secured contemporaneously in the same exchange offer solicitation.[108] The exit amendments are binding on holdout creditors that failed to tender their debt instruments.[109] The goal of exit amendments is to weaken the enforcement mechanism of the old bonds—such as sovereign immunity, forum selection, and choice of law clauses—and by so doing, reduce their post-restructuring value and make them unattractive for potential holdouts.[110] Thus, like the redesignation and pacman strategies, exit amendments can be used together with CACs to minimize incidences of holdouts and neutralize vulture funds in sovereign debt restructurings.

(iv) Model Pari Passu Clauses

Parri Passu[111] clauses gained spotlight in the aftermath of the controversy generated by the infamous court battles between Argentina and vulture funds in connection with its 2001 restructuring. Prior to the controversial decision in *NML v.*

---

[106] *Ibid.*

[107] *Ibid* at 26.

[108] Apostolos Gkoutzinis, "Law and Practice of Liability Management" (2013) at 29, CAMBRIDGE UNIVERSITY PRESS.

[109] *Ibid.*

[110] *See* Lee C. Buchheit & Elena L. Daly, "Minimizing Holdout Creditors: Sticks" in SOVEREIGN DEBT MANAGEMENT, Rosa M. Lastra & Lee Buchheit eds. (2014) at 18-19, OXFORD UNIVERSITY PRESS; IMF (2020) at 26.

[111] The term *Pari passu* means "equal footing" in Latin. *See* African Legal Support Facility, "Understanding Sovereign Debt, Options and Opportunities for Africa" at 68.

Argentina, pari passu clauses were geared towards reducing intercreditor inequality among unsecured creditors in public and private debt transactions despite variations in the language of these clauses.[112] However, contrary to this market understanding, the *NML* court held that *pari passu* clauses include a requirement that debtor countries must make ratable payment to all their creditors including holdouts.[113] Based on this interpretation, the court enjoined Argentina from making further payments to all its creditors, including those that received new bonds in the 2001 restructuring unless it simultaneously makes payment to the holdout creditors.[114] Constrained by this injunction, Argentina settled the case and paid the vulture funds that rejected its 2005 and 2010 restructuring.[115]

In response to the NML decision, a new pari passu clause was developed by ICMA that expressly excludes this ratable payment interpretation.[116] The ICMA model clause has been widely adopted in new issuances since coming on stream and can help sovereigns to avoid NML-type situations.

(v) Trust Structures and Sharing Clauses

The issuance of debts under a trust arrangement is another mechanism for minimizing disruptive vulture fund litigations.[117] In general, sovereign bonds are issued under fiscal agency agreements (FAA) or trust structures. Under FAA, the fiscal agent serves as an agent of the debtor country, and its primary role is to make principal and coupon payments to the bondholders.[118] In contrast to agents, a trustee acts for and on behalf of all the bondholders which prevents unilateral action by hostile creditors and owes several responsibilities to the bondholders as a group.[119] For instance, in

---

[112] *Supra* note 8; For a broader discussion of NML Capital v. Argentina see Georges Affaki, "Revisiting the Pari Passu Clause" in SOVEREIGN DEBT MANAGEMENT, Rosa M. Lastra & Lee Buchheit eds., (2014) at 39–48 OXFORD UNIVERSITY PRESS; Rodrigo Oliveres-Caminal, "The Pari Passu Clause in Soveriegn Debt Instruments: Developments in Recent Litigation" BIS PAPERS NO 72, available at https://www.bis.org/publ/bppdf/bispap72u.pdf.
[113] *Ibid.*
[114] *Ibid.*
[115] *Supra* note 31.
[116] *Supra* note 8.
[117] *Supra* note 95 at 37.
[118] *Ibid.*
[119] *Ibid.*

bonds issued under trusts structures, only the trustee can sue to collect accelerated payments under the bonds and must distribute the proceeds pro rata among all the bondholders.[120] By preventing individual creditor enforcement actions and requiring pro rata distribution of litigation proceeds among all bondholders, issuing debts using trust structure compared to the FAA disincentivizes rogue creditors from initiating disruptive litigations that undermine restructurings.[121]

Despite the above comparative advantage of trustee structures, FAAs remains the dominant means of sovereign debt issuance under English law and many low-income countries (including those in Africa) still issue their debts under FAA given the relatively higher cost of using trustees.[122] However, sharing clauses can be wired into FAAs which ensures that the proceeds of any recovery by individual creditors (in this case vulture funds) will be shared ratably among all the creditors as a whole.[123] In other words, countries that want to keep issuing debts under FAA can use sharing clauses to capture some of the benefits of having a trustee from the perspective of preventing quick acceleration and the race to the courthouse by holdouts.

(vi) Natural Disaster Clauses

Low-and middle-income countries, especially the small island developing countries, are disproportionately impacted by environmental and climate-related catastrophes like drought, flooding, earthquakes, and hurricanes among others that undermine their fiscal sustainability. To balance the ability of these countries to meet their debt service obligations while retaining enough fiscal space to whether severe natural disasters, natural disaster clauses were developed to provide them with debt relief in these situations.

In general, natural disaster clauses provide sovereigns impacted by natural disasters with interest forbearance and maturity extensions pending their recovery from

---

[120] *Ibid.*

[121] *Ibid.*

[122] The preference for FAAs, especially by lower-income countries that issue bonds under English law has been attributed to the slightly higher costs of trusts structures; *Supra* note 95 at 38.

[123] Lee Buchheit and Sean Hagan, "From Coronavirus Crisis to Sovereign Debt Crisis" (2020), FINANCIAL TIMES, available at https://www.ft.com/content/05ca6c2c-0270-4e9b-b963-3812ae7fd32b; *Supra* note 95 at 37.

such natural disasters.[124] They generally operate as a kind of "insurance" against natural disasters for countries that are prone to climate and environmental-related hazards.[125] Grenada and Barbados incorporated natural disaster clauses in their restructurings in 2015 and 2018 respectively.[126] The trigger event for Grenada's natural disaster clause is a payout by the Caribbean Catastrophe Risk Insurance Facility (CCRIF) for natural disaster-related losses of more than $150m (except for Paris Club debts which provide for a flexible trigger) while for Barbados, a payout by CCRIF above $5m. The Eastern Caribbean Central Bank, in collaboration with ICMA, is promoting the adoption these clauses by more countries.[127]

Although natural disaster clauses were developed in the context of climate-related disasters, they can be extended to other disaster situations like Covid-19 pandemic and the Ebola crisis in Sub-Saharan Africa.[128] By using natural disaster clauses to expand the range of situations in which a sovereign can obtain debt relief without defaulting and/or resorting to debt restructuring, natural disaster clauses will enable vulnerable countries to avoid a dance with vulture funds.

(c) Creation of non-profit funds to counter vulture funds
Non-profit funds or anti-vulture funds can also be used to counter vulture funds.[129] These anti-vulture funds will act like white knights by taking positions in the debts of distressed countries and using their voting power to neutralize the vulture funds.[130]

---

[124] *Supra* note 95 at 11.
[125] *Ibid.*
[126] *Ibid.*
[127] *Ibid.*
[128] Economic Commission for Latin America and the Caribbean, "An Innovative Financing for Development Agenda for the Recovery in Latin America and the Caribbean" (2021) at 25, SPECIAL REPORT No.12 (COVID-19); Sui-jim Ho and Stephanie Fontana, "Sovereign Debt Evolution: The Natural Disaster Clause" (2021) at 11, EMERGING MARKETS RESTRUCTURING JOURNAL.
[129] Daniel J. Brutti, "Sovereign Debt Crises and Vulture Hedge Funds: Issues and Policy Solutions" (2020) at 61, B.C.L. REV. 1819, available at https://lawdigitalcommons.bc.edu/cgi/viewcontent.cgi?article=3888&context=bclr.
[130] In takeover situations, target companies usually defend themselves by selling themselves to a friendly individual or company (a "white knight") at a fair consideration. *See* Investopedia "White Knight" https://www.investopedia.com/terms/w/whiteknight.asp.

In the context of the Covid-19 crisis, Bradlow advocated for the establishment of an anti-vulture fund—the Debts of Vulnerable Economies (DOVE)—that would protect African countries in debt distress from the scourge of vulture funds.[131] The DOVE Fund domiciled with African multilateral institutions like the African Union or African Development Bank, managed by stakeholders independent of debtor countries and creditors and funded via contributions from governments, international organizations and individuals.[132]

According to Bradlow, the DOVE fund will reduce speculation in African sovereign debts by buy African sovereign bonds at their steeply discounted market prices and implement a repayment standstill until abatement of the Covid-19 pandemic crisis.[133] Furthermore, the DOVE would have "urge all other creditors to commit to a standstill on African debt payments" while the global pandemic crisis lasts, and thereafter consider restructuring these debts on a case-by-case basis.[134] In this regard, the DOVE fund would ensure that sovereign debts does not unduly burden post-pandemic economic recovery efforts in Africa.[135] The DOVE fund will raise money from multilateral institutions and other donors which it will use to acquire the debts of debt-distressed African countries in the secondary markets just like vulture funds and then use their votes as a counterweight against vulture funds in restructurings.

6 Conclusion

As presently constituted, the international debt architecture provides little or no protection for poor countries against vulture funds. As a result, vulture funds profit by worsening the cost and pain of debt-distress for poor countries and their citizens. While some countries have passed anti-vulture statutes to deter these debt vultures, they are still waxing strong. Thus, fundamental reforms in the form of an SDRM and

---

[131] Daniel Bradlow, "Deterring the Debt Vultures in Africa," available at https://www.project-syndicate.org/commentary/new-fund-can-deter-africa-sovereign-debt-vultures-by-daniel-d-bradlow-2020-05.
[132] *Ibid.*
[133] *Ibid.*; *See also* Danny Bradlow, "Doves, Vultures and African Debt in the Time of COVID-19" (2020) at 3, available at https://www.afronomicslaw.org/2020/05/22/doves-vultures-and-african-debt-in-the-time-of-covid-19.
[134] *Supra* note 131.
[135] *Supra* note 133.

similar mechanisms at domestic levels are needed to protect low-and-middle income countries from these sovereign debt speculators. However, given the influence enjoyed by vulture funds in the global financial system and domestically in advanced countries whose concurrence are needed for these fundamental reforms, core reforms to the global financial architecture may not materialize in the short to medium term even though they are in the interest of the international community as a whole.[136] Nevertheless, African countries should adopt a common position on this issue possibly that proposed by the African civil society organizations like the African Forum on Debt and Development and African Sovereign Justice Network and galvanize other developing countries to continue pressuring the Global North to back these overdue reforms.[137] In this book Marie-Louis Aren's chapter makes a compelling case for Africn countries to adopt a common position on sovereign debt matters. Pending the reforms highlighted above, African countries should utilize contractual mechanisms like collective action clauses, exit consent and amendments, and model *pari passu* clauses to protect themselves from debt vulture.

---

[136] AFRODAD, 'World leaders continue to kick debt reform down the road', available at https://csoforffd.org/2021/03/30/press-release-world-leaders-continue-to-kick-the-can-down-the-road-on-debt-reform/.

[137] Message to the African Ministers of Finance, 'Planning and Economic Development On Mounting Sovereign Debt of African Countries' (2021), available at https://afrodad.org/wp-content/uploads/2021/04/AfSDJN-AFRODAD-FES-Statement-March_232021.pdf.

CHAPTER FOUR

The Case Against International Arbitration in Sovereign Debt Contexts

Geoffrey Adonu*

1 Introduction

With many African countries either in debt distress or already in debt default, Africa faces yet another wave of debt crisis.[1] The fact many African Eurobonds are due for repayment over the next few years amid rising interest rates and tough market conditions compounds the continent's debt situation.[2] If the current situation persists, the continent could be faced with more debt defaults, debt restructurings as well as enforcement actions by creditors in the coming years.

Litigation in creditor-friendly jurisdictions like New York and London has been the primary means of enforcing sovereign debt claims.[3] In order to facilitate such

---

* Geoffrey Adonu is an international lawyer and a sovereign debt consultant at Afronomicslaw. He received a J.D. from University at Buffalo School of Law in 2023, an LLM from New York University School of Law in 2020 and has an LLB from Babcock University. The author would like to thank the editors of Afronomicslaw, in particular James Thuo Gathii and Olabisi D. Akinkugbe, for their useful suggestions, comments and mentorship.

[1] *See* Daniel Bradlow & Magalie Masamba, *Debt Distress in Africa: Biggest Problems, and Ways Forward*, THE CONVERSATION (May 11, 2022 9:28 AM), https://theconversation.com/debt-distress-in-africa-biggest-problems-and-ways-forward-182716; INTERNATIONAL MONETARY FUND, *Regional Economic Outlook. Sub-Saharan Africa: Living on the Edge,* 1 (October 2022); Gregory Smith, *Where Credit is Due—How Africa's Debt can be a benefit, not a Burden*, 14–15 (Hurst & Company, London 2021).

[2] Anna Gross, *African Countries Face "Wall" of Sovereign Debt Repayments*, FINANCIAL TIMES (February 9, 2020), https://www.ft.com/content/8c232df6-4451-11ea-abea-0c7a29cd66fe.

[3] Lee C. Buchheit & G. Mitu Gulati, *Restructuring Sovereign Debt after NML v. Argentina*, 12 CAP. MKT. L. J. 244, 224 (2017).

litigation, most sovereign debt contracts require debtor countries to waive their sovereign immunity and submit to the jurisdiction of foreign courts.[4] Although most sovereign debt suits result in judgments against the sovereign debtors, the paucity of attachable sovereign assets abroad limits the likelihood of recovery and discourages many creditors from pursuing litigations in favor of negotiated settlement with the sovereign.[5] In addition to the limited chance of ultimate recovery, sovereign debt litigation is very complex, costly and protracted in nature (sovereign debt cases last between three to ten years on average in domestic courts).[6]

Despite the foregoing constraints of sovereign debt limitations, international loan contracts "rarely provide for arbitration"[7] which has been attributed to the fact that sovereigns rarely default on their debts given the enormous reputational and political costs, especially loss of market access.[8] Since *Abaclat v. Argentina* however (which ruled that sovereign bond claims can be enforced via investment treaty arbitration) international arbitration has emerged as a viable alternative enforcement mechanism for sovereign creditors.[9] African countries are signatories to over 200 international investment agreements (IIA). Many of these African IIAs were signed around the same time and have provisions that are similar or resemble those in the Italy-Argentina Bilateral Investment Treaty (BIT) under which Abaclat was decided and may be construed to cover sovereign bonds as well.[10] Consequently, Abaclat-like

---

[4] Karen Halverson Cross, *Sovereign Arbitration, in* Sovereign Debt Management 152 (Rosa M. Lastra & Lee Buchhei eds., 2014) (noting that until sovereign borrowing ceased in the wake of the Great Depression arbitration clauses were used featured in sovereign debt contracts in the early part of the twentieth century. Also, sovereign loan documentations from multilateral institutions like the World Bank typically contain arbitration clauses).

[5] Lee C. Buchheit et. al., *supra* note 3 at 224.

[6] *See* African Development Bank Group, *Vulture Funds in the Sovereign Debt Context*, https://www.afdb.org/en/topics-and-sectors/initiatives-partnerships/african-legal-support-facility./vulture-funds-in-the-sovereign-debt-context (last visited May 16, 2023).

[7] Cross, *supra* note 4 at 151, 153.

[8] Stratos Pahis, *The African Debt Crisis and the Perils of International Arbitration,* Afr. Sovereign Debt Just. Paper Series, 5 (2022); Stephen Kim Park & Tim R Samples, *Tribunalizing Sovereign Debt: Argentina's Experience with Investor-States Dispute Settlement,* 50 Vand. L. Rev. 1033 (2021).

[9] Id.

[10] *See* Stratos Pahis, *The African Debt Crisis and the Perils of International Arbitration,* African Sovereign Debt Justice Paper Series No.4, (2022).

arbitrations could play a significant role in future debt defaults and restructurings involving African governments.

Against the above background, this chapter explores the emergence of international arbitration as a recourse for creditors in enforcing sovereign debt obligations. The chapter argues that despite its merits in other contexts, international arbitration would do more harm than good in the sovereign debt contexts. Specifically, the chapter contends that the stronger enforcement regime of international arbitration and the principle of confidentiality in arbitral proceedings can worsen holdout problems, prevent accountability in public debt transactions, exacerbate intercreditor asymmetry and threaten debt sustainability of debt-distressed countries by undermining their debt restructurings.

For instance, in the absence of bankruptcy protection for sovereigns, the stronger and swifter enforcement regime provided by international arbitration via the Convention on the Recognition and Enforcement of Foreign Arbitral Awards (New York Convention) and International Center for Settlement of Investment Disputes (ICSID) Convention provides holdout creditors with an additional weapon with which to disrupt sovereign debt restructurings.[11] Additionally, the confidentiality of arbitral proceedings could undermine the principles of transparency and equitable treatment of creditors under the 2015 United Nations' Basic Principles on Sovereign Debt Restructuring Processes (UN Restructuring Principles).[12] For example, the opacity of arbitral proceedings can conceal the very existence or extent of a sovereign debt obligation and any fraudulent or corrupt practices relating to such debt transactions.

This chapter proceeds as follows: Part 2 examines international arbitrations as it relates to sovereign debt obligations while Part 3 explores the negative implications

---

[11] *See* Dilini Pathirana, *Sri Lanka Gone Broke: Sovereign Debt Restructuring and Challenges Ahead*, AFRONOMICS L., (Sept. 5, 2022), https://www.afronomicslaw.org/category/analysis/sri-lanka-gone-broke-sovereign-debt-restructuring-and-challenges-ahead (arguing that arbitrations by holdouts is one of the potential challenges Sri Lanka may face in its debt restructuring efforts).

[12] G.A. Res. 69/319 (Sept. 10, 2015). (The resolution sets out 9 principles, including good faith, transparency, impartiality, equitable treatment, sovereign immunity from jurisdiction and enforcement, legitimacy, and majority restructurings that should guide sovereign debt restructurings. Being soft law principles, these principles have no binding force)..

of international arbitration for vulnerable sovereign debtors. Part 4 provides policy recommendations for African sovereigns and Part 5 concludes the chapter.

2 International Arbitration in Sovereign Debt Context

Arbitration is an alternative dispute resolution mechanism in which parties consensually submit disputes for adjudication by a tribunal consisting of arbitrator(s) chosen by the parties.[13] International arbitration refers to arbitral proceedings that affect two or more jurisdictions—either with respect to the parties' nationality or otherwise—in contrast to domestic arbitrations. There are two forms of international arbitrations: investment treaty arbitrations which relate to claims brought under international investment treaties and international commercial arbitrations that result from arbitration agreements in commercial contracts between sovereigns and private parties.[14] Both types of international arbitration can be used in respect of "commercial, interstate, and foreign investment"[15] disputes between "states, between private actors, or a combination of each."[16]

International arbitrations are conducted pursuant to the rules of international institutions like the United Nations Commission on International Trade Law (UNCITRAL Rules),[17] ICSID Rules[18] and the London Court of International Arbitration.[19]

---

[13] *See* CORNELL LAW SCHOOL, *Arbitration,* Legal Information Institute https://www.law.cornell.edu/wex/arbitration (last visited May 16, 2023); *See also* Pahis, *supra* note 8, at 3.

[14] Pahis, *supra*, note 8 at 3.

[15] PEACE PALACE LIBRARY, *International Arbitration,* https://peacepalacelibrary.nl/research-guide/international-arbitration (last visited May 16, 2023).

[16] Pahis, *supra*, note 8 at 3.

[17] United Nations Comm'n on Int'l Trade L.[UNCITRAL], *Arbitration Rules* (2021), https://uncitral.un.org/sites/uncitral.un.org/files/media-documents/uncitral/en/21-07996_expedited-arbitration-e-ebook.pdf.

[18] Int'l Cent. for Settlement Inv. Disp. [ICSID], *Convention, Regulations and Rules,* (Apr. 2006), https://icsid.worldbank.org/sites/default/files/ICSID%20Convention%20English.pdf.

[19] London Ct. of Int'l Arb.[LCIA] *Arbitration Rules,* (Oct. 2020), https://www.lcia.org/Dispute_Resolution_Services/lcia-arbitration-rules-2020.aspx.

2.1 Investment Treaty Arbitration

Investment-treaty arbitrations are initiated pursuant to multilateral or bilateral IIAs.[20] In general, IIAs require state parties to protect investments in their territories by nationals of counterparties from expropriation and unfair, inequitable, or discriminatory treatment.[21] IIAs also protect foreign investors against contractual breaches by their host states and grant them the right to directly commence arbitration against the host country and seek damages for violations of the applicable IIA.[22]

As noted above, international loan contracts including sovereign bonds rarely contain arbitration agreements and most disputes arising from sovereign bonds especially in connection with restructurings have mostly been litigated in New York and London courts.[23] However, the protections and guarantees provided by IIAs (for instance the protection against expropriation may be implicated by sovereign debt disputes especially in respect of restructuring making investment treaty arbitration an enforcement option for sovereign creditors.[24] However, IIAs generally cover only investments within the scope of the treaty.[25] As a result, the arbitrability of a sovereign debt claims particularly those arising from sovereign debt restructurings or involving sovereign bonds under an IIA depends on the specific provisions of the IIA in issue, particularly the definition of covered investment thereunder.[26] Although the arbitrability question has not been settled conclusively, recent arbitral rulings

---

[20] Pahis, *supra*, note 8 at 3.

[21] *Id.*

[22] *Id.; See Fedax N.V. v. Republic of Venezuela,* ICSID Case No. ARB/96/3, Award, (March 9, 1998), 37 I.L.M. 1391 (1998) (finding that Venezuela violated the BIT in issue and awarded damages to the holders of Venezuelan sovereign debt instruments); *Fedax N.V. v. Republic of Venezuela,* ICSID Case No. ARB/96/3, Decision of the Tribunal on Jurisdiction, ¶ 34, (July 11, 1997).

[23] *See* Indermit Gill & Lee Buchheit, *Targeted Legislative Tweaks Can Help Contain the Harm of Debt Crisis,* BROOKINGS (June 27, 2022), https://www.brookings.edu/blog/future-development/2022/06/27/targeted-legislative-tweaks-can-help-contain-the-harm-of-debt-crises/ (arguing that it is time to rectify the imbalance in the sovereign debt architecture).

[24] Pahis, *supra*, note 8 at 3.

[25] *Id.*

[26] *See* NORTON ROSE FULBRIGHT, *Are We Facing a Sovereign Debt Crisis? Disputes Risk Implications for Investors,* (Dec. 2021), https://www.nortonrosefulbright.com/en/knowledge/publications/9807d68b/are-we-facing-a-sovereign-debt-crisis accessed on April 25.

suggest that IIAs that define investments to include "every kind of asset" or "all assets" may be construed to cover sovereign debt obligations.[27] For instance, thousands of bondholders were allowed to commence arbitral proceedings against Argentina and Greece in connection with their recent sovereign debt restructurings.[28]

2.2 International Commercial Arbitration

Most international investment and large-scale infrastructure project contracts between foreign investors and developing countries contain arbitration clauses that give the private parties the right to initiate arbitrations against the state for contractual breaches. Arbitrations arising from such contracts and that involve foreign nationals or affect more than one jurisdiction are known as international commercial arbitrations.

International commercial arbitration differs from investment treaty arbitration in several respects.[29] First, while sovereign consent to arbitration in investment-treaty arbitration context comes from being a signatory to an investment treaty, sovereign consent for international commercial arbitration purposes are based on direct contractual agreements with the claimant.[30] Second, while investment treaty arbitration claims focus on substantive treaty obligations by the sovereign, international commercial arbitration claims involve for breach of commercial contracts.[31] Third, while the applicable investment treaty itself is governing law in an investment treaty arbitration, the governing law for international commercial arbitration is the domestic or foreign law chosen by the parties in their contract.[32]

Since international loan contracts rarely contain arbitration clauses, international commercial arbitrations do not directly implicate sovereign debt obligations in the same way as investment treaty arbitrations could. However, the resulting awards from commercial arbitrations increase the debts of the relevant country and as such,

---

[27] Pahis, *supra* note 8, at 3. *See* Stratos Pahis, *BITs and Bonds: The International Economies of Sovereign Debt,* 115 AM, J, INT'L L. 242, 244 (2021).

[28] Stratos Pahis, *BITs and Bonds: The International Economies of Sovereign Debt,* 115 AM, J, INT'L L. 242, 244 (2021); Pahis, *supra* note 8, at 3-4.

[29] *See* Pahis, *supra* note 8, at 4.

[30] *Id.*

[31] *Id.*

[32] *Id.*

constitute a significant source of sovereign debt risks for developing countries who have billions of commercial arbitration awards issued against them from time to time. In addition, commercial arbitrations awards can be purchased by vulture funds at steep discount and used to extract preferential payments from debt-stricken countries which could undermine debt restructurings efforts.[33]

2.3 *Abaclat v. Argentina: Sovereign Debt Arbitration Gains Traction*

As discussed above, the arbitrability of sovereign debt claims under IIAs has not been conclusively resolved.[34] However, going by the rulings in *Abaclat v. Argentina*[35] and its progenies, bondholders can now enforce their debt claims via investment treaty arbitration subject to the language and provisions of the IIA in issue.

In *Abaclat*, 180,000 Italian investors holding Argentine bonds (reduced to 60,000 bondholders after many of the original claimants participated in Argentina's subsequent restructuring in 2010) refused to participate in Argentina's 2005 restructuring and initiated ICSID arbitration against Argentina.[36] Initially, these holdouts sued Argentina in multiple jurisdictions (hundreds of lawsuits were filed against Argentina over its 2001 and 2005 restructurings in Italy, Germany, and New York among others).[37] However, after unsuccessful litigation efforts (because Argentina's sovereign immunity was upheld in most cases and the paucity of attachable Argentine foreign assets),[38] these holdouts turned to ICSID arbitration under the Italy-Argentina BIT.[39]

Argentina challenged the jurisdiction of the ICSID tribunal on multiple grounds. Firstly, Argentina argued that sovereign bonds are not 'investments' under

---

[33] IMF (2020), *See* Pathiarana, *supra* note 11.

[34] Pahis, *supra* note 8, at 3.

[35] *Abaclat and Others v. Argentine Republic,* ICSID Case No. ARB/07/5, Decision on Jurisdiction and Admissibility (Aug. 4, 2011). [*hereinafter* Abaclat].

[36] *Id.*

[37] *Abaclat, supra* note 35, at ¶ 82.

[38] Cross, *supra* note 4, at 157. *See e.g., Borri v. Argentine Republic,* Request for a Ruling on Jurisdiction, No. 6532, (May 27, 2005) (holding that although the issuance of bonds is a private act, Argentina's unilateral extension of the payment term on the debt instrument was a sovereign act subject to immunity).

[39] Treaty between the Republic of Italy and the Republic of Argentina for the Promotion and Protection of Investments, It.-Arg., May 22, 1990. [*hereinafter* the Italy-Argentina BIT); *see Abaclat, supra* note 35, at ¶ 312.

the Italy-Argentina BIT and the ICSID Convention.[40] The tribunal however dismissed this argument. The tribunal reasoned that since the Italy-Argentina BIT defined investment as "obligations, private or public titles or any other right to performances or services having economic value," the sole consideration is whether the bonds "create the value" that Argentina and Italy intended to protect under the applicable BIT.[41] Consequently, the tribunal concluded that bonds in issue fell within the applicable BIT's definition of investments and constitutes an eligible investment under Article 25(1) of the ICSID Convention.[42] In his dissenting opinion, Professor George Abi-Saab disagreed with the tribunal on the ground that bonds make limited contribution to the host state's development and the bonds in this case lacked any jurisdictional link to Argentina.[43]

Secondly, Argentina challenged the tribunal's jurisdiction to conduct a class arbitration against it. Argentina submitted that even if it had consented to arbitration under the BIT, such consent cannot be construed to cover a class-action like proceeding. Again, the tribunal ruled against Argentina, holding that Argentina's specific consent was not required as to the "form" of collective proceedings in ICSID arbitrations.[44] In other words, the tribunal characterized the mass arbitration question—whether an ICSID arbitration can be conducted in a class-action format—as a procedural matter rather than a question of consent to arbitration.[45] Thus, despite the silence of the ICSID Convention on the issue, the tribunal ruled that it would be contrary to the purpose of the BIT and to the spirit of ICSID Convention to interpret such silence in the rules as a prohibition and rejecting the claim of the bondholders would constitute a "shocking" denial of justice.[46]

---

[40] *Abaclat, supra* note 35, ¶ 341; Convention on the Settlement of Investment Disputes Between States and Nationals of Other States, (Oct. 14, 1966), 17 U.S.T. 1270, 575 U.N.T.S. 159, at Art. 25(1). [*hereinafter* ICSD Convention].

[41] *Id.*, ¶ 352, 265.

[42] *Id.*, ¶ 361, 387.

[43] *Abaclat,* ICSID Case No. ARB/07/15, Dissenting Opinion of Professor Georges Abi-Saab, ¶ 46, 78–87.

[44] *Abaclat, supra* note 35, at ¶ 489, 491, 517–19.

[45] *Id.*

[46] *Id.,* at ¶ 531, 537.

The *Abaclat* decision has various implications for sovereign debt enforcement.[47] First, as a result of the "mass claims" procedure developed in *Abaclat*, bondholders can now pursue their claims against a sovereign as a class in a single arbitration against sovereign debtors.[48] Second, *Abaclat* was the first known investment treaty arbitration against a sovereign arising out of a debt restructuring transaction and, since then, more creditors increasingly consider treaty arbitrations in respect of their sovereign debt claims.[49] For example, following *Abaclat*, investment treaty arbitration was initiated against Greece in connection with its 2012 restructuring.[50]

Thus far, no African country has been subject of an Abaclat-like arbitration. However, over 200 IIAs in force across the continent. Many of these BITs were signed before *Abaclat* and likely contain provisions that are similar or resembles those in the Italy-Argentina BIT in *Abaclat* and could be construed to cover sovereign debt claims as well. Hence, thousands of bondholders may bring Abaclat-like claims against African governments if they default on their debts or seek to restructure their bonds in the future.[51] Further, given the menace of vulture funds already in the continent, there is a heightened risk that as more African countries are forced to pursue restructure, vulture funds may pounce and seek to take advantage of the stronger enforcement regime of international arbitration to extract preferential payments from African states.[52]

3 The Case Against International Arbitration in the African Sovereign Debt Landscape

Although African countries are signatories to over 200 IIAs already and cannot do much to avoid international arbitration claims in respect of their extant debt obligations under those IIAs as well as other international commercial agreements containing arbitration agreements (theoretically they can be terminated), there are strong reasons African counties to avoid international arbitration in respect of their future

---

[47] Cross, *supra* note 4, at 161.
[48] Norton Rose Fulbright, *supra* note 26.
[49] Cross, *supra* note 4, at 161.
[50] Pahis, note 8, at 3–4; Norton Rose Fulbright, *supra* note 26
[51] Pahis, *supra* note 8, at 5.
[52] *See* Pathirana, *supra* note 11 (noting that holdout creditors might use investment treaty arbitration to disrupt Sri Lanka's 2022 restructuring process).

debt obligations. First, while the strong enforcement mechanisms provided by international arbitration may be beneficial to creditors in various contexts,[53] they can be used to scuttle and disrupt debt restructurings of African states. Second, given the confidentiality of arbitration which has strong benefits in private commercial transactions,[54] public debt transactions are repaid from public funds and confidentiality can be used to prevent accountability and conceal corrupt practices in transactions that incur debt obligations for African government. Third, the secrecy of arbitrations can also be exploited to undermine the transparency and the principle of equal treatment of creditors in sovereign debt transactions.

3.1   A Strong Enforcement Regime Can Undermine Orderly Restructurings
International arbitration awards are enforced New York and ICSID Conventions more easily "with greater finality" and "broader reach" than domestic court judgments.[55] The New York Convention has 161 signatories and requires each contracting state to recognize arbitral awards as binding and enforce them."[56] The contracting states are prohibited from imposing more onerous conditions or higher fees or charges for recognition or enforcement of foreign arbitral awards than those applicable for domestic awards.[57] Thus, subject to limited exceptions like public policy and non-arbitrability of the subject matter of the dispute,[58] holders of foreign arbitral awards against a state party can rapidly seize their reachable assets in any of the other 160 countries that are parties to the Convention.[59] Further, since there are broader exceptions to sovereign immunity against attachment of sovereign assets for arbitral awards under United States' law,[60] there has been a "long history of successful asset

---

[53] Pahis, *supra* note 8, at 5.
[54] Pahis, *supra* note 8, at 6.
[55] Cross, *supra* note 4, at 152. *See also* Pahis, *supra* note 8, at 4.
[56] The New York Arbitration Convention on the Recognition and Enforcement of Foreign Arbitral Awards, Jun. 10, 1958, 21 U.S.T. 251, 330 U.N.T.S 38, at Art. 3. [*hereinafter* New York Convention].
[57] *Id.*
[58] *See* New York Convention, supra note 56, at Art. 5.
[59] Libby George, *Explainer: Nigeria Fights Back, but Threat of $9 Billion Penalty Looms,* REUTERS (Sept. 27, 2019), https://www.reuters.com/article/us-nigeria-arbitration-explainer/explainer-nigeria-fights-back-but-threat-of-9-billion-penalty-looms-idUSKBN1WC1IR.

seizures using the New York Convention."[61] Like the New York Convention, the ICSID Convention has 153 members and requires the contracting parties to enforce ICSID awards "as if [they] were a final judgment of a court in that state."[62]

In contrast to the New York Convention and ICSID enforcement regimes, the enforcement of foreign judgments is based on "bilateral or less comprehensive multilateral treaties" or the local law of the enforcing state and somewhat "muddy."[63] In addition, domestic court judgments can be "thwarted by resistance from the State and its [judicial branch]."[64]

In the absence of an "international framework" or "independent arbiter between debtors and creditors," the balance in sovereign debt restructurings is "tilt[ed] in favor of creditors more than the debtor in distress."[65] The constraints to enforcement of foreign court judgments coupled with the paucity of attachable foreign assets outside their territory serves as a counterbalance against creditors and reduced holdout problems by incentivizing potential holdout creditors to come to join restructuring negotiations instead of racing to courts.[66] International arbitration and its swift and stronger enforcement regime viz-a-viz domestic court litigation will however hand holdout creditors additional weapon with to disrupt restructurings, tilting the balance even further in favor of creditors thereby exacerbating holdout problems.[67]

Rather than all creditors, the primary beneficiaries of a stronger enforcement regime will be vulture funds who exploit lacunas in the sovereign debt architecture to profit from debt crisis in poor countries.[68] Given that even the threat of holdouts

---

[60] Cross, *supra* note 4, at 152–3.

[61] Libby George, *supra* note 59.

[62] ICSID Convention, *supra* note 40, at Art. 54(1).

[63] Pahis, *supra* note 8 at 5–6.

[64] Pahis, *supra* note 8 at 6.

[65] Magalie Masamba, *Africa's Dance with Unsustainable Debt: Is it Time for a Comprehensive Mechanism for Sovereign Debt Restructuring?* AFR. SOVEREIGN DEBT JUST. PAPER SERIES (2021).

[66] Buchheit et al., *supra* note 3 at 224.

[67] Masamba, *supra* note 67 at 6.

[68] *See* Indermit Gill & Lee Buchheit, *Targeted legislative Tweaks can help contain the harm of Debt Crisis,* BROOKINGS (June 27, 2022), https://www.brookings.edu/blog/future-development/2022/06/27/targeted-legislative-tweaks-can-help-contain-the-harm-of-debt-crises/ (arguing that it is time to rectify the imbalance in the sovereign debt architecture).

can undermine a necessary restructuring,[69] a higher chance of successful recovery via arbitration (under the New York and ICSID Conventions) will incentivize more creditors to holdout (and initiate arbitral proceedings to obtain full payout) to the detriment of other creditors thereby compounding the holdout problem and undermining the distressed-country's chances of quickly returning to debt sustainability.[70] For instance, Argentina settled the Abaclat arbitration in 2016 for $1,350 million[71] to the detriment of bondholders whose bonds were restructured which can discourage even benevolent creditors from participating in debt restructurings and providing debt relief to vulnerable countries.

Relatedly, by making it easier for holdouts to recover, international arbitration will exacerbate intercreditor competition.[72] For instance, vulture funds can purchase arbitral awards cheaply from original judgment creditors and use it to secure preferential recovery via the "enhanced enforcement of international arbitration"[73] at the expense of creditors that make concessions during restructurings and those whose debt instruments have no arbitration agreement.[74] Even among creditors whose debt instruments contain arbitration agreements, a race to arbitration could ensue as creditors seek to capture the available foreign assets of the debtor country while restructuring negotiations are underway.[75] Furthermore, creditors holding arbitral awards may not be bound by Collective Action Clauses (CACs)—even if the underlying debt instruments contains CACs—pursuant to the doctrine of merger.[76] The doctrine of merger under United States and English law states that the legal obligations of the parties under a debt

---

[69] Pahis, *supra* note 8, at 8.

[70] Pahis, *supra* note 8, at 10; *See* Indermit Gill et. al., *supra* note 68. (arguing that it is time to rectify the imbalance in the sovereign debt architecture).

[71] Investment Policy Hub "Investment Dispute Settlement Navigator" https://investmentpolicy.unctad.org/investment-dispute-settlement/cases/284/abaclat-and-others-v-argentina.

[72] Pahis, *supra* note 8, at 8.

[73] Pahis, *supra* note 8, at 8.

[74] INTERNATIONAL MONETARY FUND, *The International Architecture for Resolving Sovereign Debt Involving Private-Sector Creditors—Recent Developments, Challenges, and Reform Options,* 31, 33 (September 23, 2020).

[75] Libby George, *supra* note 59 (noting successful asset seizures via arbitral awards under the New York Convention).

[76] International Monetary Fund, *supra* note 74, at 31, 33 (under the doctrine of merger, legal obligations under a debt instrument are extinguished by a court judgment on liability).

instrument is extinguished by a judgment liability, i.e., the judgment debtor's obligation to repay the principal and interest in the underlying contract merges into the judgment.[77] Conversely, the creditor obtains the right to enforce its judgment through the judicial mechanisms for enforcing judgment debt rather than relying on the contractual terms.[78] If this doctrine is extended to arbitral awards, then holdouts creditors can extricate themselves from CACs by securing an arbitral award against the debtor country.[79] These additional dimensions to creditor asymmetry will further exacerbate intercreditor competition, increase the incidence of holdouts in restructurings and result in additional costs for both debtor countries and creditors as a whole.[80]

3.2 Confidentiality of Arbitrations Impedes Accountability in Public Debt Transactions

Confidentiality is one of the fundamental principles of arbitration. Thus, the rules, and procedures of most arbitral institutions explicitly make arbitral proceedings, the documents pertaining to thereto and even the eventual award confidential unless the parties agree otherwise. In effect, international arbitration is largely a secret affair between the parties.[81]

While confidentiality may be desirable in private commercial situations (to protect of trade secrets of the parties for instance), sovereign debts issuances and other transactions that lead to incurrence of public debts are matters of public concern and information regarding any dispute relating to them ought to be accessible to the public.[82] As such, keeping arbitrations (including the underlying transactions) secret will undermine accountability in public debt governance by helping to conceal corrupt

---

[77] International Monetary Fund, *supra* note 74, at 33 *fn* 48 (these arguments were espoused by some bondholders in Casa Express Corp. v. Venezuela, U.S. District Court for the Southern District of New York case involving Venezuela's debt default).

[78] *Id.*

[79] *Id.*

[80] Pahis, *supra* note 8, at 8.

[81] *Id.,* at 9.

[82] Jonathan Bonnitcha, *Corruption and Confidentiality in Contract-Based ISDS: The Case of P&ID v Nigeria,* INVESTMENT TREATY NEWS (March 23, 2021), https://www.iisd.org/itn/en/2021/03/23/corruption-and-confidentiality-in-contract-based-isds-the-case-of-pid-v-nigeria-jonathan-bonnitcha/ (noting that the burden of paying this kind of arbitral awards would fall on the citizens and taxpayers of the debtor country not the government officials involved in the allegedly corrupt transaction).

practices and making it harder for civil society to hold government officials accountable.[83] The arbitrations involving Processing and Industrial Development's investment in Nigeria and Mozambique's tuna bonds scandal (discussed below) are illustrative.

3.2.1 NIGERIA V. PROCESSING AND INDUSTRIAL DEVELOPMENT ARBITRATION The arbitration between Nigeria and P&ID[84] illustrates how the opacity of arbitral proceedings can undermine anti-corruption efforts in developing countries. In 2010, the Nigerian government signed a contract with P&ID to build a gas processing plant in support of the country's gas-to-power initiatives.[85] P&ID was incorporated in the British Virgin Island by two Irish citizens, Michael Quinn and Brendan Cahill.[86] However, without even commencing construction, P&ID commenced arbitration against Nigeria in 2012 and the arbitral tribunal awarded P&ID $6.6 billion as well as pre-and post-judgment interest of 7% in 2017.[87] Nigeria missed the deadlines to appeal the award and P&ID applied to an English court to enforce the award in March 2018.[88] However, although the English court allowed P&ID to enforce the award in September 2019, it later granted Nigeria the right of appeal.[89]

In December 2019, Nigeria applied for extension of time to appeal and alleged that the "underlying contract, the arbitration clause in the [underlying contract] and the awards were procured as the result of a massive fraud perpetrated by P&ID."[90] In particular, Nigeria contended that the underlying contract was procured through bribery and corruption of government officials[91] as well as its legal counsel.[92] In granting

---

[83] Pahis, *supra* note 8, at 9.

[84] *Federal Republic of Nigeria v. Process & Industrial Developments Limited* [2020] EWHC 2379 (Comm), [*hereinafter* Nigeria v. P&ID] available at https://www.bailii.org/ew/cases/EWHC/Comm/2020/2379.html (for analysis, see generally Kate Beioley & Neil Munshi, "The $6bn Judgment putting Nigeria against a London Court," Financial Times (July 12, 2020) https://www.ft.com/content/91ddbd53-a754-4190-944e-d472921bb81e); *See also* Jonathan Bonnitcha, *supra* note 84.

[85] *Federal Republic of Nigeria v. Process & Industrial Developments Limited, supra* note 84, at para. 20.

[86] *Id.,* at para. 6.

[87] *Id.,* at para. 2.

[88] *Id.,* at para. 77.

[89] *Id.,* at para. 79.

[90] *Id.,* para. 3.

[91] *Id.,* at para. 117–129, 185–199.

[92] *Id.,* at para. 185, 211–225.

the application and allowing Nigeria to challenge the award, the court held that there is a "strong prima facie case" that the underlying contract was "procured by bribery paid to insiders as part of a larger scheme to defraud Nigeria.[93] The court also noted that there is a "possibility" that Nigeria's counsel in the arbitration had been corrupted.[94]

The case is still *sub judice*, but irrespective of the final outcome, the mere fact that an award that constitutes about 20% of Nigeria's foreign reserves and 2.5% of Nigeria's GDP[95] was issued without any public scrutiny or public access to the underlying contract shows how the secrecy of international arbitration can be used to undermine accountability and transparency in public debt transactions.[96] If the case has been litigated in courts rather than arbitration, it is inconceivable that the case would have gone on for more than a decade without the details of the alleged corruption coming to the fore. For example, public interest litigation was instrumental in uncovering the fraud and corruption associated with the Mozambican tuna bonds and invalidation of the illegal debt.[97]

3.2.2 THE MOZAMBIQUE TUNA BOND SCANDAL   A scandal that brought the country to debt crisis, Mozambique's "Tuna Bond" scandal involved $2 billion of secret bank loans and bonds issued by Mozambique state-owned entities via Credit Suisse and Russian bank VTB and guaranteed by the government without parliamentary approval as required under Mozambique law.[98] Between 2013–2016, three Mozambican wholly owned state companies—Proindicus SA (Proindicus), Empressa Mocambicana de Atum SA (EMATUM) and Mozambique Asset Management (MAM)—entered three supply contacts with three subsidiaries of Privinvest, a

---

[93] *Id.*, para. 226.

[94] *Id.*, at 225.

[95] Libby George, *supra* note 59.

[96] Jonathan Bonnitcha, *supra* note 84.

[97] Denise Namburete, *How Public Interest Litigation Led to invalidation of Illegal Mozambican Debt*, AFRONOMICSLAW (Aug. 4, 2020), https://www.afronomicslaw.org/2020/08/04/how-public-interest-litigation-led-to-invalidation-of-illegal-mozambican-debt.

[98] Denise Namburete, *Keynote Address to Civil Society Forum on African Sovereign Debt ahead of the March 17–21 African Finance, Development and Planning Ministers Meeting*, AFRONOMICSLAW (Mar. 22, 2021), https://www.afronomicslaw.org/category/african-sovereign-debt-justice-network-afsdjn/keynote-address-denise-namburete-civil.

Lebanese-UAE-based shipbuilder for the supply of goods and services in connection with the development of Mozambique's Exclusive Economic Zone (EEZ).[99]

The contract between Proindicus and Privinvest Shipbuilding SAL was for the supply of "ships, aircraft and local infrastructure so as to enable the Republic [of Mozambique] to police its extensive coastline and exclusive territorial waters."[100] The second contract was between EMATUM and Abu Dhabi Mar Investments LLC for the supply of a "large fishing fleet" for Mozambique.[101] The last contract was between MAM and Privinvest Shipbuilding Investment LLC, for the creation of a shipyard for and provision of related services and further vessels.[102] The Proindicus and EMATUM contracts are governed by Swiss law and provided for ICC arbitration in Geneva while the MAM contract was governed by Swiss law as well with a provision for arbitration under rules of the Swiss Chamber of Commerce Arbitration Institution.

The Privinvest companies later sub-contracted the supply contracts to third parties under agreements that are governed by English law and granted exclusive jurisdiction to English courts.[103] The payment obligations of the state companies were payable upfront for the supply contracts to be effective and funded through borrowings from Credit Suisse (for the Proindicus and EMATUM contracts) and from Russian bank VTB (for the MAM contract). The loan contracts as well as the sovereign guarantee provided by Mozambique are governed by English law.

In 2018, the United States Department of Justice indicted certain employees of Credit Suisse and a representative of Privinvest for fraud and bribery in connection with their roles in the Privinvest transactions with Mozambique.[104] Consequently, Mozambique commenced an English court proceeding to set aside the transactions on the basis that the Minister of Finance had no parliamentary authority to enter the transactions as required by its law. The republic also alleged that the contracts were

---

[99] *Mozambique v. Credit Suisse,* [2021] EWCA Civ 329 (appeal from Eng. and Wales) (for the high trial court proceedings, see Mozambique v. Credit Suisse, Claim No: CL-2019-000127 available at https://jubileedebt.org.uk/wp-content/uploads/2020/01/Amended-Particulars-of-Claim_08.19.pdf).

[100] *Id.,* at ¶ 10(i).

[101] *Id.,* at ¶ 10(ii).

[102] *Id.,* at ¶ 10(iii).

[103] *Id.,* at ¶ 15–16.

[104] *U. S. v. Boustani,* Case No: CR 18/681 available at https://www.justice.gov/criminal-fraud/file/1150716/download .

instruments of bribery, conspiracy, and fraud against the country. Privinvest then applied for a stay of proceeding under the section 9 of the English Arbitration Act 1996[105] on the ground that the while some of the contracts involved are governed by English law and subject to the jurisdiction of English courts, the underlying supply contracts are subject to Swiss law and arbitration. In its ruling, the trial court held that Mozambique's allegations of fraud, conspiracy and bribery fell outside the scope of the arbitration agreements contained in the supply contracts.[106]

Privinvest appealed and the appellate court held that Mozambique's claims against the Privinvest companies fall within the scope of the arbitration clauses in the supply contracts. In doing so, the appellate court reasoned that the "bribes" allegedly paid to procure the supply contracts or bribes paid to secure the loan agreements guaranteed by the government "cannot be sensibly divorced" since the bribes were allegedly paid "in furtherance of the alleged fraudulent scheme involving all three transactions."[107] Consequently, the appellate court granted a stay of proceedings pending arbitration.

In 2020, the Mozambique Constitutional Court[108] declared the debts null and void on constitutional grounds, a ruling that was hailed as a "victory for the rule of law."[109] Also, the country's former Finance Minister responsible for contracting the debts was held up in South Africa pending a U.S. extradition request. Credit Suisse has

---

[105] See *Mozambique v. Credit Suisse, supra* note 125, at ¶ 61–62 (section 9(1) states that "[a] party to an arbitration agreement against whom legal proceedings are brought (whether by claim or counterclaim) in respect of a matter which under the agreement is referred to arbitration may ... apply to the court in which the proceedings have been brought to stay the proceedings so far as they concern that matter." Section 9(4) states that "on an application under this section the court shall grant a stay unless satisfied that the arbitration agreement is null and void, inoperative, or incapable of being performed." These provisions are based on Article II of the New York Convention and are aimed at ensuring that matters submitted by parties to arbitration are not decided by courts).
[106] *Mozambique v. Credit Suisse, supra* note 125, at ¶ 40.
[107] *Id.,* at ¶ 101.
[108] Republic of Mozambique, CONSTITUTIONAL COUNCIL, Case No: 05/CC/2019, Judgment, (Jun. 3, 2019).
[109] See Daniel Bradlow, *Prudent Debt Management and Lessons from the Mozambique Constitutional Council,* AFRONOMICSLAW (Aug. 5, 2020), https://www.afronomicslaw.org/2020/08/05/prudent-debt-management-and-lessons-from-the-mozambique-constitutional-council; James Thuo Gathii, *Introduction: Sovereign Debt under Domestic and Foreign law: Lessons from the Mozambique Constitutional Council Decision of May 8, 2020,* AFRONOMICSLAW (Aug. 3, 2020), https://www.afronomicslaw.org

admitted fraud in the US and UK in connection with this scandal.[110] The final words regarding Mozambique's liability for the debts however rests with the international arbitration tribunal constituted pursuant to the supply contracts and potentially the English courts that may be called upon to enforce the resulting award. If Privinvest secures a favorable award, the English courts are likely to enforce it against Mozambique going by a recent English the decision in involving Ukraine's debts to Russia.

In *The Law Debenture Trust Corporation Plc v Ukraine*.[111] Ukraine sought to avoid repayment of $3 billion of bonds held by Russia on the ground that its officials who signed the instruments did not have the requisite authority under Ukrainian law, the English court ruled against Ukraine. The courts emphasized that under English law, they will defer to the UK government on the issue of state recognition and since Ukraine is recognized by the UK as a sovereign state, it must be deemed to have the relevant capacity to enter valid contracts. The court also noted that since Ukrainian officials have entered into 31 prior valid agreements that bind Ukraine, it was not unreasonable for Russian creditors to assume that the relevant government officials had the requisite authority to enter this transaction. Based on this decision, the fate of Mozambique and its population with respect to repayment of this "odious" and "secret debt" rests with ICC arbitration tribunal[112] as the ensuing award may be enforced by English courts.[113]

/2020/08/03/introduction-sovereign-debt-under-domestic-and-foreign-law-lessons-from-the-mozambique-constitutional-council-decision-of-may-8-2020; Denise Namburete, *Keynote Address to Civil Society Forum on African Sovereign Debt ahead f the March 17–21 African Finance, Development and Planning Ministers Meeting*, AFRONOMICSLAW (Mar. 22, 2021), https://www.afronomicslaw.org/category/african-sovereign-debt-justice-network-afsdjn/keynote-address-denise-namburete-civil.

[110] Joseph Cotterill & Owen Walker, *Mozambique Reels from Credit Suisse "Tuna Bond" Scandal*, FINANCIAL TIMES (Oct. 24, 2021), https://www.ft.com/content/f8288871-6a21-447c-8031-f69aa8ee80fa.

[111] The Law Debenture Trust Corporation plc v. Ukraine, [2018] EWCA Civ 2026; Daniel Bradlow, *Prudent Debt Management and Lessons from the Mozambique Constitutional Council*, AFRONOMICSLAW (Aug. 5, 2020), https://www.afronomicslaw.org/2020/08/05/prudent-debt-management-and-lessons-from-the-mozambique-constitutional-council.

[112] *Abu Dhabi Mar Investments LLC and Privinvest Shipbuilding Investments LLC v. The Republic of Mozambique*, Case No. 24325/GR/PAR (ICC Int'l Ct. Arb.), https://jusmundi.com/fr/document/decision/en-abu-dhabi-mar-investments-llc-and-privinvest-shipbuilding-investments-llc-v-the-republic-of-mozambique-proindicus-sa-and-empresa-mocambicana-de-atum-sa-ematum-judgment-of-the-high-court-of-justice-of-england-and-wales-2021-ewca-329-thursday-11th-march-2021.

[113] Bradlow, *supra* note 111

3.3 Confidentiality Undermines Transparency and Equitable Treatment of Creditors in Debt Restructurings

Transparency is one of the nine principles of sovereign debt restructurings under the 2015 United Nations' Basic Principles on Sovereign Debt Restructuring Processes (UN Restructuring Principles).[114] Although non-binding, the UN Principles on Sovereign Debt Restructurings provides for transparency, including prompt sharing of both data and processes relating to sovereign debt restructurings to enhance accountability. In addition, creditors typically demand full disclosure of both the debts and creditors of a debtor country at the time of extending financing and during restructurings.[115] With international arbitration however, the details of a sovereign debt and any settlements thereof may be kept secret and without adequate disclosures, creditors may be discouraged from lending at all or to lend at a higher premium for new issuances and/or from participating at all in a restructuring.[116]

Equitable treatment of creditors is another core principle of sovereign debt restructuring under the UN Restructuring Principles. Under this principle, states shall not discriminate among creditors unless a different treatment is justified under the law, is reasonable, and is correlated to the characteristics of the credit. This guarantees inter-creditor equality among creditors.[117] It also implies that creditors have the right to receive comparable treatment in accordance with their credit and its characteristics and no creditor should be excluded ex ante from the sovereign debt restructuring process. Confidentiality is however antithetical to this principle. The opacity of arbitral proceedings will make it harder for creditors to access information

---

[114] G.A. Res. 69/319 (Sept. 10, 2015) (the resolution sets out 9 principles, including good faith, transparency, impartiality, equitable treatment, sovereign immunity from jurisdiction and enforcement, legitimacy, and majority restructurings that should guide sovereign debt restructurings. Being soft law principles, these principles have no binding force)

[115] Pahis, *supra* note 8, at, 9.

[116] *Id.*

[117] United Nations General Assembly, Resolution A/69/L.84 available at https://unctad.org/system/files/official-document/a69L84_en.pdf. The resolution sets out 9 principles, including good faith, transparency, impartiality, equitable treatment, sovereign immunity from jurisdiction and enforcement, legitimacy, and majority restructurings that should guide sovereign debt restructurings. Being soft law principles, these principles have no binding force.

about the debt status and creditors of debtor countries.[118] Further, the opacity of arbitral proceedings means that states can secretly offer preferential settlements terms to certain creditors to the detriment of all the creditors which is capable of undermining creditor participation in restructurings.[119]

The ongoing Zambian restructuring illustrates the foregoing points. Zambia defaulted on its debts in 2020 and has been undergoing restructuring. However, bondholders have been reluctant to accept the restructuring terms proposed by Zambia partly because Zambia did not disclose the full extent of its exposure to China and how much it committed to pay China.[120] While the Zambia situation did not arise due to arbitration, it shows that the ability to keep the details of sovereign debt agreements and settlements secret through arbitration will encourage sovereigns debtors to engage in opportunistic behavior like offering discriminatory terms to different creditor groups and even concealing the very existence of some of its debts to certain creditors.[121]

3.4 Arbitration Increases Debt Burdens and Undermines Debt Sustainability

In 2020, the International Monetary Fund (IMF) observed that arbitral awards now constitute a significant portion of the debt stock of many countries and constitutes "a sizable share of GDP" in some countries.[122] Arbitral awards are contingent liabilities[123] and as such, not captured in the debt data of the affected countries. Thus, unlike bonded or syndicated debts that are predictable, arbitral awards can make debt sustainability assessments (DSA) upon which the IMF's financial assistance to financially-distressed countries and debt restructurings are based uncertain and inaccurate.[124] As a result, a sovereign's debt problems might be understated in the DSA resulting in

---

[118] Pahis, *supra* note 8, at, 9.

[119] *Id.*

[120] *Id.*

[121] *Id.*

[122] International Monetary Fund, *supra* note 76, at 33.

[123] *See* IFRS, *IAS 37 Provisions, Contingent Liabilities and Contingent Assets,* (2022), https://www.ifrs.org/issued-standards/list-of-standards/ias-37-provisions-contingent-liabilities-and-contingent-assets/ (refers to liabilities that are not predictable and may or may not materialize depending on events that are outside the control of the obligor).

[124] International Monetary Fund, *supra* note 76, at 33.

more of the economic burdens of restructuring being pushed to the sovereign and its citizens in the form of austerity.[125] For instance, until the $6.6 billion arbitration case against Nigeria in the P&ID (the equivalent of 20% of its foreign reserves, half of its crude oil revenue in 2018 and 2.5% of its GDP)[126] became public, such a gigantic liability may not have been reflected Nigeria's DSAs.

4 Conclusion

Over 200 IIAs are in force across Africa and African countries may be subject of arbitral proceedings either arising either from their sovereign bonds or other commercial obligations that could result in significant public debt burden. As such, international arbitrations and awards emanating from such proceedings are likely to play a more significant role in sovereign debt resolutions involving African governments as the continent confronts yet another wave of debt distress. While nothing can be done regarding arbitral proceedings that may arise under the existing IIAs, African states should take steps to minimize their exposure to international arbitration in the future. African governments should explicitly exclude arbitration agreements from their debt instruments going forward. Relatedly, African countries should explicitly exclude sovereign debts from the scope of their new IIAs. For instance, to reduce its exposure to international arbitrations, India terminated fifty-seven of its BITs between 2013–2016 and started excluding investment-treaty arbitrations from its newly negotiated treaties.[127] Where sovereign debts cannot be totally excluded, they should be accorded limited protections.[128] Additionally, in general commercial matters that could result in significant sovereign debt exposure, African sovereigns should adopt a default policy of no submission to international arbitration except where the debts are inseparable from infrastructure projects in which the expertise and neutrality of arbitrators may add value that outweighs the adverse implications arbitration.[129]

---

[125] Karina Patricio Ferreira Lima, *Reforming the International Monetary Fund's Debt Sustainability Assessments towards Achieving the UN's Sustainable Development Goals (SDGs): A Crucial Post-Pandemic Recovery Agenda* 2 AFR. J. INT'L ECON. L. 32 (2021); Oxfam (2021).

[126] George, *supra* note 59

[127] *Id.*

[128] Kavaljit Signh, *Letters to the Editor: ISDS is Unsuited to Meet Today's Global Challenges*, FINANCIAL TIMES (May 7, 2017), https://www.ft.com/content/ed08cd0c-2fea-11e7-9555-23ef563ecf9a (generally describing India's revamp of its BIT practices in response to investor-state dispute concerns).

Furthermore, when international arbitration cannot be avoided, African sovereigns should ensure that their submission to arbitration is contingent on waiver of confidentiality to ensure that all aspects of the arbitration, including the underlying contracts, the submissions, hearings and the resulting awards or settlements, being accessible to the public.[130] In all these respects, this chapter is therefore in substantial agreement with Ohio Omiunu and Titilayo Adebola's chapter in this book.

---

[129] Pahis, *supra* note 8, at 13.
[130] *Id.*

CHAPTER FIVE

Sovereign Debt as Investments: Dispute Resolution and Restructuring in Times of Crises

Ohio Omiunu* and Titilayo Adebola**

I Introduction

Over the years, a patchwork of International Investment Agreements (IIAs), including Bilateral Investment Treaties (BITs), Free Trade Agreements (FTAs), and Economic Partnership Agreements (EPAs) with clauses or chapters on investment and financial services, have played a crucial role in shaping the international investment protection landscape for foreign investors.[1] These IIAs often contain provisions for dispute resolution between investors and host governments.[2] Controversially, the scope of IIAs has widened over the years to cover sovereign debt instruments as investments to be protected.[3] It is imperative to unpack the link between investment

---

* Reader/Associate Professor of Law, Kent Law School and Editor, Afronomicslaw.org.
** Lecturer, University of Aberdeen School of Law; Associate Director, Center for Commercial Law and Editor, Afronomicslaw.org

[1] According to the United Nations Committee on Trade and Development (UNCTAD), as of March 2023, there are a total of 2831 Bilateral Investment Treaties (BITs), of which 2220 are in force. There is a total of 435 Treaties with Investment Provisions (TIPs), of which 364 are in force. *See International Investment Agreements Navigator*, INVESTMENT POLICY HUB (Accessed on 13 May 2023) https://investmentpolicy.unctad.org/international-investment-agreements. *See also* Jeswald W. Salacuse, THE LAW OF INVESTMENT TREATIES (Oxford U. Press, 3rd ed. 2021); Rudolf Dolzer, Ursala Kriebaum and Christoph Schreuer, PRINCIPLES OF INTERNATIONAL INVESTMENT LAW (Oxford U. Press, 3rd ed. 2022).

[2] *See generally,* Stephan W Schill, THE MULTILATERLIZATION OF INTERNATIONAL INVESTMENT LAW (Cambridge U. Press 2009).

[3] According to Park and Samples, "Many IIAs expressly include debt instruments as an investment, and a broad definition of investment that does not expressly exclude sovereign bonds (or similarly defined

protection under IIAs and sovereign debt because the traditional shield of sovereign immunity has been eroded over time, leading to an increase in litigation and arbitration following sovereign debt defaults. This exposes countries to potential risks in the context of international dispute resolution.[4]

This controversial trend has significant ramifications for sovereign debt restructuring. As UNCTAD pointed out in a 2011 issue note, 'investor-state dispute settlement (ISDS) mechanisms allowing individual bondholders to arbitrate against the State, especially where the majority have agreed to a restructuring, can pose an obstacle to efficient debt restructuring'.[5] This policy advice by UNCTAD remains instructive today and is particularly pertinent in the current terrain where the coronavirus (COVID-19) pandemic has triggered a series of defaults by sovereign states.[6] As the global community attempts to find amicable solutions to the debt crises, there is a

---

debt instruments) qualifies." See Stephen K. Park and Tim R. Samples, *Tribunalizing Sovereign Debt: Argentina's Experience with Investor-State Dispute Settlement* 50 (4) VANDERBILT J. OF TRANSNAT'L L., 1033, 1041 (2017).

[4] Sovereign debtors have traditionally been shielded from litigation and arbitration through the international law principle of sovereign immunity, which recognises the equality of sovereign countries and prevents dispute resolution procedures against sovereigns without their consent. See Stratos Pahis, *The African Debt Crisis and the Perils of International Arbitration* PAPER IV AFRICAN SOVEREIGN DEBT JUSTICE NETWORK PAPER SERIES (2021); Michael Waibel, *Opening Pandora's Box: Sovereign Bonds in International Arbitration*. 101(4) THE AM J. OF INT'L L., 711–759 (2007); David Gaukrodger Gaukrodger and Kathryn Gordon *Investor-State Dispute Settlement: A Scoping Paper for the Investment Policy Community*, OECD WORKING PAPER No.2012/3 (Dec. 15, 2012); Panizza, Ugo, Federico Sturzenegger, and Jeromin Zettelmeyer. 2009. *The Economics and Law of Sovereign Debt and Default* J. OF ECON. LITERATURE, 47 (3): 651–98; Sean Hagan, *Designing a Legal Framework to Restructure Sovereign Debt*. 36 GEO J. OF INT'L L. 299–402 (2004).

[5] See UNCTAD, SOVEREIGN DEBT RESTRUCTURING AND INTERNATIONAL AGREEMENTS' IIA Issue Note, No. 2, 8 (July 2011) https://unctad.org/system/files/official-document/webdiaepcb2011d3_en.pdf.

[6] According to Fitch Ratings, "there have been 14 separate default events since 2020, across nine different sovereigns, a marked increase compared with 19 defaults across 13 different countries between 2000 and 2019." See Fitch, *Sovereign Defaults Are at Record High*, FITCHRATINGS (29 March, 2023) https://www.fitchratings.com/research/sovereigns/sovereign-defaults-are-at-record-high-29-03-2023#:~:text=Moreover%2C%20Fitch%20rates%20eight%20sovereigns,%27%20by%20Fitch%20was%2040.6%25

danger that countries in the Global South may face judicial challenges from holdout creditors who may seek to exploit the wide berth given to the definition of "investments" under financial service chapters of extant investment-related agreements.

Given the abovementioned issues, this chapter maps the United States of America's (US), and the European Union's (EU) approaches to conceptualising sovereign debt in their FTAs. These two jurisdictions have been selected for appraisal because they are critical stakeholders in the international debt architecture.[7] Although the primary focus of this chapter is on FTAs, BITs have also been at the center of the controversial expansion of investment protection measures to sovereign debt instruments. As such, this chapter will also briefly explore the issues that emerge in interpreting sovereign debt issues in BITs.

The central objectives of this chapter can be broken down into two: firstly, to evaluate the degree to which the US and EU acknowledge and safeguard sovereign debt as a form of investment in their FTA practice, and secondly, to scrutinise the obligations and potential consequences for Global South countries, particularly regarding the protection of their interests during sovereign debt crises and restructurings.

A key finding of the chapter is that the US and the EU have been selective in applying safeguards against ISDS for sovereign debt issues. Accordingly, we advocate for vigilance on the part of Global South Countries contemplating FTAs with these countries to ensure that future agreements model the generous carve-outs adopted in EU and US FTAs with other Global North partners. In addition, we support the growing calls for eradicating ISDS from IIAs due to the broad powers it gives private corporations, including opportunistic private creditors, to challenge and override democratically enacted laws and regulations that protect *inter alia* public health, the environment, and workers' rights during debt restructuring.

2. Sovereign debt instruments as protected instruments under ICSID and BITs.

When considering the scope of protection offered under international investment agreements (IIAs), "sovereign debt" does not immediately come to mind. Instead,

---

[7] These two countries also play a crucial role in financing development projects and providing economic support to Global South countries through concessional loans.

cross-border investments in enterprises, shares, stocks, or other forms of equity participation typically dominate the discussion.[8] To better understand the connection between sovereign debt and investment/finance chapters of IIAs, examining the controversial interpretation of "investment" under BITs and Article 25 (1) of the ICSID Convention is an important starting point. This is important because the definition and conceptualisation of "investment" under the BIT/ICSID Convention regime have played a crucial role in determining whether creditors were entitled to protection under specific IIAs and the application of investor-state dispute resolution mechanisms.[9] Conventionally, IIAs adopt a broad asset-based definition of investment that covers "every kind of asset" owned or controlled by an investor.[10] This is quite nebulous and can be interpreted narrowly or widely. In other instances, IIAs are more specific in what is covered under the definition of investment, i.e., a closed list approach. Where the scope of "investment" is interpreted to be broad enough to include sovereign debt instruments, creditors have sought to rely on ICSID or international commercial arbitration as adjudication forums for sovereign debt claims.[11] This requirement establishes what is known as the "double-barrelled test," which necessitates fulfilling the applicability requirements stipulated in both the ICSID Convention and the invoked BIT.[12]

Although the ICSID Convention does not define the term "investment," there have been attempts in several ICSID cases to stretch the scope of Article 25(1) of the ICSID Convention, which states that the International Centre for the Settlement of Dispute Resolution (Centre) has jurisdiction, ratione materiae (subject-matter jurisdiction), over "any legal dispute arising directly out of an investment, between a Contracting State (…) and a national of another Contracting State" to include sovereign

---

[8] Dolzer, Kriebaum & Schreuer, supra note 1; Salacuse, *supra* note 1.
[9] Christoph Schreuer, *Travelling the BIT Route: Of Waiting Periods, Umbrella Clauses and Forks in the Road*. 5(2) J. OF WORLD INV. & TRADE 231–256 (2004).
[10] UNCTAD, *supra* note 5.
[11] Michael Waibel, SOVEREIGN DEFAULTS BEFORE INTERNATIONAL COURTS AND TRIBUNALS (Cambridge U. Press 2011).
[12] Schill, *supra* note 2.

debt cases.[13] The variations in the interpretation of Article 25(1) are in part as a result of the so-called "Salini test" (i.e. a list of requirements that emanated from the Salini v. Morocco case), which tribunals have been used in a prescriptive way to determine whether the ICSID Convention should be regarded as applicable to disputes involving sovereign debt issues.[14]

The implications of this interpretation of sovereign debt instruments as investments under the BIT/ICSID regime have played out prominently during sovereign debt crises in the last two decades. Notably, during the restructuring operations undertaken by Argentina at the turn of the millennium, "holdout bondholders" pursued different dispute resolution strategies to secure their interests.[15] In particular, the Argentine debt crisis of 2001 marked a seismic shift in the international sovereign debt default landscape as investors filed a series of lawsuits against Argentina in the US and UK alongside arbitration proceedings following Argentina's default.[16] These lawsuits and arbitration proceedings culminated in a second default in 2014 and repayment of approximately USD$9.3 billion to hold out creditors in 2016.[17]

---

[13] Dan Sarooshi, *Investment Treaty Arbitration and the World Trade Organization: What Role for Systemic Values in the Resolution of International Economic Disputes?* 49 (3) TEXAS INT'L L. J. 445, 445 (2014).

[14] Matthias Goldmann, *Foreign Investment, Sovereign Debt, and Human Rights,* SOVEREIGN DEBT AND HUM. RTS (Oxford U. Press 2018).

[15] Anna Gelpern, *A Skeptic's Case for Sovereign Bankruptcy.* 50(3) HOUS. L. REV. 1095–1127 (2013); Martin Guzman and Joseph Stiglitz *Creating a Framework for Sovereign Debt Restructuring that Works* in TOO LITTLE, TOO LATE 43–78 (Columbia U. Press 2016).

[16] Julian Schumacher, *Sovereign Debt Litigation in Argentina: Implications of the Pari Passu Default* 1 (1) J. OF FIN. REGUL. 143–48 (2015), Giselle Datz and Katharine Corcoran, *Deviant Debt: Reputation, Litigation, and Outlier Effects in Argentina's Debt Restructuring Saga* 25 (2) NEW POLITICAL ECONOMY 300–13(2020); Mark C Weidemaier and Anna Gelpern, *Injunctions in Sovereign Debt Litigation* YALE J. ON REGUL, 31. 189 (2014), Benjamin Hebert and Jesse Schreger *The Costs of Sovereign Default: Evidence from Argentina* 107 AM. ECON. REV. (2017).

[17] For more details of Argentina's settlement of the 14-year-long legal battle with holdout creditors *See* Alexandra Stevenson, How Argentina Settled a Billion-Dollar Debt Dispute With Hedge Funds, NEW YORK TIMES (25 April 2016) https://www.nytimes.com/2016/04/25/business/dealbook/how-argentina-settled-a-billion-dollar-debt-dispute-with-hedge-funds.html.

The domestic cases which were filed against Argentina over 14 years had significant implications for resolving sovereign debt disputes, as they demonstrated the willingness of domestic courts, especially in New York and London, to enforce the rights of holdout bondholders and the potential challenges faced by sovereign nations in restructuring their debt.

In addition to domestic litigation cases, some holdout bondholders commenced investment treaty arbitration proceedings against Argentina *"... arguing that the "haircut" amounts to a violation of international obligations arising out of the applicable investment treaty."*[18] Several ICSID arbitration cases focused on this, including *Abaclat v. Argentina, Ambiente Ufficio v. Argentina,* and *Giovanni Alemanni v. Argentina.*

In the *Abaclat v Argentina*, Italian holdout bondholders initiated ICSID proceedings against Argentina under the Argentina-Italy BIT. They argued that Argentina's restructuring of its sovereign debt amounted to violating the State's obligations arising from the BIT. The Tribunal did not apply the Salini test to determine whether the bondholders' contributions qualified as "investments" under the ICSID Convention. Instead, the Tribunal concluded that the Salini test was unnecessary to decide the case because the bondholders' claims fell within the scope of the Argentina-Italy BIT.[19] The Tribunal also noted that if the bondholders were not considered investors under the Convention, they would be deprived of the procedural protections afforded by the ICSID Convention, which could create a risk of unequal treatment and unfairness in the proceedings. In the *Ambiente v Argentina* case, which also concerned claims by Italian nationals against Argentina for purported violations of the Argentina-Italy BIT in connection with the respondent State's default on paying its sovereign debt in 2001, the Tribunal reached similar conclusions as to the Abaclat tribunal, holding that the term "investment" is to be given a broad meaning encompassing sovereign bonds and security entitlements.

---

[18] *See* Abaclat v. Argentina, ICSID Case No. ARB/07/5; Ambiente Ufficio v. Argentina, ICSID Case. No. ARB/08/9; and Giovanni Alemanni v. Argentina, ICSID Case No. ARB/07/8.

[19] The Tribunal declined to apply the Salini test to resolve the problem of the applicability *ratione materiae* of the ICISD Convention, justifying its refusal on the basis that if the bondholders' contributions were to fail the Salini test, they would be deprived of the procedural protections afforded by the ICSID Convention.

SOVEREIGN DEBT AS INVESTMENTS   137

Although the decisions from these two cases support an interpretation that sovereign debt is an investment for protection under IIAs, it is instructive to note that there was a sharply worded dissent in the *Abaclat* decision by Georges Abi-Saab who argued *inter alia* that the definition of investment emerging from financial markets was too broad.[20] Abi-Saab argued in his dissenting judgment that the lack of an explicit definition of investment in the ICSID Convention did not justify an expansion of the ambit of the definition to cover sovereign bonds. In Abi-Saab's words, *"sovereign debt instruments (whether we call them "bonds," "obligaciones," "security entitlements" or otherwise") that are at the basis of these claims, do not constitute a "protected investment"* under the ICSID Convention.[21] He explained that the types of investments contemplated by the ICSID Convention contributed to the host country's economic development, i.e., to expand its productive capacity. According to him, foreign direct investment is the ideal investment contemplated for ICSID purposes, not sovereign bonds. While he did not suggest that all portfolio-style financial investments are outside ICSID's protective scope, he argued that they are not necessarily covered.

He also raised concerns that the majority decision in the *Abaclat* case had failed to distinguish between purchases on the primary market, involving the issuer (Argentina) and the first buyers of the issue (the underwriters), and the secondary market, where previously issued securities are traded, without any involvement of the sovereign debtor. In his words, *"an ICSID Tribunal cannot look only at the economics of a transaction, without taking into consideration its legal framework and structure, to determine whether it qualifies as a protected 'investment' or not."*[22] This argument is informative, emphasising the implications of interpreting secondary market transactions involving intricate intermediation chains as covered investments under BITs and other IIAs. Such a broad interpretation exposes sovereigns to numerous potential

---

[20] Abaclat Paragraph 42. In light of the above, Pietro Ortolani questions whether sovereign debt instruments qualify as investments for the purposes of Article 25 of ICSID. He believes that the notion of "investment" currently enshrined in international investment law is overbroad and should be re-modulated. See Pietro Ortolani, Are Bondholders Investors? Sovereign Debt and Investment after Pastova, 30 Leiden Journal of International Law 383–404 (2017).

[21] Dissenting opinion, Professor Georges Abi-Saab. Paragraph 2(a).

[22] Abaclat Paragraphs 71–72.

claimants, regardless of their distance from the initial investment envisioned by the State Parties under the IIA. This type of decision by an ISDS tribunal incentivises vulture funds and other predatory practices by rogue creditors. These types of creditors are typically profit-driven and often target the securities of vulnerable countries.[23]

Abi-Saab was also critical of the majority's decision to use a "mass claim" procedure, which allowed over 60,000 investors to bring a single claim against Argentina. He argued that this procedure was inappropriate for the case, violating Argentina's due process rights and was incompatible with the ICSID arbitration rules. Specifically, he argued that an ICSID tribunal could not accept jurisdiction over mass claims without consent from the State Parties to the BIT. This is particularly instructive because the majority decision in the *Abaclat* case attempted to expand the treaty's scope beyond what the state parties intended. The broader concern is that the majority decision effectively allowed the claimants to use ISDS to challenge measures taken by Argentina to address its economic crisis, which was not the original intention of the treaty. As we would see with the case study countries discussed later, this could encourage holdout creditors to use ISDS mechanisms to challenge legitimate measures taken by states in response to economic crises, thereby undermining the ability of states to govern in the public interest.

Subsequently, in *Poštova Banka SA and Istrokapital SE v Hellenic Republic*, the debate took another decisive turn when an arbitral tribunal in a landmark decision dismissed a claim brought by private creditors against the Hellenic Republic (the "Respondent" or "Greece") during the Greek financial crisis for lack of jurisdiction. This is a critical case because it has cast significant doubt on the viability of arbitration (ICSID and/or International Commercial Arbitration) as the appropriate forum for

---

[23] Jonathan I Blackman and Rahul Mukhi, *The Evolution of Modern Sovereign Debt Litigation: Vultures, Alter Egos, and Other Legal Fauna* 73 (4) L. & CONTEMP. PROBS 47, 49 (2010). Vulture funds are hedge funds or other investment funds that buy the debt of poor countries at a discount, often from other creditors who have lost patience with the debtor country's inability to pay. The vulture fund then sues the debtor country for the full amount of the debt, plus interest and penalties, using the ISDS mechanism if available. This can lead to the debtor country being forced to pay much more than it would have if it had negotiated a settlement with the original creditor. Vulture funds have been widely criticized for their practices, which are seen as exploiting the debt problems of poor countries for profit.

SOVEREIGN DEBT AS INVESTMENTS 139

resolving disputes relating to sovereign debt restructurings. In this case, a claim was brought against Greece by a Slovak bank—Poštová Banka, a.s. ("Poštová banka"). Moreover, its shareholder Istrokapital SE ("Istrokapital"), a European Public Limited Liability Company, organised under the laws of Cyprus pursuant to the Slovak Republic-Hellenic Republic BIT ("Slovakia-Greece BIT") and the Cyprus-Hellenic Republic BIT. The claimants sought compensation for illegal expropriation, failure to accord fair and equitable treatment, and violating umbrella clauses regarding the bank's interests in Greek government bonds ("GGBs") exchanged in 2012. Greece objected to the jurisdiction of the Tribunal on the grounds *inter alia* that the Tribunal lacked jurisdiction ratione materiae because (a) Poštová banka's interests in GGBs were not protected investments under the Slovakia-Greece BIT and the ICSID Convention; and (b) Istrokapital never made an investment protected under Article 1(1) of the Cyprus-Greece BIT or Article 25(1) of the ICSID Convention.[24]

In considering whether it had jurisdiction *ratione materiae* over the dispute, the Tribunal had to determine if the interests in the GGBs held by Poštová banka met the definition of a protected investment under Article 1(1) of the Slovakia-Greece BIT. Specifically, the Tribunal considered the chapeau for Article 1 of the *Slovakia-Greece BIT*, which provides that *"[i]nvestment means every kind of asset."* Article 1(1)(b) refers to *"shares in and stock and debentures of a company and any other form of participation in a company."* Furthermore, Article 1(1)(c) refers to *"loans, claims to money or any performance under contract having a financial value."*[25] The Tribunal noted a variation in the terminology and scope used across several BITs signed by Greece. As such, the Tribunal was hesitant about ascribing a blanket interpretation to Greece's treaty practice, noting that in some Greek BITs, there is a reference to the term "loans." In contrast, there is a reference to "long-term loans" or loans "connected to an investment" in others. It was also noted that some of Greece's BITs excluded the term "loan" in its entirety (para 292). Given this, the Tribunal was keen to interpret the Slovakia-Greece BIT on its merits to determine if the State parties intended to include "sovereign debt" within the scope of definition for investments under the Slovakia-Greece BIT.

---

[24] Paragraph 91 *Poštová*.
[25] *See* Paragraph 278 *Poštová* Award.

Even though Article 1 of the Slovakia-Greece BIT provided a broad asset-based definition instead of a closed list (para 286), the Tribunal held that the careful drafting of protected investments in the Slovakia-Greece BIT indicated that there were limits to the definition (para 294). Following this line of reasoning, the Tribunal argued that there was a difference between the language of the Slovakia-Greece BIT and the Argentina-Italy BIT discussed in the prior Argentina cases (i.e., *Abaclat* and *Ambiente Ufficio*) (paras 306–308). As such, the Tribunal was persuaded to reach a different conclusion from the Argentina cases. In doing so, the Tribunal dealt extensively with the differences between private and sovereign debt, making the latter a particular type of indebtedness that should not be bunched up with the kind of investments envisaged under Article 1 of the Slovakia-Greece BIT (paras 318–338). According to the Tribunal, "in sum, sovereign debt is an instrument of government monetary and economic policy. Its impact at the local and international levels makes it an important tool for handling a State's social and economic policies. *It cannot, thus, be equated to private indebtedness or corporate debt (emphasis added)*."[26]

3 The Treatment of Sovereign Debt in FTAs by the US and the EU

From the preceding analysis, it is evident that the conceptualisation of sovereign debt as an investment for protection remains a highly contentious and problematic issue, mainly because of interpretive difficulties regarding the coverage of sovereign debt instruments as covered investments, especially in first-generation BITs. Up to this point in the analysis, we have discussed the debates surrounding this issue concerning BITs. That raises the obvious question: Is there a different approach to conceptualising sovereign debt under FTAs compared to BITs? The answer to the above question depends on the generation of FTAs under consideration. The process adopted also varies from country to country, depending on the general attitude to investment protection and the use of ISDS mechanisms in their international economic interactions. There is also a noticeable difference when the FTA involves two or more developed country partners.

---

[26] *See* Paragraph 324 *Poštová* Award. *See also* Laurie Achtouk-Spivak and Paul Barker, *Landmark Sovereign Debt Restructuring Award*, OPINIOJURIS (30 April 2015) https://opiniojuris.org/2015/04/30/guest-post-landmark-sovereign-debt-restructuring-award.

Like BITs discussed in the previous section, investment and financial services chapters of FTAs have similar clauses on what constitutes investment which may therefore include sovereign bonds. FTAs signed by countries such as the US or the EU either explicitly list bonds as covered by the treaty or exclude them from their scope. For example, in his analysis of several BITs and FTAs, Kevin Gallagher found that *"almost all of the agreements by major capital exporters from industrialised nations include 'any kind of asset' as covered investments and thus likely cover sovereign bonds."*[27] He also found that *"some treaties, such as the 1994 North American Free Trade Agreement (NAFTA), the majority of Peru's IIAs and others (such as the Australia-Chile FTA) exclude or safeguard sovereign debt."*[28] Gallagher's observation proves true across several FTAs signed by the US, which includes Financial Services and/or Investment Chapters. A perusal of these investment agreements/FTAs in section 3.1 reveals some inconsistency in coverage of debt as an investment, which bears the hallmark of issues that have proved problematic under BITs discussed previously.

3.1. US FTAs

The US approach to conceptualising sovereign debt in its FTAs reflects the country's broader stance on investment protection and investor-state dispute settlement mechanisms.[29] One of the critical features of the US approach is the inclusion of financial services chapters in its FTAs.[30] These chapters are designed to facilitate cross-border trade in financial services with FTA partners while providing a framework for protecting investments in sovereign debt instruments.[31] Across several US FTAs, sovereign debt is acknowledged as a form of investment, and the provisions on

---

[27] Kevin P Gallagher, *Mission Creep: International Investment Agreements and Sovereign Debt Restructuring*, INVESTMENT TREATY NEWS (Jan. 12 2012) https://www.iisd.org/itn/en/2012/01/12/mission-creep-international-investment-agreements-and-sovereign-debt-restructuring-3.

[28] *Id.*

[29] Michael A. Bailey, Judith Goldstein & Barry R. Weingast (1997). *The Institutional Roots of American Trade Policy: Politics, Coalitions, and International Trade* 49(3) WORLD POLITICS 309–38 (1997).

[30] *See Free Trade Agreements,* OFFICE OF THE UNITED STATES TRADE REPRESENTATIVE https://ustr.gov/issue-areas/services-investment-digital-trade/services/free-trade-agreements.

[31] David Gaukrodger and Kathryn Gordon (2012). *Investor-State Dispute Settlement: A Scoping Paper for the Investment Policy Community* OECD WORKING PAPERS ON INT'L INV. (02), 1–60 (2012).

investment protection cover sovereign debt instruments.[32] For instance, the US-Singapore FTA contains a financial services chapter that recognises sovereign debt as a form of investment and provides investment protection.[33] However, the US approach often includes specific exclusions and limitations related to sovereign debt, which can limit the applicability of investor-state dispute settlement mechanisms to sovereign debt-related disputes.[34] The US also employs a model BIT, which serves as a template for its negotiations on investment protection and investor-state dispute settlement provisions in FTAs. The 2012 U.S. Model BIT contains provisions related to sovereign debt, recognising it as a form of investment and providing investment protection. However, the Model BIT also includes an annexe that sets out exceptions and limitations for sovereign debt-related disputes, which can limit the scope of investor-state arbitration in addressing such disputes.

Focusing on a sample of US FTAs, there is a consistent pattern in the conceptualisation of debt across the board. For example, the US-Morocco FTA, the US-Oman FTA, and the US-Columbia FTA had identical language related to debt. The only noticeable difference was that for the US-Columbia TPA, the definition of investment under Article 10.28 (c): which stipulates forms that investment could take (i.e., bonds, debentures, other debt instruments, and loans), includes a footnote (footnote 13) explanation stating that: *Loans issued by one Party to another Party are not investments.*[35]

Although NAFTA provided stipulations safeguarding sovereign debt restructuring in its annexe, these annexes are not standard options across US treaties post-NAFTA. The US was initially very reluctant to include such annexes in its agreements. More recent FTAs such as the US-Australia, US-South Korea, US-Morocco, US-Oman, US-Panama, and US-Singapore agreements expressly include bonds and

---

[32] Robert Howse *The Concept of Odious Debt in Public International Law*, UNITED NATIONS CONFERENCE ON TRADE AND DEVELOPMENT DISCUSSION PAPERS, No 185, 1–38 (2007).
[33] US-Singapore FTA, 2003.
[34] Waibel, supra, note 11.
[35] US-Colombia FTA, https://ustr.gov/sites/default/files/uploads/agreements/fta/colombia/asset_upload_file630_10143.pdf (Accessed on May 15, 2023).

debt as covered investments, without the NAFTA-type annexe addressing the issue of sovereign debt restructuring. Gallagher points out that the *"absence of such a safeguard in the US-South Korea agreement is striking given that South Korea engaged in a historic restructuring of its sovereign debt following its financial crisis in the late 1990s."*[36] Drawing from interviews with US negotiators for his report, Gallagher notes that the US does not initiate discussions regarding sovereign debt but only responds to them when raised by negotiating partners.[37] This observation should be a point of caution for Global South countries, especially African countries, who are contemplating negotiating FTAs and other IIAs with the US. It demonstrates the shrewd nature of US negotiators, who will only remove these clauses if the negotiating team from the other side raise issues with their inclusion.

Chile and Uruguay are examples of nations that expressed such concerns when negotiating FTAs with the US. The concerns expressed by negotiators from these South American countries forced the US to agree to a ban on claims by creditors during restructuring. These provisions were included in the US-Chile FTA[38] and later the US-Dominican Republic-Central America Free Trade Agreement or DR-CAFTA.[39] However, these bans came with caveats because they do not preclude claims if the restructuring by the sovereign violates National Treatment or Most

---

[36] Kevin P. Gallagher, *The New Vulture Culture: Sovereign Debt Restructuring and Trade and Investment Treaties* The Ideas WORKING PAPER SERIES PAPER NO. 02/2011/; *See also* Paul Blustein, *The Chastening: Inside the Crisis that Rocked the Global Financial System and Humbled the IMF*, New York PUBLICAFFAIRS (2003).

[37] Gallagher, *supra* note 26.

[38] *See* Annex 10-B of the Investment Chapter of the Chile-US FTA which states that: *The rescheduling of the debts of Chile, or of its appropriate institutions owned or controlled through ownership interests by Chile, owed to the United States and the rescheduling of its debts owed to creditors in general are not subject to any provision of Section A other than Articles 10.2 (NT) and 10.3 (MFN).*

[39] *See* Annex 10-A of the Investment Chapter of the CAFTA-DR which states that: The rescheduling of the debts of a Central American Party or the Dominican Republic, or of such Party's institutions owned or controlled through ownership interests by such Party, owed to the United States and the rescheduling of any of such Party's debts owed to creditors in general are not subject to any provision of Section A other than Articles 10.3 (NT) and 10.4 (MFN).

Favored Nation clauses.[40] The US strongly opposed including a provision for "negotiated restructuring" in the US-Uruguay BIT negotiations.[41] This issue proved to be a deal-breaker for Uruguay, which forced the US negotiators to eventually agree for provisions on "negotiated restructuring" to be included in the US agreements with Uruguay.[42] Similar clauses are found in the US-Peru TPA[43] and US-Colombia FTAs, respectively stipulating that *"any country can engage in a 'negotiated restructuring' without being liable for the losses of foreign investors."*[44]

The USMCA (NAFTA 2.0) carries on with this approach stipulating in Chapter 14 Annex 2 that:

> 1. *For greater certainty, no award shall be made in favour of a claimant for a claim under Article 14.D.3.1 (Submission of a Claim to Arbitration) concerning default or non-payment of debt issued by a Party unless the claimant meets its burden of proving that such default or non-payment constitutes a breach of a relevant obligation in the Chapter.);*
> 2. *No claim that a restructuring of debt issued by a Party, standing alone, breaches an obligation in this Chapter shall be submitted to arbitration under Article 14.D.3.1 (Submission of a Claim to Arbitration), provided that the restructuring is effected as provided for under the debt instrument's terms, including the debt instrument's governing law.*

---

[40] *Id.*

[41] *See* Senate Executive Report 109-17, which describes the objections raised by Uruguay and its insistence on the inclusion of Annex G, which was consider a departure or at least an exception to the 2004 US Model BIT. https://www.govinfo.gov/content/pkg/CRPT-109erpt17/html/CRPT-109erpt17.htm.

[42] *See* Annex G.

[43] Under Article 10:28 of the US-Peru TPA, negotiated restructuring means the restructuring or rescheduling of a debt instrument that has been effected through (i) a modification or amendment of such debt instrument, as provided for under its terms, or (ii) a comprehensive debt exchange or other similar process in which the holders of no less than 75 percent of the aggregate principal amount of the outstanding debt under such debt instrument have consented to such debt exchange or other processes.

[44] *Id.*

SOVEREIGN DEBT AS INVESTMENTS   145

From the preceding, the U.S. approach to conceptualising sovereign debt in its FTAs is summarised below:

Key Features	Description
The conceptualisation of debt and inclusion of sovereign bonds as covered investments	The conceptualisation of debt across US FTAs/TPAs depends on the era and the dynamics of each negotiated deal. For example, the US-Morocco FTA, the US-Oman FTA, and the US-Columbia FTA had identical language related to debt. More recent FTAs such as the US-Australia, US-South Korea, US-Morocco, US-Oman, US-Panama, and US-Singapore agreements expressly include bonds and debt as covered investments. The US-Peru TPA, 1994 NAFTA exclude sovereign debt as covered investments.
Presence of safeguards for sovereign debt	Although the 1994 NAFTA provided stipulations safeguarding sovereign debt restructuring in its annexe, these annexes are not standard options across US treaties post-NAFTA. The US was initially very reluctant to include such annexes in its agreements.
Responding to issues on sovereign debt during negotiations	The US does not initiate discussions regarding sovereign debt but only responds to them when raised by negotiating partners.
Negotiated restructuring of sovereign debt	US agreements with Uruguay, Peru, and Colombia include provisions for "negotiated restructuring" that allow countries to engage in a restructuring without being liable for the losses of foreign investors. These agreements also have caveats that do not preclude claims if the restructuring violates NT or MFN clauses.
Ban on claims during the restructuring	The US-Chile FTA and US-Dominican Republic-Central America Free Trade Agreement or DR-CAFTA include bans on claims by creditors during restructuring. However, these bans do not preclude claims if the restructuring violates NT or MFN clauses.
Opposition to "negotiated restructuring."	The US vehemently opposed including a provision for "negotiated restructuring" in the US-Uruguay BIT negotiations but eventually agreed to include it due to Uruguay's insistence.

Key Features	Description
The USMCA's approach	The USMCA (NAFTA 2.0) includes provisions that no award shall be made in favour of a claimant for a claim under Article 14.D.3.1 concerning default or non-payment of debt issued by a Party and that no claim that a restructuring of debt issued by a Party breaches an obligation shall be submitted to arbitration.

IIAs	Scope of Debt as Covered Investment	Safeguard for Sovereign Debt Restructuring
US-Morocco FTA	Includes bonds and debt	No specific annexes for sovereign debt restructuring
US-Oman FTA	Includes bonds and debt	No specific annexes for sovereign debt restructuring
US-Colombia FTA	Includes bonds, debentures, other debt instruments, and loans	No specific annexes for sovereign debt restructuring; loans issued by one Party to another Party are not investments
NAFTA	Excludes sovereign bonds	Included specific annexes for sovereign debt restructuring safeguards
US-Peru TPA	Excludes sovereign bonds	No specific annexes for sovereign debt restructuring
US-Australia FTA	Includes bonds and debt	No specific annexes for sovereign debt restructuring
US-South Korea FTA	Includes bonds and debt	No specific annexes for sovereign debt restructuring
US-Panama FTA	Includes bonds and debt	No specific annexes for sovereign debt restructuring
US-Singapore FTA	Includes bonds and debt	No specific annexes for sovereign debt restructuring
US-Chile FTA	It has the scope to include bonds and debt.	Specific provisions for a ban on claims by creditors during a restructuring with exceptions for NT and MFN clauses
US-DR-CAFTA	It has the scope to include bonds and debt.	Specific provisions for a ban on claims by creditors during a restructuring with exceptions for NT and MFN clauses

IIAs	Scope of Debt as Covered Investment	Safeguard for Sovereign Debt Restructuring
US-Uruguay BIT		Negotiated restructuring provisions included after Uruguay insisted

3.2. EU-FTAs

Like the US, the EU includes financial services and cross-border trade in services chapters in its FTAs and other IIAs. These agreements often contain provisions addressing sovereign debt. Several prominent EU FTAs, such as the EU-Canada Comprehensive Economic and Trade Agreement (CETA) and the EU-Singapore Investment Protection Agreement (EUSIPA), include provisions that classify sovereign bonds as investments to be protected within their financial services and cross-border trade in services chapters. Chapter Eight of CETA covers investment, and Annex 8.1 defines "investment" as including debt securities issued by a Party, which would encompass sovereign bonds. Conversely, the EUSIPA is a standalone investment protection agreement that complements the EU-Singapore Free Trade Agreement. The agreement defines "investment" in Article 1.2, which includes debt securities issued by a Party, thus covering sovereign bonds. Like the EUSIPA, the EU-Vietnam Investment Protection Agreement (EVIPA) also has a standalone investment protection agreement that complements the EU-Vietnam Free Trade Agreement. The definition of "investment" under Article 1.2 of the Agreement includes debt securities issued by a Party, classifying sovereign bonds as protected investments.

Agreement	Type of Agreement	Definition of "investment"
CETA	FTA (Mega-regional)	Debt securities issued by a Party are considered "investments."
EUSIPA	Investment Protection Agreement	Debt securities issued by a Party are considered "investments."
EVIPA		Debt securities issued by a Party are considered "investments."

Due in part to the sovereign debt crises experienced by some EU member states and the broader implications for the stability of the European financial system, in recent years, the EU has paid greater attention to the issue of sovereign debt in its FTAs.[45] As a result, the EU has sought to incorporate more detailed provisions related to sovereign debt in its agreements to provide a more robust framework for treating sovereign debt and resolving related disputes.[46]

While the EU widely acknowledges sovereign debt within its FTAs, Agreements such as the CETA contain specific exclusions and reservations, such as excluding disputes arising from the restructuring of sovereign debt from the scope of the agreement's investor-state dispute settlement mechanism.[47] This means that investors cannot use the ISDS mechanism to challenge sovereign debt restructuring measures the host state takes. In addition, CETA includes other safeguards to protect the regulatory sovereignty of the parties, such as a requirement that investors exhaust local remedies before initiating an ISDS claim and a "right to regulate" clause that affirms the right of the parties to regulate in the public interest. Under the EU-Singapore FTA, although less comprehensive than the CETA, specific provisions limit the role of investor-state arbitration in addressing sovereign debt-related disputes.

Like the US, the EU's approach to conceptualising sovereign debt in its FTAs is characterised by an increasing focus on incorporating detailed provisions related to sovereign debt while maintaining specific exclusions and reservations to limit the role of investor-state arbitration in addressing sovereign debt-related. However, these safeguards are more detailed in some FTAs, such as the CETA and less so in FTAs, such as the EU-Singapore FTA. It is also evident that the EU has varying treatment on safeguard mechanisms for sovereign debt issues across different agreements. For example, although the EU-Cariforum Economic Partnership Agreement (EPA) contains safeguards (under Article 234) from measures relating to public health, safety, and the environment, it does not appear to extend to disputes relating to sovereign debt. The absence of a specific safeguard against ISDS for sovereign debt issues in some EU-FTAs and EPAs, especially with Global South partners, is problematic,

---

[45] Giuseppe Bianco, *European Union's Investment Agreements and Public Debt. 28(2)* EUR. BUS. L. REV. 119–33 (2017).
[46] Bianco, *supra* note 45 at 119–33.

particularly given the controversies around the use of ISDS mechanisms to challenge sovereign debt restructurings.

4 An Inconsistent Approach to Safeguards against ISDS for Sovereign Debt Issues

From the preceding analysis, it is evident that IIAs without safeguards from ISDS mechanisms for sovereign debt disputes provide an avenue for legal recourse for uncooperative creditors seeking full repayment of their distressed sovereign debt instruments. This can undermine debt restructuring efforts and limits an indebted country's ability to address its socioeconomic priorities during a sovereign debt crisis.[48] The possibility of claims being brought by uncooperative creditors using ISDS mechanisms in FTAs creates a disincentive for debt restructuring, discouraging countries from undertaking necessary debt restructuring, prolonging the crisis, and delaying the economic recovery of the indebted nation. Invariably, this also leads to unequal treatment of creditors, as those who have access to ISDS would be less inclined to negotiate during restructuring and could potentially gain preferential treatment over those who do not.

The analysis in the previous section shows that the US has not been consistent in its negotiating tactics with several countries. While agreements like the US-Mexico-Canada Agreement (USMCA) include explicit carve-outs for sovereign debt restructuring, others do not.[49] It is plausible to argue that, unlike the older generation FTAs, the carve-outs in the USMCA reflect advancements in the thinking around the potential problems posed by sovereign debt disputes subject to ISDS mechanisms. However, it remains to be seen if this progressive stance in the USMCA will be reflected in future US-FTA practices, especially FTAs with Global South partners.

---

[47] Gaukrodger and Gordon, *supra* note 29; Comprehensive Economic and Trade Agreement (CETA) between the European Union and Canada (CETA) 2016.

[48] Matthias Goldmann, *Foreign Investment, Sovereign Debt, and Human Rights* (August 24, 2018) in Ilias Bantekas and Cephas Lumina (eds.), SOVEREIGN DEBT AND HUMAN RIGHTS, (Oxford U. Press 2018).

[49] Specifically, Article 17.6.3 of the USMCA states that a Party may adopt or maintain non-discriminatory measures that are designed and applied to ensure the equitable treatment of creditors in the context of a sovereign debt restructuring and that such measures shall not be considered a breach of the investment-related obligations of the agreement.

Conversely, including carve-outs may be more reflective of the specific circumstances of the USMCA negotiations and the parties' negotiating positions rather than a broader shift in approach to FTAs. Furthermore, the carve-outs may only apply to a limited range of situations, which may not fully address the complex issues involved in sovereign debt restructuring. The US may also revert to a more traditional approach to FTA negotiations, particularly in negotiations with Global South partners. In these negotiations, the US may seek to include more conventional ISDS provisions, which could limit the policy space of Global South countries to address their socio-economic priorities during a sovereign debt restructuring. Therefore, while the USMCA may represent a positive step forward in safeguarding policy space during sovereign debt restructuring, it remains to be seen if this approach will be reflected in future US-FTA practices, particularly concerning Global South partners.

The EU may have to a greater degree, taken a more consistent approach to safeguarding against ISDS for sovereign debt issues in its FTAs, such as the CETA and the EU-Singapore FTA.[50] However, the EU-Cariforum Economic Partnership Agreement (EPA) does not explicitly exclude sovereign debt restructuring from the scope of ISDS. Like the US, could this be excused with the argument that more recent FTAs, including FTAs with global South countries, will benefit from the approach adopted in the CETA?

Like the US, the fact that the EU has included explicit carve-outs in some agreements, such as the CETA and the EU-Singapore FTA, is a positive step forward. The lack of similar carve-outs in other agreements, such as the EU-Cariforum EPA, raises questions about the consistency and reliability of the EU's approach to safeguarding policy space in sovereign debt restructuring. Like the USMCA, it is again possible that the EU's approach to safeguarding against ISDS for sovereign debt issues may be influenced by various factors, including the negotiating positions of the parties involved, the political context of the negotiations, and the specific circumstances of each agreement. Therefore, while the EU may have taken a more consistent approach to safeguarding against ISDS for sovereign debt issues in some of its FTAs, it is essential to carefully examine the specific provisions of each agreement to determine the

---

[50] CETA provides for the adoption of non-discriminatory measures to ensure the equitable treatment of creditors in the context of a sovereign debt restructuring. Article 13.7 of the CETA states that such measures shall not be considered a breach of the investment-related obligations of the agreement.

extent to which they provide sufficient safeguards for policy space during sovereign debt restructuring.

5 Conclusion

Stakeholders seeking reforms to the international debt architecture must maintain vigilance on potential crises that could emanate from future North-South IIA relationships. This is imperative because, as Park and Samples remind us, *"the absence of a formal bankruptcy regime or binding regulatory oversight [for sovereign debt issues] makes it ... fertile ground for rogue behaviour by opportunistic debtors and creditors alike."*[51] As such, future IIAs without safeguards against ISDS mechanisms for sovereign debt issues open the door for predatory "tribunalization" of sovereign debt issues. Global South countries negotiating FTAs with Global North trade and investment partners must insist on safeguards against applying ISDS mechanisms to sovereign debt disputes, as seen in the approaches taken by South American countries such as Chile and Uruguay, to protect their policy space and legitimate investor rights. Recalling the point made by Gallagher that the US does not initiate discussions regarding sovereign debt but only responds to them when raised by negotiating partners, it is imperative for Global South countries negotiating FTAs with the US to be aware of the complications that can arise if safeguards are not built in to exclude the application of ISDS mechanisms to sovereign debt disputes. Although there is a need to attract foreign investment and access international capital markets, Global South countries must have the requisite policy space to address economic crises without fear of investor challenges while also protecting the legitimate rights of investors.

Alternatively, ISDS should be eliminated entirely from Agreements of this nature to discourage predatory and opportunistic "tribunalization" of sovereign debt issues. This stance is supported by a growing number of US lawmakers who advocate for the removal of ISDS from US trade agreements due to private corporations' predatory use of the ISDS regime.[52] In light of the mounting scepticism regarding the

---

[51] Park and Samples, *supra* note 2.
[52] *See* "Senator Warren, *Representative Doggett Call for Elimination of Investor-State Dispute Settlement System, Action on Behalf of Honduran Government*," ELIZABETH WARREN (May 03 2023) https://www.warren.senate.gov/oversight/letters/senator-warren-representative-doggett-call-for-elimination-of-investor-state-dispute-settlement-system-action-on-behalf-of-honduran-government.

efficacy of ISDS provisions in facilitating beneficial investment in host countries[53] and the broad powers it gives private corporations to challenge and override democratically-enacted laws and regulations that protect public health, the environment, and workers' rights, a group of lawmakers is calling on the US Trade Representative Office to avoid including ISDS in future trade negotiations and to address the exploitative use of existing ISDS mechanisms by private corporations.[54] Over 30 US lawmakers made this call in reaction to a case brought against the Honduran government by a US company Honduras Próspera under the ISDS system.[55] These US Lawmakers are supporting the Honduran government's call for eliminating ISDS provisions in the Central America Free Trade Agreement (CAFTA) because they undermine the ability of governments to regulate in the public interest.[56] These concerns apply in the context of sovereign debt restructuring, with holdout creditors less keen to join negotiations for debt restructuring if they have the ISDS option available.

As such, eliminating or implementing safeguards against ISDS mechanisms for sovereign debt disputes is crucial and essential for Global South countries negotiating IIAs with Global North trade and investment partners. Failure to do so will discourage holdout creditors from joining debt-restructuring negotiations. As recent events have shown, holdout creditors' reluctance to participate in debt restructuring negotiations is due to the availability of ISDS options, which inevitably prolongs economic crises and hampers efforts to promote economic recovery. Overall, Global South countries must carefully consider how to balance the competing concerns they confront: access to capital versus the risk of ISDS.

---

[53] *See* Mavluda Sattorova, Mustafa Erkan, Ohiocheoya Omiunu, *"How Do Host States Respond to Investment Treaty Law? Some Empirical Observations"* in John D. Haskell and Akbar Rasulov (eds) NEW VOICES AND NEW PERSPECTIVES IN INTERNATIONAL ECONOMIC LAW, EUROPEAN JOURNAL OF INTERNATIONAL ECONOMIC LAW.

[54] *Ibid.*

[55] *Ibid. See also* Honduras Próspera Inc., St. John's Bay Development Company LLC, and Próspera Arbitration Center LLC v. Republic of Honduras, ICSID Case No. ARB/23/2.

[56] *Ibid.*

CHAPTER SIX

Debt Restructuring under the G20 Common Framework: Austerity Again? The Case of Zambia and Chad

Nona Tamale[*]

1 Introduction

In the immediate aftermath of the outbreak of the COVID-19 pandemic, several African countries grappled with limited fiscal space to respond to the needs of their populations. Severe social and economic impacts, compounded by liquidity constraints, affected the capacity of some governments to meet their debt obligations, with Zambia becoming the first country to default on its debt repayments during pandemic.[1] In response, the international community offered debt relief through the G20 Debt Service Suspension Initiative (DSSI) and the International Monetary Fund (IMF) Catastrophe Containment and Relief Trust (CCRT). While these initiatives mostly eased liquidity pressures, countries facing solvency issues required a more comprehensive solution. Consequently, the G20 Common Framework for Debt Treatments beyond the DSSI (Common Framework) was created as a platform for low-income countries to restructure their debt. To date, four countries—Chad, Ghana, Zambia, and Ethiopia—of the 41 DSSI eligible countries at high risk or in debt distress have applied to the Common Framework.[2]

---

[*] Nona Tamale is an Assistant Lecturer under the Department of Public and Comparative Law at the School of Law, Makerere University and the Legal and Policy Officer for Afronomicslaw.

[1] Deborah Brautigam & Yinxuan Wang, *Zambia's Chinese Debt in Pandemic Era*, CHINA AFR. RSCH. INITIATIVE, (Briefing Paper) (2021).

[2] Guillame Chabert et. al., *Restructuring Debt of Poorer Nations Requires More Efficient Coordination*, INT'L MONETARY FUND BLOG (Apr. 7, 2022), https://blogs.imf.org/2022/04/07/restructuring-debt-of-poorer-nations-requires-more-efficient-coordination/.

Negotiations with creditors under the Common Framework are still underway for Chad, Ghana, and Zambia. This chapter seeks to ascertain whether these countries intend to adopt austerity measures amid their restructuring in order to guarantee repayment of debt to their creditors. It demonstrates that even prior to the conclusion of these negotiations, there are indications that austerity is a pre-condition for a successful debt restructuring for Zambia, Ghana, and Chad. It shows that these countries are already implementing austerity measures, on the advice on the IMF, during the negotiations with their creditors, arguably to prove to their willingness to meet their debt servicing obligations and guarantee successful outcomes in the restructuring process. It cautions against and argues that taking the austerity path is counter-productive in achieving long term debt sustainability and is inconsistent with the principle of shared responsibility between lenders and debtors espoused in various soft law instruments, including the G20 Operational Guidelines for Sustainable Finance.

This chapter is organized as follows. Part 1 discusses the progress in debt restructuring for Zambia and Chad under the Common Framework. Part 2 provides a brief historical recap of austerity as a condition for debt relief in Africa, right from the structural adjustment era. Part 3 reveals how Zambia and Chad are already undertaking austerity measures amidst their debt restructuring negotiations. Part 4 of the chapter discusses the implications of undertaking austerity amidst debt restructurings. Part 5 concludes.

2 Debt Restructuring under the G20 Common Framework in Chad and Zambia

The COVID-19 pandemic and its associated economic downturn exposed the debt-related vulnerabilities of numerous countries, Zambia and Chad inclusive. As of end-2021, Zambia's public external debt had almost doubled over a five-year period with the largest proportion owed to private creditors (45%), followed by multilateral

---

[3] *See* BANK OF ZAMBIA, *Annual Report 2021,* at 37 (by end-2021, Zambia's public external debt stood at US$13.04 billion up from US$ 6.85 billion in 2016); *See also* BANK OF ZAMBIA, *Annual Report 2016,* at 23.

creditors (30%) and bilateral creditors (25%).[3] For Chad, its external debt was equivalent to more than a third of its gross national income (GNI).[4] Similar to Zambia, commercial creditors hold the bulk of Chad's debt, 97% of which is owed to a single creditor, Glencore Energy.[5]

While both countries were beneficiaries of debt relief from the G20 Debt Service Suspension Initiative (DSSI) and IMF Catastrophe Containment Relief Trust (CCRT),[6] this assistance turned out to be miniscule in light of their heavy debt burdens as well its composition. Private and multilateral creditors, who hold a substantial amount of sovereign debt, did not participate in the DSSI thus they continued to receive debt repayments amidst the pandemic. Though Zambia's external debt servicing fell in 2021,[7] private creditors received the bulk of repayments (50.8%).[8] Similarly, Chad's estimated repayments to its private creditors between 2021–2024 are equivalent to 43% of its financing gap over the same period.[9]

With a rise in the number of countries with unsustainable debt burdens and the absence of a sovereign debt restructuring mechanism, the G20's Common Framework for debt treatments beyond the DSSI (Common Framework) was meant to

---

[4] *See* UNITED NATIONS CONF. ON TRADE AND DEV., *Helping Chad Strengthen Public Debt Management,* (Feb. 25, 2022), https://unctad.org/news/helping-chad-strengthen-public-debt-management (Chad's public external debt amounted to US$3.6 billion in 2020).

[5] *See* IMF, *Chad: Request for a Three-Year Arrangement Under the Extended Credit Facility,* Country Report 2021 (Dec. 2021) (commercial creditors hold the bulk of Chad's debt (36.7%) while multilateral and bilateral creditors are owed a 35.5% and 27.8% share respectively).

[6] *See* WORLD BANK, *Debt Service Suspension Initiative,* Brief (Mar. 10, 2022), https://www.worldbank.org/en/topic/debt/brief/covid-19-debt-service-suspension-initiative (Zambia's deferred debt repayments under the DSSI amounted to an estimate of US$700 million while Chad saved approximately US$102 million. Chad also received relief of US$14 million under the IMF CCRT); *See also* IMF, *COVID-19 Financial Assistance and Debt Service Relief,* https://www.imf.org/en/Topics/imf-and-covid19/COVID-Lending-Tracker#REGION (last visited Jun. 20, 2022).

[7] *See* Bank of Zambia, *supra* note 1 (external debt servicing dropped from US$1,196.2 million in 2019 to US$207 million in 2021).

[8] *Id.* (multilateral creditors and non-Paris Club bilateral creditors received 37.3% and 11.9% of Zambia's total debt servicing in 2021).

[9] *See* IMF, *supra* note 5 (Chad is expected to pay an estimate of US$717 million to its private creditors between 2021–2024 which amounts to 43% of its financing gap (US$1.6 billion) over the same period).

provide a platform for low-income countries to restructure their debt.[10] Negotiating an IMF programme and obtaining comparable treatment from private creditors are among the key requirements for participating countries.

Chad was the first country to apply to the Common Framework in January 2022. Chad's creditor committee,[11] co-chaired by France and Saudi Arabia, backed the proposed IMF loan arrangement and shortly thereafter, Chad entered an extended credit facility (ECF) with the Fund in December 2021. The country's main creditor, Glencore also established a creditor committee and indicated its interest in negotiating with the Chadian government.[12]

Zambia applied to the Common Framework shortly after Chad in February 2021. China, the country's largest bilateral creditor, and France agreed to co-chair its creditor committee formed in February 2022. While it negotiated a staff level agreement with the IMF for US$ 1.3 billion, the approval of the loan arrangement is contingent on progress in the country's engagement with private creditors "to help secure a deal on comparable terms to official creditors."[13] In July 2022 the IMF indicated that its likely to approve the loan arrangement following a pledge by Zambia's creditor committee to provide debt relief.[14] However the government is still required to continue negotiations to bring its commercial creditors on board on similar terms.[15]

The process has stalled and none of the countries which applied one and half years ago have succeeded in arriving at a comprehensive debt workout. The long

---

[10] GROUP OF 20, *Extraordinary G20 Finance Ministers and Central Bank Governors' Meeting: Statement,* 2-3 (Nov. 13, 2020), https://www.sciencespo.fr/psia/sovereign-debt/wp-content/uploads/2020/11/English_Extraordinary-G20-FMCBG-Statement_November-13.pdf.

[11] PARIS CLUB, *Statement of the 4th Meeting of the Creditor Committee for Chad under the Common Framework,* (Jun. 11, 2021), https://clubdeparis.org/en/communications/communique-presse/4th-meeting-of-the-creditor-committee-for-chad-under-the-common.

[12] IMF, *supra* note 5.

[13] IMF, *IMF Staff Reaches Staff-level Agreement on an Extended Credit Facility Arrangement with Zambia,* Press Release (Dec. 2021).

[14] IMF, *IMF Managing Director welcomes the Statement by the Creditor Committee for Zambia under the Common Framework for Debt Treatments,* Press Release (Jul. 2022).

[15] Group of 20, *First meeting of the creditor committee for Zambia under the Common Framework for debt treatments beyond the DSSI,* (2022), https://g20.org/first-meeting-of-the-creditor-committee-for-zambia-under-the-common-framework-for-debt-treatments-beyond-the-dssi/ (last vistied Jun. 25, 2022).

process and absence of debt relief during negotiations for countries which applied to the Common Framework has arguably deterred other African countries struggling with heavy debt burdens from participating in the mechanism.[16] The delays have primarily been attributed to creditor coordination challenges and enforcement of the requirement of obtaining comparable of treatment of commercial creditors remains vague,[17] to the detriment of the borrowing countries. Amidst this, these countries undergoing restructuring have limited fiscal space to respond to the ongoing economic shocks and their pandemic recovery needs, yet they have resumed debt repayments to their lenders. This chapter argues that, as a result, these governments are implementing austerity measures to demonstrate their willingness to restore debt sustainability, as discussed in Section 4.

3 History of Austerity as a Condition for Debt Relief in Africa

The terms austerity and fiscal consolidation are often used synonymously[18] to refer to policies adopted by governments with the ultimate aim of reducing their deficits and high debt levels.[19] Specifically, austerity measures may be revenue or expenditure based and include cuts in public expenditure, labour reforms, wage bill reform, removal or reduction of subsidies, rationalizing of social protection programs and consumption revenues such as Value Added Tax (VAT).[20]

---

[16] Masood Ahmed & Hannah Brown, *Fix the Common Framework for Debt Before it is too Late*, CTR. FOR GLOB. DEV. (Jan. 8, 2022), https://www.cgdev.org/blog/fix-common-framework-debt-it-too-late (an IMF article implies that the confidence in the Common Framework is low among eligible countries due to the prolonged delays experienced by Chad, Zambia and Ethiopia); *See also* Kristalina Georgieva and Ceyla Pazarbasioglu, *The G20 Common Framework for Debt Treatments Must be Stepped Up*, IMF (Dec. 2, 2021), https://blogs.imf.org/2021/12/02/the-g20-common-framework-for-debt-treatments-must-be-stepped-up/.

[17] *Id.*

[18] *See e.g.,* Alberto Alesina et al, *Austerity and Elections,* (IMF Working Paper, WP/21/121, 2021), https://www.imf.org/en/Publications/WP/Issues/2021/04/30/Austerity-and-Elections-50245.

[19] OECD, *Fiscal Consolidation: The Need for Evidence-Based Decision Making,* in Government at a Glance 2011 31 (2011).

[20] Isabel Ortiz & Matthew Cummins, *Global Austerity Alert: Looming Budget Cuts in 2021–25 and Alternative Pathways,* (INITIATIVE FOR POLICY DIALOGUE Working Paper, 2021), https://policydialogue.org/files/publications/papers/Global-Austerity-Alert-Ortiz-Cummins-2021-final.pdf.

For decades, policy prescriptions of international financial institutions (IFI), specifically the IMF and World Bank, to Africa countries facing economic and debt crises have typically included austerity measures. This trend and its disastrous impact has been observed from the infamous stabilization and structural adjustment programs of the 1990s,[21] through the poverty reduction agenda of the 1990's and 2000's,[22] to the post 2009 financial crisis period,[23] and most recently, in the COVID-19 pandemic response.[24] While there are claims that IMF austerity is a concern of the past, these have been debunked by recent studies showing that IMF is prescribing austerity for the post-pandemic period, through conditionalities in its loan programmes.[25]

Despite opposition from civil society groups, academics and global institutions, austerity assumes a hegemonic position and has become deep-rooted in the region's fiscal policy. This is demonstrated by the fact that even in the absence of IFI loan

---

[21] *See, e.g.,* JOHN CLARK & CAROLINE ALLISON, ZAMBIA: DEATH AND POLICY, (1989) (some of the policy prescriptions under the SAPs, also referred to as the Washington Consensus, include currency devaluation, trade liberalization, privatization and deregulation accompanied by austerity measures such as cuts in public expenditure, introduction of user fees for public services, public service wage bill cuts, and elimination of subsidies); *See also* Fantu Cheru (Independent Expert), *Effects of Structural Adjustment Policies on the Full Enjoyment of Human Rights,* U.N. Doc. E/CN.4/1999/50 (Feb. 24, 1999); *See also* RODWAN ABOUHARB & DAVID CINGRANELLI, HUMAN RIGHTS AND STRUTURAL ADJUSTMENT, (2007), *and* Lotsmart Fonjong, *Rethinking the Impact of Structural Adjustment Programs on Human Rights Violations in West Africa,* 13 PERSP. ON GLOB. DEV. 87 (2014).

[22] *See* Demba Moussa Dembele, *The International Monetary Fund (IMF) and World Bank in Africa: A "Disastrous" Record,* 35 INT'L J. OF HEALTH SERV. 389 (2005).

[23] *See* Isabel Ortiz et al., *The Decade of Adjustment: A Review of Austerity Trends 2010–2020 in 187 Countries,* (ILO, The S. Ctr., The Initiative for Pol'y Dialogue, ESS Working Paper No. 53, 2015) (according to Ortiz, the most common austerity measures in Africa following the global financial crisis were subsidy reform, wage bill cuts/caps, increase in consumption taxes, pension reform and further targeting of social protection programmes).

[24] *See, e.g.,* NONA TAMALE, ADDING FUEL TO FIRE: HOW IMF DEMANDS FOR AUSTERITY WILL DRIVE UP INEQUALITY (2021) (Briefing Paper); *How the IMF is Pushing an Austerity-based Recovery,* OXFAM INT'L, WASH. OFF. (Apr. 18, 2022), https://medium.com/@OxfamIFIs/how-the-imf-is-pushing-an-austerity-based-recovery-f19c6040e918, *and* Daniel Munevar, ARRESTED DEVELOPMENT: INTERNATIONAL MONETARY FUND LENDING AND AUSTERITY POST COVID-19, (2020) (Briefing Paper).

[25] *See* e.g., Alexander Kentikelenis & Thomas Stubbs, *Austerity Redux: The Post-Pandemic Wave of Budget Cuts and the Future of Global Public Health,* 13 GLOB. POL'Y 5 (2021); *See also* Isabel Ortiz et. al., *supra* note 23.

programmes, countries undertake budget austerity in order to retain market access. Indeed, credit rating agencies, in assessing ability of countries to repay debt obligations, also consider whether a country is maintaining tight fiscal policies.[26] The global financial system is designed foremost to secure repayments for creditors, and the absence of a sovereign debt restructuring mechanism allows for creditor-led debt workouts, commonly accompanied by prescriptions of austerity.[27]

Looking at the cases studies, both Chad and Zambia have previously adopted austerity measures to resolve their debt problems. Zambia had to cancel its IMF reform programme in 1987 following public protests over its austerity measures including removal of food subsidies which had drastic consequences for Zambians, affecting low-income households the most.[28] In more recent years, IMF, through its lending and surveillance advised Zambia to implement wage bill freezes,[29] further targeting of cash transfer programs,[30] reform of agricultural subsidies,[31] removal of fuel and electricity subsidies,[32] and cut its public expenditure.[33]

---

[26] Dep't. Of Econ. and Soc. Aff. [UNDESA], *Credit Rating Agencies and Sovereign Debt: Challenges and Solutions,* (2021), https://www.un.org/development/desa/financing/document/credit-rating-agencies-and-sovereign-debt-challenges-and-solutions; *See also* Fritz Sager & Markus Hinterleitner, *Austerity Programs and their Assessment by Credit Rating Agencies during the European Debt Crisis—an Implementation Perspective,* https://boris.unibe.ch/88014/2/CRAs_Austerity_Programs_Sager_Hinterleitner.pdf (last visited Jun. 23, 2022) (the authors argue that CRAs cause a "'vicious circle' of downgrades" and escalate refinancing costs for countries, ultimately affecting their capacity to repay their debt. For countries whose austerity packages CRAs perceive will be unsuccessful in achieving the aim of reducing debt and deficit levels (and by extension, those which do not undertake austerity despite high debt levels), rating downgrades can result into even higher borrowing costs and loss of market access); *See* Civil Society Financing for Development Group, *Submission to the UN Independent Expert on Foreign Debt and Human Rights Report on 'Debt Relief, Debt Crisis Prevention and Human Rights: The Role of Credit Rating Agencies',* (Nov. 2020), https://www.ohchr.org/sites/default/files/Documents/Issues/IEDebt/CreditRatingAgencies/civil-society-FdDgroup-credit-rating-2020.pdf (this source provides a more detailed discussion on the role of CRAs in promoting austerity).

[27] Bhumika Muchhala, *The IMF in Debt Restructuring, the Resurgence of Austerity, and the Urgency of Fiscal Justice,* COMM. FOR THE ABOLITION OF ILLEGITIMATE DEBT (May 27, 2022), http://www.cadtm.org/The-IMF-in-Debt-Restructuring-the-Resurgence-of-Austerity-and-the-Urgency-of.

[28] John Clark et.al., *supra* note 21.

[29] IMF, *Zambia: Staff Report for The 2015 Article IV Consultation,* Staff Country Report (Jun. 2015).

[30] *Id.*

[31] *Id.*

[32] IMF, *Zambia: Staff Report for The 2017 Article IV Consultation,* Staff Country Report (Oct. 2017).

[33] IMF, *Zambia: Staff Report for The 2019 Article IV Consultation,* Staff Country Report (Aug. 2019).

Chad has also undergone a wave of austerity following an economic crisis in 2015 resulting from a fall in global oil prices. The country restructured its debt with its main creditor, Glencore in 2015 and 2018. Chad entered an IMF programme in 2017 under which it was advised to cut its expenditure, including the public wage bill, in order to ensure that it met its debt repayment obligations and secured a debt workout from Glencore.[34] Subsequently, it adopted severe austerity measures including cuts to the health and education expenditure which triggered anti-austerity protests in 2018.[35] The following section illustrates that Zambia and Chad are already undertaking austerity measures amidst their debt restructuring negotiations.

4 Austerity in the Context of the Zambia and Chad Debt Restructuring under the G20 Common Framework

This chapter argues that even prior to the conclusion of the negotiations under the Common Framework, there are indications that austerity prescriptions are going to feature in the debt restructurings of Zambia and Chad. It demonstrates that these countries are already implementing austerity during the negotiations with their creditors in order to prove to their willingness to meet their debt repayment obligations and guarantee successful outcomes in the restructuring process.

Debt restructuring under the G20 Common Framework is hinged on negotiation of an IMF loan program,[36] which typically includes austerity measures to secure resources for debt repayments to creditors.[37]

Chad entered a loan arrangement with the IMF in December 2021 which is centered around bringing debt to a sustainable level through restructuring under the Common Framework and a projected four year fiscal consolidation plan.[38] The fiscal adjustment entails cutting expenditure, particularly reducing the wage bill and

---

[34] Amnesty Int'l, *Strangled Budgets, Silenced Dissent: The Human Cost of Austerity Measures in Chad*, AI Index AFR 20/8203/2018 (Jul. 16, 2018).

[35] *Id.*

[36] Group of 20, *supra* note 15.

[37] Daniel Munevar, The G20 "Common Framework for Debt Treatments beyond the DSSI": Is It Bound to Fail? (2020) (various studies have documented trends of austerity in IMF's recent lending including its COVID-19 response); *See, e.g.,* Tamale, *supra* note 24.; Oxfam Wash. Off., *supra* note 24., *and* Munevar, *supra* note 24.

[38] IMF, *supra* note 5.

removal of electricity subsidies.[39] Wage bill reform has been a controversial issue in Chad since the 2016 and 2018 budget cuts which resulted in social discontent and anti-austerity protests.[40] The government signed a three year "social pact" with the public-sector trade unions in October 2021 reinstating the benefits that civil servants lost as a result of expenditure cuts in 2016,[41] which are at stake under the new loan arrangement. Key to note is that even under its COVID-19 loan programme, Chad committed to undertake wage bill reform and reduce its public spending once the pandemic subsided.[42]

Zambia, on the other hand, negotiated a staff level agreement in December 2021 which it is already implementing even though it is pending approval of the Board.[43] The agreement is not available to the public thus the proposed policy measures are shrouded in secrecy, which has raised concern among Zambian nationals.[44] However, shortly before applying to the Common Framework, the government adopted the Zambia Economic Recovery Program 2020–2023 which lays out the country's plan for economic recovery following the pandemic and its 2020 debt default.[45] It includes austerity policies such as cuts in public expenditure, wage cuts,[46] further streamlining of subsidies,[47] and privatization of state owned enterprises.[48] While the contents of

---

[39] *Id.*

[40] Amnesty International, *supra* note 34.

[41] IMF, *supra* note 5.

[42] Nona Tamale, Behind the Numbers: A Dataset on Spending, Accountability, and Recovery Measures Included in the IMF COVID-19 Loans, (2021).

[43] IMF, *Statement by IMF Deputy Managing Director Antoinette M. Sayeh at the Conclusion of her Visit to Zambia,* Press Release No. 22201 (Jun. 16, 2022).

[44] *Options for Equitable Economic Growth and Development in Zambia,* Fight Ineq. Alliance Zam. (Apr. 12, 2022), https://www.fightinequality.org/news/fia-zambia-alternatives-imf.

[45] *See, e.g.,* IMF, *IMF Staff Completes Virtual Mission to Zambia,* Press Release No. 21/50 (Mar. 4, 2021) (the Zambian government consulted with the IMF on their Economic Recovery Plan); *See also* IMF, *IMF Completes High-Level Staff Visit to Zambia,* Press Release No .20/365 (Dec. 9, 2020); *See also* Gov't of the Republic of Zam., Zambia Economic Recovery Programme 2020–2023 (2020).

[46] The plan proposes to reduce administration costs in government operations which can be interpreted to mean wage bill reform.

[47] The plan envisages a reduction in the beneficiaries of the country's agricultural subsidies program, Farmer Input Support Programme (FISP) from 80% to 60%.

[48] Government of the Republic of Zambia, *supra* note 45.

the staff level agreement remain undisclosed, drawing from its recovery plan, it can be concluded that the country is taking the austerity route amidst its restructuring.

There is notable resistance against taking on an IMF programme in Zambia due to concerns that the country will undertake policy reforms akin to those adopted during the 1980's and 1990's economic crisis, including austerity, renown for the devastating impact on the socio-economic well being of Zambians.[49] Recent studies estimate cuts in government expenditure worth US$ 4 billion by 2026,[50] five times the country's annual health budget.[51] The following part of the chapter discusses the implications of prescribing austerity during debt restructuring for Zambia and Chad.

5 Implications of Austerity Amidst Debt Restructuring

While austerity is often proposed as a means to restoring debt sustainability, this chapter argues that to the contrary, ultimately, these policies are counteractive and could instead keep countries in a cyclical trap of indebtedness. Austerity policies have been linked to increased inequality,[52] with research by the IMF concluding that fiscal consolidation can result in falls in income and employment in the short-term, with a risk of substantial rise in long-term unemployment.[53] Taking the austerity path thus raises the risk of further prolonging economic recovery from the COVID-19 pandemic for Zambia and Chad and slowing their progress in achieving their socio-economic development targets, including under the Sustainable Development Goals Agenda 2030 and the African Union's Agenda 2063.

The UN Basic Principles on Sovereign Debt Restructuring Processes (UN Basic Principles) are instructive on debt sustainability during sovereign debt restructuring workouts. The aim of good faith restructuring is to arrive at "a prompt and durable re-establishment of debt sustainability and debt servicing."[54] It is imperative to note at this point that restructuring under the Common Framework is reliant on a debt

---

[49] FIGHT INEQ. ALLIANCE ZAM., *supra* note 44.

[50] *Id.* (IMF projects that that public expenditure will drop from 31% of GDP to 21% of GDP by 2026).

[51] MATTHEW MARTIN, THE CRISIS OF EXTREME INEQUALITY IN SADC: FIGHTING AUSTERITY AND THE COVID-19 PANDEMIC, (2022).

[52] Laurence Ball, et al., *The Distributional Effects of Fiscal Consolidation,* (IMF Working Paper WP/13/151, 2013).

[53] *Id.; See also* Laurence Ball, et al., *Painful Medicine,* 48 IMF FIN. AND DEV. 20 (2011).

[54] U.N. Charter art. 2, ¶ 1–5.

sustainability analysis (DSA) undertaken by the IMF and World Bank. These have been widely critiqued for focusing primarily on economic considerations (a country's capacity to service its debt obligations), disregarding other sustainability criteria, including investment in SDGs and climate needs.[55] In adopting austerity measures, the focus is predominantly on ensuring repayment of debt, negating the broader debt sustainability concerns, economic and social costs of austerity as well as the human rights implications.

Literature over the last three decades has publicized the negative impact of austerity policies on the lives of Africans. Studies have demonstrated that these measures disproportionately affect the most vulnerable and marginalized groups who heavily rely on public services and social protection programmes[57] including the poor,[58] women,[59] persons with disabilities, older persons and children.[60] Austerity inhibits

---

[55] Human Rights Council Rep. 20/23 at ¶ 65 (April 10, 2011); *See also* ULRICH VOLZ, ET AL., ADDRESSING THE DEBT CRISIS IN THE GLOBAL SOUTH: DEBT RELIEF FOR SUSTAINABLE RECOVERIES, THINK7 (2022); *See also* Karina Patricio, *Reforming the International Monetary Fund's Debt Sustainability Assessments Towards Achieving the UN's Sustainable Development Goals (SDGs): A Crucial Post-Pandemic Recovery Agenda,* 2 AFR. J. OF INT'L ECON. L. 32 (2021); *See* Magalie Masamba, The Pressing Call for an International Debt Restructuring Framework and the Potential Gains its Creation will have for African Countries, (Jul. 21, 2022) (unpublished article) (this article discusses incorporating human rights into the definition of debt sustainability).

[56] *See* John Clark et. al., *supra* note 21; Rose Wanjiru, IMF Policies and Their Impact on Education, Health and Women's Rights in Kenya: The Fallacies and Pitfalls of the IMF Policies, (2009), *and* Amnesty Int'l, *supra* note 34.

[57] Rep. of the Independent Expert on the Effects of Foreign Debt and Other Related International Financial Obligations of States on the Full Enjoyment of All Human Rights, Particularly Economic, Social and Cultural Rights, U.N. Doc. A/67/304 (Aug. 13, 2012); *See also* Cephas Lumina & Nona Tamale, *Sovereign Debt and Human Rights: A Focus on Sub-Saharan Africa,* AFR. SOVEREIGN DEBT JUST. NETWORK PAPER SERIES (2021).

[58] Busi Sibeko, *The Cost of Austerity: Lessons for South Africa,* (Inst for Econ. Just. Working Paper Series, No. 2, 2018); *See also* Thomas Stubbs et al., *Poverty, Inequality, and the International Monetary Fund: How Austerity Hurts the Poor and Widens Inequality,* (Glob. Econ. Governance Initiative Working Paper 46, 2021).

[59] *See* Rep. of the Independent Expert on the Effects of Foreign Debt and Other Related International Financial Obligations of States on the Full Enjoyment of All Human Rights, Particularly Economic, Social and Cultural Rights on the Impact of Economic Reforms and Austerity Measures on Women's Human Rights, U.N. Doc. A/73/179 (Jul. 18, 2018); *See also* Kate Donald & Nicolas Lusiani, *The Gendered Costs of Austerity: Assessing the IMF's Role in Budget Cuts Which Threaten Women's Rights,* BRETTON WOODS PROJECT (2017).

[60] *See e.g.,* Nona Tamale, *surpa* note 24.

the enjoyment of social and economic rights of citizens of borrower countries who bear the consequences of budget cuts in crucial sectors such as health and education, wage cuts and removal of subsidies and other regressive measures.[61] Infringements of civil and political rights such freedom of assembly and expression have also been reported especially during anti-austerity protests frequently quashed by governments,[62] often with use of violence.[63]

Sovereign debt restructuring literature has highlighted the conflicting interests of creditors and citizens of debtor governments. Particularly, the property rights of creditors at stake when governments fail to meet their debt obligations vis a vis the human rights of citizens infringed upon when governments adopt retrogressive measures.[64] Masamba argues that a balance is required in managing the conflicts of the two groups during debt restructuring.[65] I agree and argue that resolving debt problems through austerity tips the scale even more towards creditors' interests (freeing resources to ensure payment of their claims) at the cost of citizens of borrower countries who are forced to shoulder the devastating effects of austerity, moving further away from the possibility of achieving such balance.

Central to balancing of interests is the principle of shared responsibility between creditors and borrowers to achieve debt sustainability which is recognized in various sovereign debt soft law instruments, including the G20 Operational Guidelines for

---

[61] Rep. of the United Nations High Commissioner for Human Rights, U.N. Doc. E-2013-82 (May 13, 2013).

[62] Amnesty International, *supra* note 34 (the report covers the anti-austerity protests in Chad in 2018. Other African countries in which anti-austerity protests have been held include: Cote d' Ivoire (1990), Sudan (1985), Tunisia (1983), Morocco (1980s), Mauritania, Algeria). See David Seddon & Leo Zeilig, Class and Protest in Africa: New Waves, 32 REV. OF AFR. POL. ECON. 9 (2005); *See also* Tafadzwa Maganga, *Youth Demonstrations and their Impact on Political Change and Development in Africa*, ACCORD (Aug. 20, 2020), https://www.accord.org.za/conflict-trends/youth-demonstrations-and-their-impact-on-political-change-and-development-in-africa/.

[63] Amnesty International, *supra* note 34.

[64] Magalie Masamba, *Sovereign Debt Restructuring and Human Rights: Overcoming a False Binary*, in COVID-19 AND SOVEREIGN DEBT: THE CASE OF SADC, (Daniel Bradlow & Magalie Masamba eds., 2022).

[65] *Id*

Sustainable Financing.[66] Lumina argues that shared responsibility imposes joint obligations on both creditors and borrowers: i) ensure that their lending and borrowing does not result in unsustainable debt burdens and ii) mutual accountability for their role in creating debt problems.[67] This principle is embodied in the UNCTAD Principles on Promoting Responsible Sovereign Lending and Borrowing which require creditors to make responsible lending decisions."[68]

I argue that requiring debtor countries to take the austerity path during restructuring, as evidence that the country is working towards managing its fiscal situation to resolve its debt problem, demonstrates a reluctance to recognize the shared responsibility by lenders and debtor governments. It also reinforces the narrative that indebtedness is primarily a result of debt mismanagement by borrower countries, a problem which can be rectified by tightening their belts. However, this misses the role that creditors play in creating the debt problem and minimizes their role in its alleviation and ultimately, achieving debt sustainability. Thus, as a result of this narrative, it follows that priority is often given to creditors interests over citizens of debtor countries who are forced to shoulder debilitating austerity measures.

Further, the obvious conflicts between creditors rights and rights of citizens of borrower countries notwithstanding, I argue that in the context of a debt restructuring, both creditors and citizens can be impacted by austerity, albeit at a varying severity. It is in the interest of citizens that public debt is paid back so that their governments can exercise autonomy over their policy making space and increase fiscal space to make investments which benefit them. Conversely, austerity could slow

---

[66] *See* GROUP OF 20, G20 OPERATIONAL GUIDELINES FOR SUSTAINABLE FINANCING, ¶ 3 (2017) ("As emphasized in the Addis Ababa Action Agenda, borrowing countries and lenders, including sovereign lenders, share responsibilities in maintaining debt on a sustainable path." Other instruments include the UNCTAD principles on Promoting Responsible Sovereign Lending and Borrowing (UNCTAD Principles); *See also* Human Rights Council Rep. 20/23 at ¶ 23, 24 (April 10, 2011).

[67] Cephas Lumina, *Sovereign Debt and Human Rights* in Sovereign Debt and Human Rights, (Ilias Bantekas & Cephas Lumina eds. 2019).

[68] UNITED NATIONS CONF. ON TRADE AND DEV., PRINCIPLES OF PROMOTING RESPONSIBLE SOVEREIGN LENDING AND BORROWING 6 (2012) (responsible lending entails undertaking a "realistic assessment of the sovereign borrower's capacity to service a loan based on the best available information and following objective and agreed technical rules on due diligence and national accounts).

down recovery from the pandemic and potentially affect future economic growth, increasing the risk of failure to meet the future repayments to creditors. As such, a borrower country which successfully concludes debt restructuring without imposing harsh austerity policies, has a relatively good opportunity to increase growth and boost recovery by improving its capacity to meet future debt repayments, a win for the creditors.

6 Conclusion

The COVID-19 crisis set back the progress the continent had achieved in alleviating poverty and improving the socio-economic wellbeing of people. In offering debt relief to countries through the Common Framework, it is imperative to tread cautiously and avoid repeating history, particularly prescribing austerity measures whose debilitating impact on the lives of people in Africa over the past decades has been well documented. Austerity is neither inevitable nor the only solution to reducing high debt and deficit levels. Ortiz and Cummins have presented a list of alternatives to austerity through which governments can expand their fiscal space, allowing them to invest in their post pandemic recovery and their development goals and reduce reliance on external debt financing.[69]

---

[69] Isabel Ortiz et al., *supra* note 56 (the proposed alternative financing options include: increasing tax revenues using progressive approaches (wealth taxes, corporate taxes, taxation of the digital economy; curbing illicit financial flows including leakages through tax evasion, tax avoidance and trade misinvoicing; re-allocating public expenditures for instance cutting military expenditure, utilizing fiscal and central bank foreign exchange reserves, where possible; and borrowing on concessional terms).

CHAPTER SEVEN

Covid-19 and Balance-of-Payments in Africa: A Critique of the IMF-WTO Convergence of Roles in the Balance-of-Payments Surveillance of Developing Countries

Akinyi J. Eurallyah*

1 Introduction

The COVID-19 pandemic has caused major economic disruptions and significant adverse impacts on the flow of international trade and investments in Africa.[1] At the same time, the Russian invasion of Ukraine has also shaken the global commodity markets and compounded Africa's already difficult policy outlook.[2] These events are happening at a time when these countries' policy and fiscal space to respond to the resulting shocks is non-existent or minimal, if any.[3] Notably, most of these countries are experiencing surging oil and food prices which are already straining the external and fiscal balances of commodity-importing African countries and have increased food security concerns in the region.[4] Besides, these countries are also facing a decrease of export revenues which consequently exerts a strong pressure on the exchange rate

---

* Phd Candidate, (Sovereign Debt & International Financial Regulation) Schulich Law School, Dalhousie University. Advocate of the High Court of Kenya.
[1] *See generally* African Dev. Bank Group, *Regional Economic Outlook 2021: From Debt Resolution to Growth—The Road Ahead for Africa,* (Mar. 12, 2021), https://www.afdb.org/en/documents/african-economic-outlook-2021.
[2] IMF, *A New Shock and Little Room to Manoeuvre,* Regional Economic Outlook: Sub-Saharan Africa, 1, (Apr. 2022).
[3] *Ibid.*
[4] World Bank, *Global Economic Prospects: Sub-Saharan Africa,* (2022) https://thedocs.worldbank.org/en/doc/cb15f6d7442cadedf75bb95c4fdec1b3-0350012022/related/Global-Economic-Prospects-January-2022-Regional-Overview-SSA.pdf; *See also* Tim Collins, *Economic Outlook 2022: Africa Faces Rickety Rebound,* Africa Business (Jan.10, 2022), https://african.business/2022/01/trade-investment/economic-outlook-2022-africa-faces-rickety-rebound/.

of their national currencies, capital outflow and a sharp decline in international reserves.[5]

Consequently, the region has undertaken appropriate measures to mitigate the impact and prevent the deepening of the economic crisis caused by the pandemic.[6] These measures include providing tax and credit holidays, exemptions from rental charges, as well as sovereign borrowing from foreign sources to provide essential social services.[7] However, the need to finance development programs aimed at supporting the economy in response to the COVID-19 pandemic has resulted in a significant increase in foreign debt among African countries.[8] This means that serious debt challenges on the continent might be looming, and debt defaults such as those of Zambia[9] and Mali[10] as well as lengthy debt resolutions are already a major obstacle to Africa's progress toward sustainable development.

---

[5] *See* Abhijit Mukhopadhyay, *The Search for Sustainable Solutions to Debt Accumulation in Sub-Saharan Africa* OBSERVER RESEARCH FOUNDATION OCCASIONAL PAPER, Feb. 2022, at 1.

[6] *See generally* Olumuyiwa Odedeji, *Pandemic, Debt Accumulation, and a Balance Sheet Approach to Fiscal Analysis in African Countries,* CENTER FOR GLOBAL DEVELOPMENT (Mar. 8, 2022, 9:30 AM) https://www.cgdev.org/publication/pandemic-debt-accumulation-and-balance-sheet-approach-fiscal-analysis-african-countries (During 2020–21, Nigeria implemented 2.4 percent of GDP in various forms of fiscal interventions to contain the economic impact of the virus, and South Africa spent about 6 percent of GDP. Equity, loans, and guarantees were also used in the case of South Africa, amounting to about 4 percent of GDP).

[7] WORLD BANK, *Government Financial Reporting in Times of the COVID-19 Pandemic,* (Oct. 2020) https://openknowledge.worldbank.org/handle/10986/34792; *See also COVID-19 and Africa: Socio-Economic Implications of and Policy Responses,* (OECD 2020).

[8] *See generally Debt Sustainability Analysis (June 2021),* WORLD BANK, https://www.worldbank.org/en/programs/debt-toolkit/dsa [last accessed Jun. 2021].; *see also* François Faure & Perrine Guérin, *Dealing with Africa's Risk of Debt Distress,* 2 BNP PARIBAS ECO CONJUNCTURE 1 (Feb. 2021).

[9] *See* Elliot Smith, *Africa's Reliance on Chinese Loans Has Experts Concerned About More Debt Defaults,* CNBC (Feb. 17, 2021 6:44 AM), https://www.cnbc.com/2021/02/17/africas-reliance-on-chinese-loans-has-experts-concerned-about-more-debt-defaults.html. (Zambia became the first country on the continent to formally default on its debt in November 2020, opting out of a $42.5 million Eurobond repayment).

[10] *See Mali Defaults on Bond Payments Amid Regional Sanctions,* AFRONOMICSLAW (Feb. 5, 2022), https://www.afronomicslaw.org/category/african-sovereign-debt-justice-network-afsdjn/mali-defaults-bond-payments-amid-regional (Mali became the first African country in 2022 to renege on its obligation to service treasury bonds that matured in January 2022 in the value of 15.6 billion CFA (approximately $26.6 million)).

To this end, at least theoretically, the international economic order allows governments to utilise either monetary or trade policy to overcome their debt crisis and balance-of-payment (BOP) challenges, subject to their respective international economic obligations.[11] For example, Article XVIII:2 of the World Trade Organisation's (WTO) General Agreement on Tariff and Trade (GATT) allows developing countries to apply quantitative restrictions for balance-of-payments purposes in a manner which takes full account the continued high level of demand for imports likely to be generated by their programmes of economic development. However, successfully invoking this provision is somewhat problematic for developing countries. This has been nowhere more clearly demonstrated than by the WTO Panel resolution of the dispute between the United States and India.[12] In the wake of a sovereign debt crisis and consequent balance-of-payments challenges on the continent, it is timely to clarify the challenges that African countries (and other developing countries) will face in their attempt to invoke GATT Article XVIII. Against this background, this chapter proceeds as follows: section 2 explores the challenges of sovereign debt, foreign exchange reserves, and balance-of-payments experienced by African countries; section 3 problematises the IMF/WTO relationship and convergence of roles in the balance-of-payments surveillance of developing countries; and finally, section 4 offers concluding remarks.

2.1. *COVID-19 and the Nature of Balance-of-Payments Problems of African Countries*

One of the determining factors of a country's BOP is the sensitivity of that country's economy to external stimuli.[13] Most African countries are characterised by a high degree of dependence on the outside world, shown by the relatively large share of both exports and imports in their gross domestic product (GDP).[14] The region's

---

[11] *See e.g., General* Agreement on Tariffs and Trade 1994, Apr. 15, 1994, 1867 U.N.T.S. 190. (Articles XII and XVIII). [*hereinafter* GATT 1994].

[12] Panel Report, *India —Quantitative Restrictions on Imports of Agricultural, Textile and Industrial Products,* WTO DOC. WT/DS90/R (adopted Apr. 6, 1999) [*hereinafter* India-Quantitative Restrictions case).

[13] *Ibid.;* See also 1 J. E. Meade, *The Theory of International Economic Policy,* 11 (1951).

[14] *See generally* AFR. DEV. BANK GROUP, *Regional Economic Outlook 2021: From Debt Resolution to Growth—The Road Ahead for Africa* (2021)..

dependence on international trade is acute because of the impossibility of obtaining capital goods locally and hence development depends on import of equipment, which in turn must be paid for largely out of export proceeds.[15] The consequence is that this basic structure of production and of foreign trade renders the economic growth of African countries highly sensitive and vulnerable to developments in external trade, unless the countries' production patterns are radically altered by the process of industrialisation.[16]

By way of illustration, fiscal deficits of African countries were estimated at 8.4% of GDP in 2020, having doubled from 4.6% in 2019.[17] This was as a result of the heavy stimulus spending by many countries to mitigate the economic impacts of the COVID-19 pandemic. As shown in Figure 1, the average size of these fiscal stimulus packages as deployed by African governments were about 3% of GDP, even though there are significant variations, from about 32% in Mauritius, 10% in South Africa, and less than 1% in Tanzania.[18]

In addition to the COVID-19-related spending, 2020 fiscal deficits also resulted from revenue shortfalls for oil-exporting companies, reduced tax base as a result of the economic contractions caused by the pandemic, and a sharp decline in both imports and exports.[19] As far as general financial flows from foreign direct investment (FDI), remittances, tourism, portfolio investments, and official development assistance are concerned, AfDB observed that these inflows declined between 2019 and 2020 (Figure 2), mainly as a result of the uncertainty of the investment climate.[20] This decline is broad-based, thereby affecting all sectors, including tourism, leisure, energy,

---

[15] Evita Schmieg, *Global Trade and African Countries: Free Trade Agreements, WTO and Regional Integration,* (SWP Berlin, Working Paper No. 2, 2016).

[16] *Ibid.*

[17] *See generally* African Development Bank, *supra* note 14. (These fiscal measures comprised above-the-line budgetary support by way of investments in health systems, expansion of social protection programs, as well as private sector support through tax reliefs and other below-the line measures such as business guarantees for the ailing ones).

[18] *Ibid* at 17.

[19] *Ibid.*

[20] *See* African Development Bank, *supra* note 14, at 18-20; *See also* IMF, *supra* note 2, at 5. (For example, FDI flows declined by 18% from approximately $45 billion in 2019 to approximately $37 billion in 2020. Likewise, portfolio investments reversed in 2020 from a net inflow of $23 billion in 2019 to a net outflow of $27 billion in 2020 mainly because of liquidation by investors on their investments in search of safer

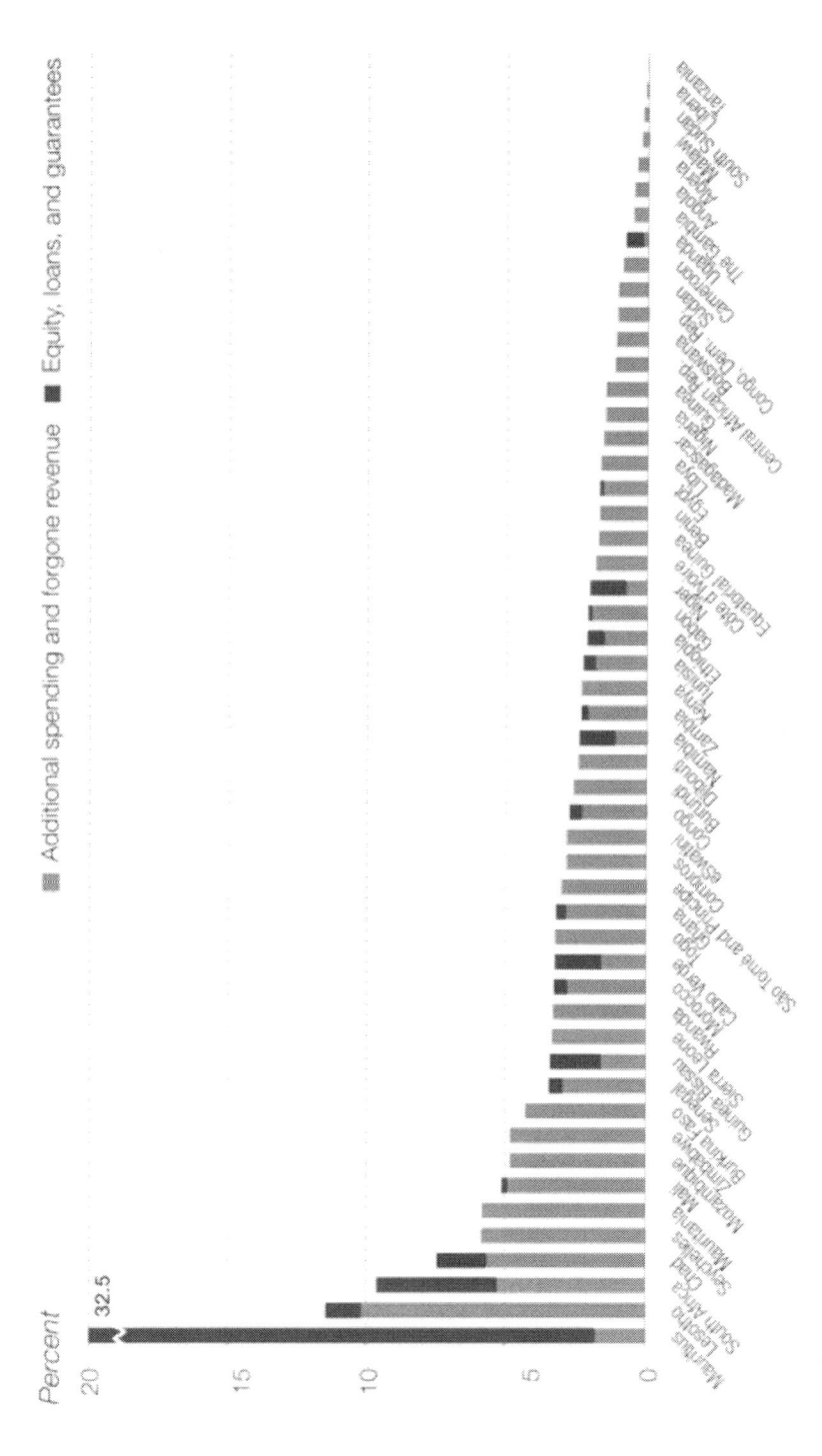

FIGURE 1 Above-the-line measures and liquidity support of African Countries, 2020. (Source: AfDB calculations based on IMF Fiscal Affairs Department database)

aviation, hospitality, and manufacturing.[21] Consequently, the external positions of these countries significantly deteriorated during the pandemic but were expected to recover, with the overall current account deficit for Africa estimated at 5.5% of GDP in 2020, narrowing to 4.1% of GDP in 2021, and further down to 2.7% in 2022.[22] The narrowing largely reflected the expected recovery of GDP and of Africa's major commodity exports. Weak domestic demand and fewer capital projects were also expected to lower import demand in the medium term.[23]

In yet another shock that exacerbates Africa's BOP challenges, the Russian invasion of Ukraine has shaken global commodity markets, consequently resulting in geopolitical tensions.[24] For example, the war has prompted a surge in commodity prices by disrupting energy and food exports from Russia and Ukraine (Figure 3).

Although this may result in a windfall gain for some large commodity African exporters of oil, copper, gold, diamonds, and palladium, rising commodity prices are seriously undermining fiscal and external balances in commodity-importing African countries, while also threatening food security and energy affordability for the

---

assets elsewhere. Similarly, AfDB estimates that official development assistance decreased by 10% in 2020, from $52.88 billion in 2019 to $47.59 billion in 2020. Moreover, remittances—the most significant source of external financial inflows to Africa, had been increasing until the inception of the pandemic in 2020. However, they too declined from $85.8 billion in 2019 to $78.3 billion in 2020, with countries such as Lesotho, Mozambique, Cabo Verde, Mauritius, and Seychelles being the most hit. As far as tourism is concerned, Africa had the second-fasted growing tourism sector before the pandemic, accounting for 8.5% of the continent's GDP. With the halting of international tourism in 2020 as a result of the pandemic, international tourist arrivals dropped by 98% between April and June 2020 as compared to the same period in 2019. Aviation was not spared either, with the International Air Transportation Association estimating that Africa's aviation industry lost $2 billion in 2020).

[21] African Development Bank, *supra* note 14, at 19.

[22] *Ibid* at 20.

[23] *Ibid.* (The projected improvement in current account balances is, however, particularly uncertain for countries with contact-intensive sectors such as tourism, hospitality, entertainment, and transportation).

[24] *See* IMF, supra note 2, at 2. (IMF acknowledges the modest direct links between Sub-Saharan Africa and Russia and Ukraine, making up less than 2.5% of the region's total trade with the outside world. The modest direct links notwithstanding, the war has and continues to affect the region through its effect on global commodity prices).

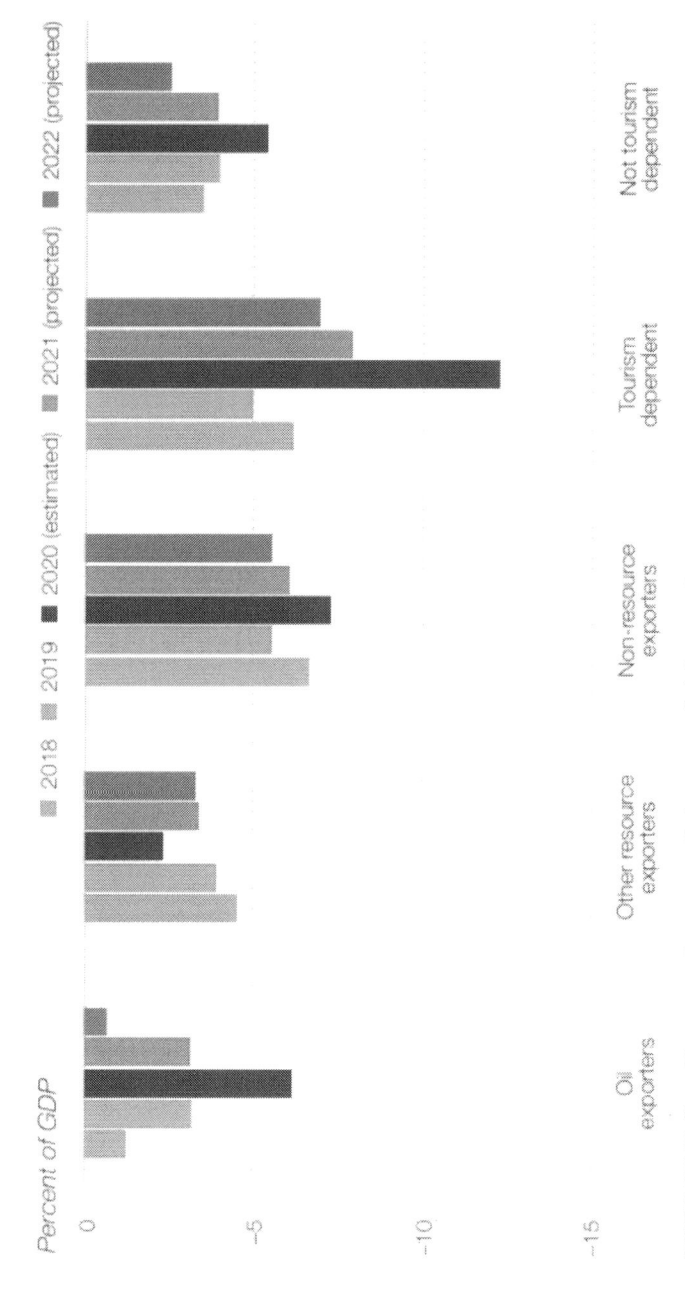

FIGURE 2 Current Account Balances of African Countries by Economic Region, 2018–2022. (Source: *African Development Bank REO 2021*)

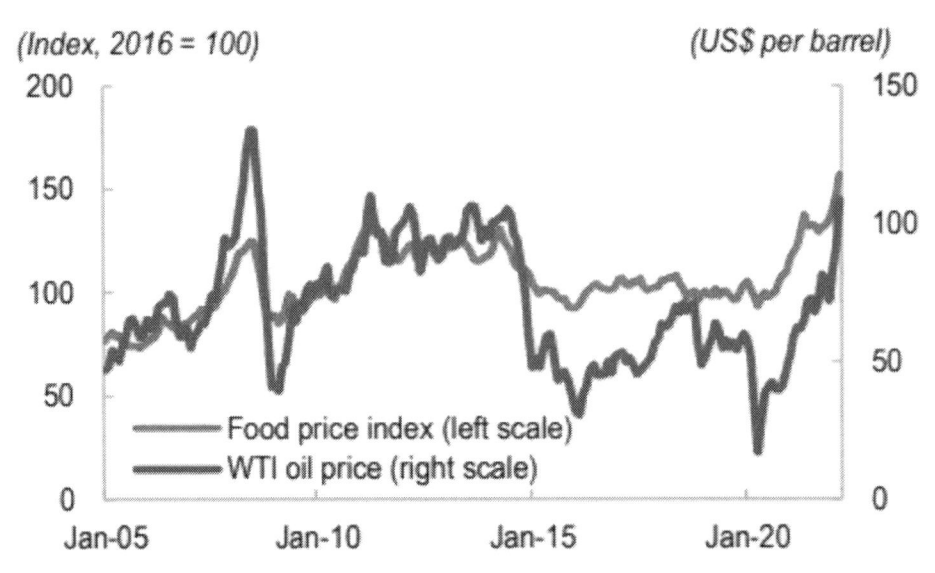

FIGURE 3 Commodity Prices, 2005–2022. Note: WTI = West Texas Intermediate (*Source: African Development Bank REO 2021*)

continent's most vulnerable populations.[25] The aftermath of increased oil and gas prices, especially for 37 non-oil-exporting African countries, is the massive negative terms-of-trade shock—which has (and will continue to) worsened trade balances, increased transport and living costs, and deteriorated fiscal balances, particularly for those with fuel subsidies.[26]

Looking beyond April 2022, the IMF projects that an escalation in geopolitical tensions between Russia and the West, as well as the continuation of the war in Ukraine, compounded with restrictions on imports from Russia will potentially place additional upward strain on food and energy prices.[27] This will weigh heavily on the continent's commodity-importing countries, thereby exacerbating social

---

[25] *See generally* IMF, *supra* note 2, at 2. (Sub-Saharan Africa imports almost 85% of its wheat, with some sourcing a large proportion of their imports from either Russia or Ukraine. This makes them very vulnerable to global disruptions in supply of these food products. The top 8 wheat importers in Africa are Tanzania, Cote d'Ivoire, Senegal, Mozambique, Angola, Ethiopia, Kenya, and South Africa).

[26] *Ibid.* (For oil importers, IMF estimates that the crisis will increase the region's import bill by almost $19 billion, even as they are expected to experience a 0.8% deterioration of their fiscal balances, in comparison to October 2021, twice the average of all oil importing countries).

[27] *Ibid.* at 6.

tensions, increasing global risk aversion, and raising borrowing costs, especially for countries with more precarious fiscal positions.[28] The region is also vulnerable due to a slowdown in China, which accounts for more than 20% of sub-Saharan Africa's exports.[29] To the IMF, over the medium term, most countries will need to continue fiscal consolidation in order to reduce debt vulnerabilities and boost resilience while protecting development spending.

2.2. COVID-19, Dwindling Foreign Exchange Reserves, and Sovereign Debt in Africa

Figure 4 below shows how growing debt levels and debt service burdens have also narrowed the available fiscal space for African countries, exacerbating their strains on debt sustainability.[30] According to the AfDB, debt service burdens accounted for

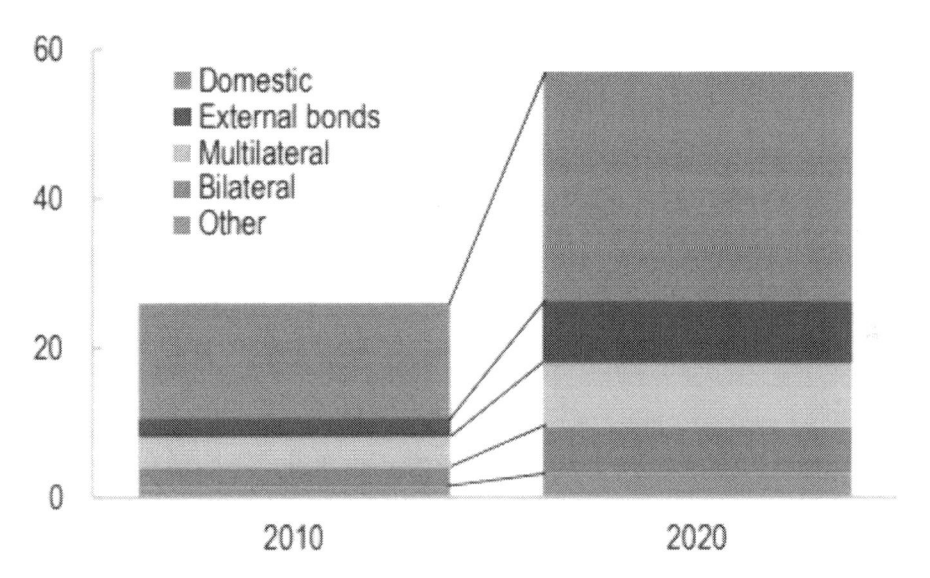

FIGURE 4 Composition of Public Debt of Sub-Saharan Africa as a % of GDP, 2010–2020 (SOURCES: World Bank International Debt Statistics; IMF World Economic Outlook database)

---

[28] Ibid.
[29] Ibid.
[30] See generally African Development Bank, supra note 14.

more than 20% of tax revenues for many African countries. The increasing debts have left most African countries in debt distress (Figure 5). However, in 2020, the AfDB projected that the temporary debt service suspension initiative, its successor G20 Common Framework for Debt Treatments beyond DSSI and other emergency budget supports offered by multilateral institutions would give the countries some breathing space to alleviate some financing constraints (Figure 6).[31] However, contrary to this projection, the reality on the ground has been demoralising.[32] For example, after

(Number of countries)

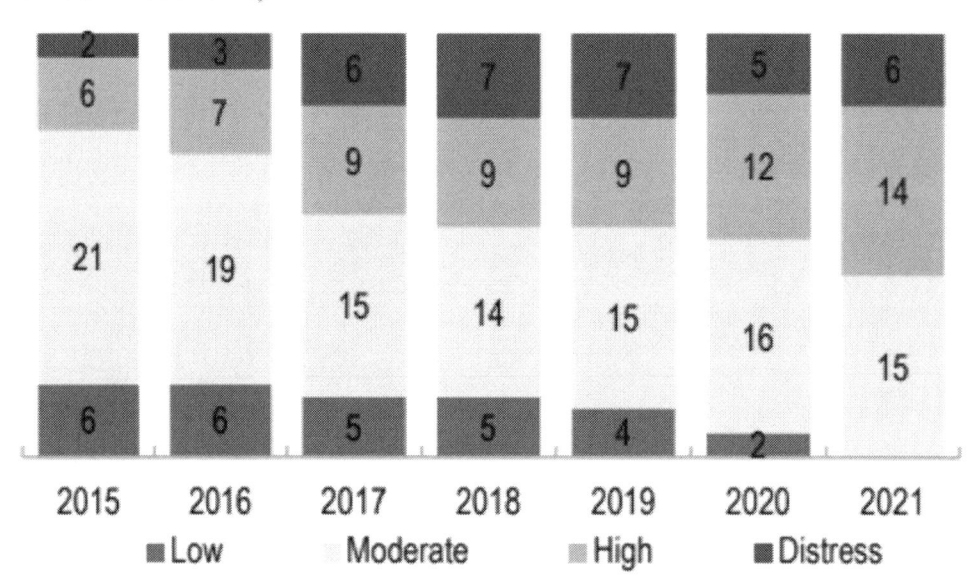

FIGURE 5 Debt Risk Status of Sub-Saharan Africa for PRGT Eligible LIDC, 2015–2021. Note: PRGT = Poverty reduction and growth trust; LIDC = Low-income developing countries (*Source: IMF, Debt Sustainability Analysis Low-Income Developing Countries database*)

---

[31] African Development Bank, *supra* note 14, at 17.
[32] William N Kring, *The failures of the G20's Debt Service Suspension Initiative*, East Asia Forum (Sept. 7, 2021), https://www.eastasiaforum.org/2021/09/07/the-failures-of-the-g20s-debt-service-suspension-initiative/.

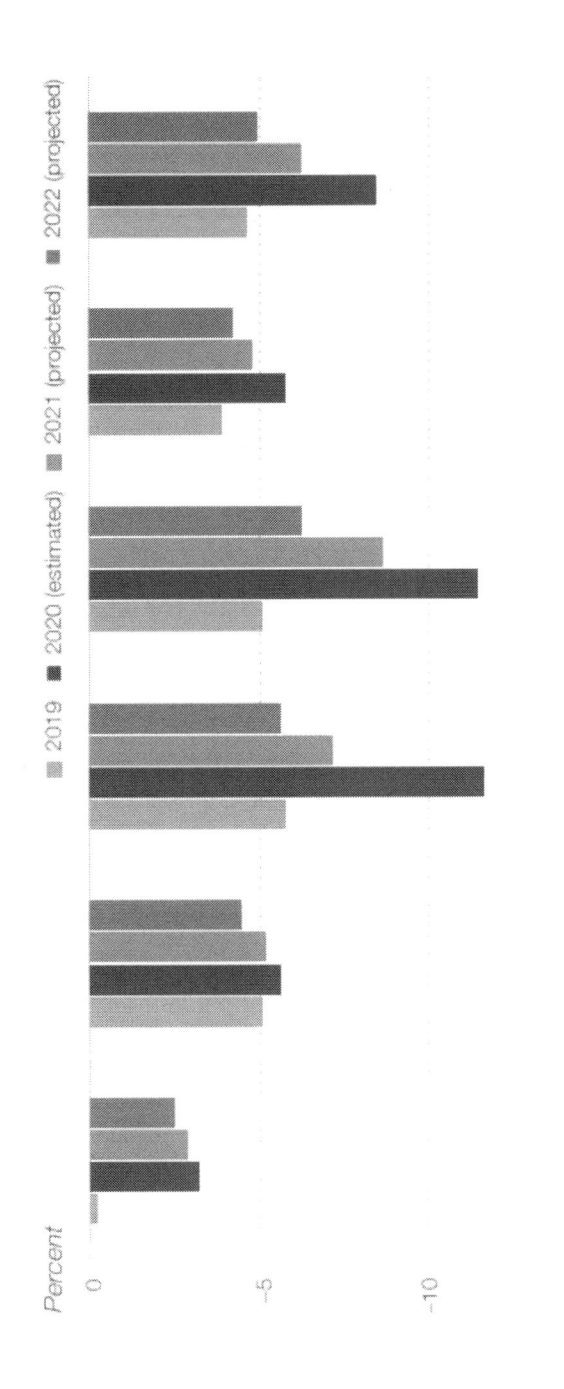

FIGURE 6 Fiscal Balance to GDP of African Countries by Region, 2019–2022. (Source: *African Development Bank*)

the expiry of the DSSI in 2021, many African countries have experienced loan payment spikes which have been exacerbated by the IMF's austerity measures.[33]

The foregoing notwithstanding, according to AfDB, the Continent's current account has primarily been driven by trade deficits and net factor payments abroad[34] and significantly bolstered by current transfers, including remittance inflows and foreign aid.[35] Figure 7 below gives a historiographical account of the region's current account balance decomposition between 2000 and 2019. Import covers by countries' foreign exchange reserves plummeted as a result of depletion of their external reserves to finance pandemic-related expenses, with external buffers as a percentage of GDP falling in 31 of the 52 African countries between 2019 and 2020 (Figure 8). Depleting buffers might lead to foreign exchange shortages, which could put further depreciation pressures on a country's exchange rate and undermine its ability to service debt denominated in a foreign currency.

This shows how efforts to offset exchange rate pressures led to a conspicuous drop in external reserves in many Sub-Saharan African countries. However, the forex status slightly improved in late 2020 as shown in Figure 9 below due to a slight injection of liquidity to countries in the form of special drawing rights. The downside of the SDR is that the formula for its allocation is based on a country's quota, meaning that richer countries receive more SDR than poorer ones.[36] Shockingly, barely 3%

---

[33] James Thuo Gathii, *Sovereign Debt as a Mode of Colonial Governance: Past, Present, and Future Possibilities*, JUST MONEY (May 13, 2022), https://justmoney.org/james-thuo-gathii-sovereign-debt-as-a-mode-of-colonial-governance-past-present-and-future-possibilities/; *See also* UNICEF EASTERN AND SOUTHERN.

[34] Net factor payments abroad are the value of earnings on foreign investments less payments to foreign investors.

[35] African Development Bank, *supra* note 14, at 22.

[36] Ali Zafar, Jan Muench, & Aloysius Uche Ordu, *SDRs for COVID-19 Relief: The Good, the Challenging, and the Uncertain*, BROOKINGS (Oct. 21, 2021), https://www.brookings.edu/blog/africa-in-focus/2021/10/21/sdrs-for-covid-19-relief-the-good-the-challenging-and-the-uncertain/; *See also*, AFRODAD, *Civil Society Organisations Call for Principles for Fair Channelling of Special Drawing Rights: Open Letter to G20 Finance Ministers, Central Bank Governors, and the IMF,* (Sept. 20, 2021), https://afrodad.orgcivil-society-organizations-call-for-principles-for-fair-channeling-of-special-drawing-rights/?utm_source=rss&utm_medium=rss&utm_campaign=civil-society-organizations-call-for-principles-for-fair-channeling-of-special-drawing-rights.

FIGURE 7 Africa's Current Account Balance Decomposition, 2000–2019. (Source: *African Development Bank REO 2021*)

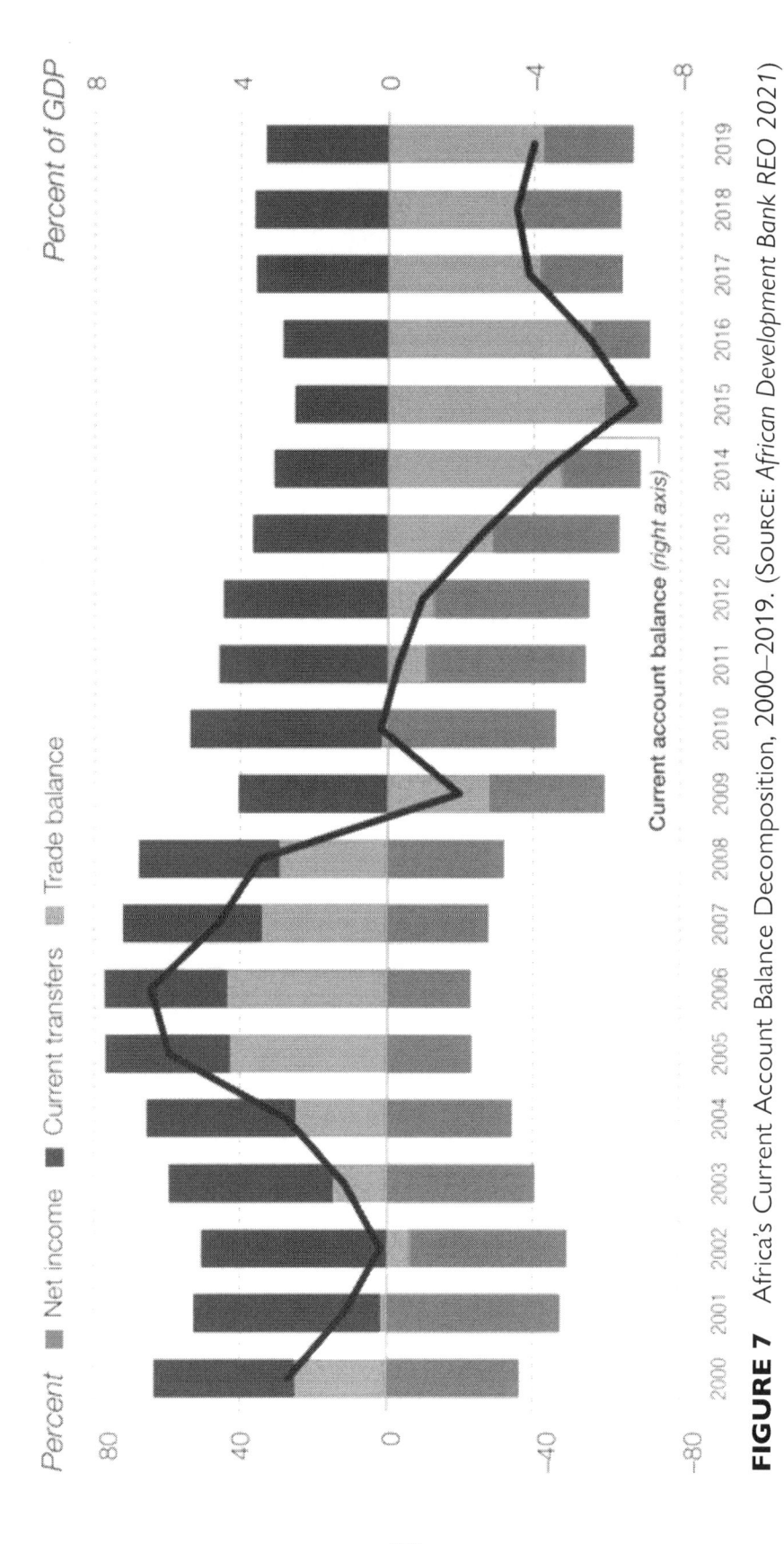

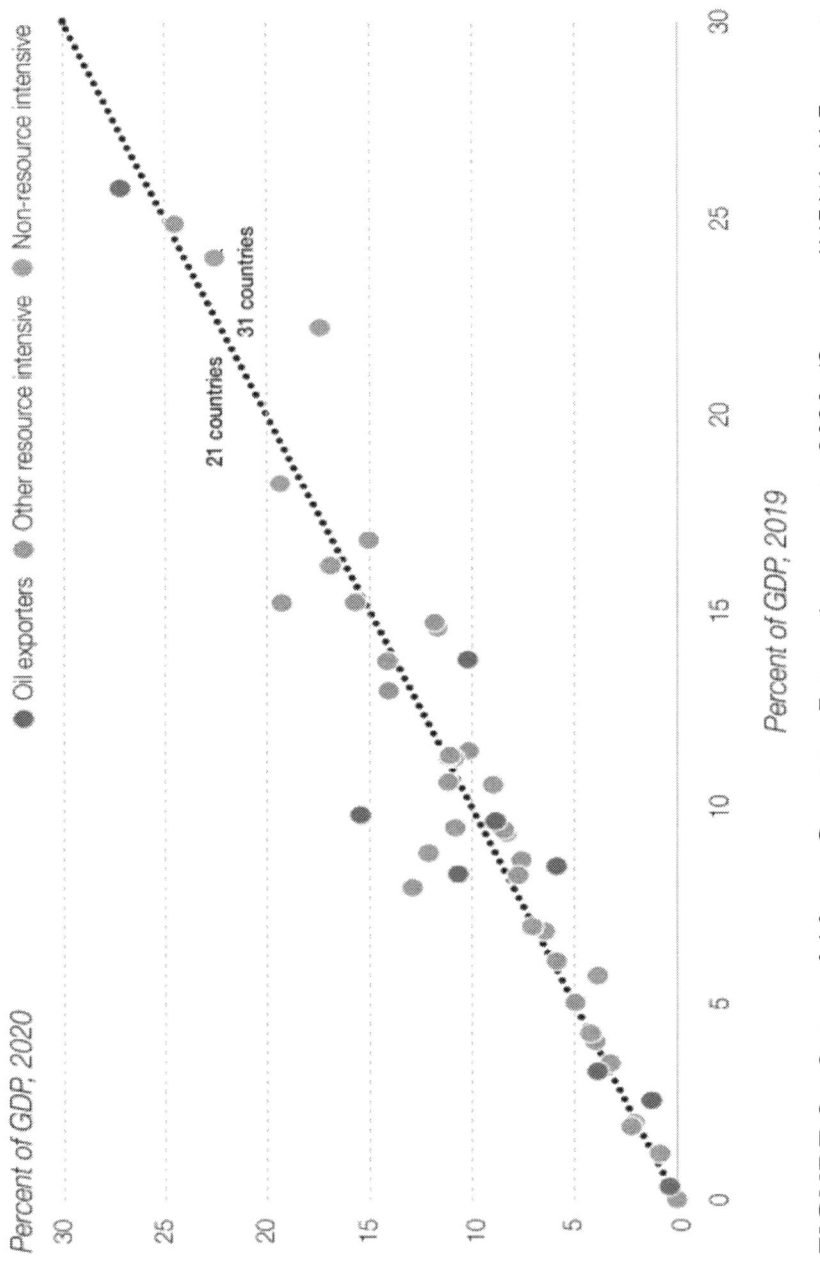

FIGURE 8 Status of African Countries External reserves in 2020. (SOURCE: *IMF World Economic Outlook database*)

(Months of imports)

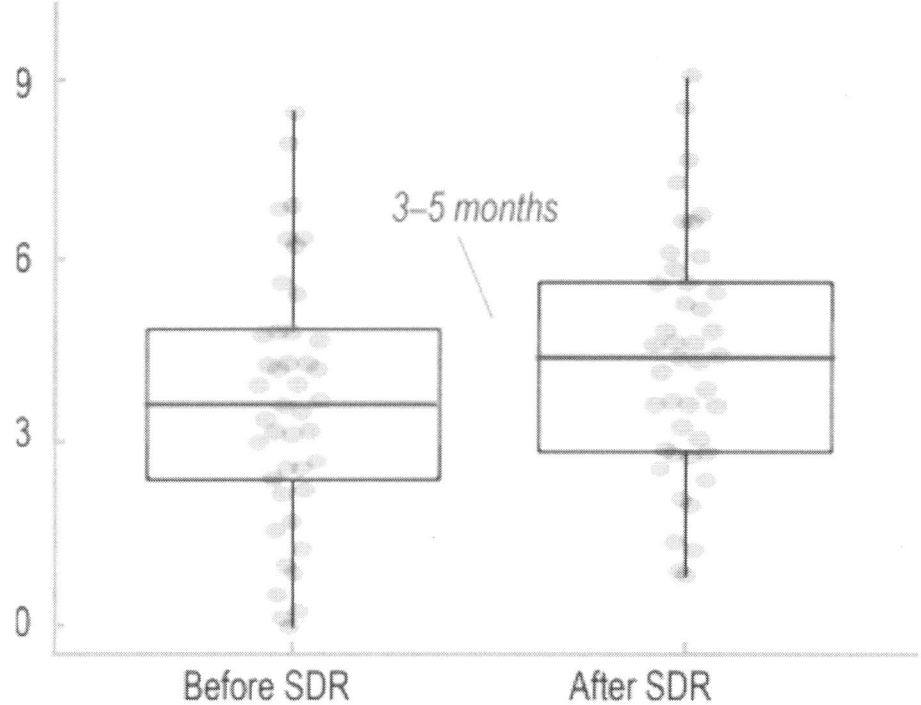

FIGURE 9 Status of African Countries' International Reserves, 2021. Note: SDR = *Special drawing rights* (SOURCE: *IMF Regional Economic Outlook 2022—Sub-Saharan Africa*)

of the $650 billion in pandemic response was allocated to low-income developing countries, with approximately 30% going to emerging frontiers.[37] Simply put, those countries that needed liquidity the most barely benefitted from the relief.

Nonetheless, the 2021 SDR allocation was most timely by strengthening countries' external positions besides providing resources for urgent spending programs. However, for a large portion of sub-Saharan Africa, their reserve levels are still uncomfortably low, with many countries still falling short of the standard import-cover

---

[37] *Ibid.*

benchmark.[38] For example, there is already increased concern that Kenya is spending more of its already dwindled forex reserves for imports and to service its national debt.[39] At the same time, Kenya has raised several Eurobonds to fund the fast-depleting forex reserves, further adversely exacerbating the country's debt burden.[40] This shows how with low interest rates emerging countries ramped up their dollar-denominated borrowing. However, the debt is serviced from forex earnings, and with dwindling earnings, especially as a result of the tightened monetary policies of the US Federal Reserve, the increased interest rates equally increase the debt servicing burdens of the borrowing countries.[41] With dwindling external reserves, it is impossible to pay for the required imports of goods and services, and the country may also default on its debt service obligations, just like Mali and Zambia.[42]

Despite the foregoing gloomy BOP situation, some scholars have contended that African countries do not have BOP problems, and instead have BOP deficits that

---

[38] *See* Jochen Schanz, *Foreign Exchange Reserves in Africa: Benefits, Costs, and Political Economy Considerations,* 105 BIS PAPERS (2019). (There is no unique framework for assessing reserve adequacy, but import cover is often the prime motive for maintaining reserves in the region and 3 to 5 months is a common standard).; *See also* Olivier Jeanne & Damiano Sandri, *Optimal Reserves in Financially Closed Economies,* (IMF Working Paper WP 16/92, 2016).

[39] Eric Olander, *Kenya's Weakening Currency is Pushing Up the Costs of Imports and Debt Servicing Costs,* THE CHINA-GLOBAL SOUTH PROJECT (Mar. 2, 2022), https://chinaglobalsouth.com/2022/03/02/kenyas-weakening-currency-is-pushing-up-the-cost-of-imports-and-debt-servicing-costs/.

[40] David Herbling, *Kenya Presses on with Eurobond Plan as Yields Rise,* BLOOMBERG (May 11, 2022 5:02 AM), https://www.bloomberg.com/news/articles/2022-05-11/kenya-in-a-corner-presses-on-with-eurobond-plan-as-yields-rise#xj4y7vzkg.; Victor Amadala, *IMF Loan, Eurobond Boosts Kenya's Forex reserves by 76 Billion,* THE STAR (Jun. 28, 2021 8:38 AM), https://www.the-star.co.ke/business/kenya/2021-06-28-imf-loan-eurobond-boosts-kenyas-forex-reserves-by-sh76-billion/; Misheck Mutize, *African Governements have Developed a Taste for Eurobonds: Why it's Dangerous,* THE CONVERSATION (Aug. 5, 2021 11:11 AM), https://theconversation.com/african-governments-have-developed-a-taste-for-eurobonds-why-its-dangerous-165469.

[41] Dominik Leusder, *The Third World Debt Crisis Reveals the Rot at the Heart of the Global Economy,* JACOBIN (Jun. 6, 2022), https://jacobin.com/2022/06/developing-world-dollar-debt-crisis-inflation.

[42] Shin-ichi Fukuda & Yoshifumi Kon, *Macroeconomic Impacts of Foreign Exchange Reserve Accumulation: Theory and International Evidence* (Asian Dev. Bank Inst., Working Paper No. 197, 2010).

[43] ERIN E. JUCKER-FLEETWOOD, MONEY AND FINANCE IN FRICA: THE EXPERIENCE OF GHANA, MOROCCO, NIGERIA, THE RHODESIAS AND NYASALAND, THE SUDAN, AND TUNISIA FROM THE ESTABLISHMENT OF THEIR CENTRAL BANKS UNTIL 1962, Chapter XXV (1964).

are innocuous if covered in time by external loans and grants.[43] However, this assertion has been challenged by other scholars who have made it clear that indeed most African countries have BOP problems, otherwise known as structural disequilibria.[44] Structural disequilibrium could result from accommodated unplanned deficits or exigent unplanned deficits.[45] On the one hand, accommodated unplanned deficits occur when the excess of autonomous outpayments over autonomous in-payments arising out of inadvertent action by the country, is readily financed by an inflow of foreign capital such as grants or loans.[46]

On the other, exigent unplanned deficits arise from the inadvertent action of the country, which cannot be readily annihilated through accommodating finance, thereby calling for emergency measures such as quantitative import and export restrictions, and equilibrating measures such as manipulation of the exchange rate and the level of internal prices, costs, and incomes.[47] Both deficits can be temporary or chronic, or even transitional resulting from force majeure acts such as droughts, pandemics, crop failures, or other seasonal irregularities, or the continuing disequilibrium in the structure and growth of exports and imports[48] as has always been the situation in African countries' economies, exacerbated by the COVID-19 pandemic. Both accommodated unplanned deficits or exigent unplanned deficits can either be innocuous or harmful, depending on the temporary or chronic nature of the deficit. Therefore, with the foregoing African countries' BOP statistics, there should be no doubt that recent and current developments in the balance-of-payments of many African countries are actually balance-of-payments problems which are harmful and need to be addressed.

The foregoing notwithstanding, perhaps the question we should be asking is, how possible is it for African countries—and the larger network of Third World countries—to address their BOP problems within the extant international BOP landscape?

---

[44] Osman Hashim Abdel-Salam, *Balance-Of-Payments Problems of African Countries,* 4 J. OF MOD. AFR. STUD. 155 (1966).
[45] Econ. Comm'n for Afr., Economic Bulleting for Africa, U.N. Doc. E /CN.14/400 (1966).
[46] *Ibid.* at 2.
[47] *Ibid.*
[48] A disequilibrium in the structure and growth of exports and imports is an economic situation where the actual propensity to import is higher than the ability to export.

3.1. The IMF/WTO Convergence of Roles in the Balance-of-Payments Surveillance

The IMF's Articles of Agreement and the WTO's Agreements[49] provide the legal basis for cooperation between the IMF and the WTO as far as BOP is concerned. At the WTO, the primary legal provisions governing balance-of-payments are contained in Articles XII, XV, and XVIII of the General Agreement on Tariffs and Trade (GATT), 1994. Article XV of the GATT 1994 is the cornerstone of the IMF/WTO legal relationship on matters concerning trade in goods. It sets out the WTO obligation to consult with the IMF as well as the scope and effect of such consultation. For context, Article XI GATT generally prohibits its Member States from maintaining quantitative import and export restrictions. However, in order to safeguard its external financial position and its balance-of-payments, a Member State may restrict the quantity or value of merchandise permitted to be imported.

Nevertheless, in order to pursue a co-ordinated policy with regard to exchange questions within the jurisdiction of the IMF and questions of quantitative restrictions and other trade measures within the WTO jurisdiction, the WTO must seek co-operation with the IMF.[50] Put differently, in the event the WTO is called upon to consider the problems concerning monetary reserves, balance-of-payments or foreign exchange arrangements, it must consult *fully* with the IMF.[51] The plain meaning of the statement "the WTO *shall consult fully with the IMF*" creates a binding obligation on the WTO Members to consult with the IMF on matters concerning monetary reserves, balance-of-payments or foreign exchange arrangements.[52] Such consultation is done at the institutional level, with the point of contact at the IMF being the Executive Board. This requirement, however, is "one-sided" not only because there is no corresponding requirement on the IMF, but also because it does not per se impose on the IMF the obligation to respond.[53] However, this was remedied by the IMF/WTO

---

[49] *See e.g.,* GATT 1994 *supra* note 11; General Agreement on Trade in Services, Apr. 15, 1994, Marrakesh Agreement Establishing the World Trade Organization, Annex 1B, 1869 U.N.T.S. 183 at 293–294. [*hereinafter* GATS 1994].

[50] *Ibid.* at 296.

[51] *Ibid.*

[52] Deborah E. Siegel, *Legal Aspects of the IMF/WTO Relationship: The Fund's Articles of Agreement and the WTO Agreements,* 96 AM. J. OF INT'L L. 561, 561–599 (2002).

[53] *Ibid.* at 569.; *See also* Frieder Roessler, *Selective Balance-of-Payments Adjustment Measures Affecting Trade: The Roles of the GATT and the IMF,* 9 J. WORLD TRADE L. 622, 622–644 (1975).

Cooperation Agreement which serves as, inter alia, the source of the IMF's obligation to respond to WTO's consultation request.[54]

On the face of it, it seems that the effect of the WTO's consultation with the IMF is that the WTO is required to *accept* determinations of statistical and other facts presented by the IMF relating to foreign exchange, monetary reserves and balance-of-payments.[55] It also seems that the WTO is to accept the determination of the IMF as to whether an action of a WTO Member in exchange matters is in accordance with the IMF's Articles of Agreement, or with the terms of a special exchange agreement between that WTO Member and the WTO. However, Article XV:2 does not require the WTO to accept any of the IMF's views; rather, it identifies factual findings within the IMF's assigned competence, such as balance-of-payments, and legal determinations by the IMF concerning consistency of exchange measures with the Articles of Agreement.[56]

In sum, given the legal consequences for the WTO as to whether or not a balance-of-payment measure is consistent with the IMF's Articles of Agreement, the IMF agreed in the Cooperation Agreement to "inform the WTO of any decisions approving restrictions on the making of payments or transfers for current international transactions, as well as participate in consultations carried out by the WTO Committee on Balance-of-Payments Restrictions on measures taken by a WTO member to safeguard its balance-of-payments"[57]

4.1. Developing Countries, the Challenge of the IMF/WTO Relationship on Balance-of-Payments Surveillance, and the Legacy of India Quantitative Restriction Case

Historically, developing countries have utilised their right to impose quantitative restrictions for balance-of-payments purposes.[58] Since 1995, however, the

---

[54] Agreement Between the International Monetary Fund and the World Trade Organization, Dec. 9, 1996, at ¶13 reprinted in Selected Decisions and Selected Documents of the International Monetary Fund, 877 (Forty-Second Issue, 2021). [*hereinafter* Agreement Between the IMF and WTO].
[55] GATT 1994 *supra* note 11, at art. 15 ¶2.
[56] Siegel *supra* note 52, at 570.
[57] Agreement between the IMF and the WTO *supra* note 54, at ¶3 and 4.
[58] WTO, *World Trade Report 2014: Trade and Development—Recent Trends and the Role of the WTO*, (2014) https://www.wto.org/english/res_e/booksp_e/world_trade_report14_e.pdf; *See also* Robert Hudec, Developing Countries in the GATT Legal System, 24-25 (1987).

Understanding on the Balance-of-Payments Provisions of the General Agreement on Tariffs and Trade 1994, which forms an integral part of the GATT 1994, tightened the rules for the use of quantitative restrictions for balance-of-payments purposes.[59] The increasing pushback against the use of quantitative restrictions to protect a member's balance-of-payments gave rise to dispute settlement proceedings at the WTO.[60] This may be one of the reasons why only three developing countries have employed these measures to protect their balance-of-payments since 2005.[61]

Nonetheless, Article XVIII:2 of GATT allows developing countries to apply quantitative restrictions for balance-of-payments purposes in a manner which takes full account of the continued high level of demand for imports likely to be generated by their programmes of economic development.[62] At the same time, GATT Article XV:2 obligates the IMF to analyse the existence and nature of a balance-of-payment problem for a member invoking the balance-of-payment exception to GATT. Consequently, the legal decision of the WTO on the overall justification of the balance-of-payments exception is made on the basis of the IMF's factual findings and determinations on the underlying economic situation on whether a WTO member has the specified balance-of-payments problem.[63] These issues have been nowhere more clearly demonstrated than by the WTO's Panel resolution of the India restriction case.[64]

4.1.1. SOME SELECTED ISSUES IN THE INDIA QUANTITATIVE RESTRICTION CASE 4.1.1.1. *Whether there is Need to Consult the IMF* Over the years, the distinction between the IMF's role in factual determination under Article XV GATT and the WTO legal conclusion on the overall justification for the Article XVIII BOP exception has been blurry. Frieder Roessler, a former director of the legal affairs

---

[59] Sonia Rolland, Development at the World Trade Organization, Annex 2 (2012).
[60] *Ibid.*
[61] *Ibid.*
[62] *See generally* GATT 1994 *supra* note 11, at art. 18. (*See* for a comprehensive framework on special and differential treatment as it relates to developing countries and their balance-of-payments actions).
[63] Siegel *supra* note 52, at 580.
[64] Panel Report, *India—Quantitative Restrictions on Imports of Agricultural, Textile and Industrial Products,* WTO Doc. WT/DS90/R (adopted Apr. 6, 1999). [*hereinafter* India-Quantative Restrictions case].

division of the GATT, once stated that GATT is institutionally ill-equipped to collect and evaluate data on financial matters.[65] Likewise, Chantal Thomas noted that "the relatively loose application of Article XVIII" may be interpreted "as arising partially out of an institutional decision to leave scrutiny of balance-of-payments measures to the IMF. The IMF's structure and focus allowed it a more extensive role in regulating those aspects of policy that relate to a country's balance-of-payments situation."[66]

The United States proffered similar arguments in the India quantitative restriction case, urging that the panel was required, in all cases concerning monetary reserves, balance-of-payments, and foreign exchange arrangements, to consult with the IMF.[67] India, on the other hand, insisted that based on a notion of institutional balance, it was the contracting parties that were required to consult the IMF and not the panel.[68] The Panel, however, side-stepped this issue and instead relied on Article 13:1 of the WTO Understanding on Rules and Procedures Governing the Settlement of Disputes (DSU) provisions allowing it to seek expert opinion.[69] Although it reached the correct conclusion, the Panel erred by relying on Article 13:1 DSU to hold that it had the discretion to decide on whether or not to seek evidence from the IMF.[70] This is because once the subject matter "... concern[s] monetary reserves, balance of payments or foreign exchange arrangements ... [the WTO] *shall* consult fully with the International Monetary Fund."[71] The position advanced by the United States thus mirrored better the requirement contained in Article XV:2 GATT 1994. Accordingly, whether it is a developing or a developed WTO Member, the IMF will at all times be involved in the scrutiny of its balance-of-payment situation.[72]

---

[65] Roessler *supra* note 53, at 648.

[66] Thomas, Chantal, *Balance-of-Payments Crises in the Developing World: Balancing Trade, Finance and Development in the New Economic Order,* 15 AM. U. INT'L L. REV. 1249, 1261 (2000).

[67] India-Quantitative Restrictions case *supra* note 64 at ¶ 3.305.

[68] *Ibid* at ¶ 3.306.

[69] WTO Understanding on Rules and Procedures Governing the Settlement of Disputes (DSU) Article 13:1.

[70] Ugochukwu C. Ukpabi, *Juridical Substance or Myth Over Balance-of-Payment: Developing Countries and the Role of the International Monetary Fund in the World Trade Organization,* 26 MICH. J. INT'L L. 702, 720. (2005).

[71] GATT 1994 *supra* note 11, at Article XV:2.

[72] Ukpabi *supra* note 70, at 720.

4.1.1.2. SCOPE OF THE IMF'S BALANCE-OF-PAYMENTS DETERMINATION

India sought to delimit the scope of the information that IMF could validly furnish the BOP Committee or a panel asked to assess a WTO Member's balance-of-payment situation.[73] In particular, the Panel deliberated on whether the information obtained from the IMF regarding the state of a Member's BOP must be solely of a statistical nature or could it in addition include an evaluation of the statistical information. It failed to address this issue and instead seemed to assume that the information from the IMF was not just statistical but also an evaluation of the data. This holding reflects De Vries' observation to the effect that the IMF's "[Executive] Board decided that the Fund was to supply to the GATT not only relevant statistical data but also conclusions as to the current need for restrictions."[74] In a similar vein, Deborah Siegel observed that a custom developed for the IMF's determination to include views about the appropriateness of the measure, including the scope and how long such exception would be needed.[75]

A controversial component of this BOP architecture is not only that the WTO Members should consult the IMF, but also that they would accept as dispositive IMF's determinations based on its expertise. Nonetheless, the fact that this consultation clause uses terms from the criteria identified in Article XII could raise a question about the precise scope of what must be accepted in cases arising under Article XVIII:B. For example, since the consultation requirement refers to a "very low level" of reserves, should it extend to whether a developing country's reserves are 'inadequate' under Article XVIII:B? The reference to "the criteria set forth in Article XVIII:9" and the institutional role for the IMF represented in this provision overall suggest that it should be interpreted to apply to facts concerning members' level of reserves in both Article XII and Article XVIII cases. Nonetheless, the panel's definitive pronouncement on this issue could have aided in determining whether indeed such a limitation regarding the scope of the BOP information required from the IMF exists or not.

---

[73] India-Quantitative Restrictions case *supra* note 64, at ¶ 3.356.
[74] Margaret Garritsen De Vries, Balance of Payments Adjustment, 1945 To 1986: The IMF Experience, 339 (1987).
[75] Siegel *supra* note 52, at 580.

4.1.1.3. EFFECT OF THE IMF'S CONSULTATION   As previously noted, based on GATT Article XV:2, Siegel observed that IMF's determinations on BOP should be accepted as dispositive. However compelling, this contention should not be accepted for a number of reasons. First, although helpful in shedding light on the ancestry of Article XV:2, it certainly would be anachronistic in the contemporary times to conclude that as it was in the former Article XV:2 so should a panel faced with a BOP dispute, presently, accept the determinations of the IMF without questioning or assessing them.[76] Secondly, the contention is inconsistent with the core objective of the DSU process which is to "make an objective assessment of the matter before it, including an objective assessment of the facts of the case."[77] It therefore follows that accepting IMF's determinations on a country's BOP, however definitive, without a corresponding opportunity of challenging it, would impede the achievement of the DSU's aim of objective assessment. To achieve this, a panel has to consider IMF's determinations alongside those furnished by other experts, and not to accord IMF's determinations any better treatment than those of available expert reports. Doing this will enhance the distillation of objective findings and the panel's ability to reach a fair and impartial decision on BOP disputes. Following this approach would ensure that the WTO retains the final word on the state of a Member's BOP situation, because doing otherwise would certainly fail the test of a fair adjudicatory process.

4.2. Developing Countries and Concerns on the Regulatory Convergence of the IMF and the WTO in the Post-Pandemic Economic Recovery

Ensuring that gains already made in managing global fiscal policy by the IMF were not circumvented was a central preoccupation connected to the emergence of the GATT [later WTO].[78] However, the India quantitative restrictions case showed that substantively, the paradigms of global financial architecture have shifted from the relative acceptance of "special and differential treatment" for developing countries

---

[76] Ukpabi *supra* note 70, at 725.
[77] Understanding on Rules and Procedures Governing the Settlement of Disputes art. 1, Apr. 15, 1994, Marrakesh Agreement Establishing the World Trade Organization, Annex 2, 1869 U.N.T.S. 401 at Article 11 [hereinafter DSU].
[78] Ukpabi *supra* note 70, at 703.

undergoing balance-of-payment problems to an assertive intolerance of the principle.[79] Likewise, institutionally, the order has also substituted "pragmatism" with "legalism," with the Global North exerting its dominance and leverage on the Global South.[80] The substantive approach has moved to an increasing belief that endogenous factors such as "wayward' government policies help create such problems and that economic discipline is necessary to help prevent such difficulties.[81] However, the contemporary balance-of-payments crises of African countries and other developing countries, coupled with the unsustainable sovereign debts, proves that the primary concern should be that developing economies are not out of the woods yet with respect to chronic balance-of payments difficulties.

At the same time, the IMF/WTO BOP surveillance should not forget the social and economic development costs these crises exert, and how difficult it can be for these economies to recover from them.[82] Therefore, although the Panel dismissed it as irrelevant, India's argument for caution during the adjudication of the case deserves some consideration. This was so despite the onslaught of the Asian financial crisis immediately after the establishment of the Panel. Besides, the current sovereign debt and balance-of-payments crisis amidst the COVID-19 pandemic among these developing economies warrants the global rethinking of the IMF/WTO BOP surveillance.

It is shocking to see how Western countries insisted on the expansion of quantitative restrictions provisions in GATT yet the historical parallels with the situation

---

[79] Thomas, Chantal, *Balance-of-Payments Crises in the Developing World: Balancing Trade, Finance and Development in the New Economic Order,* 15 AM. U. INT'L REV. 1250, 1250 (2000); *See also* Karen McCusker, *Are Trade Restrictions to Protect the Balance of Payments Becoming Obsolete?,* 35 INTERECONOMICS 89 (2000).

[80] Chantal *supra* note 79, at 1250.

[81] *Ibid.*.

[82] Lars Jensen, *Sovereign Debt Vulnerabilities in Developing Economies: Which Countries are Vulnerable and How Much Debt is at Risk?,* UNITED NATIONS DEVELOPMENT PROGRAMME GLOBAL POLICY NETWORK (March 2021) available at https://www.undp.org/sites/g/files/zskgke326/files/publications/54241%20-%20UNDP%20WP%20Debt%20Vulnerability-web.pdf.

in most developing countries today—especially African countries—leap to the eye.[83] History reminds us that developed countries reached their current economic status not through open trade policies, but rather through protecting their domestic markets.[84] As established in section 2 above, most of these African countries are neck deep in foreign debts and trade deficits. Besides, as it was then in pre-WTO times for most Western countries, these African countries and other developing countries presently lack the requisite capacity to produce locally most of their imports. Therefore, an insistence on harmful trade liberalisation could be incurably detrimental to these countries. What the decision of the Panel, anchored mainly on IMF's determinations, signals is that Western countries, with WTO as a conduit, will curtail developing country Members' resorting to import restriction's necessary exception to limit disproportionate importation pursuant to Article XVIII GATT. It therefore imposes pressure on developing countries to import more—a position that, in the absence of a significant and measurable improvement in their productive capacity base, puts their economies under pressure.[85]

Additionally, the institutional difference in the IMF/WTO relation poses further challenges. The most significant difference between the two institutions is the asymmetrical power relationship as far as decision-making process at the IMF is concerned. Whereas decision-making at the WTO is mostly by consensus,[86] at the IMF,

---

[83] *See* Christian Vincke, *Trade Restrictions for Balance of Payments Reasons and the GATT—Quotas v. Surcharges,* 13 HARV. INT'L. L. J. 289, 298–299 (1972); Ukpabi *supra* note 70 at 706. "In the post-war period, the United States was running an $11 billion surplus. On the other hand, Great Britain, for instance, had accumulated an external debt of $15 billion. Furthermore, the currencies of the Western European countries were not convertible. *Their ruined economies could not or would not (because of reconstruction policies) produce certain goods for which there was a very high internal demand. Since those goods were available only from the dollar countries, a free international trade system would have worsened the existing imbalance* ... At that time the necessity for deficit countries to use QR was probably an obvious and consequently little discussed fact."

[84] Simon Lester, Bryan Mercurio, & Arwel Davies, World Trade Law: Text, Materials and Commentary 910 (3rd ed. 2018).

[85] Ukpabi *supra* note 70, at 729.

[86] Of course, consensus is not the only mode of decision-making at the WTO. If consensus cannot be achieved, Article IX:1 allows majority voting on the basis of one Member one vote, implying that unlike IMF's weighted voting system, all WTO Members vote in equal proportion.

the voting structure is based on a quota system[87] which was designed to reflect the shares each Member country holds in the IMF. The actual quota formulas are quite complex, and the resulting shares of votes do not always accurately reflect the economic size of some members.[88] This institutional difference in terms of decision-making is particularly disturbing. As noted by a former IMF Secretary:

> Fund governance of its system of quotas and voting power has not been satisfactory because of growing distortions which have developed over time are only now beginning to be addressed in discussions in the Board. *The system as it exists is geared to defending the status quo, and this has played to the advantage of Western Europe and to the detriment of Asia and of the developing countries as a group, which is the overwhelming majority of the Fund members and of the global population.*[89]
> [Emphasis mine]

Nothing so far suggests that this asymmetrical dimension in the decision-making process of the IMF is about to change in favour of developing countries, a predisposition that may influence the determinations of the IMF on BOP matters concerning developing countries. As a result, just like as it is in sovereign debt cases of the Global South,[90] IMF's BOP determinations risk being the present mode of colonial governance. This is a danger that less-developed Members of the WTO should be aware of. Another concern on the IMF/WTO relation as may be drawn from the case is the real danger of eviscerating the special and differential treatment (SDT) accorded to less-developed WTO Members.[91] This treatment is barely present at the

---

[87] *See* IMF, *IMF Quotas,* https://www.imf.org/en/About/Factsheets/Sheets/2016/07/14/12/21/IMF-Quotas (last accessed Mar. 4, 2021) (IMF quota is defined as "the building blocks of the IMF's financial and governance structure" where a "member country's quota broadly reflects its relative position in the world economy" and determines its voting share on the IMF executive board).

[88] *IMF Survey: A More Transparent IMF Quota Formula,* IMF NEWS (Feb. 26, 2007) https://www.imf.org/en/News/Articles/2015/09/28/04/53/soint057a.

[89] Economic Forums and International Seminars, *Governing the IMF,* INT'L MONETARY FUND (Sept. 17, 2002).

[90] Gathii *supra* note 33.

[91] Ukpabi *supra* note 70, at 732.

IMF and may thus fail to reflect this in its BOP determinations. Ugochukwu Ukpabi correctly observes that:

> The extension of [SDT] to developing countries evidences the WTO's sensitivity to the peculiar difficulties of those Members as late comers to a trade architecture designed mainly by wealthy nations. Short of those provisions being no more than mere rhetoric, the close connection of the Fund and the WTO, at the very least, obscures that carefully articulated arrangement peculiar to the WTO.[92]

In this regard, IMF's factual review of BOP situations in developing countries must reflect the SDT nuance of developing countries underpinning Article XVIII GATT 1994 provisions. It is, therefore, a cardinal obligation of the dispute settlements panels of the WTO to ensure that the SDT provisions in relation to balance-of-payments are not nullified in the course of the IMF's factual review. This also further underscores the need to ensure that the WTO has the final say in IMF BOP determinations of developing countries. This, however, does not negate the fact that WTO's legitimacy is equally in question.[93] Nonetheless, the WTO is the lesser threat compared to the IMF given its quite elaborate SDT framework. This is notwithstanding that the SDT provisions are couched as best endeavours.[94] This, therefore, brings to question the intentions of Article XV:2 GATT, a provision that needs to be revisited.

Finally, the strengthened compulsory jurisdiction of the WTO panel in relation to balance-of-payments disputes resulted in a questionable conclusion of the issue that had been lingering for quite some time.[95] As a result, the decision created a

---

[92] *Ibid.*

[93] Michael Fakhri, *Reconstructing the WTO Legitimacy Debates Towards Notions of Development,* 5 Compar. Rsch. L. & Pol. Econ. (Rsch. Paper) 1 (2009).

[94] Aniekan Ukpe & Sangeeta Khorana, *Special and differential treatment in the WTO: framing differential treatment to achieve (real) development,* 20 J. Int'l Trade L. & Pol'y 83 (2021).

[95] *See generally* GATT Negotiating Group on GATT Articles, *Note on Meeting of 27–30 June 1988,* MTN.GNG/NG7/8 (Jul. 21, 1988) (During the Uruguay Rounds negotiations, it was observed that "85 percent of all quantitative restrictions in force were imposed under Article XVIII," with the number of countries invoking Article XVIII:B since 1958 averaging 15 yearly); Richard Eglin, *Balance-of-Payments Measures in the GATT,* 10 World Econ. 1, 8 (1987); *See also* Ji Yeong Yoo, *Restructuring GATT Balance-of-Payments Safeguard in the WTO System,* 53 J. World Trade 528 (2019).

spill-over effect towards future policy choice on BOP problems of other less developed WTO Members. At the same time, if the conclusions of a WTO panel and the decision of the IMF on the state of a BOP position differ, how the obligation under GATT Article XV:2 and the DSU could be accommodated remains unanswered and perhaps warrants further research. Additionally, given the difference in the institutional operations of both entities, how the SDT is to be implemented by the WTO in BOP measures without undue influence from the North remains largely uncertain. To this end, history reminds us that Article XVIII GATT is a toothless bulldog.

4.3. *The Need for a Harmonised BOP Surveillance for Post-Pandemic Economic Recovery in African Countries*

Article XXXVIII:2C mandates WTO Members to collaborate in analysing the development plans and policies of less-developed Members with a view to devising concrete measures to promote the development of trade potential. This means that the drafters envisaged potential conflict of interests when "assistance for economic development" was utilised.[96] The impetus for harmonization of IMF/WTO BOP surveillance mechanisms stems primarily from the interrelatedness of trade and exchange issues arising in the context of a balance-of-payment difficulty already alluded to. This is mainly because quantitative restrictions for balance-of-payment purposes resonate in the WTO Member's exchange condition and vice-versa, and also because of the limited competence of the WTO in connection with balance-of-payment.[97]

Consequently, there are three ways that could foster confidence in the extant BOP framework. First, the consultations on balance-of-payment proceedings should be an opportunity to reiterate the relevant WTO Agreement provisions on SDT, ensuring that IMF deliberations adequately reflect SDT commitments.[98] For example, the WTO Committee on Balance-of-payments could direct the IMF during BOP consultations to ensure that WTO treaty provisions concerning SDT of developing countries are reflected in the IMF's factual determinations on the BOP status

---

[96] Dukgeun Ahn, *Linkages between International Financial and Trade Institutions: The IMF, World Bank and the WTO,* 34 J. WORLD TRADE 1, 25 (2000).
[97] Ukpabi *supra* note 70, at 733.
[98] *Ibid.*

of developing countries. Secondly, while cognizant of the institutional structure of IMF and its predisposition, the WTO should explore the possibility of receiving balance-of-payment statistics from other organizations for the sake of transparency.[99] Failure to explore alternative sources of balance-of-payment information, developing countries may make WTO a convenient proxy for enforcing the IMF's *de facto* juridical competence over BOP matters, consequently failing to convey the message of its impartiality to all its members.[100] Thirdly, given the obvious trade repercussions of balance-of-payment problems, the WTO should retain superior competence over the IMF in matters concerning trade, and that WTO competence in examining the overall trade ramifications of Members in redressing BOP problems should not be impaired.[101]

These proposals could go a long way in ensuring that developing countries—particularly African countries that are currently laden with unsustainable debts impacting on their development objectives—can successfully invoke Article XVIII GATT to correct the distortionary effects of imports.

5 Conclusion

The institutional differences between the IMF and WTO, and the India quantitative restriction case reveal a less than complete understanding of the legal components of the balance-of-payments relationship between the two institutions. Several decades later, unanswered questions still persist on avoiding conflicting SDT rights and obligations between their common members. In the wake of sovereign debt and balance-of-payments crises, and to the extent that there still are ambiguities or varying views on the meaning of the governing provisions on balance-of-payments, it is impossible for African countries and other developing countries to successfully invoke Article XVIII GATT to correct their balance-of-payments challenges. And like a domino, African countries may follow in the footsteps of Mali and Zambia in defaulting on their debt obligations.

---

[99] *Ibid.* at 734.
[100] *Ibid.*
[101] *Ibid.*

CHAPTER EIGHT

Supervising Sovereign Debt Restructuring Through the United Nations

Kelvin Mbithi*

1 Introduction

African countries rarely get to participate in setting up systems at the global stage because many of the processes for doing so and the governing institutions were formulated during colonization. Examples include the international trading system and the international debt architecture.[1] Article II of the Articles of Agreement of the International Monetary Fund (hereinafter, IMF) provided that the original members of the Fund would be the countries that took part in the United Nations Monetary and Financial Conference.[2] The conference is also known as the Bretton Woods Conference. Out of the three African countries that sent a delegation, South Africa was still under apartheid rule at the time.[3] The next African country to join was Sudan in 1957.[4] This was about twelve years after the entry into force of the Articles of Agreement of the IMF.[5] The World Bank is composed of the International Bank for Reconstruction and Development (hereinafter, IBRD) and the International Development

---

* Kelvin Mbithi is a lawyer and Certified Professional Mediator. He has published various works on human rights, elections, and campaign financing. He writes for his blog https://mbithiopinions.wordpress.com/.
[1] Walter Rodney, *How Europe Underdeveloped Africa* (6th edn, Bogle-L'Ouverture Publications 1983).
[2] Articles of Agreement of the IMF, Art. 2 § 2, 60 Stat. 1401, 2 U.N.T.S. 39.
[3] Kurt Schuler & Mark Bernkopf, *Who Was at Bretton Woods?*, Ctr. for Fin. Stability (Jul. 1, 2014), https://centerforfinancialstability.org/bw/Who_Was_at_Bretton_Woods.pdf.
[4] IMF, *List of Members*, https://www.imf.org/external/np/sec/memdir/memdate.htm (last visited May 7, 2022).
[5] *Id.*

Association (hereinafter, IDA).[6] These institutions were set up at the same time and constitute the foundation of the international trading system and debt architecture.

The current shackles of debt that most countries in the Global South find themselves feels like *déjà vu*. In a 2006 article, Bhupinder Chimni noted that the Global South faces a renewed threat of colonization.[7] Chimni highlighted the use of international financial and trade institutions in dictating the economic and social policies in the Global South.[8] The criticism includes the Structural Adjustment Programs (hereinafter, SAPs) which the IMF required developing countries to introduce. The SAPs included reduced government spending, removing subsidies, and eliminating restrictions on import and exports.[9] The measures that the IMF recommended, although designed to stabilize the economy, hurt the poor in the Global South. For example, the reduced spending led to the government cutting funding for important public services.[10] The international debt architecture institutions could be perceived as using international law as a tool for advancing the economic and political domination of the countries in the Global South.

Global South scholars are advancing a transformation in understanding the underlying norms of how Africa interacts with international law. The movement which is dubbed Third World Approach to International Law (TWAIL) exposes the history of subordinated groups that have resulted in current consequences.[11] It is crucial that in conversations about modern problems such as debt distress and restructuring, that the origin of the issues is not ignored.[12] TWAIL proposes changes to the existing international documents and principles to eliminate the dominance by the Global North.[13] This requires a sequential process that can be summarized into three

---

[6] David Driscoll, The IMF and the World Bank: How Do They Differ?, (IMF 1995).

[7] Bhupinder Chimni, *Third World Approaches to International Law: A Manifesto,* 8 INT'L CMTY. L REV. 3 (2006)

[8] *Id.*

[9] DORIS WANGUI GITHUA, HE IMPACT OF INTERNATIONAL MONETARY FUND (IMF) AND THE WORLD BANK STRUCTURAL ADJUSTMENT PROGRAMMES IN DEVELOPING COUNTRIES, CASE STUDY OF KENYA, (Univ. of Nairobi 2013).

[10] *Id.*

[11] James Gathii, *The Agenda of Third World Approaches to International Law in* International Legal Theory: Foundations and Frontiers (Jeffrey Dunoff and Mark Pollack eds. 2019).

[12] ATTIYA WARIS, FINANCING AFRICA (Langaa Research and Publishing CIG 2019).

[13] Gathii, *supra* note 11.

steps. First is to identify how international law supports the existing forms of inequality in the international political and economic systems.[14] The second step is to ensure history is not forgotten because the impacts of violence and colonialism continue to be felt in the previous colonies.[15] After appropriately conducting the assessment of the problem, TWAIL then seeks to introduce reforms that would turn oppressive systems into instruments of liberation.

The article is divided into five sections. Section I introduces the paper and lays a foundation for the discussions. It provides a background on the use of international law to oppress African countries. It then highlights the emerging claims of TWAIL and separation of the roles of the IMF and World Bank that will be instrumental in this paper. The introduction then gives a brief overview of the article. Section II identifies the principle of third world approaches to international law that will underpin the discussion.

Third world approaches to international law provides a framework for critiquing and restructuring the existing international debt architecture. This is crucial for the discussions in the paper as the principle also helps in providing appropriate recommendations. Section III studies the role of the existing international debt architecture in the current chaos with looming threats of mass debt distress. Section IV proposes reworking the international debt architecture to place the United Nations at the top of the supervisory framework. Section V concludes the paper.

2 PRINCIPLES FOR TRANSFORMING DEBT ARCHITECTURE

Third World Approaches to International Law
Accepting that international law as currently formulated legitimizes particular ideas that are used to resolve global problems is crucial to understanding the global debt architecture. The Global North's hold over the international law institutions enables a specific set of ideas to remain dominant as a means of evaluating policies.[16] Chimni notes that although a direct link may be difficult to point out, the functions of producing and disseminating knowledge are steered by a few dominant states.[17] When

---

[14] *Id.*
[15] *Id.*
[16] *Id.*
[17] Chimni, *supra* note 7.

evaluating the present condition of African governments on issues such as sovereign debt, the proposed causes seem to be about the inability of African people to establish good governance.[18] The blame game seeks to justify colonialism on the one hand as a necessary evil and to also support further intrusiveness in the governance of African countries on the other.[19] Although the IMF and the World Bank advocate for measures that are costly to the rights of Africans, the accountability of these institutions is still resisted. An alternative international framework is necessary to eradicate the conditions of oppression in the Global South.[20]

TWAIL allows a critique of the predominant schools of thought in international law because the interests of African countries are still not taken into account. Chimni considers TWAIL to be a form of resistance that balances optimism with a healthy dose of pessimism.[21] The optimistic view is erroneous since it believes that the world is gradually going to become more just without fundamental changes in the social order. The pessimistic approach considers the current dominance and subjugation to be a never-ending process.[22] TWAIL's commitment to non-violence means that one of the options that remains to advance the agenda of transformation is through research.[23] Makau Mutua notes that TWAIL is crucial to exposing the role of international law in advancing a hierarchy that places the Global South below the Global North.[24]

TWAIL provides a means for the Global South to expose the indirect oppression by the dominant philosophies from the Global North. The Global South is connected primarily by the historical experiences of plunder experienced at the hands of the Global North.[25] The hegemony that international law advances at the expense of the Global South can be resisted on a theoretical level. The primary aim of TWAIL is to identify the voiceless and marginalized societies and give individuals a means to critique the prevailing conditions.[26] Challenging the dominance of Global North is

---

[18] Rodney, *supra* note 1.

[19] *Id.*

[20] Makau Mutua, *What Is TWAIL?*, 94 Am. Soc'y Int'l L. 31(2000).

[21] Chimni, *supra* note 7.

[22] *Id.*

[23] Gathii, *supra* note 11.

[24] Mutua, *supra* note 20.

[25] *Id.*

crucial before any alternative norms can be presented for consideration. With more focus on the powerlessness that countries in the Global South have in economic terms, it is possible to begin to address the underlying causes.[27] TWAIL provides methodologies and theories for assessing international law institutions, but in addition to the theoretical, it is concerned with the practical application of the proposals presented.[28]

This chapter, like other TWAIL scholarship contributes to new avenues of producing knowledge. A topic that remains important for TWAIL is ensuring that international institutions remain accountable and transparent.[29] This work is hardly going to be easy because the IMF and the World Bank remain powerful institutions. However, the conversation that the international systems should be reformed can be gradually pushed forward. This chapter relies on TWAIL to show the oppression of countries in the Global South through the medium of sovereign debt. TWAIL then provides the framework that supports the United Nations and its institutions as the appropriate forums for empowering Global South countries to restructure sovereign debt.

3 CRITIQUING EXISTING INTERNATIONAL DEBT STRUCTURE

The criticism against the IMF and the World Bank is due to the use of sovereign debt to attach compulsory terms and policies for African countries. Milton Friedman noted that concentrated power is not made harmless by the good intentions of those who wield it.[30] It is important to examine instances of concentrated power to identify the objectives of the entities wielding the authority. This section delves first into the set-up of the existing international debt architecture. It then discusses why the current approach does not result in ideal outcomes for African countries compared to other nations. This discussion sets the stage for the next section which discusses possible reforms for the international debt architecture.

---

[26] Larissa Ramina, *TWAIL—"Third World Approaches to International Law" and Human Rights: Some Considerations*, 5 J. OF CONST. RSCH. 261 (2018).
[27] *Id.*
[28] Obiora Okafor, *Critical Third World Approaches to International Law (TWAIL): Theory, Methodology, or Both?*, 10 INT'L CMTY. L. REV. 371 (2008).
[29] Chimni, *supra* note 7.
[30] MILTON FRIEDMAN, CAPITALISM AND FREEDOM (Univ. of Chi. Press, 40th Anniversary ed. 2002).

3.1 International Monetary Fund (IMF)

The IMF's purpose is to foster co-operation between members to allow for stability in international financial transactions such as foreign currency exchange.[31] However, the IMF has a variety of funds that members can borrow from to improve their economic development. IMF member countries provide funds through payment of membership fees and other subscriptions. The pool of resources is available to members in need.[32] The IMF has 190 member countries since its inception in 1945.[33] The IMF ties its lending to the borrowing country implementing policies to restore sustainable growth and a stable economy.[34] IMF funds are open to all members although at varying interest rates and terms to take into account the development level of the country.[35] Low income countries are subjected to surveillance and discussion with the IMF on the policies to introduce to properly manage finances.[36] On the surface, it seems that the IMF was set up for the benefit of low income countries in the Global South.

Economists such as John Maynard Keynes proposed that placing cautious bankers in charge of the IMF would ensure development of the objectives.[37] The temporary nature of IMF assistance was emphasized as a tool to ensure the norm could be restored. The separation of the roles of the IMF and the World Bank is indicative of the desire of the founding states to avoid concentration of power. The additional separation anticipated that the IMF's work would relate to the less developing nations. Gradually, the IMF began to expand its mandate by offering more long-term assistance. For example, in 1974, the IMF offered a program for up to three years.[38] The conditionality attached to IMF loans was a topic of discussion during the Bretton Woods Conference.[39] To date, the IMF continues to impose conditions for assisting countries in the Global South. For example, the IMF has insisted that Kenya should remove fuel subsidies, important

---

[31] Driscoll, *supra* note 6.
[32] *Id.*
[33] IMF, *supra* note 4.
[34] IMF, *IMF Lending,* (Feb. 22, 2022), https://www.imf.org/en/About/Factsheets/IMF-Lending.
[35] *Id.*
[36] IMF, *Factsheet—IMF Support for Low-Income Countries,* (Jan. 5, 2022), https://www.imf.org/en/About/Factsheets/IMF-Support-for-Low-Income-Countries.
[37] SCANDINAVIAN INST. OF AFR. STUD., THE IMF AND THE WORLD BANK IN AFRICA: CONDITIONALITY, IMPACT AND ALTERNATIVES, (Kjell Havnevik ed. 1987).
[38] *Id.*
[39] *Id.*

government policy to assist the citizens, to continue accessing IMF assistance.[40] An aspect that needs to be fully appreciated is the philosophy which underlies programs presented by the IMF. This is because the IMF takes strong positions on the preferred policy objectives.[41] Some of the measures include reduced spending by governments on important social services. The impacts of the 1980s policies continue to be felt to this date as the situation in African countries continue to deteriorate. Nona Tamale's chapter in this book discusses these policies and their impacts at length.

3.2 World Bank

Another institution that plays an important role in the international debt architecture is the World Bank. The World Bank's main role is to fund economic development. The World Bank is composed of the International Bank for Reconstruction and Development (hereinafter, IBRD) and the International Development Association (hereinafter, IDA).[42] The IBRD secures money for loans through issuing bonds to private institutions and individuals. The IDA gets its funds from donor nations' grants.[43] The IDA and IBRD after securing funds, loan the money to countries in need of development aid. The World Bank has 189 members since it was formed in 1945.[44] On the other hand, the World Bank requires a country to have a per capita income of less than $1,085 to be eligible to borrow from the IDA.[45] Upper-middle-income countries ($1,046–$12,535) can borrow from the IBRD.[46] Lower middle-income countries ($1,036 and $4,045) can borrow from IDA and IBRD.[47] Just like the IMF, on the surface, it seems that the World Bank was also set up to help developing countries.

---

[40] Macharia Kamau, *Treasury to Scrap Fuel Subsidy in next Two Months, IMF Says,* THE STANDARD (Jul. 21, 2022), https://www.standardmedia.co.ke/entertainment/business/article/2001450854/treasury-to-scrap-fuel-subsidy-in-next-two-months-imf-says.

[41] Githua, *supra* note 9.

[42] Driscoll, *supra* note 6.

[43] *Id.*

[44] WORLD BANK, *Member Countries,* https://www.worldbank.org/en/about/leadership/members (last visited May 1, 2022).

[45] Bretton Woods Project, *Who Can Borrow from the World Bank?,* (Dec. 10, 2020), https://www.brettonwoodsproject.org/2020/12/art-320866/.

[46] *Id.*

[47] *Id.*

3.3 Sovereign Debt Crisis

The modern connection between sovereignty and sovereign debt consists of the IMF and World Bank imposing conditions on countries that are in debt distress. In addition to impacting sovereignty, the imposition of these policies results in harmful consequences for human rights. The countries lending to African nations have interests that are pursued in exchange for the funding.[48] The Global North has pushed for a separation of roles that gradually pushed United Nations Conference on Trade and Development (hereinafter, UNCTAD) from involvement in discussing political and organizational reforms of international economic institutions.[49] UNCTAD's mandate was reduced to assisting with the technical aspects of implementing proposals by the IMF and World Bank.[50] UNCTAD's activities in sovereign debt restructuring are discussed in the next section. This section highlights how the World Bank and the IMF's domination of the international debt structure has resulted in negative impacts for African countries.

Sovereign debt crises have been taking place for a long time and may likely strike African countries again. According to the International Law Association, virtually all countries have defaulted on their external debt.[51] The default by countries in the Global North such as England took place as early as 1340. Others include Spain and France.[52] These countries have defaulted severally but are not the only countries to do so.[53] Between 1930–1950, half of countries in the world were in debt default. At that time, the debt crisis was resolved by countries giving up territories.[54] At the moment, there are increasing predictions that African countries are moving towards

---

[48] Magalie Masamba, *Sovereign Debt Restructuring and Human Rights: Overcoming a False Binary*, in COVID-19 and Sovereign Debt: The Case of SADC (Daniel Bradlow & Magalie Masamba eds. 2022).
[49] Quentin Deforge & Benjamin Lemoine, *The Global South Debt Revolution That Wasn't: UNCTAD From Technocratic Activism to Technical Assistance*, in Sovereign Debt Diplomacies: Rethinking Sovereign Debt from Colonial Empires to Hegemony (Pierre Penet & Juan Flores Zendejas eds. 2021).
[50] *Id.*
[51] Muhammad Bello, The Place of Socio-Economic Rights in Sovereign Debt Governance, (Mar. 2020) (LLD Thesis, University of the Free State) (on file at the University of the Free State Kovsie Scholar Repository).
[52] *Id.*
[53] *Id.*
[54] *Id.*

debt distress.[55] The reasons are varied but generally revolve around over-borrowing and misuse of resources.[56] While these factors have a role to play, the original sin should not be forgotten. It is as a result of colonialism that African countries were left in the hands of the corrupt elite. The hold that the elites have over power in the continent has been reinforced by the Global North's support for African leaders viewed as friendly to the interests of the developed countries.

These are not the only reasons for the present situation that African countries find themselves. The IMF and World Bank's role in encouraging African countries to indulge in the debt spree should also not be forgotten.[57] As noted by economist Dr. David Ndii, the IMF and the World Bank are lending institutions which have a conflict of interest in the debt debate.[58] Continued borrowing by African countries justifies the existence of institutions such as the IMF and the World Bank to help out in cases of looming debt crises. IMF loans are based on the quotas that have been in existence since the 1940s.[59] Voting power is also tied to the quotas which means that the Global North retains control of the IMF. The industrial countries control 57.6% of the vote.[60] The United States alone controls 19.3% of the vote.[61] A vote to change the quotas would require 85% of the vote which means the existing structure of the IMF remains difficult to change.[62] As a result, the IMF policies are heavily skewed towards the wishes of the Global North with little regard for the African nations.

---

[55] Francisca Kibabu, Impact of External Debt on African States Development: A Case Study of Kenya (2000–2016), (2018) (MA in International Studies, University of Nairobi) (on file with the University of Nairobi Research Archives).

[56] *Id.*

[57] David Ndii, Of Tigers, *Debt Merchants and 2020 Vision,* THE ELEPHANT (Jan. 10, 2020), https://www.theelephant.info/op-eds/2020/01/10/of-tigers-debt-merchants-and-2020-vision/.

[58] *Id.*

[59] *See* Rep. of the Independent Expert on the Effects of Foreign Debt and Other Related International Financial Obligations of States on the Full Enjoyment of All Human Rights, Particularly Economic, Social and Cultural Rights on the Impact of Economic Reforms and Austerity Measures on Women's Human Rights, U.N. Doc. A/73/179 (Jul. 18, 2018); *See also* Kate Donald & Nicolas Lusiani, *The Gendered Costs of Austerity: Assessing the IMF's Role in Budget Cuts Which Threaten Women's Rights,* BRETTON WOODS PROJECT (2017).

[60] *Id.*

[61] *Id.*

[62] *Id.*

The position of the IMF as a lender is firmly entrenched in the international debt architecture. For example, about 85 nations have sought credit facilities from the IMF.[63] The IMF surveillance program is based on international soft law developed in 2002 as a set of rules and guidance notes for its orderly business.[64] However, the program is sometimes flawed as it is based on assumptions about the present and future sustainability of debt in a country. Generally, projections underestimate the debt distress situation in a country.[65] As a temporary lending institution, the focus on short-term debt requirements overlooks the long-term consequences for a country.[66] The controlling members of the IMF are not usually the same set of countries that rely on the lending facilities which further skews IMF governance in favour of creditors rather than borrowers.[67] As part of the institutions that continue to deepen the debt crisis in the Global South, the IMF would not be best placed to supervise debt restructuring.

The increasing pressure of debt servicing on resources of African countries continue to make it difficult for the nations to provide for their citizens.[68] $240 billion was spent by African countries servicing debt leading up to 2000.[69] Despite the payments, the African countries continued to owe over four times the amount owed before the debt payments started. The example of Nigeria is indicative. In 1978, the nation had borrowed $5 billion yet despite paying $16 billion for loan servicing, the nation still owed $31 billion.[70] The phenomenon that was evident in the past, is still ongoing as

---

[63] Karina Lima, *Reforming the International Monetary Fund's Debt Sustainability Assessments towards Achieving the UN's Sustainable Development Goals (SDGs): A Crucial Post-Pandemic Recovery Agenda*, 2 AFR. J. OF INT'L ECON. L. 32 (2021).

[64] *Id.*

[65] *Id.*

[66] James Gathii, *Retelling Good Governance Narratives on Africa's Economic and Political Predicaments: Continuities and Discontinuities in Legal Outcomes Between Markets and States*, 45 Vill. L. Rev. 971 (2000).

[67] 50YEARS, *Who Is The IMF?*, (Nov. 1, 2014), http://www.50years.org/.

[68] Dr. Masamba, Magalie, "The Pressing Call for an International Debt Restructuring Framework and the Potential Gains its Creation will have for African Countries." Upcoming 2022.

[69] Demba Moussa Dembele, *The International Monetary Fund and the World Bank in Africa: A "Disastrous" Record*, 35 INT'L J. OF HEALTH SERV. 389 (2005).

[70] *Id.*

debt servicing continues to become more difficult. The role of over borrowing by governments cannot be denied. For example, Kenya's public debt has consistently grown higher than the GDP growth in the country since June 2013.[71] However, the interest terms continue to remain high.[72] This shows that African countries debt distress may not be solely attributable to about the mismanagement and corruption accompanying government policies.

3.4 Sovereign Debt and Sovereignty

The link between sovereign debt and sovereignty is historical where territories were given up in exchange for debt repayment. In the 1800s, the lending nations used crude means to enforce payment such as taking over territories.[73] The methods of rectifying default were based on the military strength of the defaulting nation. For example, when in 1882 Egypt defaulted on its loans, Britain readily used military power to enforce payment.[74] This can be contrasted with the United States which defaulted on various loans in the 1840s but did not face similar threats.[75] In the modern context, the use of diplomacy to encourage repayment is also coupled with other models of economic pressure such as denying credit facilities to a country. The results of a country attempting to exercise sovereignty in matters of sovereign debt has negative economic consequences for the borrower nation.[76] The creditors have great power and blocking or reducing access to credit can raise the cost of living and slow down development in a country. The imperialism in the past is maintained in the present through more indirect means such as economic pressure on a country.

Although contracts should be binding, sometimes, it may be contrary to the interests of the citizens and the nation for the country to be required to pay the debt in the terms previously agreed. The Mozambique case represents one of the first

---

[71] THE NATIONAL TREASURY AND PLANNING, ANNUAL PUBLIC DEBT REPORT 2020/2021, (Government of Kenya 2021).
[72] Id.
[73] Introduction Sovereign Debt Diplomacies: Rethinking Sovereign Debt from Colonial Empires to Hegemony (page 4) (Pierre Penet & Juan Flores Zendejas eds. 2021).
[74] Id.
[75] Id.
[76] Id.

instances in Africa, of the courts safeguarding the interests of the Mozambicans from having to repay illegally obtained loans. Three Mozambican state-owned enterprises, Ematum, Proindicus, and Mozambique Asset Management, borrowed from two London-based banks, Russian VTB and Credit Suisse.[77] Ematum received $850 million, Proindicus received $623 million while Mozambique Asset Management received $535 million as loans.[78] When the Constitutional Council of Mozambique heard the case, it held that such a secretive contract was contrary to Mozambique laws. The loans had been obtained without Parliament's approval which violated Mozambique's constitution and budget law.[79] The Council also examined the high interest rates on the loans and found the agreements to be unconstitutional.[80] A country's need to protect its citizens and uphold the law is a crucial aspect of sovereignty threatened by debts.

The threat to sovereignty looms over countries in Africa because of the lender nations' ability to influence negotiations of loan agreements. Countries in Africa sign secretive agreements and are bound through confidentiality provisions not to disclose the contents of the contracts.[81] In Kenya, the result of the secretive loan agreements has been uncertainty as to what the government has promised the lender. The lack of transparency resulted in several citizens instituting cases to compel disclosure of the agreements. For example, the government of Kenya constructed a Standard Gauge Railway that was funded by loans from the Chinese Government.[82] The High Court

---

[77] James Gathii, *Introduction: Sovereign Debt Under Domestic and Foreign Law: Lessons from the Mozambique Constitutional Council Decision of May 8, 2020,* AFRONOMICSLAW (Aug. 3, 2020), https://www.afronomicslaw.org/2020/08/03/introduction-sovereign-debt-under-domestic-and-foreign-law-lessons-from-the-mozambique-constitutional-council-decision-of-may-8-2020.

[78] Denise Namburete, How Public Interest Litigation Led to Invalidation of Illegal Mozambican Debt, AFRONOMICSLAW (Aug. 4, 2020), https://www.afronomicslaw.org/2020/08/04/how-public-interest-litigation-led-to-invalidation-of-illegal-mozambican-debt/.

[79] Gathii, *supra* note 77.

[80] Louis Koen, *The Renegotiation of Sovereign Debt Tainted by Corruption: Mozambique's "Secret" Debt in Perspective, in* COVID-19 and Sovereign Debt: The Case of SADC (Daniel Bradlow & Magalie Masamba eds. 2022).

[81] Farai Mutondoro et. al., *Resource-Backed Loans, COVID-19 and the High Risk of Debt Trap: A Case Study of Zimbabwe, in* COVID-19 and Sovereign Debt: The Case of SADC (Daniel Bradlow & Magalie Masamba eds. 2022).

[82] Khelif Khalifa & Wanjiku Gikonyo v Principal Secretary, Ministry of Transport & 4 Others [2022] KEHC 368 (KLR) (Kenya).

held that Kenya's constitution provides citizens with the right to access information.[83] As a result, the court ordered the government to provide the citizens who had filed the case, with the contracts.[84] Despite the binding nature of contract law, nations in Africa are capable of exercising their sovereignty to demand transparency.

The Kenyan high court case set the stage for a review of the contract to determine the exact terms of the agreement. The Attorney-General indicated that the government would file an appeal which suggests that the battle for transparency may not yet be over.[85] However, the High Court ruling provides an important guide on the interpretation of the right of citizens to access information. The judgment notes that although Cabinet Secretaries have the power to declare that some information should remain a state secret, the power should not be arbitrarily exercised.[86] Further, the burden is on the government to prove that the information sought is likely to negatively affect national interest if disclosed.[87] The court held that this burden cannot solely be discharged through reliance on the words of the Cabinet Secretary.[88] There must be evidence and reasons that justify withholding information on the basis of national interest.[89] The High Court judgment is further proof that the terms of an agreement or statute cannot override constitutional obligations imposed on the government.

The input of civil society groups can be crucial in exposing state-capture by foreign entities under the guise of development loans. A coalition of civil society groups pressured the Mozambican government to institute an audit to determine how the loans were sourced and used.[90] In a concerted effort, the pressure was also applied on the United States and the United Kingdom to carry out corruption investigations on the persons who were instrumental in procuring the illegal loans.[91] In the Kenyan

---

[83] *Id.*

[84] *Id.*

[85] Muyanga, Attorney-General Appeals Court Order to Make SGR Tenders Public, BUSINESS DAILY (May 20, 2022), https://www.businessdailyafrica.com/bd/economy/ag-appeals-court-order-to-make-sgr-tenders-public-3821018.

[86] Khalifa v Ministry of Transport, supra note 82.

[87] *Id.*

[88] *Id.*

[89] *Id.*

[90] Gathii, *supra* note 77.

[91] *Id.*

case, the civil society groups had for a long time being pressuring the government to publicise the contract awarding Kenya's most expensive infrastructure project to the Chinese government-backed banks.[92] In Kenya and Mozambique, the civil society groups also filed the court cases that led to the successful outcomes.

The collaboration by the civil society, media, and development partners advanced the argument that loans obtained by the government should be subject to public scrutiny.[93] The United States investigation led to the arrest of three Credit Suisse employees in London that were part of the deal. Manuel Chang, the former Mozambican minister of finance was also arrested in South Africa.[94] The corruption involved in obtaining the loans formed the basis for the court case seeking to declare that the loans had been illegally obtained. While the Mozambican litigation has been successful, the Kenyan court case is still at the preliminary stage of fact gathering. The court case allowing access to the loan agreements has set the stage for the contracts to be subjected to scrutiny to assess their legality or illegality. The two cases are indicative of the role of public interest litigation in the success of the initiatives challenging the illegally obtained loans.

There is need to recognize a country's sovereign right to cancel an illegal loan agreement in international law as some have argued through the doctrine of odious debt. If the process to acquire a loan that is followed is not compliant with the international and legal standards, the fraud should be sufficient basis for voiding a loan agreement.[95] One country's actions may not be sufficient or desirable to terminate a loan agreement. This is because there are also economic implications if a country is considered capable of reneging on loan agreements. For Mozambique, once it became public that the loans were not obtained in compliance with the country's

---

[92] Carlos Mureithi, *Kenya Is Refusing to Release the Loan Contracts for Its Chinese-Built Railway*, QUARTZ AFR. (Jan. 20, 2022), https://qz.com/africa/2115070/kenya-refuses-to-release-contracts-for-china-debt/.

[93] Denise Namburete, How Public Interest Litigation Led to Invalidation of Illegal Mozambican Debt, AFRONOMICSLAW (Aug. 4, 2022), https://www.afronomicslaw.org/2020/08/04/how-public-interest-litigation-led-to-invalidation-of-illegal-mozambican-debt/.

[94] *Id.*

[95] *Id.*

laws, creditors viewed the country as a greater investment risk.[96] The IMF cancelled a credit facility arrangement with the government and eight countries also suspended the support offered to the government through aid and loans.[97] The World Bank noted that the economic growth rate in the country reduced to 3.8% from 7.5% within a span of three years.[98] Since multiple jurisdictions and entities are involved in the process of granting loans, a concerted effort on the international front can help protect a country exercising its sovereign right to cancel a debt.

4 TRANSFORMATION: THE ROLE OF THE UNITED NATIONS

4.1 The United Nations General Assembly

The framework for sovereign debt restructuring remains undeveloped despite attempts to establish an international mechanism. In the past, restructuring has depended on the ability to negotiate with the lending nation for an extension. As noted by Dr. Magalie Masamba, the fragmented framework has given creditors more power over the debtors and there is need to balance the scales.[99] The IMF and World Bank solutions have focused on austerity as a pre-condition to granting debt relief which has resulted in negative impacts on the policy objectives of African governments to reduce poverty. This has been due to the unwillingness of creditors to share responsibility for debt restructuring with the borrowers which delays any achievement of debt sustainability. This has placed the rights of citizens in borrower countries at risk as autonomy over policy making is ceded to the creditor's proposals.[100]

---

[96] James Mutua, *Hell Breaks Loose in Mozambique: Is This the Beginning of the End of Irresponsible Sovereign Borrowing? Or a Wakeup Call to Address Benignity of the International Capital Markets?*, AFRONOMICSLAW (Aug. 7, 2020), https://www.afronomicslaw.org/2020/08/07/hell-breaks-loose-in-mozambique-is-this-the-beginning-of-the-end-of-irresponsible-sovereign-borrowing-or-a-wakeup-call-to-address-benignity-of-the-international-capital-markets/.
[97] *Id.*
[98] *Id.*
[99] COVID-19 and Sovereign Debt: The Case of SADC (Daniel Bradlow & Magalie Masamba eds. 2022).
[100] Tamale Nona, "Debt Restructuring under the G20 Common Framework: Austerity Again? The Case of Zambia and Chad." Upcoming 2022.

While an IMF proposal for a debt restructuring framework was blocked by the United States, on 10 September 2015, the UNGA adopted Resolution 69/319 on Basic Principles of Sovereign Debt Restructuring.[101] The resolution came as a result of Resolution 68/304 which sought to establish a multilateral legal framework on sovereign debt restructuring.[102] Resolution 69/319 sets out the core principles that should guide restructurings. The principles include good faith, majority restructuring, sustainability, sovereign immunity, equitable treatment, impartiality, transparency, sovereignty, and sustainability.[103] The principles seek to advance the realisation of the right of states to apply for restructuring of sovereign debt. Sovereign immunity involves considering the various aspects of a nation's authority that could be limited if sovereign debt cannot be restructured at the option of the government.[104] The foregoing principles represent an important step forward. However, Resolution 63/319 is non-binding and creditors still retain approval rights meaning that the rights of the states are qualified. Thus, despite the good work in identifying and passing a framework, it remains insufficient.

International law places UNGA resolutions within the framework of soft law. Soft law does not create binding obligations onstates. This is because it only sets out what a majority of members of the United Nations hold as the dominant views.[105] The treaty making process ought not be circumvented because states should have an opportunity to accept to be bound under international law. However, the nature of UNGA resolutions is that decisions can only be made based on the views of the majority.[106] The general consensus should not be dismissed as inconsequential because it is indicative of a desire to have some framework on certain issues. The role the United Nations can play begins at UNGA and continues to other aspects of international

---

[101] Sangwani Ng'ambi, *Sovereign Debt Restructuring in Zambia: A United Nations Principles-Based Approach?,* in COVID-19 and Sovereign Debt: The Case of SADC (Daniel Bradlow & Magalie Masamba eds. 2022).

[102] James Gathii & Harrison Mbori, *Proposals on Sovereign Debt Restructuring Over the Years,* Background Paper Prepared for the 2022 AfSDJN Summer Debt Academy ' 2022.

[103] Ng'ambi, *supra* note 101.

[104] *Id.*

[105] *Id.*

[106] *Id.*

law such as treaty making. The presence of consensus indicates that UN members may be open to having more binding international law provisions to codify their views.[107] Thus, despite being non-binding, the UNGA resolutions present a desire for nations to move forward with developing international law provisions on sovereign debt restructuring.

The UNGA resolution stands in sharp contrast to arguments to the effect that sovereign debt restructuring is best determined on a case-by-case basis. Sovereign debt has generally remained outside the scope of formal international law despite involvement of several international institutions such as the IMF and the G7 countries.[108] It is expected that developing countries in distress ought to turn to the IMF approved policies to steer the economy to safe harbor.[109] However, there is rarely any debt forgiveness because the IMF, creditors, and other institutions merely restructure the loans owed.[110] There is need for an international system and general rules that will guide the process of debt restructuring. For example, the establishment of an international court would ensure that while each country and case would be determined separately, an overarching set of rules would be applied.[111] Evidently, the case-by-case basis argument needs to be supplemented by an internationally binding framework of rules.

4.2 Role Other UN Institutions Can Play

The Secretary-General's office can support the United Nations role in supervising debt restructuring. The United Nations Secretary-General is generally responsible for ensuring that treaties have been adopted and executed as required under international law. There are currently over 500 treaties deposited with the Secretary-General.[112] As depositary, one of the crucial functions is to maintain impartiality. The involvement

---

[107] *Id.*

[108] Rep. of the Commission of Experts of the President of the United Nations General Assembly on Reforms of the International Monetary and Financial System, (Sept. 21, 2009).

[109] Gathii, *supra* note 66.

[110] Rep. of the Commission of Experts of the President of the United Nations General Assembly *supra* note 108.

[111] *Id.*

[112] TREATY SECTION OF THE OFFICE OF LEGAL AFFAIRS, TREATY HANDBOOK, U.N. Sales No. E.12.V1 (2013).

of the Secretary-General is primarily in instances where the negotiations were conducted at conferences convened by the United Nations.[113] The Secretary-General's office is also consulted in case about questions arising under a particular treaty.[114] The office is also capable of providing legal opinions and updating parties on progress towards a particular treaty.[115] The Secretary-General's office can provide important administrative assistance that would improve progress towards development of a treaty on sovereign debt restructuring.

UNCTAD can also contribute to the debt restructuring conversation. During its formation in 1964, UNCTAD's goal was to assist developing countries to integrate in the world economy.[116] The organization made it possible for critical analysis of problems plaguing developing nations and discussion of solutions. As early as 1971, in Lima, UNCTAD was sharing suggestions from Global South scholars on frameworks for debt restructuring.[117] Between 1973 and 1975, after various discussions, Global South countries were willing to discuss international guidelines coupled with supervising institutions to manage debt relief.[118] In addition, UNCTAD has also participated in more contemporary initiatives. In 2015, UNCTAD Secretariat was requested to assist the Ad Hoc committee set up to discuss an international legal framework on debt restructuring.[119] The result of the discussions was the September 2015 UNGA resolution on sovereign debt restructuring.[120] The role played by UNCTAD and the proposals presented further reinforce the position that the UN should be the supervisor of debt restructuring.

---

[113] *Id.*

[114] Treaty Section of the Office of Legal Affairs, "Summary of Practice of the Secretary-General as Depositary of Multilateral Treaties," U.N. Sales No. E.94.V.15 (1999).

[115] *Id.*

[116] Deforge et al., *supra* note 49.

[117] *Id.*

[118] *Id.*

[119] UNCTAD, *Sovereign Debt Restructuring,* https://unctad.org/topic/debt-and-finance/sovereign-debt-restructuring (last visited Jun 5, 2022).

[120] *Id.*

4.3 UN Charter

The UN as presently established consists of the UNGA, the Security Council, an Economic and Social Council, a Trusteeship Council, and an International Court of Justice and a Secretariat.[121] The Security Council's role under the Charter is primarily on international peace and security.[122] At the present moment, the disputes over sovereign debt have yet to become a conflict likely to threaten international peace and security. However, as noted earlier in the paper, in the past, countries took the territory of other countries as payment for debts. In the event that the Security Council's intervention is required, it would be appropriate that other organs of the UN had attempted to resolve the situation. Members of the UN are allowed to bring to the Security Council or the UNGA, any dispute that may be likely to result in international friction that could endanger peace and security.[123] In this regard, with the UNGA carrying out the primary role of establishing a multilateral framework with the support of UNCTAD, it is possible that sovereign debt restructuring may achieve peaceful resolution.

The Economic and Social Council is empowered to recommend how the UN can ensure observance of human rights and fundamental freedoms.[124] The Economic and Social Council should be allowed to participate in preparation of necessary conventions and agreements. This is because sovereign debt restructuring falls within the competence of the UN. In terms of an appropriate court or forum, the UN framework provides for an International Court of Justice. In the preparation of a multilateral framework, a venue for dispute resolution needs to be selected. Other appropriate forums could include setting up an arbitration or separate court to handle international debt restructuring. As highlighted above, sovereign debt restructuring deserves international attention.

---

[121] U.N. Charter art. 7.
[122] U.N. Charter art. 24.
[123] U.N. Charter art. 34, 35.
[124] U.N. Charter art. 62 ¶ 2.

5 CONCLUSION

Sovereign debt is incurred by countries in pursuit of socio-economic objectives such as infrastructure and delivery of services. However, the absence of an international framework on sovereign debt restructuring means that it remains a lender-controlled process. The potential of sovereign debt to reduce the fiscal space for countries through high interest rates means that it impacts their sovereignty. As lending institutions, the IMF and the World Bank would have a conflict of interest if they were to supervise sovereign debt restructuring. Moreover, voting powers in the IMF and the World Bank are heavily skewed in favour of creditor countries such as the United States. The United Nations is therefore the appropriate forum for ensuring that each country gets a fair vote on the principles that should govern sovereign debt. If sovereign debt crisis is not appropriately resolved, the human rights of Africans and the sovereignty of African nations could be in jeopardy.

CHAPTER NINE

The African Sovereign Debt Crisis: Is the African Repo Market the Solution?

Horman Chitonge[*]

1 Introduction

Concerns around the rising levels of sovereign debt in Africa have resurfaced in the last decade, making headlines in international and local news media. This is not the first time that sovereign debt in Africa has dominated economic development policy debates; several countries on the continent entered the New Millennium with a crippling public debt burden, which was partly resolved through the MDRI in the first decade of the 2000s. After the debt cancellation, sovereign debt in most African countries declined with the average public debt-to-GDP ratio dropping from over 100 precent in 2000 to below 30 percent by 2010 (Senga et al., 2018; see also table 1). Although the debt levels declined in most countries, the MDRI only placated the problem; sovereign debt levels have risen sharply in several countries in the last decade, raising fears around debt sustainability amid rising cost of debt servicing (ECA, 2020; Fofack, 2021; Heitzig et al., 2021; Gabor, 2021a).

The onset of the Covid-19 pandemic has aggravated the debt situation on the continent, forcing many African governments to borrow in order to respond to the economic, social, and health challenges induced by the pandemic (Fofack, 2021; Heitzig, et al., 2021; UNCTAD, 2022). This paper looks at the current sovereign debt crisis in Africa, focusing on the proposed measures intended to alleviate the impact of rising levels of public debt on Africa. The paper focuses mainly on the proposed Africa-wide repo market by the United Nations Economic Commission for Africa (ECA). This paper argues that sovereign debt crises in Africa are a symptom of

---

[*] Professor of African Studies at the Centre for African Studies, University of Cape Town.

a deeper fundamental economic problem related to the way African economies are structured. The paper further argues that while the LSF (the Africa repo market) proposed by the ECA can provide immediate liquidity relief to African countries with stronger economies, the measures are unlikely to address the fundamental economic challenges (which are at the root of the African debt crises in the past and currently) of most African economies, especially the small and weaker economies.

Although the details of the LSF are still being worked out, the proposed structure and operation modalities are not likely to contribute significantly to addressing the core economic challenges in Africa. The main reason for this is that it reproduces the structures and modalities of the global financial system which only favours stronger and bigger economies. For instance, the LSF has adopted the same risk evaluation mechanisms and credit rating modalities from the global financial system, and this will reproduce the "African Premium" and impose penalties on smaller and weaker economies on the continent (Morsy & Moustafa, 2020). As Gabor (2021a) has highlighted, it is the few economies on the continent which issue sovereign bonds that may benefit from the LSF. Even for those countries that are likely to benefit from the LSF, it is not clear that this would resolve the economic structural problems which are the root cause of unsustainable public debt. Without addressing the fundamental structural problem, the sovereign debt crisis will keep resurfacing for a long time to come. As it has been observed, "debt relief … is not sufficient to ensure long-term debt sustainability. Excessive debt is often a symptom of deeper structural and institutional weaknesses that need to be addressed first to achieve debt sustainability." (World Bank, 2022:209).

Measures adopted to respond to the debt crisis in Africa should be linked to efforts aimed at supporting structural transformation of African economies. This claim applies to the African repo market which has been proposed as an instrument for providing cheaper development finance resources and is expected to contribute to achieving debt sustainability. While the ECA (2020) sees the LSF as a game changer," revolutionalising global development financing", this paper shows that given the proposed LSF structure and modalities, it has mimicked the global financial architecture.

2 Outline

The paper starts with an overview of public debt trends in Africa, focusing on the period between 2000 and 2020. This is followed by a discussion of the key factors behind the rising sovereign debt levels. The next section then looks at the issues of debt sustainability in the context of the rising cost of borrowing and the related issue of the "African premium" or the "perception deficiency." This is followed by a discussion of the proposed LSF. The concluding section sums up the key points made in the paper.

3 Africa's Sovereign Debt: An Overview

The issue of sovereign debt in Africa has generated a rapidly growing body of literature, which can be classified into six major strands:

The first strand of debates has focused on the sustainability of public debt (Coulibaly, 2021; IMF, 2021; UNCTAD, 2022, World Bank, 2022). Here, the main concern is that the rising levels of debt and the costs of servicing the debt is likely to undermine the developmental efforts in most countries. As shown below in the case of Zambia, some countries are spending more than a third of public expenditure on debt servicing only. This diverts resources from other critical services such as education, health, and social protection. The second concern that has emerged in the last two years is the impact of the Covid-19 pandemic on African economies and public debt (Heitzig et al., 2021; IMF, 2021; World Bank, 2022; UNCTAD, 2022). African governments have been forced to borrow from local and international markets to support measures implemented to respond to the challenges induced by the pandemic. Data presented below confirm the rise of public debt in several countries following the Covid-19 outbreak. While several countries were already in debt distress even before the pandemic broke, there is no doubt that the pandemic has clearly contributed significantly to the rising debt burden on the continent (UNCTAD, 2022; World Bank, 2022). The third major arear of concern in the literature is that African sovereign bonds are incurring higher interest rates compared to countries with similar economic fundamentals (Olabisi & Stein, 2015; Morsy & Moustafa, 2020; ECA, 2020; Fofack, 2021; Gabor, 2021a). This is largely connected to the unfair way in which the global financial system relates to poorer countries which are penalized for being poor. They are made to pay higher interest rates because they have weaker economic fundamentals, while richer countries pay the lowest premium on their sovereign bonds. The fourth issue is related to the third and involves the behaviour and impact of Credit Rating Agencies (CRAs) on Africa's sovereign debt (Broto &

Molina, 2014; Barta & Johnston, 2018; Chirikure et al., 2022). Several analysts have noted that Africa suffers from the perception deficiency syndrome which in most cases has nothing to do with the real economic situation on the ground. As a result of this, rating agencies sometimes act on their poor perception of African economies, a situation that contributes to raising the cost of borrowing for African countries. The fifth issue that has been highlighted in the literature is around the growth of domestic sovereign bond markets (Dafe et al., 2017; Beirne et al., 2021). This has been lauded as a positive move because it reduces the risk associated with foreign currency denominated bonds, which exacerbate the cost of debt servicing when the local currency depreciates against major global currencies. Lastly, there have been growing calls, in the wake of the current debt crisis, to restructure the global financial system to promote fair access to development finance resources (G20 EPG, 2020; Stiglitz, 2020; Tiftik & Mahmood, 2021). Calls to restructure the global financial system have come not only from NGOs, but also from governments of the developing countries as well the United Nations.

4 Trends in Africa's Sovereign Debt

In terms of the current sovereign debt crisis in Africa, the literature has highlighted three key common trends. The first is that sovereign debt in Africa has been rising at alarming rates in several countries in the last decade, with the situation becoming critical following the outbreak of the Covid-19 pandemic as countries scrambled to find resources to cover the pandemic-induced expenditure (UNCTAD, 2022). This is partly evident in the number of countries in debt distress rising from 8 in 2014 to 18 in 2020, with public debt-to-GDP ratio rising to an average of 58 percent of GDP for the continent (IMF, 2021)[1] and 70 percent for the sample of countries discussed in this paper (see Table 1).

The second major emerging trend is that African countries, even after taking into account the various domestic macroeconomic fundamentals, are paying more to borrow from international capital markets. This has been attributed to an over-inflated risk assessment of African sovereign debt, aggravated by the Covid-19

---

[1] For countries such as Angola, Congo Republic, Ghana, Mozambique, Seychelles, South Africa and Zambia, public debt is higher than the average for the region (see Table 1).

TABLE 1 Public Debt to GDP Ratio (2000-2022), %

	2000	2005	2010	2015	2016	2017	2018	2019	2020	2021	2022
Angola	133.9	133.5	37.2	57.1	75.7	69.3	93.0	113.6	136.5	103.7	90.8
Cameroon	79.3	47.7	14.7	32.9	33.3	37.7	39.6	42.3	45.8	45.8	43.8
DRC	135.0	101.5	30.6	17.0	19.5	19.2	15.1	15.0	15.2	11.9	10.1
Congo Rep	145.0	99.8	43.5	74.2	91.0	94.2	77.1	81.7	101.1	85.4	76.9
Côte d'Ivoire	74.0	58.2	45.6	29.5	31.7	33.5	36.0	38.8	47.7	50.2	51.1
Ethiopia	93.6	78.2	39.6	54.5	54.9	57.7	61.1	57.9	55.4	57.1	n/a
Gabon	72.5	49.3	21.3	44.7	64.2	62.9	60.9	59.8	77.4	72.1	63.7
Ghana	80.2	34.0	34.5	53.9	55.9	57.0	62.0	62.6	78.9	83.5	84.9
Kenya	27.9	28.4	39.1	44.4	46.7	54.8	57.3	59.0	67.6	69.7	70.2
Mozambique	100.5	62.4	39.6	87.4	119.9	99.6	107.1	105.4	128.5	133.6	127.6
Namibia	20.4	26.0	16.0	41.3	44.8	43.2	50.4	59.6	65.3	69.9	72.6
Nigeria	57.6	18.9	9.4	20.3	23.4	25.3	27.7	29.2	35.0	35.7	36.9
Rwanda	86.0	59.0	18.8	32.4	36.6	41.3	44.9	50.2	60.1	74.8	78.2
Senegal	57.5	36.1	28.5	44.5	47.5	61.1	61.5	63.8	68.7	71.9	70.1
Seychelles	177.8	144.1	82.2	67.1	69.1	62.1	59.1	57.7	96.5	81.9	82.8
South Africa	37.9	29.6	31.2	45.2	47.1	48.6	51.6	56.3	69.4	68.8	72.3
Tanzania	n/a	46.1	27.6	39.2	39.8	40.7	40.5	39.0	39.1	39.7	39.6
Zambia	261.0	75.7	18.9	65.8	61.0	66.3	80.4	97.4	128.7	101.0	106.8
Average	96.5	62.7	32.1	47.3	53.5	54.1	57.0	60.5	73.2	69.8	69.3

SOURCE: AUTHOR BASED ON DATA FROM INTERNATIONAL DEBT STATISTICS DATABASE (https://www.worldbank.org/en/programs/debt-statistics/ids) [IDS DATABASE, 2023]

pandemic, leading to what some analysts have referred to as the "perception premium" (Fofack, 2021) or the "African Premium" (Gabor, 2021a). This reflects the international capital markets' open bias against African sovereign bonds. Olabisi and Stein (2015) estimate that, even after controlling for differences in economic fundamentals, African sovereign bonds on average attract a premium of about 2.9 percentage points compared with other countries. On the basis of this high premium on African sovereign bonds, some analysts have argued that African sovereign bonds are "mispriced" (Morsy & Moustafa, 2020).

Although the average spread of African bond coupons has declined from about 700 basis points in 2018, to around 450 basis points in 2020 and 2021, this is still way higher than comparable sovereign bonds (IMF, 2021:2). The highest yield on sovereign bonds was reported on Zambia's 10-year bond, at 44.3 percent in March 2021, though this dropped to 35.5 percent in August 2021 (Fofack, 2021). To put this into context, in the aftermath of the 2008/2009 global financial crisis which triggered the EU Debt Crisis, Italy's average interest on sovereign bonds at 7 percent were deemed unsustainable even in the short run, and radical measures were taken to restructure the debt (Lombardi & Amand, 2015). With the high interest rates African countries are facing, it is not surprising that debt servicing has "become one of their highest and fastest-growing budgetary expenditures, exceeding several countries' health budgets" (Fofack, 2021:14). This has led to a situation where most of the resources in the country are diverted to merely servicing the debt. This means indebted countries are left with meagre resources to finance development projects that can support structural transformation of the economy. Further, given the high interest rates, sovereign debt has become "default-driven" with default almost guaranteed because economically distressed economies are unlikely to sustain such levels of debt servicing.

The third major trend on Africa's sovereign debt is the rising component of foreign currency-denominated debt in sovereign debt, mostly Eurobonds (World Bank, 2020; AEO, 2021). A World Bank report on public debt has observed that most Sub-Saharan African countries have increasingly borrowed from international financial markets as opposed to concessional borrowing which accounted for the largest of sovereign debit since the early 1980s (World Bank, 2022:4). Prior to 2006, access to international bond markets on the continent was limited to South Africa, Tunisia, Egypt and Morocco, which according to Moody's (2013), have "mature domestic capital markets."

5 Sovereign Debt Dynamics in Africa

To provide a sense of the dynamics of sovereign debt in Africa, this section presents an overview of public debt on 18 selected African countries. The 18 countries are selected on the basis that they have been active in the international bond market, and they have accumulated large public debt. The section first looks at sovereign debt in general, which includes domestic and external. From the sample of countries in this paper, it is evident that most of these countries, except Kenya, Namibia, and South Africa, entered the new millennium with a huge debt burden, defined as public debt of more than 60 percent of GDP.[2] For countries such as Angola, DRC, Republic of Congo, Mozambique, Seychelles and Zambia, their debt-to-GDP ratio was over 100 percent in 2000, and the large portion of this was external debt. After a series of debt cancellations between 2005 and 2007, we see that public debt in most of these countries fell sharply, from the average (for this sample) of 97 percent in 2000 to 32 percent by 2010.[3] Although the debt levels in most countries dropped after the MDRI, most of these countries were subjected to more stringent regulatory measures attached to the debt relief package. The Bush administration for instance imposed stricter conditionality on relief given to poorer countries to ensure that they complied with Bush's war on terrorism after 9/11 (Williams, 2008).

But from 2010 onwards, public debt started to rise steadily in most countries, with sovereign debt-to-GDP ratio peaking at 73 percent in 2020 and declining slightly to 69 percent in 2021 and 2022 (Table 1). For the sample of countries in this paper, the average sovereign debt levels grew by 50 percent between 2010 and 2015, with public debt-to-GDP ratio more than doubling in countries such as Zambia, Namibia, Mozambique, Gabon, and Cameroon (Table 1). Rising debt in African countries mirrors the global trend after the onset of the Covid-19 pandemic which pushed up sovereign debt as countries implemented measures to respond to the pandemic. At the global level, the average public debt-to-GDP ratio rose from 88 percent

---

[2] The IMF uses 60 percent of GDP of public debt as a threshold for determining whether a country has a sustainable public debt or not. Debt distress is determined by looking at several indicators including projected public revenue, economic growth, debt-to-GDP ratio, foreign currency reserves, current account position, etc. (IMF, 2021).

[3] A combination of the Highly Indebted Poor Country (HIPC) initiative, together with the Multilateral Debt Relief Initiative (MDRI), coordinated by the Inter-American Development Bank, provided over US$100 billion in debt relief to 38 eligible countries by 2007 (World Bank, 2022a).

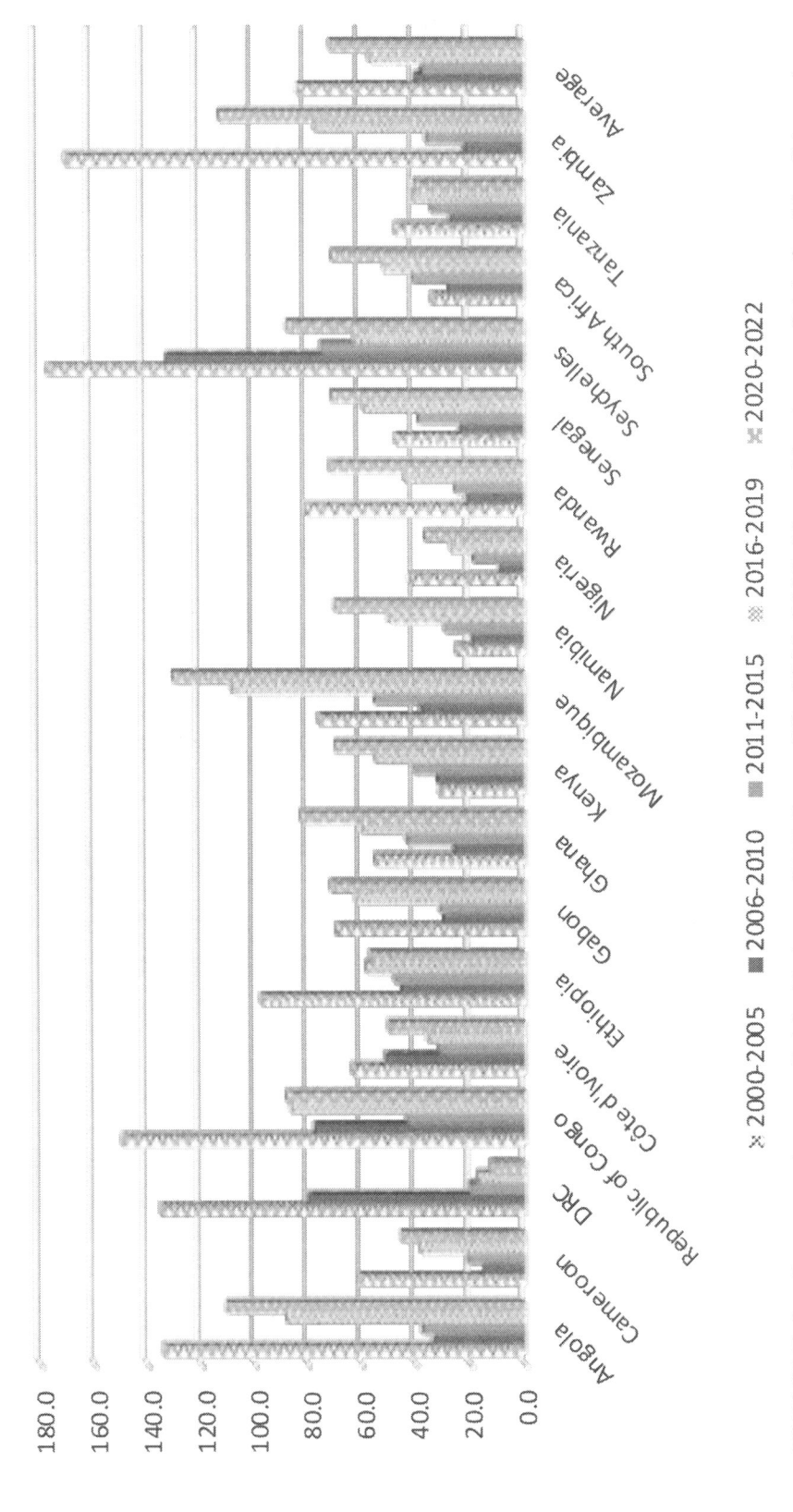

FIGURE 1 Five-year Average Public Debt-to-GDP Ratio (%) 2000–2022. Note: No data available for Namibia and Seychelles. (Source: Author based on data from International Debt Statistics database (https://www.worldbank.org/en/programs/debt-statistics/ids) [IDS Database, 2023].)

in 2019 to 105 in 2020 (Tiftik & Mahmood, 2021). For advanced economies, debt-to-GDP ratio increased to 124 percent in 2020, and close to 140 percent for the USA (Gaspar et al., 2021).

In the case of the African sample of countries discussed here, increased public borrowing begun before the pandemic as Table 1 shows, though the borrowing has risen sharply after the pandemic (Heitzig et al., 2021). If we look at the five-year average, we see that the average annual rate of public debt growth doubled from 7 percent in the 2011–2016 period to over 14 percent in the 2016–2019 period (Figure 1).

Apart from the DRC and Republic of Congo, public debt in all selected countries increased between 2006 and 2020, with countries such as Angola, Mozambique, Ghana, Zambia, Rwanda, and Namibia experiencing sharp increases over this period (Figure 1).

Average annual public debt growth rate for the 2020-2022 period rose by almost 10 percentage points from 14 percent before the Covid-19 pandemic to 24 percent. In half of the countries in the sample (Cameroon, Cote d'Ivoire, Ghana, Namibia, Nigeria, Rwanda, Seychelles, and Zambia) average annual public debt growth rates doubled compared to the growth rates before the onset of the Covid-19 pandemic, reflecting the Covid-19 pandemic induced borrowing.

6 Drivers of Rising Sovereign Debt in Africa

There are many factors which have contributed to rising sovereign debt in Africa. These include the low public debt following the debt cancellation after 2007 and the robust economic growth resulting from rising commodity prices on the global market between 2003 and 2014, which signal stronger capabilities among African countries (AEO, 2021). Other factors include the expansionary monetary policy adopted in most advanced economies after the 2008/2009 financial crisis, which lowered borrowing costs, lowered interest rates, and increased money supply. This pushed investors to look for high yields on investments largely in emerging markets (World Bank, 2020). Low interest rates on the global financial markets partly explain why we are seeing a shift in the composition of Africa's external debt from predominantly concessional borrowing to private capital markets after the 2009 financial crisis (Dafe et al., 2017; IMF, 2021; AEO, 2021). It has been estimated that the number of African countries borrowing on international markets increased from 3 in 2003 to 21 by 2020

(Fofack, 2021:13). Although concessional borrowing is still a large portion of Africa's public debt, there has been significant growth of non-concessional borrowing which is sometimes interpreted as a sign of confidence in the growth prospects of African economies (AEO, 2021).

Although interest rates have been low in advanced countries, the cost of borrowing has been relatively higher for African countries (Gabor, 2021a; Fofack, 2021, Morsy & Moustafa, 2020. The low interest rates in advanced economies made African sovereign assets attractive to investors, leading to several instances when most of the bonds issued by African governments were oversubscribed. A World Bank report that that all the sovereign bonds issued by African governments in 2019 were oversubscribed, following earlier trends (World Bank, 2020). For example, the 2012 10-year Zambian Eurobond was 16 times oversubscribed (Olabisi & Stein, 2015:88). Nigeria's 2018 12 and 20-year Eurobonds were also 4.6 times oversubscribed, while Senegal's bonds were 4.5 times; and Ghana's 2019 Eurobond was 7 times oversubscribed (Cyton, various years). The foregoing shows that investors are keen to seek out African sovereign bonds. This is mainly because the yields on African sovereign bonds are on average are much higher than in any part of the world, suggesting that lenders are getting more than what they can get elsewhere. The World Bank confirms this when it argues that African sovereign bonds are oversubscribed because African sovereign bonds "offered investors the highest yields available globally" (World Bank, 2020:4).

7   Chinese Loan Commitment to Africa

The public debt reported in Table 1 above does not include borrowing commitments from other lenders like China. There have been complaints about lack of transparency among African countries when it comes to public debt, such that the actual debt burden may be higher than what is officially reported (World Bank, 2022). Gelpern et al. (2021), who based on their review of 100 contracts between Chinse lenders and 24 borrowing countries, report that Chinese loans have unique confidentiality clauses written into the contract which constrain the borrower from revealing not only the terms of the loan, but even the existence of the loan. They conclude that due to the secrecy surrounding most loans from Chinese lenders, it seems as though Beijing is pursuing what they refer to as "debt trap diplomacy" because the terms of contract are not subject to public scrutiny. (Gelpern et al., 2021:4).

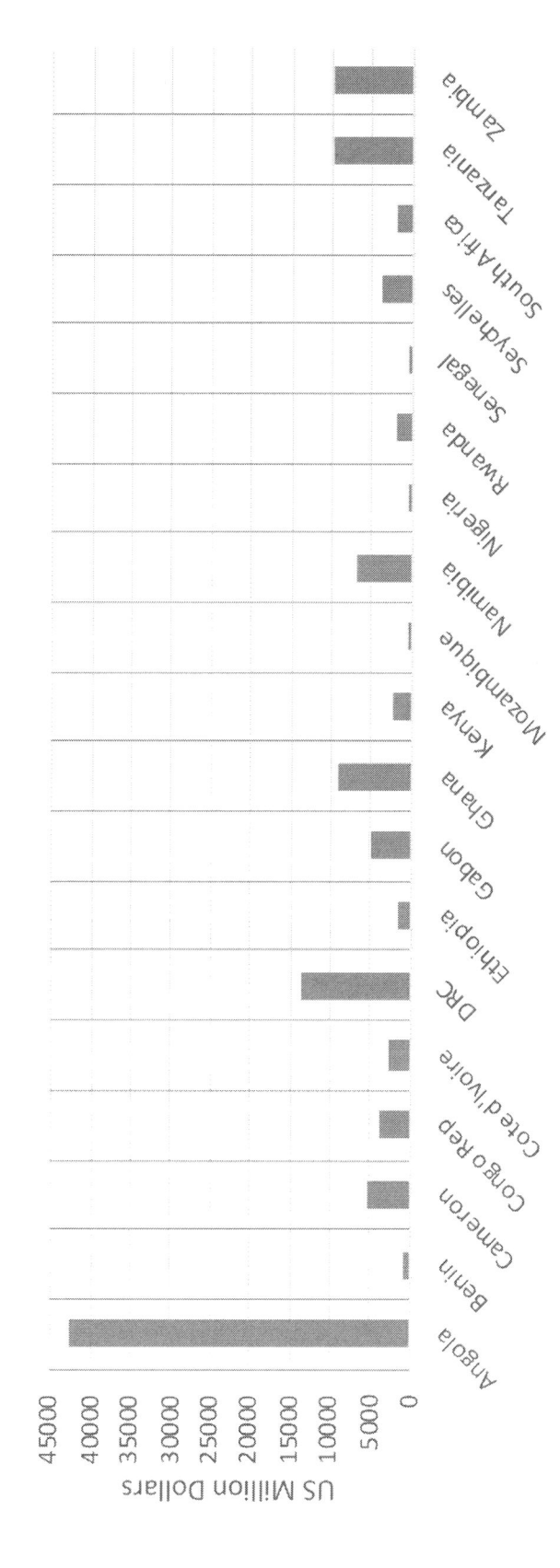

FIGURE 2 Chinese Loan Commitment to African Countries (2000–2019). (SOURCE: Author based on data from the Chinese Loans to Africa Database (http://www.bu.edu/gdp/Chinese-loans-to-africa-database/) [CLA Database, 2022].

Overall, Chinese loan commitments to Africa have been low compared to loans from international capital markets. Between 2000 and 2019, the total loan commitment from China to African countries added up to US$153.4 billion, with a third of this going to Angola alone. If we look at the sample of countries we are considering in this chapter, it is evident that Chinese loan commitments to Africa are dominated by a few countries mainly Angola, Congo Republic, Ethiopia, Nigeria, and Zambia.

The Chinese loan commitments to Africa data show that the larger portion of the loan (80 percent) go into infrastructure, mainly transport, communication, energy and mining. If this is true, these loans seem to support the effort to transform African economies.

The overall picture of the sovereign debt dynamic in Africa that one gets is that levels of public debt have been rising in most countries, and that the nature of the debt has shifted from being overwhelmingly concessional to relying on international capital markets, particularly the non-Paris-Club lenders. The other dominant feature in the sovereign debt dynamics is that although there has been significant growth of the Local Currency Bond Markets (LCBMs) in a number of countries in recent years, (Essers et al., 2014; Mecagni et al., 2014; AEO, 2021; IMF, 2021), external debt in most countries is still denominated in foreign currency, making up a significant share of sovereign debt.

8 External Debt

Since local capital markets in most African countries, outside of South Africa, Egypt, Morocco, and Mauritius, are small and developing (Moody's, 2013; Essers et al., 2014), African governments have been relying on external borrowing to access development finance. It has been estimated that external debt accounted for 60 percent of public debt in Africa in 2019, up from 57 percent in 2018 (AEO, 2021:53). For the sample of African countries we are focusing on in this chapter, the average external debt-to-GDP in 2000 was over 90 percent, but this dropped sharply to just 26 percent in 2010 (Figure 3).

From 2010, external debt has been rising steadily reaching the average of 62 percent of GDP in 2020.

In terms of the debt stock, although South Africa, Nigeria, Angola, and Kenya have relatively low external debt-to-GDP ratios, they have the largest share of external debt stock among African countries, reflecting the big size of these economies (Figure 4).

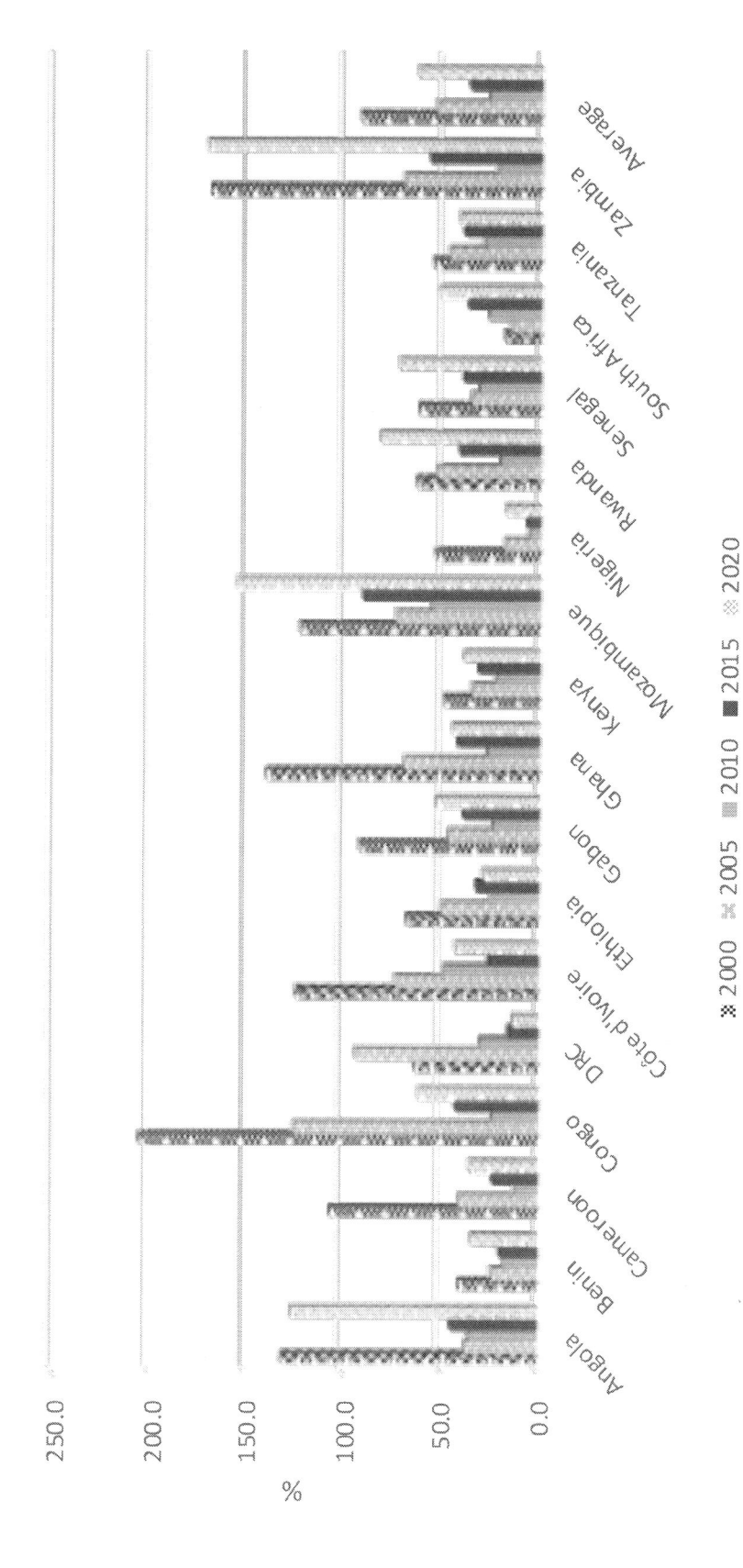

FIGURE 3 External Debt to GDP Ratio (2000-2020) %. Note: No data available for Namibia and Seychelles. (Source: Author based on data from World Bank Development Indicators Database (https://databank.worldbank.org/source/world-development-indicators) [WDI Database, 2022]).

FIGURE 4 External Debt (Billion US$ Current Prices) 2000–2020.
Note: No data available for Namibia and Seychelles. (SOURCE: Author based on data from World Bank Development Indicators Database (https://databank.worldbank.org/source/world-development-indicators) [WDI Database, 2022].)

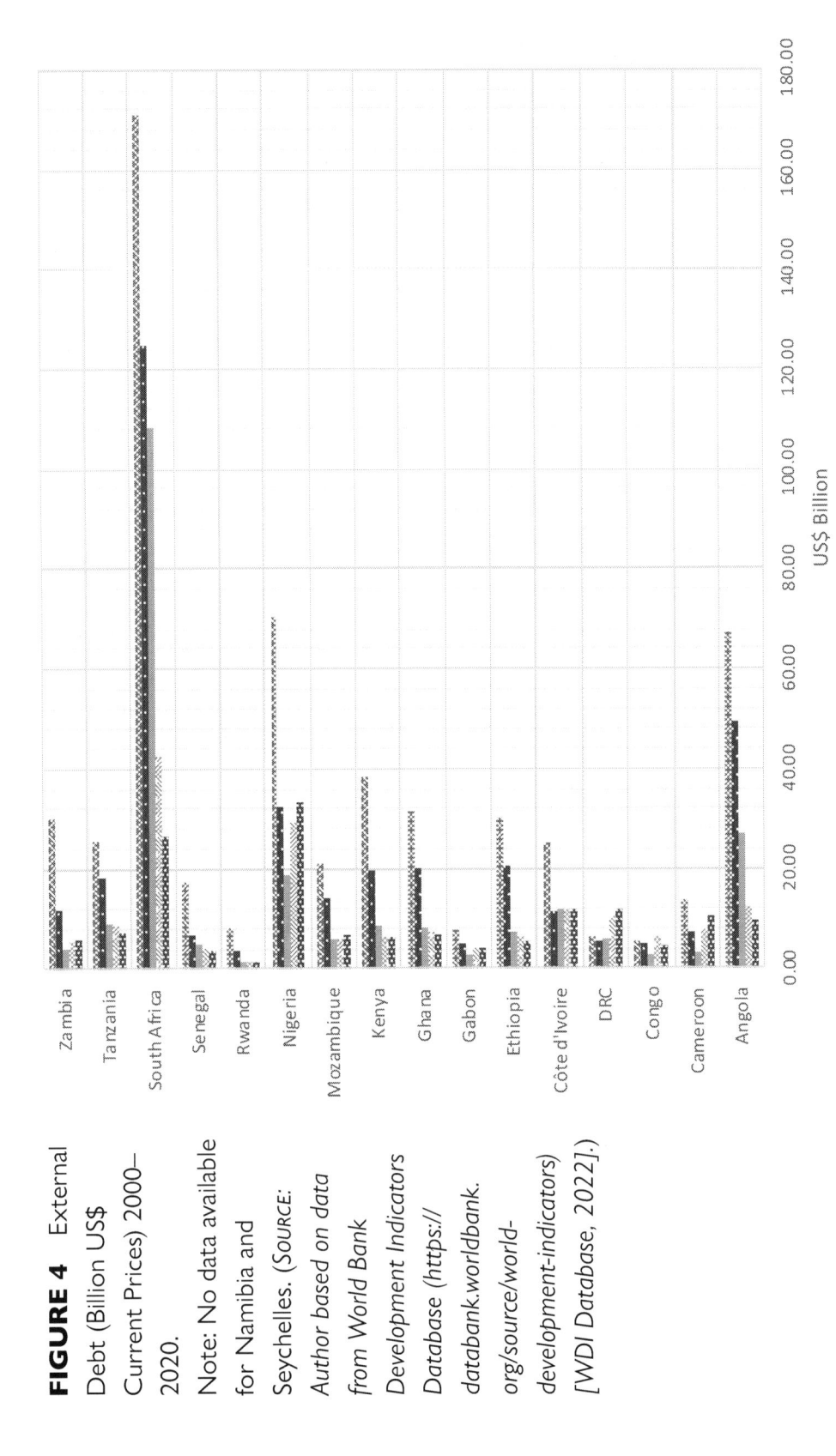

South Africa, Nigeria and Angola have the largest stock of international bond assets, which together account for 50 percent of the external debt for countries in the sample.

As noted earlier, starting from 2006, a larger number of sovereign bonds in Africa were issued on international capital markets. As of 2021, there were 21 African countries (the 18 countries we have focused on in this chapter plus Egypt, Morocco, and Tunisia) which had issued sovereign bonds on international capital markets. Several countries have issued multiple international sovereign bonds in the last decade, with Benin entering the bond market for the first time in 2019 (Table 3).

TABLE 2 Sovereign Bond Issued by African Countries *(Note: South Africa has been issuing sovereign bonds on international capital markets since the lifting of sanctions in 1994).*

	Year Issued	Bond Amount (Million $US)	Tenor	Maturity Year	Yield on Coupon
Angola	2012	1000	7	2019	7,19
	2015	1500	10	2025	8,25
	2019	3000	10 & 30	2029/2049	8,6
Benin	2019	567.5	6	2026	5,9
	2021	1213	11/31	2032/2052	5,9
Cameroon	2015	750	10	2025	9,5
	2021	700	10	2031	5,9
Republic of Congo	2007	478	—	—	—
Côte d'Ivoire	2010	2500	22	2032	6,25
	2014	750	10	2024	6,5
	2015	1000	12	2027	6,62
	2017	1875	16	2033	6,12
	2018	1700	11 & 29	2029 & 2047	5,9
	2020	1191	12	2032	4,6
	2021	850	11	2032	4,3
Ethiopia	2014	1000	10	2024	6,62

TABLE 2 Sovereign Bond Issued by African Countries *(Note: South Africa has been issuing sovereign bonds on international capital markets since the lifting of sanctions in 1994).*

	Year Issued	Bond Amount (Million $US)	Tenor	Maturity Year	Yield on Coupon
Gabon	2007	1000	10	2017	8,25
	2013	1500	11	2024	6,38
	2020	1000	10	2030	6,62
Ghana	2007	750	10	2017	8,5
	2013	750	10	2023	8
	2014	1000	12	2026	8,13
	2015	1000	15	2030	7,9
	2016	750	6	2022	9,3
	2018	2000	11 & 31	2029 & 2049	8,2
	2019	3000	31	2051	8,4
	2020	3000	7, 15 & 41	2027, 2035 & 2061	—
	2021	3000	4,7, 12 &20	2025, 2028, 2032 & 2041	8,3
Kenya	2014	2750	10	2024	4,8
	2018	2000	10 & 30	2028 & 2048	6,8
	2019	2100	8 & 13	2027 & 2032	6,2
	2021	1000	12	2033	6,3
Mozambique	2013	850	7	2020	7,85
	2018	500	7	2025	8,5
Namibia	2011	500	10	2021	5,5
Nigeria	2011	500	10	2021	7,13
	2013	1000	10 & 5	2018 & 2023	6
	2017	4800	30	2047	8,2
	2018	5368	12 & 20	2030 & 2038	7,8
	2021	3000	7,12 &30	2028, 2033 & 2051	6,8
Rwanda	2013	400	10	2023	6,87
	2021	620	10	2031	5,5

TABLE 2 (cont'd.)					
	Year Issued	Bond Amount (Million $US)	Tenor	Maturity Year	Yield on Coupon
Senegal	2009	200	5	2014	9,12
	2011	500	10	2021	8,3
	2014	500	10	2024	6,3
	2017	1000	16	2033	7,3
	2018	2000	10	2028	5,4
	2021	800	30	2051	7,2
Seychelles	2006	200	5	2011	9,46
	2010	168	16	2026	5
South Africa	2016	1250	10	2026	4,87
	2017	19000	30	2047	5,7
	2019	5000	10 &30	2029 & 2049	5,2
Tanzania	2013	600	7	2020	float
Zambia	2012	750	10	2022	5,37
	2014	1000	10	2024	8,5
	2015	1250	12	2027	9
(SOURCE: Compiled by author from various sources.) [Moody's, 2013]					

We see from Figure 4 that in six countries (Cameroon, Cote d'Ivoire, Kenya, Nigeria, Rwanda Senegal, and Zambia) the total value of external debt stock doubled between 2015 and 2020. If we take 2010 as a base year, we see that there is sharp increase in external debt in all countries except DRC and Congo.

When we look at the external public debt growth, although there are differences between countries, the common trend observed is that external debt started to rise in several countries in the period between 2005 and 2010, with the highest growth reported in the period between 2010–2015 (Table 3).

The slowdown in the annual growth rate of external public debt between 2015-2020 can be attributed to the fall in commodities especially after 2014, which most creditors use to measure risks and ability to pay the loans (IMF, 2021; Fofack, 2021).

While the total value of external debt gives us a sense of what amounts are owed non-resident creditors, the annual growth rate of external public debt, one of the most important indicators, used to measure a country's ability to meet its financial

TABLE 3 Five-Year Average Annual Growth of External Debt (%) 2000–2020 *(Data for Namibia and Seychelles not available.).*

	2000–2005	2005–2010	2010–2015	2015–2020
Angola	5.1	23.8	16.8	7.3
Cameroon	−5.4	−11.7	25.8	18.0
Congo	6.9	−11.0	15.1	1.0
DRC	−1.9	−8.5	−2.6	3.0
Côte d'Ivoire	−0.1	−0.5	−0.5	24.0
Ethiopia	2.4	3.6	36.1	9.7
Gabon	0.3	−5.3	15.0	9.8
Ghana	1.8	2.8	28.0	11.2
Kenya	1.1	7.3	24.6	18.7
Mozambique	−2.1	−0.2	27.5	9.7
Nigeria	−2.6	−7.1	14.4	23.5
Rwanda	3.7	−3.8	36.0	27.5
Senegal	1.1	5.6	7.5	30.7
South Africa	11.8	31.2	3.0	7.4
Tanzania	3.4	1.2	20.6	8.1
Zambia	−1.5	−4.2	35.4	31.0
Average	1.5	1.5	18.9	15.0

(Source: *Compiled by author from various sources.*) [IDS Database, 2023]

obligations to creditors (World Bank, 2022). In the sample of countries presented in this paper, we see that there is heterogeneity among these countries, with countries such as Angola, Mozambique, Rwanda, Senegal, and Zambia showing higher levels of debt burden (Figure 4).

Like other public debt indicators discussed above, the external public debt service-to-export revenue ratio declined from 2000, with the lowest ratio reported in 2010 for most countries. But in several countries, the ratio has been increasing since 2010.[4] External debt service, as a proportion of export revenue, shows the country's

---

[4] The 2020 ratios were obviously affected by the contracting GDPs in most countries due to the impact of the Covid-19 pandemic. The IMF (2021) estimates the on average, Sub-Saharan African economies contracted by 1.9 percent in 2020, with some countries recording much higher contraction.

ability to service debts and this ratio in 2020 was more in many countries than it was in 2000 (Table 4). These rising levels of debt service are a worrying concern in many countries mainly because this imposes a huge fiscal burden in terms of servicing the debt. This often results in governments diverting scarce resources from social and developmental spending, aimed at structural transformation of these economies, to meet debt service obligations. As argued above, this situation does not only make the debt burden unsustainable, but perpetuates the debt crisis (UNCTAD, 2022; World Bank, 2022).

The unsustainability of the debt service burden becomes more evident in the Zambia example where the country is expected to spend almost half of government revenue on debt service in 2022 (Table 5).

TABLE 4 Debt Service to Export Revenue Ratio (%).

	2000	2005	2010	2015	2020
Angola	20.62	10.52	4.45	19.46	32.07
Benin	12.95	5.87	2.28	2.75	..
Cameroon	14.26	14.35	2.63	6.02	14.09
Congo, Rep.	0.56	2.25	1.45	8.26	—
Congo, Dem. Rep.	..	7.78	3.05	3.73	2.27
Cote d'Ivoire	15.85	1.35	3.97	3.56	—
Gabon	9.23	3.47	4.78	8.50	—
Ghana	16.96	7.93	2.83	5.85	11.61
Ethiopia	13.63	4.30	3.78	18.16	25.77
Kenya	17.30	9.46	4.13	6.98	25.49
Mozambique	8.05	2.82	3.43	9.43	31.33
Nigeria	8.21	15.41	0.38	0.80	3.81
Rwanda	24.67	10.77	2.00	4.06	7.30
Senegal	14.74	6.36	4.37	6.34	—
South Africa	5.91	5.63	2.88	15.24	11.44
Tanzania	11.23	3.92	1.33	4.86	14.26
Zambia	18.51	6.53	0.76	4.21	7.15
Average	13.29	6.98	2.85	7.54	15.55

(SOURCE: *Author based on data from the International Debt Statistics*)
(*https://www.worldbank.org/en/programs/debt-statistics/ids*) [IDS Database, 2023]

Total debt service-to-public revenue in Zambia rose rapidly from 34 percent in 2020 to almost half of the national expenditure in 2022 (Table 5). Debt servicing in 2020 and 2021 in Zambia was higher than expenditure on health, education, public infrastructure, social protection, housing and community services, defense and environmental protection put together. Projected debt servicing in 2022 is 2.5 times higher than all these public expenditure line items put together![5] On average, public debt service to GDP ratio in African countries is very high compared to advanced economies which spend on average only 1 percent of GDP on public debt servicing, and certainly higher than the average of 8 percent for emerging economies (World Bank, 2022:204). The rising external debt service in the Zambian case can be attributed to the rising interest rates following Zambia's default on debt services in 2020, but also the depreciation of the local currency (Kwacha).

Rising debt servicing commitments have pushed many countries into debt distress or are already in debt distress, with diminishing liquidity. The IMF Debt Sustainability Analysis Test shows that 17 African countries in 2020 were either at high risk of or in debt distress (IMF, 2021). This situation has led to calls on the global community to find ways to address the unsustainable debt burden not just in African countries, but in low and middle-income countries in other regions. The IMF's DSA itself is highly problematic in poor countries because it forces countries to stick to an austerity plan. This leads to the reprioritisation of resource allocation from social expenditure to meeting debt service obligations (Lima, 2021). Further, the IMF's DSA does not lead to sustainability in poor countries because it focuses on short-term interventions in a situation that requires long-term strategies.

The dynamics of high debt burdens are characterized by a vicious circle in which a country's need for financing rises with rising borrowing costs. This is mainly due to the unfavourable risk assessment which low-income countries in Africa and the Global South receive from creditors. For example, in the case of Zambia, the country's default on the US$42.5 million debt service in 2020 led to skyrocketing yield on its sovereign bonds as indicated above. The rising interest rates on debts has pushed up the cost of servicing debt in most countries with debt servicing in Zambia rising

---

[5] In 2022, the 2012 Eurobond principal payment is due, and that is what has pushed the debt payment share in public expenditure (see National Budget Speech, 2022).

TABLE 5 Zambia Debts Service vs Public Expenditure.

	Government Expenditure (billion Kwacha)			Share in Government Expenditure (%)		
	2020	2021	2022	2020	2021	2022
Domestic debt Service	12.6	18.3	27.4	11.9	15.3	15.8
External Debt	21.1	27.7	51.3	19.9	23.1	29.7
Arears Payment	2.3	2.8	3.1	2.2	2.3	1.8
Total Debt Service	**36**	**48.8**	**81.8**	**34.0**	**40.7**	**47.3**
Education	13.1	13.8	18.1	12.4	11.5	10.5
Health	9.3	9.6	13.9	8.8	8.0	8.0
Social Protection	2.6	4.8	6.3	2.5	4.0	3.6
Housing & Community Services	3.5	2.2	2.4	3.3	1.8	1.4
Environmental Protection	0.61	0.95	0.97	0.6	0.8	0.6
Defence	6.5	5.6	7.6	6.1	4.7	4.4
Infrastructure	12.7	6.8	5.95	12	5.7	3.4
Total Social Expenditure	35.6	43.75	55.22	31.7	30.5	18.5
Total Revenue (estimate)	**106**	**119.6**	**172.9**			

(SOURCE: Author based on data from 2020, 2021 and 2022 National Budget)

"almost thirteenfold within a decade from around $63 million per year to more than $804 million annually by the end of 2019" (Fofack, 2021:14). This was worsened by the depreciation of the local currency (Kwacha) which by the end of the first quarter in 2021 had lost 22.7 percent of its value compared to the same quarter in 2020 (Cytonn, 2021). In 2020 alone, the country was expected to pay 4 billion dollars, which is close to 25 percent of GDP in debt servicing and payment of arrears. The average public debt service-to-public revenue in Africa was 19 percent in 2019 but this rose to more than 25 percent in 2021 (AEO, 2021:59).

9 Africa's Debt Crisis and the Global Financial System

Countries with high public debt burdens such as Angola, Mozambique, Rwanda, Ghana, Gabon, Congo, Seychelles and even South Africa are facing mounting pressure, leading to dwindling resources left to allocate for development purposes after meeting debt service obligations. In the current context of slow economic recovery, low revenue collection and strong pressure on the local currencies as advanced economies start to normalize their monetary policy, the pressure on public revenue in most countries will intensify leading to the need to access further financing support (World Bank, 2020). The current debt crisis is likely to lead to more liquidity and fiscal constraints due to further possible downgrade by the Rating Agencies (CRAs) which will push up the costs of borrowing (Chirikure et al., 2022). The systematic bias of CRAs against African sovereign bond assets makes it even more difficult for African governments to access the needed resources to stimulate growth and economic recovery (Barta and Johnston, 2017; Morsy & Moustafa, 2020; Fofack, 2021, Gabor, 2021a; ECA, 2020). Even if economic fundamentals in most African countries improve, given that CRAs tend to be slow to respond to improving economic conditions (Broto & Molina, 2014), it is likely that international capital markets will continue to over-inflate and misprice the risks of Africa's sovereign bond assets (Morsy & Moustafa, 2020; Fofack, 2021) pushing up the cost of borrowing beyond what most countries can afford. As the South African Finance Minister recently noted, the high costs of borrowing sparked by downgrades at the height of the 2020 pandemic was tantamount to kicking African countries when they were down.

The forgoing overview of the sovereign debt situation in Africa highlights the fact that the global financial system is not only creating unsustainable burdens for developing countries, but it is also grossly unfair, and in the current situation it will only intensify the already huge inequality gaps between and within nations (UNCTAD, 2022, Stiglitz, 2020). The entire financial system is biased against developing countries through an unfair system of assessing risks that contribute to spiking borrowing costs. These spikes are highly correlated with the likelihood of default as the case of Zambia highlights. Although the World Bank (2022) and IMF (2021) have been praising themselves that they have provided adequate debt relief to poor countries through various debt relief mechanisms, UNCTAD has persuasively argued that this "response has been too little too late and, to some extent, also too shortsighted" (UNCTAD, 2022:6).[6]

In particular, private creditors have remained aloof to the unfolding debt crisis in developing countries with most of them unwilling to restructure developing countries' public debts to manageable levels. For instance, according to the Jubilee Debt Campaign, Black Rock, one of the world's largest fund management entities, which holds US$220 million in Zambia's sovereign bonds, has refused to delay interest payments on Zambia's coupons, despite pressure from other lenders (Inman, 2022). As a result of the unwillingness of private creditors, the often unwieldy and large number of commercial financial entities holding debt, it has been difficult to coordinate creditor-debtor discussions (World Bank, 2022). These coordination difficulties compound the unfairness of the global financial system towards Africa.

10 The African Premium

While the increased access to international capital markets makes available the resources much needed to financing development needs in Africa, this access comes at not only a huge cost, but also with the risks attached to foreign currency denominated loans. There are at least three major risks associated with the external borrowing for countries in Africa. The first is the exchange rate risk, which makes it difficult to service loans when the local currency depreciates as alluded to earlier. This is also related to unexpected changes in monetary policy in advanced countries which tend to negatively impact the macroeconomic stability in Africa (IMF, 2021). Most of

---

[6] The IMF provided US$168 billion and the World Bank $US157 billion between March and April 2020 to 100 developing countries, but this was provided as public debt though on concessional terms, and only US$851 million debt service from low-income countries eligible for DSSI was provided (see UNCTAD, 2022:6).

the loans borrowed from international capital markets are invested in projects which generate income in local currency, and when the local currency depreciates, the cost of servicing the loans rises as well.

The second major risk associated with external debt relates to credit rating risk which occurs when a country's credit rating is downgraded, pushing up cost of borrowing including debt servicing (Heitzig et al., 2021). Morsy and Moustafa (2020) for instance have argued that the cost of borrowing is largely affected by a country's credit rating which contributes to the higher bond spread resulting into a higher premium. The important issue when it comes to the credit rating risk is that yields on international capital markets are inversely proportional to rating scores, such that lower rated bonds must pay higher interest to attract investors. In the African context, the rating risk is over-inflated by the traditional bias and perception deficit against African economies, often disregarding the economic fundamentals (Gabor, 2021b). African countries which have the same rating with non-African countries end up paying significantly higher interest rates (Olabisi & Stein, 2015; Morsy & Moustafa, 2020). An example that illustrates this is that of Italy and Mauritius: Although Mauritius had a better credit rating (Baa1) than Italy (Ba3) in 2020, the spread on the 10-year sovereign bond were 245 basis points for Mauritius and only 92.7 basis points for Italy (Fofack, 2021:10). The ECA (2020:5) reports that although Italy's public debt-to-GDP ratio is in the region of 155%, the country is still able to access capital markets resources at just 0.2 percent for a 5-year bond. These are a few examples of the blatant bias of the international financial against poorer countries. Ghana's finance Minister had to challenge Moody's decision to downgrade the country's sovereign credit rating from B3 to Caa1 in February 2022. The minister challenged the decision to downgrade the country's rating arguing that key data were omitted, and that balance of payment figures used were incorrect (Thomas, 2022). Ghana's challenge of Moody's was supported by the African Peer Review Mechanism (APRM) which appealed to Moody's to reconsider the rating decision on Ghana, arguing that the agency ignored some of key data, which if taken into account would swing the rating decision. This is one example of the biased way in which African countries are assessed by rating agencies. Ghana is not the first country to challenge the decision of rating agencies, even state officials in advanced economies have raised concerns regarding the lack of transparency and overlook of economic fundamentals.

The third major risk is that external debt in Africa is prone to risks associated with external shocks mainly the sharp decline of commodity prices on the global market. The IMF (2021) has reported that the falling commodity prices at the height of the Covid-19 pandemic increased the exchange rate risk for most African countries with large external debt.[7]

What the literature on Africa's sovereign debt has highlighted is the unfair way Africa and other developing countries are treated in the current global financial system, which make it difficult for developing countries to access the critical resources needed for development financing (ECA, 2020; G20 EPG, 2020; Gabor, 2021b). African and other developing countries find themselves pressed from all sides in the current international financial system, which is increasingly behaving like a loan shark (predatory lending) which takes advantage of a desperate borrower needing help by imposing default-driven borrowing terms that suffocates the borrower (Stiglitz, 2020). Similarly, concessional borrowing from multilateral financial institutions also come with the choking conditionality implemented through shock-therapy. As Stiglitz (2020) has observed, "[i]nternational creditors, especially private creditors, should know by now that you can't squeeze water out of stone." The increased number of African countries classified as debt distress reflect the inability of the current global financial system to respond to global challenges in a fair and sustainable manner (G20 EPG, 2020).

11 Is the Africa-wide Repo Market the Solution?

In the wake of the current debt crisis, several measures have now been proposed to address the challenges associated with the debt crisis. With specific reference to Africa, the creation of the African repurchase (repo) market to improve liquidity and sustainable access to development finance has been proposed and launched. In November 2021, the Economic Commission for Africa (ECA) announced the launch of the Liquidity and Sustainability Facility (LSF)—the Africa-wide repo market. The main objective of the LSF according to the ECA is to provide "African governments with

---

[7] For example, former Bank of England Governor, Mervyn King, questioned the credibility of rating agencies and suggested that investors ignore the rating agencies and instead base their investment decisions on yields of government bonds (Chitonge, 2015:39).

a liquidity structure on par with international standards so as to address the African [c]ontinent's specific Eurobond issuance needs" (ECA, 2021). The ECA expects the African repo market to address the challenge of rising cost of sovereign debt, and it is estimated that through the LSF, African governments will save up to US$11 billion over the next five years as a result of lower borrowing costs option. Analysts acknowledge that the idea of a facility that seeks to address Africa's rising cost of accessing development finance is welcome, but there are doubts on whether the LSF in its proposed form can address the cost of borrowing for African countries (Gabor, 2021a). While the LSF is certainly a work in progress, and it is not possible at this stage to assess how it operates, a number of observations can be made based on the proposed structure and operation of the facility. The proposed format of the LSF, while it seeks to adopt unique features, still follows the contours of the current global financial system which has worked in favour of advanced and stronger economies. For the LSF to make a difference it has to be radically different from the current global finance architecture, and the African repo market has not done that.

12   What is a Repo Market?

Repo markets are essentially a financing instrument for short-term financial needs. The Bank for International Settlements (BIS, 2017) argues that repo markets are financing structures which perform two key functions: they create low-risk investment avenues and promote efficient management of risks and collateral by financial and non-banking firms. It has also been argued that while in the 1990s, repo markets were not formally integrated into the finance industry, they have now become "integral components of the banking industry's treasury, liquidity and assets/liabilities management disciplines" (Euroclear, 2009). Many developed countries have well developed repo markets which are part of the capital markets and play an important role in providing short-term financing options to private and public borrowers. For instance, in Europe, the Euro repo markets have in the past decade "grown to become the predominant source of short-term funding in euro-denominated markets" and this has helped to lower borrowing costs when the bond assets are traded in these competitive capital markets (Fofack, 2021:9-10). Repo markets are also seen as critical tools for stabilizing the financial systems (Cullen, 2018). However, some analysts are critical of the role of repo markets and argue that these structures only serve to validate neoliberal economic interests (Gabor, 2021b; Barta & Johnston, 2018).

The African repo market proposed by the ECA is envisioned to work as a facility where private investors can borrow against African sovereign bonds at concessional interest rates (Gabor, 2021a). A private investor with an African sovereign (Eurobond or local currency bonds) can borrow from the LSF by pledging these bonds as collateral (see ECA, 2020). In a conventional capital market, private investors seeking to buy or holding African sovereign bonds often rely on their own funds or raise funds for investment from capital markets, usually at higher interest rates depending on the sovereign credit rating or the collateral status of the country in question. What the African repo anticipates is to attract private investors into African sovereign bonds by making available resources from which they can borrow against these bonds. According to the ECA (2020) since the private investors holding African bonds will be able to borrow at lower interest, it is expected that the LSF will ultimately lower African governments' cost of accessing development finance (ECA, 2021). The ECA envisions the LSF to serve two critical functions: to provide investment funds at subsidized or lower interest rates, and secondly, to attract private investors into African sovereign bonds. The concessional lending aspects is expected to lower the cost while at the same time attract more investors into the African repo. But these assumptions need to be critically assessed to see if there are grounds upon which these expectations can be realized. For instance, the view that by offering lower interests to investors with African sovereign bonds will attract private investors assumes that these investors make decisions to invest purely on the basis of interest rates. Private investors in particular take several factors into account before they decide to invest. One has to overcome the negative perception of African sovereigns to attract significant investments from private investors. That is the challenge which the African repo market should grapple with.

Like most repo markets, the LSF will have two parties in the secondary market: the seller who sells the security/bond but commits to buy back (repurchase—hence repo) the asset at an agreed date, and the buyer who pays for the asset, but commits to sell back (reverse repo) the asset at a future date (Euroclear, 2009; Cullen, 2018). In the same way, a private investor holding African sovereign bonds can sell (borrow against) these bonds by accessing the LSF resources instead of capital markets. The LSF would then give money (buy the sovereign bond) to the private investor agreeing to sell the bond to the private investor at a specified date. This then would represent the "reverse purchase" for the LSF (National Treasury, 2021). The ECA envisions that the LSF would provide an incentive for private investors to invest in African sovereign bonds, which is expected to lower borrowing costs and improve access to development finance resources for African countries on more favourable terms (ECA, 2020).

13   The African Repo Market: Opportunities and Challenges

In theory, the LSF has three major opportunities. One is that it can make sovereign borrowing transparent and potentially cheaper, but not always cheaper (see ibid). Second it has the potential to be an indirect vehicle for accessing long-term development finance necessary to support the transformation of African economies. It has the potential to ease the liquidity constraints which many African countries face due to the unfair structure of the global financial system, as alluded to above. Third, the LSF has the advantage of being a regional facility designed to further African interests which are often overlooked or discriminated against in international markets.

The ECA sees its proposal for LSF in Africa to prioritise liquidity first, with risks (collateral evaluation) coming in as a second priority as something of a game changer (ECA, 2020). Gabor, explains how the LSF is expected to operate, including the priority given to liquidity:

> Whereas public and private repo lenders use haircuts as a risk management tool [and therefore prioritise assessment of risk], the LSF would first prioritise the liquidity of sovereign bond markets, albeit without giving up entirely the risk management aspect. This is why the LSF would set concessional haircuts at below market levels (prioritized liquidity), but would retain [collateral evaluation] a ratings-based methodology (presumably accounting for the credit [rating] of the private borrowers and for the creditworthiness of the issuer of sovereign collateral)" (Gabor, 2021a:9).[8]

While the ECA touts this as a game changer that deviates from the current global financial architecture which prioritises risk evaluation over liquidity, the proposed LSF modalities and structure are not radically different from the "Wall Street Consensus"

---

[8] Haircut is the difference between the money value given to the seller (borrower) and the value of collateral the asset provides as guarantee, as assessed by the lender (buyer) (Gabor, 2021a:8).

(Gabor, 2021b). As noted above, the lowering of interest rates does not mean the private investors will overlook their "perceived" risks of African sovereign bonds. There is a high possibility that the perceived risks of African sovereign bonds can lead to raising the LSF interest rates, thereby raising borrowing cost, which eventually undermines liquidity, especially for African economies with perceived poor fundamentals. The European Central Bank adopted a similar measure, but between 2010 and 2012, raised the interest on the repo by demanding additional collateral, which led to the dampening of the mood for private investors (Cullen, 2018). The LSF might face a similar scenario which is likely to undermine its priority on liquidity because the need to cover the perceived risk of the least liquid economies override liquidity as a priority (Euroclear, 2009; BIS, 2017; Gabor, 2021a). Gabor (2021a) has argued that the LSF is likely to amplify the pro-cyclical risks among African economies due to its proposed collateral framework.

Even if the LSF has a genuine focus on liquidity, as long as the lending and borrowing modalities are linked to the current models of risk evaluation and collateral structure, this will not augur well for most African economies which suffer a perception deficiency in the current risk evaluation framework. For this to work, one has to find a different system of evaluating risk and collateral requirement or decouple the need for liquidity from risk assessment. Such a mechanism would amount to a fundamental shift from the current model that can't work without risk evaluation to protect the interest of investors. This is fundamental because it is always economies perceived to be at high risk of default which face serious liquidity constraint, and as a result face prohibitively high cost of borrowing. Thus, stating that liquidity will be prioritised, while at the same time sticking to the conventional risk evaluation model does not break the circle of high cost of borrowing, especially for poorer economies. Even if the continent was to come up with its own rating agencies as proposed by the Senegalese President, Macky Sall, in his speech at the AU in early 2022 (Africanews, 2022), this would only make a difference if the risk assessment criteria, which has always worked against African economies, are radically changed. The fact that LSF will also apply the collateral/risk assessment has serious implications on its ability to provide equitable access to finance for development among African countries.

In terms of the challenges, although the ECA (2020) argues that this is expected to revolutionalise the global financial system, the facility still mirrors conventional capital market instruments which means that it will not offer anything substantially different in the African context as elaborated on earlier. One of the basic weaknesses of the LSF as proposed is that it will still apply the same collateral evaluation or risk management criteria which is likely to discriminate against sovereign debts from poorer African countries, given that countries have different economic fundamentals upon which the risk assessment and credit ratings are based. Unless the LSF can find a way to delink liquidity needs from risk assessment, it will be difficult to provide cheaper access to development finance resources for poorer African countries. LSF, as long as it sticks to the current risk assessment and credit rating criteria, will be reproducing the same system where the richer countries have open access to development financial resources while the poorer nations are pushed into default driven borrowing (Fofack, 2020). In this sense, the facility will still favour relatively advanced economies on the continent by allowing them to borrow at lower interest rates but imposing punitive borrowing costs on poorer African countries which desperately need to borrow at lower costs (Gabor, 2021a). Ultimately, the outcome of the African repo is not likely to be very different from the highly discriminatory and unfair global financial system which punishes poor nations for being poor, while favouring richer nations which can afford to pay higher interests rates. In the African context, issuance of sovereign bonds is concentrated in five large economies (Nigeria, South Africa, Egypt, and Angola) which, together, account for over 75 percent of sovereign bonds on the continent (Gabor, 2021a:12). Given the proposed structure and operation of the LSF, it is likely that it will reproduce the same inequality, we have seen at the global level, on the continent.

The other major challenge is the size or fire power of the facility. The ECA is counting on donors, OECD central banks, multilateral and regional development banks, IMF (Special Drawing Rights), to provide the initial capital for the LSF. But it is not clear that these funders will be forthcoming to make any substantial amount available to support the African repo. Even if they do come to the party and make funds available, that would mean that they would apply the conventional neoliberal global financial framework, which does not give the LSF much room to deviate from the norm. If these institutions make the needed funds for the LSF to operate, they will impose their own view of how the facility should operate, most likely will bring the LSF within the ambit of the established CRA structure, which takes us back to square one. If past experiences are anything to go by, there is no ground to believe that these funders will commit substantial resources to the African repo market without the accompanying regulatory discipline (Williams, 2008). There are other concerns raised on the LSF including the point that its status in relation to central banks on the continent is not yet clear and that the LSF operations might be in direct conflict with and may even undermine the work of central banks (Gabor, 2021a). Similarly, the LSF does not seem to have addressed the "perception deficit" which has followed African borrowers for a long time. There is also a concern that it is not clear if the LSF will operate local or foreign currency denominated bonds. Decisions on whether the LSF will adopt a local or foreign currency bond system can have a significant impact. The other major concern is that it is not clear whether the LSF would mechanism to ensure that the resources accessed are directed to efforts which support the structural transformation of African economies by building productive capacities. If African governments borrow to run by-elections because the ruling party has "bought" an opposition MP(member of Parliament), then the LSF will not be contributing to addressing the fundamental economic challenge on the continent.

14 Long-Term Solution to the African Debt Crisis

While the various initiatives put in place to respond to the debt crisis such as the LSF are needed as short-term interventions, resolving the debt crisis in Africa, on a sustainable basis, calls for actions that focus on transforming the structure of African economies. The major root cause of the debt crisis is the heavy dependence of African economies on primary commodity export which makes them vulnerable to global price or demand shocks (UNCTAD, 2022). When commodity prices on the global market fall, revenue for African countries decline, negatively affecting the availability of resources for development. Past experiences of the debt crisis in Africa have revealed that most countries borrow when commodity prices on global markets are high, but then find it difficult to repay the loans when prices decline, and prices of commodities do fall and fall sharply often. Thus, as long as the structural issue of dependence on commodities is not addressed, the debt crisis will remain a recurrent problem for African countries. Transforming the structure of African economies to create economic resilience requires broadening both the production and export bases, as well as reducing the large productivity gaps between sectors, which is a sign of inefficient use of resources in the economy (AEO, 2020). Transforming African economies requires long-term investment in sectors to boost production, productivity and build competitiveness. Accessing resources to support structural transformation should be the main focus of strategies seeking to address the debt crisis on the continent. As the World Bank (2022) has rightly observed, creating resilient economies in Africa requires transforming the structure of these economies and that is the most sustainable way to address the sovereign debt crisis.

15 Conclusion

This paper has shown that Africa is again in the throes of an even deeper sovereign debt crisis. Although there is heterogeneity among African countries, the current levels of debt in several countries have reached alarming proportions. Public debt-to-GDP ratios for countries such as Ghana, Kenya, Mozambique, Namibia, Senegal, South Africa and Zambia are much higher in 2020 than in 2000. The rising cost of debt servicing in most of the countries with high public debt has meant that an increasingly higher proportion of public resources are being committed to meeting sovereign debt obligations, diverting the little resources available from efforts to promote economic transformation and funding social services. For example, in the Zambian case, the government is expected to spend 47 percent of total public revenue in 2022 to service debt and pay areas on debt. Part of the challenge here is that African sovereign debt incurs a high cost of borrowing in terms of interest rates charged due largely to the bias against African bonds in international capital markets. To address this challenge, the ECA has proposed and launched the LSF which is envisioned to lower the cost of accessing development finance in Africa. While this is a timely initiative with the potential to contribute to addressing the debt crisis, the LSF has several shortcomings which makes it difficult for poorer African countries to benefit from this initiative. Its proposed structure is likely to lead to the same effects as the global financial system which punishes African countries for being poor. Efforts intended to effectively address the African debt crisis need to understand the complex nature of the 21st century global capitalism underpinned by a sophisticated financial sector whose activities exacerbate global inequality and marginalization. It is argued in this paper that an effective sustainable way to address the debt crisis in Africa is to promote structural transformation of African economies to create resilience and stability.

References

Afr. Dev. Bank Grp., African Economic Outlook 2021: From Debt Resolution to Growth: The Road Ahead for Africa (2021). [AEO, 2021]. (2021). [AEO, 2021].

AU Chair Wants Pan-African Financial Rating Agency, Africanews (May 16, 2022, 4:42 PM), https://www.africanews.com/2022/05/16/au-chair-wants-pan-african-financial-rating-agency//. [Africanews, 2022].

Bank for Int'l Settlements, Repo Market Functioning (Comm. on the Glob. Fin. Sys. Papers, No. 59, 2017). [BIS, 2017].

Zsofia Barta & Alison Johnston, *Rating Politics?: Partisan Discrimination in Credit Ratings in Developed Economies,* 51 Comp. Pol. Stud. 587 (2018). [Barta & Johnston, 2018].

John Beirne et al., *Local Currency Bond Markets, Foreign Investor Participation, and Capital Flow Volatility in Emerging Asia* (Asian Dev. Bank Inst. Working Paper Series, Paper No. 1252, 2021). [Beirne et al., 2021].

Carmen Broto & Luis Molina, *Sovereign Ratings and their Asymmetric Response to Fundamentals* (Banco de Espana Working Paper, Paper No. 1428, 2014). [Broto & Molina, 2014].

Nora Chirikure et al., *How Are the 'Big Three' Rating Agencies Impacting African Countries?,* Afr. Pol'y Rsch. Inst. (Apr. 19, 2022), https://afripoli.org/how-are-the-big-three-rating-agencies-impacting-african-countries-54. [Chirikure et al., 2022].

Horman Chitonge, Economic Growth and Development in Africa: Understanding Trends and Prospects (2015). [Chitonge, 2015].

Chinese Loans to Africa Database, B. U. Glob. Dev. Pol'y Ctr., https://www.bu.edu/gdp/chinese-loans-to-africa-database/ (last updated Apr. 25, 2022). [CLA Database, 2022].

Brahima S. Coulibaly, *Debt Sustainability and Financing for Development: A Key Post-COVID Challenge, in* Foresight Africa 2021, at 9–12 (Brookings Afr. Growth Initiative, 2021). [Coulibaly, 2021].

Jay Cullen, *The Repo Market, Collateral and Systemic Risk: In Search of Regulatory Coherence, in* Research Handbook on Shadow Banking: Legal and Regulatory Aspects (Iris H.-Y. Chiu & Iain G. MacNeil, eds., 2018). [Cullen, 2018].

Florence Dafe et al., *Localising Sovereign Debt: The Rise of Local Currency Bond Markets in Sub-Saharan Africa* (SOAS Univ. of London Dep't of Econ. Working Paper Series, Paper No. 202, 2017). [Dafe et al., 2017].

U.N. Econ. Comm'n for Afr., Building Forward Together: Financing a Sustainable Recover for the Future of All (2020). [ECA, 2020].

U.N. Econ. Comm'n for Afr., *Launch of the Liquidity and Sustainability Facility (LSF) /Glasgow, Scotland,* Polity (Nov. 4, 2021), https://www.polity.org.za/article/launch-of-the-liquidity-and-sustainability-facility-lsf-glasgow-scotland-2021-11-04. [ECA, 2021].

Dennis Essers et al., *Local Currency Bond Market Development in Sub-Saharan Africa: A Stock-Taking Exercise and Analysis of Key Drivers* (U. Antwerp Inst. of Dev. Pol'y & Mgmt. Working Paper, Paper No. 2014-08, 2014). [Essers et al., 2014].

Euroclear, Understanding Repos and the Repo Markets (2009). [Euroclear, 2009].

Hippolyte Fofack, Brookings Afr. Growth Initiative. The Ruinous Price for Africa of Pernicious "Perception Premiums" (2021). [Fofack, 2021].

Daniela Gabor, *The Liquidity and Sustainability Facility for African Sovereign Bonds: A Good ECA/PIMCO Idea Whose Time Has Come?* (SocArXiv Ctr. for Open Sci., 2021), https://doi.org/10.31235/osf.io/erku6. [Gabor, 2021a].

Daniela Gabor, *The Wall Street Consensus,* 52 Dev. & Change 429 (2021). [Gabor, 2021b].

Vitor Gaspar et al., *Global Debt Reaches a Record $226 Trillion,* IMF Blog (Dec. 15, 2021), https://blogs.imf.org/2021/12/15/global-debt-reaches-a-record-226-trillion/. [Gaspar et al., 2021].

Anna Gelpern et al., AidData, How China Lends: A Rare Look into 100 Debt Contracts with Foreign Governments (2021). [Gelpern et al., 2021].

Chris Heitzig et al., Brookings Afr. Growth Initiative, Sub-Saharan Africa's Debt Problem: Mapping the Pandemic's Effect and the Way Forward (2021). [Heitzig et al., 2021].

International Debt Statistics (IDS), World Bank, https://www.worldbank.org/en/programs/debt-statistics/ids (last visited Mar. 14, 2023). [IDS Database, 2023].

IMF, *Navigating a Long Pandemic,* Regional Economic Outlook: Sub-Saharan Africa (Apr. 2021). [IMF, 2021].

Phillip Inman, *BlackRock Urged to Delay Debt Repayments from Crisis-torn Zambia,* GUARDIAN (Apr. 11, 2022, 2:04 PM), https://www.theguardian.com/world/2022/apr/11/blackrock-urged-to-delay-debt-repayments-from-crisis-torn-zambia. [Inman, 2022].

Karina Patricio Ferreira Lima, *Reforming the International Monetary Fund's Debt Sustainability Assessments towards Achieving the UN's Sustainable Development Goals (SDGs): A Crucial Post-Pandemic Recovery Agenda,* 2 AFR. J. INT'L ECON. L. 32 (2021). [Lima, 2021].

Domenico Lombardi & Samantha St. Amand, Italy's Crisis: Neither Fiscal Profligacy nor Capital Flows (Apr. 2015) (unpublished manuscript), https://www.ineteconomics.org/uploads/papers/INET-Conference_Lombardi.pdf. [Lombardi & Amand, 2015].

MAURO MECAGNI ET AL., IMF AFR. DEP'T, ISSUING INTERNATIONAL SOVEREIGN BONDS: OPPORTUNITIES AND CHALLENGES FOR SUB-SAHARAN AFRICA (2014). [Mecagni et al., 2014].

AURELIEN MALI & CYRIL AUDRIN, MOODY'S INVS. SERV., INTERNATIONAL SOVEREIGN ISSUANCE IN AFRICA 2013–14: A RATING AGENCY PERSPECTIVE (Gregory Davies ed., 2013). [Moody's, 2013].

Hanan Morsy & Eman Moustafa, *Mispricing of Sovereign Risk and Investor Herding in African Debt Markets,* (Afr. Dev. Bank Grp. Working Paper Series, Paper No. 331, 2020). [Morsy & Moustafa, 2020].

S. AFR. NAT'L TREASURY DEP'T, 2020/21 DEBT MNAGEMENT REPORT (2021). [National Treasury, 2021].

Michael Olabisi & Howard Stein, *Sovereign Bond Issues: Do Africans Countries Pay More to Borrow?,* 2 J. AFR. TRADE 87 (2015). [Olabisi & Stein, 2015].

Christian Senga et al., *Sub-Saharan African Eurobond Yields: What Really Matters Beyond Global Factors?,* 8 REV. DEV. FIN. 49 (2018). [Senga et al., 2018].

JOSEPH STIGLITZ, IMF FIN. & DEV., CONQUERING THE GREAT DIVIDE (2020). [Stiglitz, 2020].

David Thomas, *Ghana Slams 'Leviathan' Rating Agencies After Moody's Downgrade,* AFR. TRADE. (Feb. 8, 2022), https://african.business/2022/02/finance-services

/ghana-slams-leviathan-ratings-agencies-after-moodys-downgrade/. [Thomas, 2022].

Emre Tiftik & Khadija Mahmood, Inst. Int'l Fin., Global Debt Monitor: COVID Drives Debt Surge—Stabilization Ahead? (Sonja Gibbs ed., 2021). [Tiftik & Mahmood, 2021].

U.N. Conference on Trade and Development, *Financing for Development: Mobilizing Sustainable Development Finance Beyond COVID-19,* U.N. Doc. TD/B/EFD/5/2 (Jan. 11, 2022). [UNCTAD, 2022].

World Development Indicators, World Bank, https://databank.worldbank.org/source/world-development-indicators (last updated Dec. 22, 2022) [WDI Database, 2022].

Matthew S. Williams, *The Bush Administration, Debt Relief, and the War on Terror: Reforming the International Development System as Part of the Neoconservative Project,* 35 Soc. Just. 49 (2008). [Williams, 2008].

World Bank, Debt Report 2020 (2nd ed. 2020), https://pubdocs.worldbank.org/en/986781586183098371/pdf/Debt-Report-Edition-II.pdf [World Bank, 2020].

World Bank, World Development Report (2022): Finance for an Equitable Recovery. [World Bank, 2022].

CHAPTER TEN

The Challenge of Collateralisation of Public Assets in Loan Contracts and Indentures: What Is the Way Forward?

Ian M. Muriithi[*]

1 Introduction

Securitisation is the process in which certain types of assets are pooled or merged by an originator and issuer then repackaged into interest-bearing securities and sold to investors who receive the principal and interest payments from the underlying assets. This process has traditionally been used to transfer credit risk from originators of the assets to the purchasers of the securities.[1] It is noteworthy that in theory any type of financial asset can be securitised. However, in practice securitisation has been limited to loans and other assets that generate receivables or with stable cashflows. Examples have included different types of consumer or commercial debts[2] such as home mortgages, contractual debts ranging from auto loans to credit card debts[3] and subprime mortgages/collateralised debt obligations as witnessed with the role they played in the 2008 Global Financial Crisis.[4] These instruments fall under the generic name of Asset-Backed Securities (ABS).[5] In the sovereign debt space such securities which comprise of sovereign loans have been backed by public assets under what is

---

[*] Advocate of the High Court of Kenya and Legal Assistant at CPF Financial Services Limited.
[1] Andreas Jobst, "Back to Basics: What is securitization?" (2008) INTERNATIONAL MONETARY FUND, available at <https://www.imf.org/external/pubs/ft/fandd/2008/09/pdf/basics.pdf> (accessed 17 May 2022).
[2] James Chen, "Securitization" (2020) INVESTOPEDIA, available at <https://www.investopedia.com/terms/s/securitization.asp#:~:text=Securitization%2is%20the%20procedure%20where,of%2repackaged%20assets%20to%20investors.> (accessed 17 May 2022).
[3] *Ibid.*
[4] *Supra* note 1.
[5] *Ibid.*

generally referred to as collateralised financing.[6] In this regard as noted by the International Monetary Fund (IMF) "a debt instrument is collateralised when the creditor has rights over an asset or revenue stream that would allow it, if the borrower defaults on its payment obligations, to rely on the asset or revenue stream to secure repayment of the debt."[7] Sovereign loans are thus either secured by existing assets or future receipts.[8] Such mechanisms are not new to Africa with collateralized borrowing in developing and emerging markets being considerable among sovereigns.[9] Various analysts assert that "many official bilateral infrastructure loans to sub-Saharan Africa are collateralised."[10] Collateralised borrowing however presents significant challenges.[11] For instance, it could potentially lead to the loss of collateral for the sovereign which would have serious impacts on the country and its citizens.[12] It suffers from a lack of transparency through hidden and contingent liabilities.[13] It leads to protracted debt restructuring processes. It does not necessarily represent a cheaper cost of financing despite lowering risks for lenders and it leaves a sovereign vulnerable to shocks.[14] However, collateralised borrowing has historically been the only means through which some African countries can raise external finance to fund essential infrastructure development.[15]

This chapter begins by examining the composition of sovereign debt in Africa in Section 2. Section 3 will analyse the different classifications of collateralised

---

[6] International Monetary Fund, 'Collateralized Transactions: Key Considerations for Public Lenders and Borrowers' (2020) INTERNATIONAL MONETARY FUND, available at <https://www.imf.org/en/Publications/Policy-Papers/Issues/2020/02/19/Collateralized-Transactions-Key-Considerations-for-Public-Lenders-and-Borrowers-49063> (accessed 17 May 2022).
[7] *Ibid*.
[8] African Development Bank Group, "African Economic Outlook 2021" (2021) AFRICAN DEVELOPMENT BANK GROUP, at 65, available at <https://www.afdb.org/en/documents/african-economic-outlook-2021> (accessed 17 May 2022).
[9] Fiscal Affairs Department and others, "Assessing Public Sector Borrowing Collateralized on Future Flow Receivables" (2003) INTERNATIONAL MONETARY FUND available at <https://www.elibrary.imf.org/view/journals/007/2003/053/article-A001-en.xml> (accessed 17-May-2022).
[10] *Supra* note 6 at 4.
[11] *Supra* note 9 at 18.
[12] *Ibid* at 10.
[13] *Supra* note 8 at 64.
[14] *Supra* note 9 at 3.
[15] *Ibid* at 10.

borrowing and its use on the continent. Its challenges shall be evaluated in Section 4 where some myths regarding the same will also be addressed. Section 5 will then examine the potential benefits of collateralised borrowing and present a way forward before the chapter comes to a conclusion.

2 The Composition of Sovereign Debt in Africa

In January 2020 the Executive Directors of the IMF held a discussion on the evolution of public debt vulnerabilities in Lower Income Economies following a joint IMF and World Bank staff assessment paper. They noted that the "continued stability of debt levels" in many low-income economies hinged on a "continued benign global environment and relative stability of commodity prices."[16] They could not have predicted or prepared for the unprecedented and devastating impact the Covid-19 Pandemic would have on the world and global economy (the effects are still being felt more than two years later). In the meantime, many African governments had been taking on excessive debt with the expectation of continuous future economic growth and with many such countries having already crossed unsustainable debt thresholds.

Today the Covid-19 pandemic has exacerbated Africa's need for increased public funding while amplifying what was already a worrying trend of unsustainable debt levels on the continent which has plunged some nations into distress and left many others on the brink.[17] Further, global economic prospects have significantly worsened as a result of Russia's illegal war in Ukraine at a time when the world was on the path of durable economic recovery.[18] This has led to higher borrowing costs for sovereigns. Tighter financial conditions have increased debt vulnerabilities thereby risking widespread distress. A a sharp rise in commodity prices namely fuel and food, intensified

---

[16] International Monetary Fund, "The Evolution of Public Debt Vulnerabilities in Lower Income Economies" (2020) IMF POLICY PAPER. EXECUTIVE BOARD ASSESSMENT, available at https://www.imf.org/en/Publications/Policy-Papers/Issues/2020/02/05/The-Evolution-of-Public-Debt-Vulnerabilities-In-Lower-Income-Economies-49018 (accessed 1-June-2022).

[17] The World Bank, "Debt-Sustainability-Analysis-(DSA)" (2021), DEBT & FISCAL RISKS TOOLKIT, available at <https://www.worldbank.org/en/programs/debt-toolkit/dsa> (accessed 1 June 2022).

[18] International Monetary Fund, "World Economic Outlook: War Sets Back the Global Recovery" (2022) INTERNATIONAL MONETARY FUND at XV, available at <https://www.imf.org/en/Publications/WEO/Issues/2022/04/19/world-economic-outlook-april-2022#:~:text=War%20Sets%20Back%20the%20Global%20Recovery,-APRIL%202022&text=Global%20growth%20is%20projected%20to,2023%20than%20projected%20in%20January.> (accessed 1 June 2022).

supply disruptions, elevated inflation to a projected 8.7% in emerging and developing economies and increased capital outflows from these markets are all expected to last much longer.[19] Emerging markets and developing countries are also expected to bear the brunt of the scarring effects of the Russia/Ukrainewar due to limited policy support.[20]

Africa has never been a stranger to debt crises in the past. However, the predicament faced today can be attributed to the fact that bilateral Paris Club creditors are no longer the largest source of debt financing on the continent. Instead, there has been a proliferation of new and diversified creditors in the market.[21] To put this into perspective "commercial creditors accounted for 40% of Africa's total external debt by the end of 2019 compared [to] 17% in 2000."[22] In stark contrast "in 2000, bilateral lenders, mostly Paris Club members, accounted for 52% of Africa's external debt stock, but by the end of 2019, their share had fallen to 27%."[23] Bondholders are now the top creditors in Africa with China slightly trailing behind as the preferred bilateral lender with a share of 13% of the continent's external debt.[24] The shift in Africa's debt composition can be partly explained by the fact that many African countries have graduated away from low-income to low-middle-income economies.[25] This has locked them out from the traditional concessional and flexible financing that they

---

[19] *Ibid.* at 1,5,8,10–15,17; *see also* Akinyi Eurallyah, "Covid-19 and Balance of Payments Crisis in Developing Countries: Balancing Trade, Sovereign Debt, and Development in Africa's Post-Pandemic Economic Era" (2022) (for a further discussion on the effect that Covid-19 and Russia's invasion has had on trade, policy and balance-of-payments in Africa).

[20] *Supra* note 17 at xvi.

[21] Austin Hart, "Restructuring Sovereign Debt" (2021) AFRICAN SOVEREIGN DEBT JUSTICE PAPER SERIES at 1, available at <https://www.afronomicslaw.org/sites/default/files/pdf/Restructuring%20Sovereign%20Debt%20-%20Edited%20AH%20(times%20new%20roman).pdf> (accessed 17 May 2022); *see also* Marie-Louise F. Aren, "Designing an African Common Position and Strategy on Vulture Fund Litigation" (2022) (for a discussion on vulture funds which has been another problem experienced by African countries through the proliferation of a diverse creditor base).

[22] *Supra* note 8 at 50.

[23] *Ibid* at 49.

[24] *Ibid* at 50.

[25] The World Bank, "World-Bank-Country-and-Lending-Groups" (2022) THE WORLD BANK, available at <https://datahelpdesk.worldbank.org/knowledgebase/articles/906519-world-bank-country-and-lending-groups> (accessed 1 June 2022).

had become accustomed to.[26] Further, the allure of commercial debt which is not attached to conditionalities of traditional bilateral and multilateral loans has proved too strong to resist. Yet this has not been without consequences.[27]

The emergence of China as Africa's biggest bilateral lender has proved significant because many of its "loans are not transparent regarding terms and collateralisation."[28] At present it is estimated that 60% of low-income developing countries are experiencing or at high risk of debt distress.[29] Additionally most of these countries on the continent "have high exposure to Chinese loans."[30] Examples include: "Djibouti (57 percent), Angola (49 percent), Republic of Congo (45 percent), Cameroon (32 percent), Ethiopia (32 percent), Kenya (27 percent), and Zambia (26 percent)."[31] Some analysts further assert that official data reported to the IMF, the World Bank's Debtor Reporting System or the Bank for International Settlements does not paint an entirely accurate picture of such exposure with lending being much higher as a result of "hidden debts."[32] With this in mind it is important to note that the IMF has admitted that information on collateralisation remains incomplete.[33]

Traditionally, for low-income economies, collateralised borrowing has represented 20% to 32% of their commercial borrowing on average.[34] According to analysis conducted by the IMF at the end of June 2002, collateralised borrowing amounted to $28.8 billion in developing and emerging markets, accounting for "about 6.5 percent of total bonds and loans outstanding"[35] for several countries included in their dataset which featured 12 African countries. By 2020, 50 commodity-backed loans to sub-Saharan Africa alone had been identified.[36]

---

[26] Otiato Guguyu, "Kenya: China Halts Kenya Loans Amid Debt Reprieve Bid" (2021) THE EAST AFRICAN, available at <https://allafrica.com/stories/202107020719.html> (accessed 1 June 2022).
[27] *Supra* note 8 at 52.
[28] *Ibid* at 64.
[29] *Supra* note 16 at 15.
[30] *Supra* note 8 at 64.
[31] *Ibid*.
[32] *Supra* note 16 at 17.
[33] *Ibid* at 23.
[34] *Ibid*.
[35] *Supra* note 7 at 9.
[36] *Supra* note 16 at 24.

With the increasing role that such debt is playing on the continent, it is important to note that "collateralised borrowing is almost always non-concessional."[37] The impact this has had together with the proliferation of a diverse creditor-base and Africa's shift in debt composition is that debt servicing costs have risen. There has been a lengthening and complication of debt restructuring processes, higher interest rates, the lowering of external debt maturities, an increase of roll over risks and the diminishing of an already constricted fiscal space.[38] Collateralised debt has added to the discussion of an increase in opaqueness about how debt is procured, spent and repaid. The next section proceeds to analyse the different classifications of collateralised debt whilst examining its use and impact on the continent.

3 The Classifications and Use of Collateralised Debt in Africa

Collateralised debt instruments used by sovereigns are complex in nature with various technical elements. They usually involve multiple parties.[39] Data suggest that there has been an increase in such lending since 2007[40] with a race to seniority amongst creditors.[41] This has been driven by the allure to obtain collateral which "constitutes a legally enforceable right against [a] secured asset."[42] A creditor who has obtained collateral in a debt instrument with a sovereign may be able to seize or liquidate the secured asset to obtain payment in the event of the sovereign's default.[43] Sovereign lenders seek such collateral in order to hedge against and to protect themselves from the borrower's perceived risks or those presented by the transaction's nature.[44]

For a sovereign to enter into such arrangements, it first must have "assets or revenue streams that are usable for the purpose."[45] Two distinct classes of assets and

---

[37] *Supra* note 9 at 27; *see also* Moses Odhiambo, "Legal Risks of Non-Concessional Financing Arising from Chinese Debt" (2022) (for a discussion on the legal risks of non-concessional financing).

[38] *Supra* note 16.

[39] *Supra* note 6 at 11.

[40] *Ibid* at 4.

[41] *Supra* note 8 at 73.

[42] Mihalyi et al., "Resource-Backed Loans in Sub-Saharan Africa" (2022) World Bank Group at 23, available at <https://openknowledge.worldbank.org/bitstream/handle/10986/36924/Resource-Backed-Loans-in-Sub-Saharan-Africa.pdf?sequence=1&isAllowed=y> (accessed 1 June 2022).

[43] *Ibid*.

[44] *Supra* note 16 at 124.

[45] *Supra* note 6 at 5.

revenue streams used as collateral have emerged. These are non-commodity related assets and commodity related assets. Examples of non-commodity related assets and revenue streams have included future national lottery receipts as witnessed in Italy, future co-participation revenues as used in the Tucuman province of Argentina[46] and export earnings as witnessed in Venezuela.[47] Road tolls have been favoured in Africa. Examples include the Lekki toll gate that is partly used to repay foreign debts in Lagos State of Nigeria[48] and Kenya's recently opened Nairobi expressway and its tolls are currently being used by the China Road and Bridge Corporation to recoup its investment.[49] Further, physical assets such as buildings, ports and industrial plants have also been viewed as acceptable collateral.[50] For resource rich developing countries,[51] the most widely used collateral has been their natural resources (i.e. commodities) through Resource Backed Loans (RBLs) which are a subcategory of collateralized loans.[52] A RBL can thus be described as borrowing which is backed by a sovereign's natural resources or its revenue streams as collateral. Such collateral has included: oil and gas,[53] "base metals such as bauxite, copper and cobalt ... precious minerals such as diamonds and platinum, and agricultural outputs such as cocoa and tobacco,"[54] most of which are public assets. Commodities are widely used as collateral because, 1) they

---

[46] *Supra* note 9 at 20, 23.

[47] Malik et al, "Banking on the Belt and Road: Insights from a new global dataset of 13,427 Chinese development projects" (2021) AIDDATA at 20, available at <https://docs.aiddata.org/ad4/pdfs/Banking_on_the_Belt_and_Road__Insights_from_a_new_global_dataset_of_13427_Chinese_development_projects.pdf> (accessed 15 June 2022).

[48] William Ukpe, "Lekki Toll Gate to reopen because it needs to pay its local and foreign debts Commissioner" (2022) NAIRAMETRICS, available at <https://nairametrics.com/2022/03/16/lekki-toll-gate-to-reopen-because-it-needs-to-pay-its-local-and-foreign-debts-commissioner/> (accessed 15 June 2022).

[49] Jevans Nyabiage, "Nairobi tollway an example of China's new belt and road financing approach in Africa" (2022) SOUTH CHINA MORNING POST, available at <https://www.scmp.com/news/china/diplomacy/article/3177766/nairobi-tollway-example-chinas-new-belt-and-road-financing> (accessed 15 June 2022).

[50] *Supra* note 6 at 4.

[51] Examples in Africa include Angola, Chad, the Democratic Republic of Congo (DRC), Ghana, Guinea, Niger, the Republic of Congo, São Tomé and Príncipe, South Sudan, Sudan, and Zimbabwe.

[52] *Supra* note 42 at 3.

[53] *Supra* note 9 at 10.

[54] *Supra* note 42 at 10.

are widely available in certain countries and 2) they tend to be easier to collateralise with their revenue flows.[55]

Data shows that collateralised borrowing tends to be more utilised in Africa when compared to the rest of the world with such debt accounting for a higher proportion of their economies.[56] For instance, between 2004 and 2018, 52 Resource Backed Loans were analysed. Thirty were signed by African Countries with the loans totalling $164 billion and $66 billion channelled to Sub-Saharan African countries.[57] To understand the prevalent use of collateralised borrowing in Africa, it is important to bear in mind that less credit worthy countries issue more collateralised debt[58] and "poor" oil exporting countries are more prone to do so than "rich" oil exporting countries.[59] Such countries also tend to issue more collateralised debts after a credit downgrade and less after a credit upgrade.[60] At face value this suggests that collateralised borrowing is used as a means of obtaining finance where access to financial markets and more traditional debt instruments has been restricted. This is not without its challenges as further explored in Section 4.

Collateralised transactions can generally be classified by examining the economic nature of the collateral, analysing the relationship between the collateral and the original transaction, asking whether the borrowing is done directly (i.e., on balance sheet) or indirectly (i.e., off balance sheet) and finally evaluating whether the collateralised instrument is marketable or non-marketable.[61] Examining the economic value of the collateral will uncover whether it is an existing/future asset or a future cash flow/stream. Analysing the relationship between the collateral and the original transaction entails asking whether the collateral is related or unrelated to the purpose for which the borrowing has been sought. Evaluating the balance sheet treatment of the borrowing will determine whether the collateralised arrangement is direct (which is where the government itself or a public enterprise pledges collateral

---

[55] *Supra* note 16 at 24.
[56] *Supra* note 8 at 81.
[57] *Ibid.*
[58] *Supra* note 9 at 10.
[59] *Ibid.*
[60] *Ibid.*
[61] *Supra* note 6 at 6.

to secure the debt incurred) or indirect (which involves the use of a special purpose vehicle that has the collateral assigned to it). Lastly, a marketable collateralised instrument means that it is capable of being traded on the secondary market and is thus liquid (e.g., secured bonds) whereas non-marketable collateralised instruments are illiquid since they are not listed on major secondary market exchanges (e.g., secured bank loans).[62] With this in mind, it is worth noting that most collateralised debt instruments tend to be non-marketable,[63] meaning that collateralised loans generally outnumber collateralised bonds.[64] This is true both in terms of value and as a total proportion of outstanding debt. Further collateralisation appears in both bilateral official lending and commercial lending,[65] with it taking several forms in practice. For instance, the IMF has identified the use of escrow accounts (examined further in section 4), pre-purchase agreements, commodity barter transactions and collateralised repo transactions in Africa.[66] In this regard it is important to note that the definition of collateralisation extends to arrangements that do not constitute the granting of a security interest but also those that have an equivalent effect (emphasis mine).[67]

Chinese state policy banks are the most prominent example of bilateral official lenders that make use of collateral arrangements in their lending with African countries. For instance, the China Export-Import Bank (Eximbank) and China Development Bank (CDB) account for 76% of RBLs to Africa which amounts to $36 billion[68] with both contributing $17 billion and $18 billion respectively, making them the top RBL lenders on the continent by volume.[69] Examples of commercial lending institutions that have used collateral arrangements in their lending include: China National Petroleum Corporation (CNPC), the Industrial Commercial Bank of China (ICBC) and private commodities traders like Glencore and Trafigura.[70] For

---

[62] Ibid.
[63] Ibid.
[64] Supra note 9 at 7.
[65] Supra note 16 at 24.
[66] Ibid.
[67] Supra note 42 at 3; Supra note 6 at 4.
[68] Supra note 42 at 7.
[69] Ibid.
[70] Ibid at 8.

instance, CNPC lent $1billion in a RBL to South Sudan in 2015 and $2.5 billion was offered to Angola through a RBL from ICBC "for the construction of Kilamba Kiaxi New Town, to be repaid with [the] proceeds from Angola's oil sales."[71]

Collateralised borrowing has traditionally been undertaken by the sovereign's central government, but it has become increasingly common for State Owned Enterprises (SOEs) to be involved in such practices.[72] In fact, numerous analysts have observed that SOEs (many of which are commercial in nature) are often the borrowing party.[73] For instance, "of the 37 countries with outstanding collateralised bonds and loans, only 4 had issuances by the sovereigns directly, while 33 used public enterprises."[74] However, as noted by Mihalyi, et al., the distinction "between SOE and central government borrowing is sometimes blurry."[75] This is especially true since governments normally guarantee SOE debt and have a say on the approvals of such borrowing.[76] For instance, Chad's national oil company's (Société des Hydrocarbures du Tchad's) RBL loan of $2 billion was guaranteed by the State. Further the RBL between Sino Congolaise des Mines and Eximbank in the Democratic Republic of Congo provided for an express guarantee in its contract.[77] Nevertheless, collateralised borrowing on future receivables (i.e., Collateralised Future Receipt Arrangements) are "the mo[st] common form of collateralised borrowing"[78] utilized by SOEs. This is significant because future receivables are more likely to be held offshore as opposed to existing assets[79] (a matter whose consequences are analysed in next section). Additionally, SOE debt has been large in some African countries such as Zambia where it has accounted for 4.5% of GDP and 1.3.% in Ghana according to data reported in the World's Bank Debt Sustainability Analysis.[80]

---

[71] *Ibid.*
[72] *Supra* note 16 at 12.
[73] *Supra* note 42 at 6, 18.
[74] *Supra* note 9 at 7.
[75] *Ibid* at 6.
[76] *Ibid.*
[77] *Ibid* at 7.
[78] *Supra* note 9 at 10.
[79] *Ibid* at 5.
[80] *Supra* note 16 at 12.

Publicly available information on collateralised borrowing remains rare and as a result there is often no knowledge of the terms or even their very existence due to the unusual and broad confidentiality clauses that are included in such instruments.[81] This highlights the deep-rooted problem of opaqueness and transparency that has generally plagued the sovereign debt landscape and hindered a better understanding of it. The focus of this paper is limited to the collateralised arrangements where there is publicly available information and those that have been uncovered as problematic. With its prominent use, Collateralised Future Receipt (CFR) Arrangements in both RBLs and non-commodity related loans stand out. The challenges this presents and those of collateralised borrowing generally are evaluated in the next section where some myths regarding the same are also addressed.

4 The Challenges of Collateralised Borrowing

The notion that public assets should be used for the benefit of the public is of no doubt.[82] This rings true not only for commodity related assets and their revenue streams that are used as collateral in RBLs as highlighted in Section 3 but also for non-commodity related assets and their revenue streams. Regarding the former it is important to note that natural resources in many legal systems around the world are vested in the State and importantly held in trust on behalf of its citizens;[83] whereas regarding the latter it is important to note that such assets which normally consist of big infrastructure projects are usually owned by SOEs. An example of this is the Standard Gauge Railway (SGR) in Kenya which is owned and operated by the Kenya Railway Corporation (KRC). A sovereign's citizens always have a direct interest in the use of such public assets and their revenue streams which should essentially secure the greatest benefit for them.[84] Therefore, the key question is whether the use of such assets

---

[81] Anna Gelpern et al., "How China Lends a Rare Look into 100 Debt Contracts with Foreign Governments" (2021) AidData at 6, 22–25, available at https://www.aiddata.org/how-china-lends (accessed 04 August 2022).

[82] James Gathii, "Incorporating the Third-Party Beneficiary Principle in Natural Resource Contracts" (2014) Loyola University Chicago School of Law at 114, available at <https://papers.ssrn.com/sol3/papers.cfm?abstract_id=2500311> (accessed 14 June 2022).

[83] *Ibid* at 115.

[84] *Ibid*.

and revenue streams as collateral secures the greatest benefit for a sovereign's citizens? Let's unpack this below by examining the challenges of collateralised borrowing.

By far the most obvious challenge faced by sovereigns from collateralised borrowing would be the loss of its public assets in the event of default. This however is not as straight forward or as clear as it might first appear. The reason is that although lenders seek collateral as a guaranteed safety net for repayment, they are often faced with the difficulty of enforcement which at times may not even be possible where the assets used as collateral are physically located in the borrowing country. A good example of this is witnessed in Zimbabwe where platinum deposits in Selous and Northfields reserves have been used as collateral to secure a $200 milllion loan from Eximbank.[85] Such assets form poor collateral because they are highly politically and socially sensitive. Their potential loss would elicit great resistance from the sovereign and its citizens, and the lender's productive use of the asset is likely to be negatively affected upon seizure.[86] It therefore comes as no surprise that "no claims on such subsoil collateral have emerged publicly."[87] The same rationale would apply to a sovereign's non-commodity based physical assets such as buildings, ports and industrial plants. The media have at times mistakenly and falsely claimed such assets have been used as collateral and are at risk of being seized by lenders. Very prominent examples of this have included claims that Kenya's Mombasa Port has been used as collateral in the SGR loan from China's Eximbank,[88] or that Uganda stands to surrender its only international airport over Chinese loans,[89] and that the Sri Lanka government

---

[85] Supra note 42 at 9.

[86] *Ibid.*

[87] *Ibid* at 25.

[88] George Omondi, "Mombasa Port at risk as audit finds it was used to secure SGR loan" (2018) The EastAfrican, available at <https://www.theeastafrican.co.ke/tea/business/mombasa-port-at-risk-as-audit-finds-it-was-used-to-secure-sgr-loan-1408886> (accessed 14 June 2022); Samwel Owino, "MPs want deal mortgaging Mombasa port to China reviewed" (2022) BUSINESS DAILY, available at <https://www.businessdailyafrica.com/bd/economy/mps-want-deal-mortgaging-mombasa-port-to-china-reviewed-3836418> (accessed 14 June 2022).

[89] Dipanjan Chaudhury, "China reportedly takes over Uganda's airport on account of loan default" (2021) The Economic Times, available at <https://economictimes.indiatimes.com/news/international/business/china-reportedly-takes-over-ugandas-airport-on-account-of-loan-default/articleshow/87957646.cms?from=mdr; https://archive.md/gW8nZ> (accessed 14 June 2022).

surrendered Hambantota Port to China due to unpaid debts.[90] These all fit into the "debt trap diplomacy" narrative that has become associated with China.[91] The truth however is that there has been no evidence of such asset seizures from disputes involving Chinese loans.[92] The real risk that sovereigns may face in terms of losing such collateral is in relation to their physical assets located in foreign jurisdictions.[93] A rare but potent example of this can be seen with Venezuela. Here its national oil company Petróleos de Venezuela, S.A. (PDVSA) which owns Citgo Petroleum Corporation (CITGO), a petroleum company with oil refinery assets located in the United States, first pledged 50.1% of its shares in its subsidiary as collateral to secure a bond and thereafter, two months later pledged the remaining 49.9% shares as collateral for loan financing.[94] This highly valuable/profitable asset which significantly contributes towards Venezuela's "oil exports [that] account[s] for more than 90 percent"[95] of its foreign exchange, is now at imminent risk of being seized by various lenders to

---

[90] Brahma Chellaney, "China's Creditor Imperialism" (2017) PROJECT SYNDICATE, available at <https://www.project-syndicate.org/commentary/china-sri-lanka-hambantota-port-debt-by-brahma-chellaney-2017-12> (accessed 14 June 2022).

[91] Deborah Brautigam et al., "How Africa Borrows From China: and Why Mombasa Port is Not Collateral for Kenya's Standard Gauge Railway" (2022) CHINA AFRICA RESEARCH INITIATIVE at 2, available at <https://static1.squarespace.com/static/5652847de4b033f56d2bdc29/t/62575fb9c92fbc7ddb334cd8/1649893307393/WP52-Brautigam-Bhalaki-Deron-Wang-How+Africa+Borrows+From+China.pdf> (accessed 14 June 2022).

[92] Kevin Acker, "Debt Relief with Chinese Characteristics" (2020) CHINA AFRICA RESEARCH INITIATIVE, available at <https://static1.squarespace.com/static/5652847de4b033f56d2bdc29/t/60353345259d4448e01a37d8/1614099270470/WP+39+-+Acker%2C+Brautigam%2C+Huang+-+Debt+Relief.pdf> (accessed 14 June 2022).

[93] *See* Marie-Louise Aren, "Designing an African Common Position and Strategy on Vulture Fund Litigation" (2022) at 9–10 (which makes reference to the Elliott Associates LP v Republic of Peru case).

[94] Reuters, "Venezuela's PDVSA uses 49.9 pct Citgo stake as loan collateral" (2016) REUTERS, available at <https://www.reuters.com/article/venezuela-pdvsa-idUSL1N1EI1FO> (accessed 14 June 2022).

[95] Whalen and Faiola, "Venezuela's foreign creditors try to lay claim to Citgo" (2018) THE WASHINGTON POST, available at <https://www.washingtonpost.com/business/economy/venezuelas-foreign-creditors-try-to-lay-claim-to-citgo/2018/10/17/b7b96440-c369-11e8-b338-a3289f6cb742_story.html> (accessed 14-June-2022).

satisfy loan repayments[96] with significant consequences likely to be inflicted on its citizens from the forgone earnings.

The foregoing limitations of enforcing physical assets as collateral even when located in foreign jurisdictions would help explain the prominent use of CFR arrangements in sovereign borrowing[97] as highlighted in Section 3. Lenders favour and seek such arrangements due to the ability to use offshore escrow accounts, a common feature through which revenue funds are held in foreign jurisdictions for their benefit. In this regard an escrow account is used "in situations of uncertainty as to whether one or another party to a transaction will be able to meet their obligations."[98] A good example of this is the $2 billion infrastructure development loan that Angola signed with China's Eximbank in 2004. The terms of the agreement provided that the loan was to be repaid from monthly proceeds out of the sale of 10,000 barrels of oil per day which were to be deposited in an offshore account.[99] Similarly Ghana's Sinohydro loan provided that the proceeds from the sale of bauxite which were to be used to repay the loan were to be deposited in an offshore escrow account.[100] Another example arising out of a non-commodity backed loan can also be seen in the $200 million loan contract between China Eximbank and the Government of Uganda for the upgrading and expansion of Entebbe International Airport.[101] Here the lender required the borrower

---

[96] Zerpa and Fieser, "Creditors Close In on Citgo the Last Asset Guaido Has Left" (2021) BLOOMBERG, available at <https://www.bloomberg.com/news/articles/2021-08-05/creditors-close-in-on-citgo-the-last-asset-guaido-has-left> (accessed 14 June 2022); Clifford Krauss, "It's the Only Way to Get Paid": A Struggle for Citgo, Venezuela's U.S. Oil Company' (2019) THE NEW YORK TIMES, available at <https://www.nytimes.com/2019/10/17/business/energy-environment/citgo-venezuela-creditors.html> (accessed 14 June 2022).

[97] *Supra* note 81 at 26–33; B Parks, A Malik and A Wooley, "Is Beijing a predatory lender? New evidence from a previously undisclosed loan contract for the Entebbe International Airport Upgrading and Expansion Project" (2022) at 2, available at <https://www.aiddata.org/publications/uganda-entebbe-airport-china-eximbank> (accessed 04 August 2022).

[98] *Supra* note 91 at 14.

[99] *Supra* note 42 at 9.

[100] *Ibid* at 10.

[101] Export-Import Bank of China, "Government Concessional Loan Agreement on Uganda Upgrading and Expansion of the Entebbe International Airport Phase 1 Project" (2015) EXPORT-IMPORT BANK OF CHINA, available at <https://docs.aiddata.org/ad4/pdfs/Uganda_Entebbe_Loan_Agreement.pdf> (accessed 04 August 2022).

to provide liquid collateral in the form of a cash deposit through an escrow account which it could unilaterally seize in the event of the Government's failure to meets its repayment obligations.[102] Likewise in Kenya's SGR project an escrow account was set up to hold the proceeds from the railway's operations which in addition to a railway development fund would be used towards Eximbank's loan repayments.[103]

The above revenue streams are what sovereigns commonly risk losing out in collateralised borrowing with judicial treatment importantly leaning towards enforcement. For instance, the United States Federal Circuit case of *Karaha Bodas Co. v. Perushaan Petrambangan Minyak Dan Gas Bumi Negara* shows that courts in the Global North will not shy away from attaching and executing a sovereign's or SOE's foreign assets. Here the court determined that certain funds belonging to Pertamina (an Indonesian state-owned oil and gas company) located in New York banks could be used to pay a judgment debt.[104] In addition to the potential outright loss of these revenue streams, the use of escrow accounts in CFR arrangements also effectively ties up the sovereign's assets[105] and forms an inefficient use of resources by locking in cash that would otherwise be available to the government, which could be used for other essential purposes, thus reducing future fiscal flexibility.[106] In this regard it is common to find contractual limitations on a sovereign's ability to withdraw funds from such accounts,[107] meaning a sovereign could find itself in the absurd position of "building up cash balances in [an escrow account], while simultaneously borrowing at high interest rates or running arrears."[108]

As alluded to in the earlier sections, sovereign debt is characterised with opaqueness and secrecy. Collateralised borrowing adds to this with a lack of transparency

---

[102] B Parks, A Malik and A Wooley, "Is Beijing a predatory lender? New evidence from a previously undisclosed loan contract for the Entebbe International Airport Upgrading and Expansion Project" (2022) at 1 & 2, available at https://www.aiddata.org/publications/uganda-entebbe-airport-china-eximbank (accessed 04-August-2022).
[103] *Supra* note 91 at 11.
[104] 465 F. Supp. 2d 283 (S.D.N.Y. 2006).
[105] *Supra* note 42 at 24.
[106] *Supra* note 9 at 21.
[107] *Supra* note 42 at 24.
[108] *Supra* note 9 at 21.

that makes "fair burden sharing more difficult and limits co-ordination"[109] which in turn "complicates debt restructuring negotiations."[110] In fact data shows that the countries which rely the most on these forms of borrowing have weaker debt disclosure practices.[111] To put this into perspective, out of fifty-two RBL cases that were surveyed in Africa only one case had contract documents which were made public with basic information such as interest rates being identifiable in just nineteen.[112] A root cause of this problem is the broad and unusual confidentiality undertakings that have been placed on sovereign borrowers by Chinese lenders which extend beyond contract negotiations and have become increasingly common.[113] For instance, from their sample Gelpern et al identified that "all post-2014 contracts with Chinese state-owned entities [contained] or reference[d] far-reaching confidentiality clauses,"[114] which attempt and have been successful in preventing sovereign borrowers from disclosing the nature of such agreements. Coupled with the practical effect that the granting of collateral confers a priority claim over a soveign asset to a specific creditor, it is not difficult to see why such forms of borrowing have caused protracted problems. For instance, "the Republic of Congo has been in litigation with external private creditors since 2014, with collateralised debt posing a major obstacle."[115] Here, hidden debts and contingent liabilities have played a significant role with loans taken by the country's national oil company being kept off its Ministry of Finance books, with

---

[109] *Supra* note 8 at 79; *see also* The World Bank Group, "Debt Transparency in Developing Economies" (2021) THE WORLD BANK GROUP at 94, available at https://documents1.worldbank.org/curated/en/743881635526394087/pdf/Debt-Transparency-in-Developing-Economies.pdf.

[110] *Ibid*.

[111] *Supra* note 42 at 17.

[112] *Supra* note 8 at 81.

[113] *Supra* note 81 at 22-25; The World Bank Group, "Debt Transparency in Developing Economies" (2021) THE WORLD BANK GROUP at 4, available at <https://documents1.worldbank.org/curated/en/743881635526394087/pdf/Debt-Transparency-in-Developing-Economies.pdf> (accessed 04 August 2022).

[114] *Supra* note 81 at 6; *see* Moses Odhiambo, "Legal Risks of Non-Concessional Financing Arising from Chinese Debt" (2022) at 5–8 (for a further discussion on these unusual confidential Chinese clauses and their effect on African countries).

[115] *Ibid* at 78; *See also* Nciko wa Nciko, "China Have Mercy on the DRC: Is the 509.43 Million dollar Busanga Contract a Barter or an Unsustainable Collateralised Sovereign Debt?" Chapter 11 in this book.

the IMF itself only becoming aware much later once repayment problems surfaced.[116] Other countries that have experienced similar challenges because of collateralised borrowing include Mozambique which is still in litigation with private contractors over government guaranteed SOE loans and Zambia which was forced to recently default on its debts due to the government's lack of transparency and failure to ensure all creditors were treated equitably.[117] It is also worth noting that collateralised borrowing can run afoul of negative pledge clauses, particularly those included in multilateral development bank contracts. This can have the effect of locking countries out of IMF-supported financing programmes.[118] All the forgoing issues make it difficult for sovereigns and international actors to determine debt parameters required creditor contributions[119] to accurately evaluate risks and monitor debt sustainability.[120]

There is also the belief that collateralised borrowing is justified as it should result in better loan terms and cheaper financing through lower interest rates for sovereigns.[121] A deeper analysis of these transactions however reveals that this is not entirely the case. For instance, in one study it was found that on average RBLs tend to have higher interest rates when compared to other sources of finance with similar terms.[122] In this regard only bilateral lenders namely China and Korea offered extremely low interest rates in RBLs. However, even in such circumstances, it is important to note that favourable cost of financing is not solely determined by low interest rates as collateralised borrowing involves highly complex transactions with various parties and at times multiple agreements.[123] It is therefore common to find high fixed transaction costs with excessive profits going to the intermediaries putting together the arrangement.[124] Tied to this is the fact that sovereigns who make use of

---

[116] *Supra* note 42 at 7.
[117] *Supra* note 8 at 81; *see also* Nona Tamale, "Debt Restructuring under the G20 Common Framework: Austerity Again? The Case of Zambia and Chad" (2022) Chapter 6 in this book..
[118] *Supra* note 9 at 3,27.
[119] *Supra* note 8 at 81.
[120] *Supra* note 42 at 16.
[121] *Supra* note 6 at 11.
[122] *Supra* note 42 at 19–22.
[123] *Supra* note 6 at 1.
[124] *Supra* note 9 at 16,22.

collateralised borrowing are non-investment grade and non-rated countries with such borrowing being used as a means of increasing credit worthiness.[125] This means over-collateralisation often occurs, with the frequent use of guarantees and payment of significant insurance premiums all at the expense of increasing costs for the sovereign.[126]

Further, of particular importance to collateralised borrowing especially RBLs is the boom-bust cycle of commodity prices. Such borrowing tends to favour sovereigns when commodity prices are high, for instance as is presently the case following Russia's illegal war in Ukraine.[127] On the other hand, sovereigns can face repayment challenges when commodity prices are low as was the case in 2014 with the collapse of oil prices. In this regard, the African Development Bank identified that "of the 14 RBL recipients, 10 experienced serious debt problems. ..."[128] A particular example is the Chadian government which was put under fiscal pressure that led to protracted renegotiations of its loans.[129]

Clearly the challenges that collateralised borrowing present are significant and cast doubt as to whether such transactions secure the greatest benefit for a sovereign's citizens. There are however potential benefits which cannot be ignored. The next section analyses these and presents a way forward.

5 The Potential Benefits of Collateralised Borrowing and The Way Forward

Evidence suggests that Africa has a much higher public investment efficiency gap when compared to other continents, for example Europe and Asia.[130] Africa is further plagued with a severe lack of infrastructure which is significant because infrastructure

---

[125] *Supra* note 6 at 5.

[126] *Supra* note 9 at 17.

[127] Akinyi Eurallyah, "Covid-19 and Balance of Payments Crisis in Developing Countries: Balancing Trade, Sovereign Debt, and Development in Africa's Post-Pandemic Economic Era" (2022) at 8.

[128] *Supra* note 8 at 81.

[129] *See* Nona Tamale, "Debt Restructuring under the G20 Common Framework: Austerity Again? The Case of Zambia and Chad" (2022) (for a further discussion on the implications of debt restructuring on Zambia and Chad with particular emphasis on austerity).

[130] *Ibid* at 87.

is an important driving force of economies and human welfare.[131] In this regard, there is a clear correlation between infrastructure and economic development. It is therefore no surprise that with Africa standing in last place on most infrastructure indicators, so too is that ranking reflected in its economic performance.[132] The predicament Africa has found itself in, is that historically it has not had a means of funding such development. This has been due to low credit ratings, with most countries on the continent being non-investment grade or non-rated, which in turn has restricted their access to financial markets that use more traditional debt instruments as was highlighted in Section 2.[133] This is compounded by the fact that infrastructure projects are difficult to finance as they are often associated with low rates of return, have large upfront costs, and are located in countries with poor implementation or capacity challenges which makes them less attractive for commercial markets.[134]

In light of the foregoing, collateralised borrowing emerged as the only means for some African countries to raise external finance and fund essential infrastructure development.[135] The fact that most RBLs on the continent go towards funding infrastructure projects is a testament to this.[136] Angola is the quintessential example of a country whose utilization of collateralised borrowing has been transformational, beginning with its first RBL in 2004 for a sum of $2 billion which was used in at least 50 different infrastructure projects.[137] This has seen the previously war ravaged country propelled into a lower middle income status one, with the finance having a rippling effect throughout the rest of its economy.[138] So successful was its implementation of such borrowing that the use of RBLs for infrastructure become known as "the Angola

---

[131] Dunia Zongwe, "On the Road to Post Conflict Reconstruction by Contract: The Angola Model" (2010) WALTER SISULU UNIVERSITY at 10, available at https://ssrn.com/abstract=1730442 (accessed 15-June-2022).
[132] Ibid.
[133] Supra note 6 at 5.
[134] Supra note 42 at 7.
[135] Supra note 9 at 10.
[136] Supra note 42 at 2.
[137] Ibid at 13.
[138] Supra note 122 at 14.

Model." At the heart of the ngola Model lies the assumption that both parties (i.e. Africa with its abundance of resources but significant infrastructure gap, and China with its world leading construction industry but limited natural resources) stand to mutually benefit from these transactions.[139] From this perspective, the Angola Model shows how African countries can leverage their natural resources to finance capital enhancing infrastructure programs,[140] diversify their economies, create employment for citizens and construct backbone infrastructure needed to transform lives e.g., hospitals, schools, health and training centers, and universities among others.[141] Although non-commodity related, the Kenyan SGR project is another example of such big infrastructure borrowing with potential to be transformative. It has recently been mired by controversy. Yet when deeply analyzed and truly understood the SGR reveals a bankable project with significant long-term benefits for not only the country but the region and which analysts ceteris paribus forecast to be comfortably repaid.[142] Notwithstanding the significant challenges presented by collateralised borrowing as laid out in section 4, when it is effectively used on infrastructure investment that can yield both economic and social returns which offset borrowing costs, it is hard to argue against its justification.[143]

With the above in mind and with collateralised borrowing having become an important source of development finance on the continent, the focus shifts towards ensuring that it leads to beneficial outcomes. This chapter supports the key considerations that the IMF recently published which should guide both lenders and borrowers when deciding whether and how to effectively utilize collateralised borrowing for beneficial outcomes. This begins by looking at the design of such agreements with particular attention paid to incentives, the enforceability of collateral, transparency, complexity, and its terms vis a vis value.[144] Next, both parties need to evaluate the macroeconomic and financial implications of collateralised borrowing which will include analyzing project returns, impact on other creditors/future financing and

---

[139] *Ibid* at 7.
[140] *Supra* note 82 at 125.
[141] *Supra* note 131 at 24, 25.
[142] *Supra* note 91 at 23, 26-31.
[143] *Supra* note 42 at 23.
[144] *Supra* note 6 at 10, 11.

impact on the risk of debt distress.[145] Ultimately, whether these considerations are satisfied requires a case-by-case assessment due to the high degree of individuality of such arrangements.[146] However, the IMF categorically provides that beneficial development outcomes from collateralised transactions are more likely if:

> (i) it produces assets or revenue streams that can be used for repayment (i.e., "related assets/revenues"); (ii) the reduced risk resulting from collateralisation is reflected in improved financial terms; (iii) a rigorous debt sustainability assessment is passed; (iv) there is full, public transparency on all contractual terms; [and] (v) collateralisation respects and complies with any applicable Negative Pledge Clauses (NPCs).[147]

In light of the above, the use of collateralised borrowing on unrelated assets which cannot produce revenue streams for repayment e.g., to plug budget deficits should be avoided. Zimbabwe's $200 million RBL which was partly used to purchase short-term consumables like fertilizer and pesticides provides an example of such questionable borrowing with its link to increased government revenue too indirect and rife with uncertainties.[148] On the other hand, Uganda's loan contract for the upgrading and expansion of the Entebbe International Airport although revenue producing provides an example of an extremely lopsided agreement whose financial terms were not negotiated well. For instance, clause 6.12 (3) of the agreement categorically provides as follows:

> All the revenues (proceeds) of Entebbe International Airport *(including but not limited to revenues generated from the Project)* shall be applied in priority to payment of any and all amounts due and payable under this Agreement.

It is vital to point out that with such a clause the Government of Uganda has effectively agreed to use the proceeds of a pre-existing international airport that was

---

[145] *Ibid* at 11, 12.
[146] *Supra* note 9 at 21.
[147] *Supra* note 6 at 12.
[148] *Supra* note 42 at 22.

already generating public revenue prior to the loan agreement, on a priority basis for 20 years to secure its expansion and upgrade! Further China Eximbank had included "the right to reject or approve the annual operating budgets of the Uganda Civil Aviation Authority (UCAA), which is the government entity responsible for Entebbe International Airport," before this position was reversed through subsequent hard-fought concessions granted to the Government of Uganda.

Ultimately it is important to remember that collateralised borrowing should also be used to pave the way for uncollateralised borrowing/capital market access rather than a means to overborrow and run high deficits by evading financing limits.[149] The fact that multiple African countries are repeat borrowers via RBLs raises dependency concerns.[150]

Equally important is ensuring that collateralised borrowing is undertaken with full transparency because after all "public debt is public." Transparency is the only way that citizens whose taxes are used to repay such borrowing can hold their governments accountable.[151] Transparency will not only benefit citizens, but also the sovereigns themselves, lenders, and multilateral development banks. For sovereigns it will ensure that the collateral is fairly priced with better contractual terms, lead to better evaluation of risks, more accurate credit ratings, improve sound fiscal management and provide better debt restructuring outcomes where needed due to increased good faith amongst the parties.[152] For lenders it will lead to the ascertainment of a sovereign's true financial position and better pricing of a country's risk due to disclosure of any seniority or payment advantages to others.[153] Finally, for multilateral development banks and other international actors, it will lead to more accurate information on which debt sustainability assessments and reports can be based as well as the ability to design more effective crisis response policies.[154] In this regard, an area that is presently nonexistent and really lacking is reporting on the collateralised features

---

[149] *Supra* note 9 at 3.
[150] *Supra* note 42 at 16.
[151] *Supra* note 81 at 25, 45.
[152] *Supra* note 8 at 79.
[153] *Supra* note at 42 at 19-22.
[154] *Supra* note 81 at 6.

of loans and SOE debts.[155] It is worth noting that despite the prevalent use of confidentiality clauses in sovereign debt contracts particularly those entered into with Chinese lenders as highlighted in section 3, there is commonly an important carve out under such terms which generally provide that "the borrower shall not disclose any information hereunder or in connection with [the] Agreement to any third party *unless required by applicable law*."[156] This highlights the important role that national laws can play for African countries in combating these unusual and broad confidentiality clauses and ensuring transparency. A good example of this can be witnessed in Kenya through the recently decided case of *Khalifa & another v Secretary, National Treasury & Planning & 4 others; Katiba Institute & another (Interested Party)* (Constitutional Petition 032 of 2019) [2022] KEHC 368 (KLR).[157] Here, it was held that the failure by the respondents (which included the Principal Secretary for the Ministry of Transport, the Principal Secretary for the National Treasury & Planning and the Attorney General of Kenya) to provide the requested agreements entered into by the government of Kenya regarding the SGR project was in violation of the right of access to information enshrined under Article 35 of the Constitution of Kenya, 2010 and the national values and principles of governance enshrined under Article 10. The court also importantly issued an order compelling the respondents to provide the information (i.e., SGR contracts) that had been requested by the 1st Petitioner. The Attorney General of Kenya has since indicated his desire to appeal the High Court's decision, but the success of such a course of action is unlikely. Further, on the international stage, the Institute of International Finance's (IIF's) voluntary principles for debt transparency and its implementation note could prove beneficial. The principles favor the public disclosure of certain commercial terms in underlying transactions by private sector lenders to a reporting entity.[158] In this regard, it is important to note that the Organisation for Economic Co-operation and Development (OECD) has

---

[155] *Supra* note 16 at 4.
[156] *Supra* note 81 at 24.
[157] The full decision is available at: http://kenyalaw.org/caselaw/cases/view/233198/.
[158] Institute of International Finance, "Voluntary Principles for Debt Transparency" (2019) at 1, available at <https://www.iif.com/Portals/0/Files/Principles%20for%20Debt%20Transparency.pdf> (accessed 04 August 2022).

recently agreed to be the host/repository for this data.[159] However, like the criticisms levied against the voluntary nature of the G-20 Debt Service Suspension Initiative (DSSI) and thereafter its Common Framework for debt treatments beyond the DSSI for private sector creditors,[160] this is not enough. This chapter argues that there are only upsides to be gained from increased transparency which will foster trust amongst all parties and lead to a better understanding of the sovereign debt landscape with fewer false claims and misconceptions.[161]

As new lenders adapt "and innovate contract features to maximize their commercial and political advantage in an increasingly crowded field"[162] so too can borrowers and multilateral development banks adapt and innovate such instruments to ensure debt sustainability.[163] In this regard, innovative financial techniques and instruments such as State Contingent Debt Instruments (SCDIs), Value Recovery Instruments (VRIs), GDP warrants, step-up coupons and policy contingent financing can be extremely useful.[164] Such instruments can make debt easier to manage if they accommodate the appearance of shocks and provide for countercyclical debt service.[165] A great example of such innovation in action can be witnessed in Chad's 2018 restructuring operation of its RBL with Glencore. Here, as part of its IMF program, the country lowered the RBLs interest rate, increased its maturity and

---

[159] Institute of International Finance, "IIF Implementation Note: Voluntary Principles for Debt Transparency" (2022) at 1, 5-7, available at <https://www.iif.com/Portals/0/Files/content/2_Implementation%20Note_vf.pdf> (accessed 04 August 2022).

[160] *See* Magalie Masamba, "The Pressing Call for an International Debt Restructuring Framework and The Potential Gains its Creation will have for African Countries" (2022) at 15.

[161] *Supra* note 158 at 2; The World Bank Group, 'Debt Transparency in Developing Economies' (2021) The WORLD BANK GROUP at 2, available at https://documents1.worldbank.org/curated/en/743881635526394087/pdf/Debt-Transparency-in-Developing-Economies.pdf (accessed 04 August 2022).

[162] *Supra* note 81 at 9.

[163] *See* Magalie Masamba, "The Pressing Call for an International Debt Restructuring Framework and The Potential Gains Its Creation will have for African Countries," Chapter 1 in this book (for a discussion on innovative reforms that have been proposed for the reform of the sovereign debt restructuring architecture).

[164] *Supra* note 8 at 80.

[165] *Ibid.*

importantly made its debt service payments counter-cyclical by including contingencies which adjust repayment depending on oil price.[166] This approach not only provides a template for other African countries to follow but could also become a common lending design feature in sovereign borrowing to minimize debt vulnerabilities.[167] With the foregoing in mind multilateral development banks and other international financial institutions are well placed to play an essential role towards the success of such instruments. These can even be used to elicit creditor participation in debt restructurings and increase transparency.[168] For instance, the IMF could link full disclosure and transparency as a precondition to access its programs through policy contingent financing.

In the long run, only bold initiatives and reforms can transform the sovereign debt landscape. For instance, "there is no uniform public disclosure standard or practice," when it comes to such borrowing, yet it would be essential to solving one of the biggest challenges posed. This however may only be possible through an International Debt Restructuring Framework which many others have called for and this chapter also supports and with it the institutional change that would bring.[170]

---

[166] *Supra* note 42 at 26.

[167] *Supra* note 8 at 80.

[168] *Ibid* at 80,87.

[169] *Supra* note 81 at 16.

[170] *See* Magalie Masamba, "The Pressing Call for an International Debt Restructuring Framework and The Potential Gains its Creation will have for African Countries" (Chapter 1 in this book); Bharath Gururagavendran, "The Coloniality of Sovereign Debt In The Global South" (Chapter 12 in this book) (for how such a framework would have to incorporate economic and social rights at its core which is something that is missing in the current neoliberalist order); Kelvin Mbithi, "Supervising Sovereign Debt Restructuring Through the United Nations" (Chapter 8 in this book); Afronomics, "Long Term Solutions are Required to Resolve the Latest Sovereign Debt Crisis" (2021) AFRONOMICS, available at https://www.afronomicslaw.org/category/african-sovereign-debt-justice-network-afsdjn/long-term-solutions-are-required-resolve (accessed 15 June 2022); *see also* James Gathii and Harrison Mbori, "Proposals on Sovereign Debt Restructuring over the Years" (2022) (for an overview of sovereign debt restructuring proposals over the years); The World Bank Group, "Debt Transparency in Developing Economies" (2021) THE WORLD BANK GROUP at 4–8, available at <https://documents1.worldbank.org/curated/en/743881635526394087/pdf/Debt-Transparency-in-Developing-Economies.pdf> (accessed 04 August 2022).

6 Conclusion

This chapter commenced in Section 1 where securitisation and collateralised financing were defined with a roadmap of the paper given. In Section 2 the composition of sovereign debt in Africa was examined. Here the effect that the Covid-19 Pandemic and Russia's illegal war in Ukraine has had on the continent were noted. Further the shift in preferred creditors from historical bilateral lenders to commercial and Chinese lenders was shown with the growing use of collateralisation. Section 3 analysed the different classifications of collateralised debt with its use and impact on the continent. The use of non-commodity related assets and commodity related assets as collateral was highlighted. It was noted that collateralized borrowing was heavily utilized in Africa when compared to rest of the world with such debt accounting for a higher proportion of its economies. To this effect the use of RBLs was prominent with collateralised borrowing mostly undertaken by SOEs through CFR arrangements. Section 4 evaluated the challenges presented by collateralised borrowing where some myths regarding the same were also addressed. The most obvious challenge sovereigns faced was the loss of collateral in the event of default but that this was not as straight forward as it first appeared. In this regard, it was revealed that the real risk sovereigns faced was in relation to their assets located in foreign jurisdictions, particularly revenue funds held in escrow accounts. Equally, important challenges presented by collateralised borrowing were further analysed such as the lack of transparency through hidden and contingent liabilities, protracted debt restructuring processes, cost of financing which is not necessarily cheaper and shock vulnerabilities. Section 5 examined the potential benefits of collateralised borrowing and presented a way forward. Such borrowing has historically been the only means through which some African countries can raise external finance to fund essential infrastructure development. When used in such a manner which can yield both economic and social returns to offset borrowing costs it would be hard to argue against its justification. This chapter made the case that it was necessary to shift focus towards ensuring beneficial outcomes. In this regard, the chapter supported the IMF's recently published guidelines on key considerations for public lenders and borrowers in collateralised transactions with particular emphasis placed on the use of borrowing, transparency, and financial innovation.

CHAPTER ELEVEN

China, Have Mercy: The Unacceptable Collaterlised Sovereign Debt Burden that the Busanga Hydropower Plant Places on the DRC

Nciko wa Nciko*

1 Introduction

A $509.43 million[1] resource-for-infrastructure (R4I) contract led to the construction of the Busanga Hydropower Plant (Busanga HPP) in the Democratic Republic of the Congo (DRC). This R4I contract was between the DRC and a consortium of Chinese state-owned companies (the Chinese Consortium). As is often the case with these types of contracts, on the face of it, the DRC is using its copper and cobalt to reimburse the $509.43 million that the Chinese Consortium used to construct the Busanga HPP.[2] The $509.43 million was borrowed from China Eximbank.

---

* Nciko wa Nciko is an LL. M Candidate at the Geneva Graduate Institute of International and Development Studies. He is also an Amnesty International Regional Researcher on Climate Justice in Southern Africa and its lead adviser on human rights in Madagascar.

[1] République Démocratique du Congo Ministère des Finances Direction Générale de la Dette Publique, Mars 2021, Bulletin Statistique de la Dette Publique de la RD Congo, Données à la fin de 2020, No 14/2020, Mars 2021 (Many sources, however, report the value of the Busanga R4I contract as $660 million. See, for example, Gregory Pointdexter "DRC awards US$660 million contract for MW Busanga hydroelectric project in Africa" June 6, 2016 <https://www.hydroreview.com/business-finance/drc-awards-us-660-million-contract-for-240-mw-busanga-hydroelectric-project-in-africa/#gref>).

[2] In 2014, the Congolese legislature passed a law to liberalize the electricity sector. Loi Numero 14/011 du 17 Juin 2014 relative au secteur de l'électricité 2014. *See also* Expose de motifs, loi de 2014. *See* Agence Francaise de Presse, "RDC : Contrat Chinois pour la construction d'un barrage de 240 MW" 6 June 2016. *See also*, for example, the Preamble of Accord De Joint-Venture Relatif à La Construction et a l'exploitation d'une Centrale Hydroélectrique a Busanga entre La République Démocratique du Congo Et Les Investisseurs Chinois (Composes de : China Railway Ressources Group Co, Ltd And Power China Ressources Limited) en présence de la Sino-Congolaise des Mines SA, la Société

Typically, R4I contracts guarantee complementarity between economies. In this case, while China has overcapacity in its construction industry and few natural resources, the DRC has physical infrastructure deficits and a lot of natural resources.[3] Because of overcapacity in its construction industry, China started sending out its state-owned companies—such as Sinohydro and China Railway Corporation—to build infrastructure in other countries, often, in exchange for mineral resources.[4] The DRC is, therefore, strategic in this regard being the world's leading producer of cobalt (with 70% of the global production in the year 2020).[5] The DRC is also the 6th largest producer of copper globally.[6] It is in the context of this complementarity between economies, that R4I contracts guarantee, that the Busanga HPP was constructed. Therefore, it is not surprising that official records from DRC's General Directorate

---

Nationale d'Electricité S.A et le Groupe Gécamines (Compose de : La Générale des Carrières Et des Mines SA, La Société Immobilière Du Congo SAS, et le Congo Management Sarl), signed on 4 July 2016. (In subsequent citations, I will be referring to this contract as The Busanga R4I Contract (4 July 2016)). Regarding the financing of the infrastructure, see Section 9(2), The Busanga R4I Contract (4 July 2016). See also Afrewatch, IBGDH and OEARSE, "Pas au courant, pas de courant : Analyse Critique de la Gouvernance du Projet Hydroélectrique de Busanga" Lubumbashi, September 2018.

[3] Zongwe, Dunia, *The Competitive Edges of China's Resource-for-Infrastructure Investment Contracts in Africa,* 2 Peking University Journal of Legal Studies, 227, 249 (2010).

[4] *See* -< http://www.crecgi.com/en/ > on 27 June 2022. *See also* Devex "Sinohydro Corporation Limited" -< https://www.devex.com/organizations/sinohydro-corporation-limited-42902> on 27 June 2022.

[5] Statistica "Principaux pays producteurs de cobalt dans le monde de 2013 à 2021" <https://fr.statista.com/statistiques/565284/cobalt-production-miniere-par-pays-principaux/#:~:text=Cette%20statistique%20pr%C3%A9sente%20la%20production,une%20production%20de%2095.000%20tonnes> on 27 June 2022.

[6] *See* Statistica "Principaux pays producteurs de cuivre dans le monde de 2013 à 2022" -<https://fr.statista.com/statistiques/565205/production-de-cuivre-dans-les-principaux-pays/> ; Agence Ecofin " RDC : Kamoa-Kakula peut devenir le 4ème producteur mondial de cuivre dès 2023 (Ivanhoe)" <https://www.agenceecofin.com/cuivre/2302-95319-rdc-kamoa-kakula-peut-devenir-le-4eme-producteur-mondial-de-cuivre-des-2023-ivanhoe#:~:text=Cuivre-,RDC%20%3A%20Kamoa%2DKakula%20peut%20devenir%20le%204%C3%A8me%20producteur%20mondial,de%20cuivre%20d%C3%A8s%202023%20(Ivanhoe)&text=(Agence%20Ecofin)%20%2D%20Future%20deuxi%C3%A8me,en%20production%20en%20mai%202021> on 27 June 2022.

of Sovereign Debt[7] which reports the country's sovereign debt on a regular basis,[8] the Office for the Coordination and Monitoring of the Sino-Congolese Programme,[9] which is the statutory body that monitors all activities pertaining to and related to Sicomines (whose electricity needs the Busanga HPP came to meet),[10] as well as the Extractive Industries Transparency Initiative (EITI)[11] which addresses key governance issues in extractive sectors[12] and the Chinese Ambassador to DRC all maintain that the $509.43 million for the Busanga HPP was bartered in exchange for copper and cobalt from Dikuluwe and Mashamba West mines in the Lualaba province.[13]

In this chapter, I historicise, interrogate and problematise the R4I between the Democratic Republic of the Congo (DRC) and the Chinese Consortium in respect of the Busanga Hydropower Plant (Busanga R4I contract). My aim is to demonstrate that, although structured as if DRC has given minerals worth $509.43 million in exchange for the construction of the Busanga HPP, this contract is not a barter as suggested by the General Directorate of Sovereign Debt, the Office for the Coordination and Monitoring of the Sino-Congolese Programme, EITI and the Chinese Ambassador to DRC. Rather than an equal exchange, this contract forces DRC into an "unsustainable collateralised sovereign debt position" by which I mean when

---

[7] République Démocratique du Congo, Direction Générale de la Dette Publique, Mars 2021, Bulletin Statistique de la Dette Publique de la RD Congo, Données à la fin de 2020, No 14/2020, Mars 2021, viii.

[8] Id at i–ii.

[9] *See* Économie, "RDC : le BCPSC précise que les réserves minières de la RDC n'ont pas été sous-évaluées ni minorées dans les contrats Sino-Congolais" Mardi 7 décembre 2021 -< https://actualite.cd/2021/12/07/rdc-le-bcpsc-precise-que-les-reserves-minieres-de-la-rdc-nont-pas-ete-sous-evaluees-ni> on 27 juin 2022.

[10] Décret n° 08/ 018 du 26 août 2008 portant création, organisation et fonctionnement du Bureau de Coordination et de Suivi du Programme Sino-Congolais, en sigle « B.C.P.S.C ».

[11] Étude d'évaluation de la mise en œuvre de la convention de collaboration relative au développement d'un projet minier et d'un projet d'infrastructures en RD Congo Projet SICOMINES Contrat de services de consultance N° 002/ST/ITIE-RDC/2021 (Pages 25–29).

[12] *See* -< https://eiti.org/> on 27 June 2022.

[13] Dunia P. Zongwe, *Natural Resources for National Reconstruction: A New Generation of Investment Contracts,* Fifth Biennial Global Conference July 7–9, 2016 held at School of Law and Mandela Institute, University of the Witwatersrand, Working paper no. 2016/28, 38, 23.

the market value of the natural resources used by a country as collateral for a debt incurred to finance infrastructure construction exceeds the value of the infrastructure constructed. From this perspective, DRC received close to nothing in this exchange while Busanga HPP is, almost exclusively, meeting the interests of the Chinese Consortium. The excess, in terms of natural resources that DRC is providing to China, could have been used in meeting DRC's other development goals. I go on to explain how this injustice to DRC was possible due to corruption and illegal conduct by the Chinese consortium and former President Joseph Kabila's ruling clique. I end the chapter with some concluding remarks, which also spropose a way forward.

2 The Busanga R4I Contract is not a Barter

The Busanga R4I contract was entered into on 4 July 2016. Under the contract, DRC will provide copper and cobalt from Dikuluwe and Mashamba West mines in the Lualaba province to China in exchange for the Busanga HPP.

Finding the language to describe R4I contracts has been a major challenge in scholarship and general discourse on Sino-African relations. But does language matter? Pundits on Sino-African relations have often labelled R4I contracts with such contradictory names.[14] However, as Dunia Zongwe rightly perceives, the debate about how to label these contracts would have been "comparable to the notoriously futile byzantine discussions about the sex of angels if it did not disclose a deep conceptual confusion about what those [contracts] are."[15] This confusion makes it difficult to ascertain whether these R4I contracts are, for example, typical to a barter or that they force a country into an unsustainable collateralised sovereign debt position (defined in the introduction of this paper).

Language does, however, matter. For instance, Johanna Jansson cautions that looking at an R4I contract as a barter is a deceptively simplistic way of looking at an already-very-complicated financial arrangement.[16] For Zongwe, determining which language to give to the Busanga R4I contract is an exercise of looking at the common

---

[14] *Id* at 38, 4 and 8–9.

[15] *Id.*

[16] Johanna Jansson, *The Sicomines agreement revisited: Prudent Chinese Banks and Risk-taking Chinese companies,* 40 Review of African Political Economy, 135, 153 (2013).

intentions of the parties.[17] When we embark on this exercise—examining the intentions of the parties to the Busanga R4I—as posited by Zongwe, it becomes clearer that the Busanga R4I is not a barter. I propose that we embark on this exercise from two fronts: firstly, which party is required to meet the pre-contractual costs related to the maintenance of the Busanga HPP and the feasibility studies done on it and, secondly, which party is required to reimburse which portion of the $509.43 million loan from China Eximbank.

2.1 Pre-contractual costs

Before DRC's independence from the Belgians, the Union Minière du Katanga operated both mining sites and hydropower plants for the Belgian Congo (1908-1960). Gécamines, the Congolese state-owned miner, inherited the operations of the Union from the early 1960s. Although Gécamines kept on maintaining the Busanga Hydropower Plant, it passed on the management of the hydropower plants to the Société Nationale d'Electricité (SNEL).[18]

To get Busanga to 100 MW, Gécamines conducted a feasibility study—endorsed by the World Bank—which estimated that $65 million could finance full construction in the 1990s.[19] However, dictator Mobutu Sese Seko,[20] believing that allowing the construction could make the South-eastern part of the country more independent from the central government which could have incentivized secessionist ideas that were prevalent in those years, opted for an 1800-kilometre high-voltage line importing electricity from Inga Hydropower Plant which is located in the Congo

---

[17] *Supra,* note 13 at 38, 8–9.

[18] Afrewatch, IBGDH and OEARSE, "Pas au courant, pas de courant : Analyse Critique de la Gouvernance du Projet Hydroélectrique de Busanga" 14 Lubumbashi, (September 2018).

[19] Dibling Sébastien, at al, "Et si le Congo-Zaïre refusait de payer sa dette ? Essai analytique des preuves d'une dette odieuse" Etude présentée lors du Séminaire International sur la dette extérieure du Zaïre, Travail réalisé dans le cadre du groupe de recherche et d'analyse du droit du cadtm, organisé par Hugo Ruiz, Avril 2004, 22

[20] Sese Seko was the renowned dictator who, with the help of Belgium, the United States, and the United Nations, removed politics from the Congolese parliament and put it in the streets, "where the balance of power is played out in a brutal fashion, in numbers of soldiers, battalions and weapons" to orchestrate the assassination of the Congolese democratically-elected prime minister Patrice Emery Lumumba in 1961. Sese Seko ruled over the DRC, which was called Zaire under his reign, for more than 30 years.

Central at the centre of the country.[21] Gécamines continued to maintain Busanga HPP until SNEL passed it over to a private operator, Mag Energy International, in a transaction whose fine details remain unclear (even to civil society organisations in the DRC) to date.[22] Mag Energy started conducting another feasibility study regarding the construction of Busanga HPP in 2006.

Jean-Luc Kahamba, who has a professional experience of about 36 years in the Congolese mining sector, confirmed that each of the large mining companies in the DRC need roughly 200 megawatts (MW) of electricity to run at full capacity.[23] SNEL has been unable to meet this electricity demand and, therefore, most mining companies have been buying electricity from neighbouring Zambia[24] and/or relying on generators.[25] It is against this backdrop that the DRC entered the Busanga R4I contract on 4 July 2016. The goal was to upgrade the Busanga HPP to reach its full capacity and profitability[26] which Mag Energy's feasibility study put at 240MW.

The Busanga R4I contract states that construction of the power plant to 240MW capacity would cost $509.43 million.[27] However, if we are to go by Gécamines's feasibility study, that the World Bank endorsed, expanding Busanga HPP to produce 240 MW could have attracted roughly $162 million when the Gécamines's feasibility study was done.[28] If we still go by the same Gécamines's feasibility study, CPI

---

[21] *Supra,* note 19.

[22] *Supra*, note 18 at 6.

[23] Interview with Jean-Luc Kahamba at the Karavia Hotel in Lubumbashi on 18 April 2022.

[24] *Id.*

[25] Observatoire d'Étude et d'Appui à la Responsabilité Sociale et Environnementale (OEARSE), L'industrie extractive et la problématique du déficit énergétique en RDC : Avons-nous une vision et pour quel impact?, 8 (2021).

[26] The Sentry, "The Backchannel: State Capture and Bribery in Congo's Deal of the Century" 23 (November 2021).

[27] Section 4(2), The Busanga R4I Contract (4 July 2016) states that the parties to it shall put third parties to task to determine the exact cost of the construction of the Busanga Hydropower Plant. This cost has been now confirmed by Official records from the Congo General Directorate of Sovereign Debt. See République Démocratique du Congo, Ministère des Finances, Direction Générale de la Dette Publique, Mars 2021, Bulletin Statistique de la Dette Publique de la RD Congo, Données à la fin de 2020, No 14/2020, Mars 2021.

[28] This cost has been arrived that by proceeding from the fact that $65 million could only help produce 100 MW.

Inflation Calculator reveals that financing the construction of Busanga HPP could not have gone beyond present-day $305.98 million at the time the Busanga R4I contract was signed in 2016.[29] In light of this calculation, the Busanga R4I forced DRC into an Unsustainable Collateralised Sovereign Debt Position. Basically, DRC is losing minerals worth about $200 million in this contract since minerals worth $509.43 million are being used to finance the construction of a power plant that should have cost about $305.98 million when the contract was signed.[30]

Apart from the $200 million overpayment, the Busanga R4I contract places the cost of buying Mag Energy's feasibility study upon the DRC.[31] Further, the contract does not attach any precise or estimated amount corresponding to Mag Energy's feasibility study.[32] In fact, the contract states that the parties shall call upon a third party at a future date to help assess the exact cost associated with Busanga HPP's construction.[33] What then was the point of the feasibility study if such cost was not established? The contract provides an estimate of $656 million,[34] but we could take (with good reason) $509.43 million as the definite cost of the project available since it emanates from DRC's General Directorate of Sovereign Debt's March 2021 report.[35]

2.2 How will the $509.43 million be reimbursed?

Understanding how the $509.43 million will be reimbursed reinforces my argument that the Busanga R4I contract is not a barter. Here, a critical distinction needs to be made, for the sake of analysis, between what I will call Sicomines I and Sicomines II.

---

[29] CPI Inflation Calculator https://data.bls.gov/cgi-bin/cpicalc.pl?cost1=162&year1=199001&year2=201607

[30] Section 4(2), The Busanga R4I Contract (4 July 2016). *See also* République Démocratique du Congo Ministère des Finances Direction Générale de la Dette Publique, Mars 2021, Bulletin Statistique de la Dette Publique de la RD Congo, Données à la fin de 2020, No 14/2020, Mars 2021.

[31] Section 6(2)(2), The Busanga R4I Contract (4 July 2016).

[32] *See generally* The Busanga R4I Contract (4 July 2016).

[33] Section 4, The Busanga R4I Contract (4 July 2016).

[34] *Id.*

[35] République Démocratique du Congo Ministère des Finances Direction Générale de la Dette Publique, Mars 2021, Bulletin Statistique de la Dette Publique de la RD Congo, Données à la fin de 2020, No 14/2020, Mars 2021.

Sicomines I is the Sino-Congolaise des Mines—a mining company that is extracting copper and cobalt from the mines of Dikuluwe and Mashamba West in the Lualaba province. Sicomines I is using the proceeds from these mines to reimburse about $6 billion that the DRC has borrowed from China Eximbank to finance Kabila's post-war development strategy which was to provide the country with infrastructure construction (the broader DRC-China R4I contract).[36] Sicomines I is co-owned by a consortium of Chinese companies (China Railway Engineering Corporation and Sinohydro,[37] which own 68% of the venture) and the Groupe Gécamines (Gécamines and la Société Immobilière du Congo SAS (SIMCO), which own 32% of the venture).[38] The Busanga R4I contract states that 50% of the $509.43 million loan that financed the Busanga HPP's construction is to be reimbursed by Sicomines I. However, Section 3 of the contract states that, although Sicomines I will reimburse 50% of the $509.43 million loan through its mining proceeds, that repayment will not be counted towards reimbursing the $6 billion loan to Kabila's government under the broader DRC-China R4I for which *Sicomines I* was created.[39]

The Busanga R4I contract goes even further. The remaining 50% of the $509.43 million is to be reimbursed by Sicomines II.[40] To understand Sicomines II, we need to examine la Sino-congolaise hydroélectrique de Busanga SA (Sicohydro), which is a joint-venture created for the purposes of constructing and managing the hydropower plant.[41] Sicomines II owns 75% of Sicohydro. Sicomines II is simply Sicomines I but, at this point, fully owned by the Chinese Consortium. This is clear from Section

---

[36] *See also* Ana Cristina Alves, *China's "win-win" cooperation: Unpacking the impact of infrastructure-for-resources deals in Africa,* 20(2) South African Journal of International Affairs, 215 (2013). *See also* David Landry, *The Risks and Rewards of Resource-for-Infrastructure Deals,* 1–5.

[37] Sinohydro is the other name for Power China Construction. *See* Section 1(18), The Busanga R4I Contract (4 July 2016).

[38] *See* Ana Cristina Alves, China's "win-win" cooperation: Unpacking the impact of infrastructure-for-resources deals in Africa, 20(2) South African Journal of International Affairs, 215 (2013); David Landry, *The Risks and Rewards of Resource-for-Infrastructure Deals,* 1–5.

[39] Section 9(2), The Busanga R4I Contract (4 July 2016). *See also* Afrewatch, IBGDH and OEARSE, "Pas au courant, pas de courant : Analyse Critique de la Gouvernance du Projet Hydroélectrique de Busanga" Lubumbashi, (September 2018).

[40] Section 5(2), The Busanga R4I Contract (4 July 2016).

[41] *Supra,* note 26 at 23 (N.

3(3)(2) of contract which states that the Groupe Gécamines has surrendered its 32% stake in Sicomines I.[42] As such, to form Sicomines II, the Consortium took 100% ownership of Sicomines I. The contract is unequivocally clear that when Sicomines II will be reimbursing the remaining 50% of the $509.43 million, such reimbursement will not be counted as part of reimbursing the $ 6 billion loan to DRC for which Sicomines I was created.[43]

By distinguishing between Sicomines I and II, the Busanga R4I contract is simply smoke and mirrors. It is Congolese copper and cobalt coming from Dikuluwe and Mashamba West mines in the Lualaba province (and probably beyond) that will cover 100% of the cost of constructing Busanga HPP. It is important to emphasise, again, that repayment of the $509.43 million loan—which Sicomines I and II are to reimburse at 50% each—does not count towards reimbursing part of the $6 billion loan that Sicomines I was created to reimburse.

To avoid the deception of distinguishing between Sicomines I and Sicomines II in the rest of this chapter, what I am referring to as "Sicomines" in the remaining parts of this paper is Sicomines I.

There is a further point to consider. The Chinese consortium owns 75% of Sicohydro (the joint venture that the Busanga HPP contract created) and the DRC is supposed to own 25%. Strictly speaking, however, DRC owns less than 25%. Of the 25% that DRC supposedly owns, 15% belong to Congo Management S.A.R.L. (COMAN) and the remaining 10% are shared between Gécamines and SNEL. Although it appears so, COMAN is not a DRC state-owned corporation and the names of its shareholders are not readily available to the public.[44] Therefore, technically, the DRC owns just 10% of Sicohydro. This means the DRC is losing more money. The DRC's Office for the Coordination and Monitoring of the Sino-Congolese Programme has noted (bringing more specificity to Kahamba's estimates) that of the 240 MW that Busanga HPP was to produce, 170MW is allocated to the running of

---

[42] Articles 8–9, The Busanga R4I Contract (4 July 2016). *See also* Section 3(3)(2), The Busanga R4I Contract (4 July 2016).

[43] Section 9(2) The Busanga R4I Contract (4 July 2016). *See also* Afrewatch, IBGDH and OEARSE, "Pas au courant, pas de courant: Analyse Critique de la Gouvernance du Projet Hydroélectrique de Busanga" Lubumbashi, (September 2018).

[44] *Supra,* note 18 at 6.

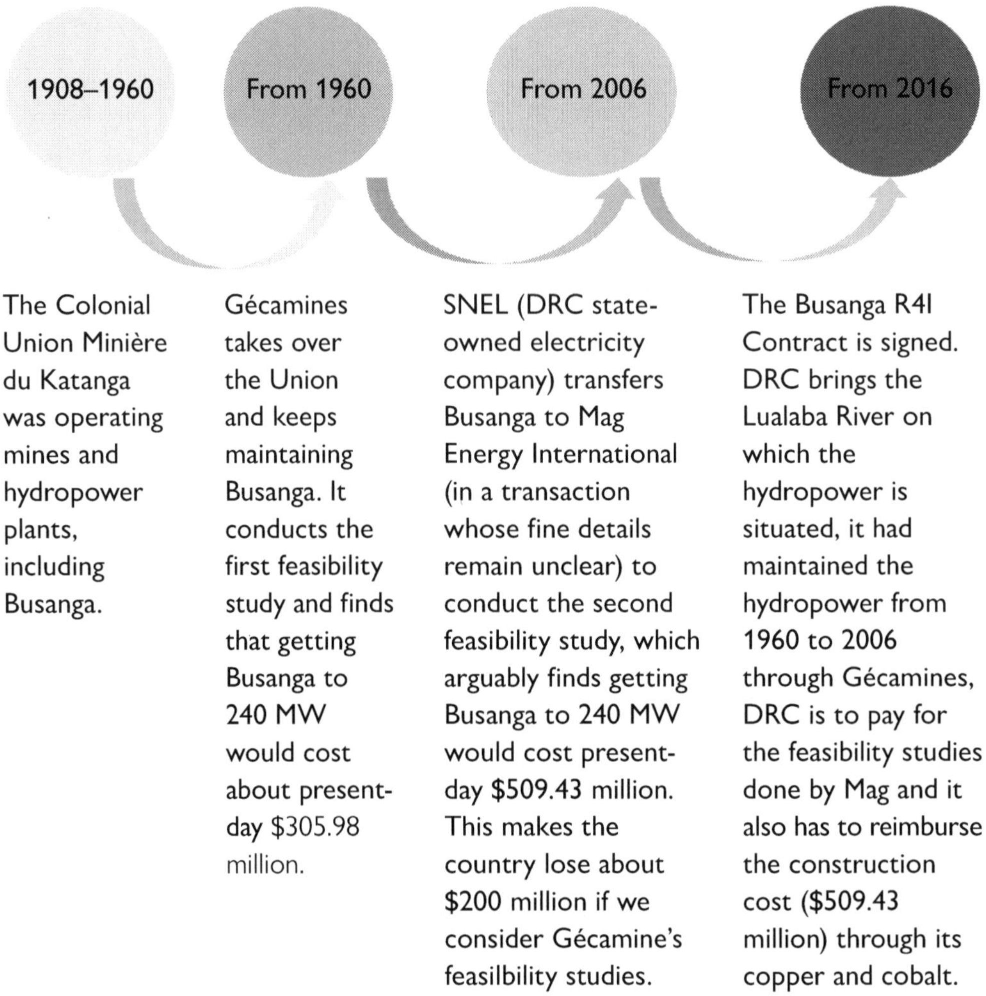

1908–1960	From 1960	From 2006	From 2016
The Colonial Union Minière du Katanga was operating mines and hydropower plants, including Busanga.	Gécamines takes over the Union and keeps maintaining Busanga. It conducts the first feasibility study and finds that getting Busanga to 240 MW would cost about present-day $305.98 million.	SNEL (DRC state-owned electricity company) transfers Busanga to Mag Energy International (in a transaction whose fine details remain unclear) to conduct the second feasibility study, which arguably finds getting Busanga to 240 MW would cost present-day $509.43 million. This makes the country lose about $200 million if we consider Gécamine's feasilbility studies.	The Busanga R4I Contract is signed. DRC brings the Lualaba River on which the hydropower is situated, it had maintained the hydropower from 1960 to 2006 through Gécamines, DRC is to pay for the feasibility studies done by Mag and it also has to reimburse the construction cost ($509.43 million) through its copper and cobalt.

Sicomines' mining operations while the excess—70MW—will be commercialized.[45] In the preamble, the Busanga R4I contract emphasizes that commercialization of electricity is part of the aims of Sicohydro.[46] However, going by ownership structure of Sicohydro, the DRC (strictly speaking) will only be getting 10% of the proceeds that would come from the commercialisation of the 70MW.

---

[45] See Économie, 'RDC : le BCPSC précise que les réserves minières de la RDC n'ont pas été sous-évaluées ni minorées dans les contrats Sino-Congolais' Mardi 7 décembre 2021 -< https://actualite.cd/2021/12/07/rdc-le-bcpsc-precise-que-les-reserves-minieres-de-la-rdc-nont-pas-ete-sous-evaluees-ni> on 27 juin 2022. See also Preamble, The Busanga R4I Contract (4 July 2016).
[46] Preamble, The Busanga R4I Contract (4 July 2016).

Ideally, as the term "resource-for-infrastructure" suggests, the DRC is required to provide resources and receive infrastructure in exchange. The language "resource-for-infrastructure" is therefore inadequate to describe the Busanga R4I contract. The Chinese Consortium bring close to nothing in this R4I contract. The DRC brought the Lualaba River on which the hydropower is situated, maintained the hydropower plant there for many years through Gécamines, is paying for the feasibility studies done on it and is also reimbursing the construction cost from its copper and cobalt. Since the Chinese Consortium did not finance the construction, it would have made perhaps more sense for the DRC to hire and pay the Consortium to construct the plant rather than giving them minerals worth $ 509.43 million.[47] They could have been hired just as a landowner would hire workers and pay them to build him/her a house.[48] We can then not help but admit that the Busanga R4I contract forces the DRC unjustly into an unsustainable collateralised sovereign debt position.

In the following part, I demonstrate that this injustice against DRC was possible thanks to corruption facilitated through unethical and illegal conduct that the Chinese Consortium and former President Joseph Kabila's ruling clique were accomplices in.

3 Unethical and Illegal Conduct

It is hard to believe the Busanga R4I contract when it states in its preamble that DRC knew from the onset that it had to provide electricity for Sicomines to be able to run its mining operations.[49] I am providing two types of evidence to the contrary. One is that, when the Sicomines R4I contract was first signed in 2008 and even when it was amended in 2009, it did not make reference to the DRC paying for the cost of the

---

[47] It is noteworthy that the Chinese Consortium and the lender, China Exim, are all Chinese state-owned companies. Hence, a broad argument may be made that, as Chinese state-owned entities, they are all instruments of the Chinese government i.e., the Chinese government is both the ultimate lender and beneficiary of the Consortium's interest in Sicomines and Busanga HPP. As such, it is arguable that the Consortium brought something—financing—in the Busanga R4I contract.
[48] This author recognizes that DRC may not have had the funds to make outright payment for Busanga HPP, hence the need for R4I approach in the first place.
[49] Preamble and Article 2, The Busanga R4I Contract (4 July 2016).

electricity that Sicomines needed to run its mining operations.[50] The Busanga R4I contract makes reference to a 2009 authorization that the DRC Minister of Energy gave to Sicomines, allowing this mining company to conduct feasibility study regarding the construction of Busanga HPP.[51] But this, in and of itself, is not proof that the country agreed to cover electricity costs. As mentioned earlier, each mining company usually meets its own electricity costs. Some have been even importing electricity from Zambia since SNEL is not providing enough. Others have been relying on generators.[52]

The other piece of evidence that Busanga R4I was never contemplated as the one that will come to meet the electricity needs of Sicomines is Du Wei. Du Wei is a Chinese scholar and businessman. It is reported that he has "freely advertised his expertise in safeguarding the African assets of Beijing's state-owned enterprises."[53] He has also closely worked with the consortium of Chinese state-owned companies that are involved in the Busanga R4I contract even when these were allegedly involved in illegal and unethical conduct.[54] He can help us understand that the DRC did not agree to pay for electricity for Sicomines operations when the Sicomines R4I was entered into in 2008 and even as revised in 2009. Just before the Busanga R4I contract was entered into in July 2016, Wei had published an academic paper the same year.

> The [paper] cited the Sino-Congolese deal [Sicomines] as a case study, pointing to the lack of stable electricity as a "power supply dilemma" that threatened to undermine the entire arrangement. Sinohydro and Sicomines had been undertaking

---

[50] *See generally* Avenant N° 2 a la Convention De Joint-Venture du 22 Avril 2008 And Avenant N° 2 A La Convention de Joint-Venture du 22 Avril 2008. See also that only two major changes were made to it in 2009 and they did not touch on Busanga. Johanna Janson, *The Sicomines Agreement: Change and Continuity in the Democratic Republic of Congo's International Relations* China in Africa Project, Occasional Paper No 97, 2011, at 20–21.
[51] Article 5, The Busanga R4I Contract (4 July 2016).
[52] *Supra,* note 25 at 8.
[53] *Supra,* note 26 at 9.
[54] *See generally* The Sentry, "The Backchannel: State Capture and Bribery in Congo's Deal of the Century" November 2021.

surveys and project feasibility studies since 2009 on a hydroelectric power station for the latter. But talks to reach a protocol agreement on construction had foundered in 2010 amid *disagreements about financing, capital contributions, personnel, and management, according to Du.*[55]

The Chinese consortium and Kabila's ruling clique joined forces, through corruption, illegal and unethical conduct, against the people. My conclusion is that this is the only explanation of the unjust Busanga R4I contract. To substantiate this conclusion, I first provide a general overview of the Chinese entities involved in the Busanga R4I contract and how they generally conduct their affairs. Then, I rely on investigations conducted by the Sentry and DRC-based Non-governmental Organisations (NGOs) to highlight how bribery was key to the conclusion of this contract.

3.1 *Of the reputation and the conduct of their affairs*

Exim's money may not actually exist or may not exist at least in the amounts we are led to believe. No one has ever seen the $509.43 million that came from Exim in the form of loans and how Exim has disbursed this amount to finance the construction of the Busanga hydropower plant. Halland et al have observed that once an R4I contract (such as the Busanga one) is signed, the loan disbursements are paid directly into the construction companies to cover construction costs.[56] Resano have complemented Halland et al by emphasizing that, strictly speaking, Exim's money to finance infrastructure construction never leaves China as both Eximbank and the consortium of Chinese construction companies have their headquarters in China.[57]

This doubt about the existence of Exim's money is yet again in line with Deborah Brautigam and Jyhjong Hwang's findings about the myths regarding China's

---

[55] *Supra*, note 26 at 23.
[56] Håvard Halland et al, with comments by Paul Collier et al., *Resource Financed Infrastructure: A Discussion on a New Form of Infrastructure Financing*, 4 The World Bank (2014).
[57] Jose Ramon Martinez Resano, *Collateralized Sovereign Debt. Missing Elements in the International Financial Arquitecture,* 7 (January 2, 2018), <https://papers.ssrn.com/sol3/papers.cfm?abstract_id=3933090>.

engagement in the construction of hydropower plants in Africa. One of these myths is the ease with which Chinese financing can be acquired.[58] Brautigam and Hwang demonstrate that finance for Chinese-built hydropower plants in Africa is misunderstood. Brautigam and Hwang conducted a detailed examination of each of the more than 100 hydropower plant projects across the continent. These 100 hydropower plant projects have been reported by the media and lists compiled by other organizations, from the year 2000 to 2013, as having been financed by Chinese policy banks and companies (China has 3 main policy banks and Exim is one of them).[59] Brautigam and Hwang found that Chinese policy banks and companies were actually involved in 'helping to build' only 23 plants.[60] This should perhaps not be surprising because Exim gets its finances from borrowing on the domestic and international capital markets and not from China's. Exim then lends so that it can be financially self-sufficient.[61] Exim's principal concern is perceived profitability of the projects it finances.[62] It may then make sense that Exim has turned a blind eye and a deaf ear to the corruption involved in the Busanga R4I contract. This is confirmed in the 2021 Congo Hold-up leak which I discuss below.

It might not be a coincidence that Chinese construction companies have failed to deliver on promised infrastructure or infrastructure of quality in many parts of the world, despite the existence of feasibility studies that are meant to determine the cost of completing the promised and quality infrastructure.[63] For instance, the consortium of Chinese companies involved in Busanga are associated with claims of prior corruption. In 2017 alone, Sinohydro was under corruption investigations in Ecuador

---

[58] Deborah Brautigam & Jyhjong Hwang, "Great Walls over African Rivers: Chinese engagement in African hydropower projects" <https://ideas.repec.org/a/bla/devpol/v37y2019i3p313-330.html>.
[59] *See* IBISWorld, "Policy Banks Industry in China—Market Research Report" -<https://www.ibisworld.com/china/market-research-reports/policy-banks-industry/#:~:text=The%20industry%20comprises%20three%20policy,development%2C%20and%20state%20investment%20projects> on 8 June 2022.
[60] *Supra,* note 59.
[61] David Dollar, *Is China's Development Finance a Challenge to the International Order?,* 13 Asian Economic Policy Review, 285 (2018).
[62] *Supra,* note 16 at 135, 157.
[63] *Supra,* note 26 at 8.

and Uganda.[64] China Eximbank loans do not come with any political, economic, or human rights conditions when it gives a loan out. This is unlike the World Bank, the International Monetary Fund (IMF), and other emerging multilateral development banks (MDBs).[65]

3.2 Bribery was key

The Congo Hold-up leak is perhaps the largest leak of African financial records and data. The Platform to Protect Whistle-blowers in Africa (PPLAAF) and Mediapart obtained it and shared it with several stakeholders. The Sentry relied on the Congo Hold-up leak in order to conduct further investigation. It found clear evidence of corruption, unethical and illegal conduct at crucial junctures in the running of Sicomines and the Busanga R4I contract.[66] In their investigation, the African Resources Watch (Afrewatch), the Initiative Bonne Gouvernance et Droits Humains (IBGDH) and the Observatoire d'Etudes et d'Appui à la Responsabilité Sociale et Environnementale (OEARSE), which are NGOs based in the DRC, also came to conclusions that are similar to those of the Sentry:[67]

> The Sentry's investigation has found clear evidence of corruption showing that Chinese corporations colluded with power players in the DRC to secure access to billions of dollars' worth of natural resources—all with an assist from the world of high finance. Put differently, a generational investment in the DRC's potential, one meant to help heal the wounds from decades of mismanagement and successive wars, in fact served another purpose all too prevalent in the world's resource-dependent economies: lining the pockets of the powerful with the wealth buried beneath the impoverished population's feet.[68]

---

[64] *Id.*

[65] Todd Moss & Sarah Rose, *China ExIm Bank and Africa: New Lending, New Challenges,* Center for Global Development, November 2006.

[66] *Supra,* note 64 at, 3.

[67] *Supra,* note 18 at 25.

[68] *Supra,* note 26 at, 3.

The Sentry's investigation demonstrates, *with proof of actual financial records and data, which are attached as annexes,* that Kabila's ruling clique captured the institutions that were meant to duly represent DRC people in the Busanga R4I contract. This resulted in the ruling clique making decisions that benefited the Chinese companies while "the money piled up within the private commercial universe surrounding the president."[69] Some of those institutions that the ruling clique captured are the Congo Construction Company (CCC), the Office for the Coordination and Monitoring of the Sino-Congolese Programme, as well as COMAN. As the investigation reveals:

> In 2016, as the Chinese stakeholders and the Congolese government were hammering out plans for the hydroelectric power [plant] in Busanga, Sicomines sent three payments totalling $25 million to CCC's accounts at BGFI Bank DRC, the vast majority of which CCC immediately routed to companies and people associated with Kabila. The remittance information—"contract costs," "payment"—offered no details on the purposes of the sizable transfers, and BGFI Bank [DRC]'s internal auditors were later unable to locate any contract underlying the payments. Citibank in New York processed at least $17 million of the money Sicomines sent to CCC.[70]

At the material time, the investigation also found that Kabila's brother, Francis Selemani, was BGFI Bank DRC's Managing Director.[71] BGFI Bank DRC, as shown in the excerpt above, was critical in helping the ruling clique launder millions.[72] Moise Ekanga was running the Office of the Coordination and Monitoring of the Sino-Congolese Programme, whose legislative mandate is to oversee the implementation of Sicomines, the operations of which are directly linked to Busanga HPP. Ekanga is Kabila's ally who allegedly helped launder millions of dollars from Sicomines through this office into businesses associated with Kabila's family.[73]

---

[69] *Id.,* at 41(Emphasis mine).
[70] *Id.,* at 24.
[71] *Id.,* at 25.
[72] *Id.,* at 4
[73] *Id.,* at 15–16

Afrewatch, IBGDH and OEARSE also found that COMAN, the mysterious company that owns 15% of the 25% of shares that the DRC owns in Sicohydro (the joint venture that the Busanga R4I contract created), has Claudine Paony Tupa as one of the main figures behind it. Tupa had strong ties with the Office for the Coordination and Monitoring of the Sino-Congolese Programme.[74] COMAN was also represented in the Busanga R4I contract by another of Kabila's allies, Norbert Nkulu, whom Kabila appointed as one of the Judges of the DRC Constitutional Court—the highest court in the land—in 2018.[75]

Afrewatch, IBGDH and OEARSE had to conduct a field study before relevant authorities and stakeholders in order to make sense of the Busanga R4I contract in the year 2018 yet the contract is of 2016.[76] The contract was hidden from public scrutiny. When the Congo Hold-up leak brought to light the bribery, the Chinese companies chose not to respond. Nor did Kabila, his associates, and family members.[77] The DRC Office for the Coordination and Monitoring of the Sino-Congolese Programme found the leak lacking in foundation. This office labelled it a move by certain western powers that are determined to tarnish the image, honour and reputation of DRC institutions and political personalities and to discourage investors, particularly those from China.[78]

4 Concluding Remarks

Europe was left in ashes after the first and second world wars. It must not be surprising then that at the Bretton Wood Conference in 1944, imperialist powers deemed it necessary to found the International Bank for Re-construction and Development—soon called the World Bank—as a way to finance infrastructure construction in Europe and, later on, in other continents.[79] From the 1980s, however, there was a growing

---

[74] *Supra,* note 18 at 25.
[75] *Supra* note 26 at 23.
[76] *Supra,* note 18 at 25.
[77] *Supra,* note 26 at 4.
[78] "Coordination du contrat Chinois éclaire l'opinion" Geopolis 7 Décembre 2021.
[79] Chris Humphrey, *Infrastructure Finance in the Developing World: Challenges and Opportunities for Multilateral Development Banks in 21st Century Infrastructure Finance,* 2 The Global Green Growth Institute and The Intergovernmental Group of Twenty-Four on Monetary Affairs and Development (2015).

consensus among development economists and NGOs that necessitated a shift in the World Bank's founding mission. This consensus was to the effect that physical infrastructure was not, in and of itself, successfully promoting development.[80] The Bank then shifted to a focus on financing health, education, and poverty relief; rather than infrastructure construction.[81]

To gain a fair understanding of this, we learn from Chris Humphrey that 70% of the main lending windows of the World Bank that were geared towards infrastructure construction in 1960s were reduced to 19% in the 2000s.[82] It also became harder for countries to tap into the 19% because it required to satisfy the political, economic, or human rights conditions that are attached to it.[83]

As financing infrastructure construction was receding in the background of the Bank's priorities, other countries became in dire post-war need for infrastructure construction. This need arose across the African continent, and the DRC was not an exception. From Belgian colonial experiences, through more than 30 years of Mobutu Sese Seko's reign of mismanagement of public funds (between 1965 and 1997), up to the first and second Congo Wars (1996–1997 and 1998–2003), failing physical infrastructure had been one of the most obvious features of the DRC.[85]

This is the country that Kabila inherited when he won the first democratic presidential election of the DRC in 2006. Disincentivised to approach the World Bank and Western donors to finance his post-war development strategy for the reasons stated above, he and his establishment turned to the East to enter an R4I contract with a consortium of Chinese state-owned construction companies.[86] Characteristically, as

---

[80] *Id.* at 2.
[81] Alex He, "China in the International Financial System: A Study of The NDB And The AIIB" 5, 12, CIGI Papers No. 106 (June 2016).
[82] *Supra,* note 80 at 3.
[83] *Supra,* note 62, at 293.
[84] See for instance Jordan Schwartz & Pablo Halkyard, *Post conflict infrastructure: Trends in aid and investment flows,* The World Bank—Private Sector Development Vice Presidency, Note No 305, March 2006.
[85] *Supra,* note 16 at 135, 152.
[86] *Supra,* note 57 at 5.

it may have been clear by now, R4I contracts compete with the World Bank's lending window that is geared towards infrastructure construction. R4I contracts are more lucrative since they are less bureaucratic and free of political, economic, or human rights accompanying conditions. Bearing these characteristics in mind, former Senegalese President, Abdoulaye Wade, for example commented that a contract that would take five years to discuss, negotiate and sign with the World Bank takes three months when it is with the Chinese.[87]

The R4I contract that Kabila's establishment signed to finance Kabila's post-war development strategy was Sicomines, the electricity needs of which led to the conclusion of yet another R4I contract—the Busanga one. One major problem surrounding this contract is what I have referred to as the "unacceptable sovereign burden that the Busanga hydropower plant places on the DRC." This is the problem of corruption. Estimating the construction of the hydropower plant to $509.43 million is inconsistent with a feasibility study done by Gecamines and endorsed by the World Bank. This study suggests that the construction of the hydropower plant could not have gone beyond $300 million. The Sentry investigation and investigations of the DRC-based NGOs, as explained in this chapter, also demonstrate that corruption is the most obvious justification of the unacceptable collateralised sovereign debt burden that the Busanga Hydropower Plant places on the DRC.

The DRC has the option to challenge this contract because it is tainted with corruption. The DRC has domesticated international instruments against corruption both at the African Union (AU) level and at the United Nations (UN) level. These are the United Nations Convention Against Corruption (UNCAC) and African Union's Convention Against Corruption (AUCC).[88] Domestic courts are obliged to help enforce these treaties in the case of the Busanga R4I contract. Although the Busanga R4I contract contemplates the ICSID as the forum for dispute resolution,[89] there is a growing body of ICSID jurisprudence denying the ICSID tribunal the

---

[87] *Supra,* note 3 at 227, 233.
[88] *See* Loi n° 06/014 du 12 juin 2006 autorisant la ratification par la République Démocratique du Congo de la Convention des Nations Unies contre la corruption.
[89] Section 17(7), The Busanga R4I Contract (4 July 2016).

jurisdiction to entertain disputes brought by investors (the Chinese consortium in our case) when it is clear that the investment treaty (the Busanga R4I in our case) has violated domestic law.[90] The 2018 case of *Cortec Mining Kenya Limited, Cortec (Pty) Limited, and Stirling Capital Limited V. Republic of Kenya* highlights this development:

> [T]he Cortec award highlights that foreign investment must be made in compliance with domestic law if it is to enjoy international protection—even in the absence of an explicit legality requirement in the applicable BIT. This finding reinforces the case for investors to exercise due diligence in order to ensure their activities comply with domestic law. The importance of legal compliance is further buttressed by the tribunal's insistence that noncompliance cannot be excused by bureaucrats or politicians. As the tribunal observed, "[n]o amount of frustration with the bureaucracy excused [the claimants] from non-performance of these legal conditions, nor could non-performance be waived by the politicians" (para. 105).[91]

There is a further point to consider. DRC judges that may be faced with a case tackling the corruption that surrounds the Busanga R4I contract should approach the UNCAC and the AUCC with caution. James Thuo Gathii has studied anticorruption treaties—including the UNCAC and AUCC[92]—and found that:

> Anticorruption treaties generally define corruption as the abuse of entrusted power for private gain. As such, global anticorruption efforts primarily target transactions involving the bribery of governmental officials. The definition excludes transactions in which multinational corporations deprive developing

---

[90] *See generally* Lorenzo Cotula and James Gathii, "Cortec Mining Kenya Limited, Cortec (Pty) Limited, and Stirling Capital Limited v. Republic of Kenya." 113(3) American Journal of International Law 574 (2019).

[91] *Id.* at 580.

[92] *See generally* James Thuo Gathii, "Recharacterizing Corruption to Encompass Illicit Financial Flows" 113 AJIL Unbound 336(2019).

[93] *Id.* at, 336–37.

states of revenue by failing to pay taxes and other monies due. Yet such transactions are equally injurious to the development agenda of poor states.'[93]

We would then expect some interpretative creativity on the part of DRC judges to expand the meaning of corruption in a way that encompasses the Chinese consortium (which is made of Chinese multinational corporations) as well since it was engaged in corruption with Kabila's ruling clique. Criminal investigations/prosecutions should be initiated into/against Kabila, his ruling clique, and the Chinese consortium.

Ideally, domestic resources such as the minerals at play in the Busanga contract should constitute the most sustainable source of investment in national development priorities. They are crucial for the DRC because they have the potential of preventing the country from borrowing more money—hence incurring sovereign debt—in order to finance its national development priorities.

---

[94] Katja Hujo & Yusuf Bangura, *The Politics of Domestic Resource Mobilization for Social Development: An Introduction,* in *The Politics of Domestic Resource Mobilization for Social Development,* 1 (Katja Hujo ed., 2020).

CHAPTER TWELVE

The Coloniality of Sovereign Debt in the Global South

Bharath Gururagavendran*

I Introduction

In the end, we will do everything but the national debt will oppress us... Regardless of the decision taken regarding this debt, it will be horrific: If we recognize it, we cease to exist, and if we do not, this nation will be the object of opprobrium.

—SIMON BOLIVAR
Former President of the Republic of Venezuela

Scholars while discussing international law, often premise their support for it on the grounds that it validates and bolsters the sovereignty doctrine,[1] guaranteeing order in an otherwise "perilous" global context muddied by the meeting of savages and saviors.[2] Relations of inequality that continue to affect nations on the periphery, were produced

---

* Bharath Gururagavendran is an incoming student at NYU's Graduate School, pursuing a Master's in International Relations. Previously, he held the position of Assistant Professor at Jindal Global Law School.

[1] Samantha Besson, "Sovereignty" (2011), MAX PLANCK ENCYCLOPEDIAS OF INTERNATIONAL LAW—OPIL, available at <https://opil.ouplaw.com/view/10.1093/law:epil/9780199231690/law-9780199231690-e1472> (accessed on 6 December 2021).

[2] Anne Orford, "Constituting Order," in James Crawford and Martti Koskenniemi (2012) at 272, THE CAMBRIDGE COMPANION TO INTERNATIONAL LAW, CAMBRIDGE UNIVERSITY PRESS; To understand the extent to which racialized beliefs about the barbarianism of the non-European world operated as a guiding principle in the development of international law, *see* Antony Anghie, "Finding the Peripheries: Sovereignty and Colonialism in Nineteenth-Century International Law" (1999) at 1, 22, 59, HARVARD INTERNATIONAL LAW JOURNAL.

through North-South interactions that took place within a broader colonial-capitalist architecture that paved the road for the domination and subjugation of the Third World. The International Financial System that mediated these interactions has in its own capacity infringed the sovereignty of those Third World nations by ravaging their economies in numerous respects.[3] And perhaps most perniciously, the disbursement of largely odious debt through such unjust frameworks has (consciously) operated as a justification to wage wars, enabling colonial rule that enslaved these nations.

The story of underdevelopment in the Global South has largely been endogenous,[4] attributing the debt crises principally to governance failures. The seizure of knowledge production and the power consolidation projects that it breathes life into, has resulted in deeply fallacious modes of economic organization, at a global scale. The popularization of such false narratives through mainstream academic discourse,[5] has helped embed colonial norms in the perceptions and practices of modern international financial institutions (*IFIs*). Moreover, these narratives that pollute our institutions are typically the sites at which racial capitalism rears its ugly head, disempowering the rights and freedoms of both Third World citizens across the global color line, and people of colour living under discriminatory conditions within First World nations.[6]

---

[3] Carlos Mariachal, "A Century of Debt Crises in Latin America: From Independence to the Great Depression, 1820–1930," PRINCETON: PRINCETON UNIVERSITY PRESS, (These measures range from using debt as a basis for military conquest, to coercively redesigning regulatory frameworks in the Third World as a criteria for entry into the global financial system).

[4] There are however critical scholars such as Eric Toussaint have produced an extensive historiography of debt crises in periphery nations that is at odds with the mainstream discourse developed by those in power who've helped formulate and spread the international system for debt disbursement. *See* Eric Toussaint, "The Debt System, A History of Sovereign Debts and Their Repudiation" (2019), HAYMARKET BOOKS [*hereafter* Eric Toussaint].

[5] For the enduring legacy of Alexander Sack who helped popularize such narratives in this treatise on the treatment of state debts in the event of regime change, *See* Sarah Ludington and Mitu Gulati, "A Convenient Untruth: Fact and Fantasy in the Doctrine of Odious Debts" (2008) at 597–602,VIRGINIA JOURNAL OF INTERNATIONAL LAW, 48(3); *See also,* Alexander Nahum Sack, "Les Effets Des Transformations Des Etats Sur Leurs Dettes Publiques Et Autres Obligations Financiers" (1927) at 46–61,PARIS: SIREY.

[6] Jodi Melamed, "Racial Capitalism" at 76–95, CRITICAL ETHNIC STUDIES, UNIVERSITY OF MINNESOTA PRESS.

The set of assumptions that underlay developmental models were constructed around the idea that laws are required to create the formal structure for macroeconomic control.[7] As such, much of the law and development doctrine that evolved in the *First Moment*, was aimed at designing laws as instruments for state intervention in the economy.[8] A process that entailed the transplanting of regulatory laws from states in the First World.[9] The *Second Moment* brought with it a neoliberal shift that was aimed at placing strict limits on state intervention, and simultaneously empowering private law.[10] In this period, the IMF and World Bank helped herald a market-oriented paradigm of development post the 1980s, instituting structural adjustment programs in developing countries as the price of entry to generate cashflow through IFIs.

Much has been written about its devastating impact on advancing poverty and income inequality in society.[11] Moreover, these reform processes have enabled massive shifts in the institutional design of several Third World nations, often entailing budget cuts to social sectors, which typically, affect the most vulnerable demographics.[12] The clearest indicator of its negative impacts on the socio-economic health of a nation, can be found in the disproportionate spending of several Sub-Saharan African countries, on debt servicing over health, during a global pandemic.[13] This has

---

[7] David M. Trubek & Alvaro Santos, "Introduction: The Third Moment In Law and Development Theory and The Emergence of A New Critical Practice" (2006), THE NEW LAW AND ECONOMIC DEVELOPMENT: A CRITICAL APPRAISAL, NEW YORK: CAMBRIDGE UNIVERSITY PRESS, Available at: https://scholarship.law.georgetown.edu/facpub/2105/, (Accessed on 11th July, 2022).

[8] *Ibid*, ¶ 2.

[9] *Ibid*, ¶ 5.

[10] To protect the facilitation of property rights and contractual exchange.

[11] Brian F. Crisp & Michael J. Kelley, "The Socio-Economic Impacts of Structural Adjustment" (1999) at 542–549, INTERNATIONAL STUDIES QUARTERLY, 43(3), WILEY.

[12] Michael Thomson offers a systematic review of the effects of structural adjustment programmes on child and maternal health, impacting social determinants of health, i.e., income, and food availability. *See* Michael Thomson et. al., "Structural Adjustment Programmes Aversely Affect Vulnerable Populations: A Systematic-Narrative Review of Their Effect on Child and Maternal Health" (2017), PUBLIC HEALTH REVIEWS, 38(13).

[13] *See* Chart 1, World Health Organization; and World Bank, International Debt Statistics, Kevin Watkins, Delivering Debt Relief for The Poorest, IMF, Finance & Development, Fall 2020, Available at: https://www.imf.org/external/pubs/ft/fandd/2020/08/debt-relief-for-the-poorest-kevin-watkins.htm#:~:text=The%20G20%20initiative%20offers%20what,one%2Dyear%20grace%20period (Accessed on 1st June 2022).

motivated a greater degree of recognition of the link between developmental policy and "human freedom", and the range of rights that they require.[14] Recognizing the importance of eradicating poverty, the IMF's SAPs have undergone several organizational transitions to be oriented towards poverty reductions.[15]

Much of these changes have emanated in the *Third Moment*. And while the IMF has utilized areas of issue linkage and aligned itself with Millennium Development Goals, its institutional logics still very much preserve neo-colonial extractive epistemologies that ought to be redesigned,[16] with a view towards generating more democratic participation (i.e., voting share reform). The international system has been attentive to these growing issue linkages between the activities of IFIs and socio-economic rights. Nevertheless, there are strong causal connections between the debt system as it currently stands, and the devastating human rights impacts on underprivileged populations in the Third World.[17] However, the Committee on Economic, Social, and Cultural Rights (*CESCR*) has stopped short of holding First World Actors accountable for perpetuating a system that exacerbates conditions of hardship for Third World peoples. By rejecting proposals for structural reform (such

---

[14] Kerry Rittich, "The Future of Law and Development: Second Generation Reforms and the Incorporation of the Social" (2004) at 202, MICHIGAN JOURNAL OF INTERNATIONAL LAW, 26(1).

[15] A good example of this has been efforts at generating Poverty Reduction Strategy Papers aimed at increasing policy ownership in the Third World. These objectives have been internalized through the creation of institutional bodies such as the Poverty Reduction and Growth Facility, now succeeded by the Extended Credit Facility. *See* Extended Credit Facility Fact Sheet, IMF, Available at: https://www.imf.org/en/About/Factsheets/Sheets/2016/08/02/21/04/Extended-Credit-Facility, (Accessed on: 31st May, 2022); *See also,* Graham Hacche, "The Evolving Role of the IMF and the Reduction of Poverty by Graham Hacche," Deputy Director, EXTERNAL RELATIONS DEPARTMENT, IMF, IMF Speech, Available at: https://www.imf.org/en/News/Articles/2015/09/28/04/53/sp021303 (Accessed on 8th July, 2022).

[16] The next section shall address how the coloniality of IFIs since the 17th century has been preserved, and is still reflected in the ongoing engagement of modern IFIs (like the IMF).

[17] In addition to the well documented effects of Structural Adjustment Programmes on socio-economic rights, there is evidence linking SAPs to worsening government respect for all types of physical integrity rights as well. *See* M. Rodwan Abouharb and David L Cingranelli, "The Human Rights Effects of World Bank Structural Adjustment" at 256, INTERNATIONAL STUDIES QUARTERLY, 50(2), WILEY.

as democratizing vote-shares), First World states intentionally maintain institutional arrangements that preserve First World hegemony. The CESCR has instead opted at recommending differential mechanisms aimed at debt relief, as a way of freeing up the fiscal resources of the state to aid its efforts to ensure socio-economic development.[18]

This chapter hopes to contribute to the growing scholarship on the human rights impacts posed by IFI's and the global debt system, by furthering issue-linkages between the IMF and other treaty bodies under the UN. Employing a TWAIL lens, this chapter hopes to interrogate the relationship between the legal regimes supporting global financial arrangements and human rights, and locate the colonial norms undergirding these systems. Part 1 of this chapter shall locate the mutually constitutive and implicative dynamics between the international regimes supporting the debt System, and ESRs, that create barriers to human rights and economic justice for the Third World. Part II of this chapter shall offer novel ways to configure extra-territorial obligations to structurally reform IFIs onto First World Nations for upholding a global financial architecture that violates the economic, and social rights of Third World citizens.

2   A Critical Investigation of the Neo-Colonial Practices of IFIs

The assumption underlying the epistemic frameworks of IFIs is that neoliberal economic policies embodied by the debt system and free trade are necessary mechanisms for economic development. And secondly, that reforming institutional structures that mandate debt repayments (through structural reform, and progressive debt restructuring) are unworkable solutions for both moral and material reasons. This section shall evaluate these assumptions with a view to demonstrating that they're historically inaccurate, empirically unsubstantiated, and rooted in colonial epistemologies that serve to entrench First World hegemony.

---

[18] Statement on the coronavirus disease (COVID-19) pandemic and economic, social and cultural rights by the Committee on Economic, Social and Cultural Rights, Committee on Economic, Social and Cultural Rights, Economic and Social Council UN E/C.12/2020/1 (6 April 2020), Available at: https://digitallibrary.un.org/record/3856957?ln=en (Accessed on 23rd May 2022).

2.1 Analysis of the Implicative Dynamics Subsisting Between Neoliberalism and the Global Human Rights Agenda

2.1.1 THE MAINSTREAMING DISCOURSES OF NEOLIBERALISM   Much of the popularization of neoliberal narratives of growth and development was fueled by the belief that it was responsible for the industrialization of Western nations. Critical scholars and historians have however put to rest the idea that the Anglophone West, and Western Europe produced high levels of accelerated growth and development, predominantly through the institution of neoliberal policies.[19] With the exception of Paraguay, all Latin American states possessed free trade systems and underwent a form of neoliberal reform. However, the British authorities employed protectionist policies to safeguard domestic producers from competition, until 1846 at which point colonial extraction and unjust appropriation had helped them consolidate vastly more economic power than the Third World.[20] Before 1860, only approximately 4 per cent of Europe's population adopted liberal free trade policies.[21] The evidence near universally confirms that the generally referred success cases for neoliberally oriented development are empirically unsubstantiated, and riddled with historical inaccuracies.

The fact that the mainstreaming of neoliberal thought[22] has persisted, despite critical reflections of the aforementioned defects, is quite apropos of its positionality as a hegemonic mode of discourse post the 1970s. The 1980s bore witness to Thatcher and Regan's assault on collectivizing institutions (trade unions, miners associations

---

[19] *Supra* note 4.

[20] Paul Bairoch, "Economics and World History: Myths and Paradoxes" (1995), CHICAGO UNIVERSITY PRESS.

[21] *Ibid.*; *See also Supra* note 4 at chapter 2.

[22] The naturalization of neoliberalism is a process that is both historical and ongoing, with its conceptual basis having become deeply embedded in people's understanding of the world. *See* David Harvey, "Neo-Liberalism as Creative Destruction" (2006) at 146–151,HUMAN GEOGRAPHY, 88(2), 2006, TAYLOR AND FRANCIS, (for a historiography of neoliberalism's effect on institutional reform, and discursive adjustment. Historically speaking, key political figures such as Thatcher and Regan have played a role in constructing global institutional attitudes favoring neoliberal policy shifts); *See* Stephen Metcalf, "Neoliberalism: The Idea That Swallowed The World" (2017), THE GUARDIAN, available at: https://www.theguardian.com/news/2017/aug/18/neoliberalism-the-idea-that-changed-the-world (Accessed on: 26th May 2022).

and unions.), and the slashing of social sector spending. The West's commitment to furthering the neoliberal agenda was greatly assisted by the efforts of US research universities that provided training in neoliberal principles to economists around the world. The era of structural adjustment programmes (as being a conditionality for loan assistance) and the displacement of Keynesian economists with neoliberal monetarists in the IMF, cumulatively produced a global diffusion of neoliberal norms that were as deep as they were wide.[23] To that effect, the relations of political power that produced the Washington Consensus, and academic discourse are a mutually constitutive set of shared phenomena, both of which, acting in concert, have been responsible for dismal economic growth that disproportionately impacts Third World nations.[24]

A critical review of the scholarship discussing the Opium wars, reveals the extent to which colonial knowledge production has shaped common understandings of global conflicts. Academic narratives typically converge around the idea that British imperial logics were manifested through a strong preference to keep trade open through Chinese ports at all costs so as to facilitate the importation of opium.[25] A comparatively lesser amount of attention has been directed at the broader set of practices that constitute the continuing tradition of obviating the Third World's sovereignty through the modalities of trade and debt. Expectedly, neoliberal frameworks

---

[23] Joseph Stiglitz, "Globalization and its Discontents" (2002), NORTON, NEW YORK.

[24] World Commission, 'On the Social Dimension of Globalization 2004: A Fair Globalization: Creating Opportunities for All" (2004), INTERNATIONAL LABOR OFFICE, GENEVA.

[25] While this is certainly true for Chinese scholarship, and select British scholarship on the subject, there have been recent accounts that challenge this account of history. See Hu Sheng, "From the Opium War to the May Fourth Movement, Beijing: Foreign Language" at vol. 1, chap. 3; *See also* for a general treatment of scholarship on the subject of historiographies of the Opium Wars, James L. Hevia, "Review: Opium, Empire, and Modern History," CHINA REVIEW INTERNATIONAL, 10(2), HAWAII UNIVERSITY PRESS. However, the undeniable importance of opium to the British Empire helps contextualize claims around British imperial rapacity as the basis for the trade wars, and this has certainly shaped common-sense understandings of the conflict, See Carl A. Trocki, "Opium, Empire, and the Global Political Economy" (1999) at 208, NEW YORK ROUTLEDGE; For a review of the ways in which China's sovereignty was damaged as a consequence of the Opium Wars by the United States (the Treaty of Wanghia), *see* Teemu Ruskola, "Canton is Not Boston: The Invention of American Imperial Sovereignty" (2005) at 13–20, AMERICAN QUARTERLY 57(3).

have been normalized in the Third World in a manner that's perversely ignorant of the realities of their most vulnerable citizens.[26]

Moreover, while there is acceptance that coercing the entry of a substance such as opium through free trade mechanisms is itself a fundamentally unjust process, it is telling that the moral intuitions underlying such consensus are focused to a greater extent on the substance in question, and not the imperial logics that undergird the larger practice of coercive market entry.[27] This explains the dissonance implicit in the inconsistent claims that converge on accepting that China's treatment by the British is condemnable, while simultaneously maintaining that the IMF and the WTO mandating free trade, as a price of entry into financial and trading systems is a justifiable position legitimated by the epistemics of comparative advantage.

2.2 The Interconnectedness of Human Rights and the Neoliberal Development Agenda
There's a striking disconnect between the idealized narrative around privatization, and studies that disconfirm these insights. And this has been noted by experts like Philip Alston and Leo Heller, who have argued that the neoliberal wave has weakened the right to water and sanitation.[28] The human rights agenda, and ESRs have been significantly eroded by neoliberal policies such as Structural Adjustment Programmes. Despite the apparent conflict between human rights and neoliberalism, neoliberals developed their own account of human rights as moral and legal supports for a liberal market order.[29] This has led to their intertwined presence in trade agreements, and the legitimization of deeply problematic instruments of the international

---

[26] For a review of the gendered effects of the sovereign debt system, see section 2 of Diana Angeret, "Women and Sovereign Debt with a Focus on East Africa," AFRICAL JOURNAL OF INTERNATIONAL ECONOMIC LAW.

[27] This is perhaps explainable by the vilification of drugs through the War on Drugs campaign (a neo-colonial undertaking itself). Paper prepared for the AFSDJN, 2022.

[28] Third Committee, General Assembly, World Altered by Neoliberal Outsourcing of Public Services to Private Sector, Third Committee Experts Stress, amid Calls for Better Rights Protection, GA/SHC/4239, 19th October 2018, Seventy-Third Session, 25th and 25th Meeting, The United Nations, Available at: https://www.un.org/press/en/2018/gashc4239.doc.htm (Accessed on: 28th May 2022).

[29] Shane Darcy, "Review: The Morals of the Market: Human Rights and the Rise of Neoliberalism" (2020) at 10, ID: INTERNATIONAL DIALOGUE, A MULTIDISCIPLINARY JOURNAL OF WORLD AFFAIRS, available at: https://www.un.org/press/en/2018/gashc4239.doc.htm (Accessed on 30th May 2022).

system such as humanitarian interventions[30] and sanctions—which are antithetically oriented to their stated purposes of protecting human rights goals.[31]

Jessica Whyte offers a compelling historiographical account of both neoliberalism and human rights, by exploring how they began to embody a shared vocabulary that is now reflected through international institutions that have hegemonized the language of human rights within the context of its neoliberal agenda. Historically speaking, the role of the Mont Pelerin Society, and the drafting processes of the Universal Declaration of Human Rights, reveal stark breakages between their conceptions of the normative content of human rights. Neoliberal thinkers like Hayek, and the Pelerin Society often hold conceptions of economic, social and cultural rights, (ESCRs), as totalitarian, and a threat to "western civilization."[32] While the Universal Declaration of Human Rights normatively offers an indivisible and unified framework of rights including civil and political rights,(CPRs), and ESCRs, their differentiated status designations in the real world tell a different story. Interest divergence in the post-World-War-II era, and the debate over the relationship between the two sets of rights rendered ESCRs a Cold War casualty, even before the final adoption of the Universal Declaration of Human Rights, (UHDR).[33]

Unlike ESCRs, civil and political rights are compatible with market-oriented reforms that neoliberal policies required, and the derecognition of ESCRs at the international system was noted in the strongest terms by the CESCR at the Vienna World Conference in 1993, *"The shocking reality [is] ... that States and the International Community as a whole contribute to tolerate all too often breaches of economic, social and cultural rights, which—if they occurred in relation to civil and political rights would provoke expressions of horror and outrage and would lead to concerted calls for immediate remedial action"*[34]

---

[30] Agata Kleczkowska, "The Illegality of Humanitarian Intervention: The Case of the UK's Legal Position Concerning the 2018 Strikes in Syria" at 35–49, UTRECHT JOPURNAL OF INTERNATIONAL AND EUROPEAN LAW, 35(1).

[31] Alena Douhan, "Unilateral Sanctions Particularly Harmful to Women, Children, Other Vulnerable Groups, Press Release," UNITED NATIONS, available at: https://news.un.org/en/story/2021/12/1107492 (Accessed on 30th May 2022).

[32] Jessica Whyte, "The Morals of the Market: Human Rights and the Rise of Neoliberalism" (2019), LONDON: VERSO BOOKS.

[33] Phil Alston & Ryan Goodman, "International Human Rights: The Successor to International Human Rights in Context: Law, Politics, and Morals" (2013), OXFORD UNIVERSIT PRESS.

[34] UN Doc. E/1993/22, Annex, III, paras. 5 and 7.

These relations of power, co-constituted by academic discourses supporting neoliberal rights-framings, have had the effect of treating the socio-economic conditions of Third World peoples as disposable resources to utilize while configuring a policy basket that helps stabilize institutional arrangements.[35] The preservation of such profoundly unequal institutional relations, is precisely what entrenches First World hegemony through IFIs like the IMF and World Bank. Despite several recorded failures of Structural Adjustment Programmes, and empirically verified linkages between the IMF's operationality and its adverse effects on ESRs, there has been no serious attempt to structurally reform its organizational structure and operational mandates.

In fact, the IMF in its 2018 Review of Program Design and Conditionality, has itself recognized that the number of structural conditions has risen in the period between 2011 and the end of 2017.[36] These findings have been echoed in its 2018 the IMF's Independent Evaluation Office update on structural conditionality, which identified several issues associated with the lack of country ownership and its associated stigma effects.[37] This is despite the fact that earlier Reviews on Conditionality (in 2007) were more positive of the changing progressive direction of the IMF. Post the COVID-19 crisis, the inequalities both between and within countries have been reinforced greatly, and the imposition of austerity measures as a fiscal response to the pandemic, is particularly pernicious, given its mal-effects on socio-economic rights.[38]

---

[35] Upendra Baxi, "Some Newly Emergent Geographies of Injustice: Boundaries and Borders in International Law" (2016) at 20–21, INDIANA JOURNAL OF GLOBAL LEGAL STUDIES 23(1), available at https://www.repository.law.indiana.edu/cgi/viewcontent.cgi?article=1601&context=ijgls (accessed on 12th July, 2022).

[36] International Monetary Fund, Strategy, Policy & Review Department, "2018 Review of Program Design and Conditionality," IMF, Policy Paper No. 19/102, available at: https://www.imf.org/en/Publications/Policy-Papers/Issues/2019/05/20/2018-Review-of-Program-Design-and-Conditionality-46910 (accessed on 25th May 2022).

[37] G Russell Kincaid & Lamdany Ruben, "IEO, Structural Conditionality in IMF-Supported Programs: Evaluation Update," INTERNATIONAL MONETARY FUND INDEPENDENT EVALUATION OFFICE, available at; https://ieo.imf.org/en/our-work/Evaluations/Updates/Structural-Conditionality-in-IMF-Supported-Programs-Eval (accessed on 26th May 2022).

[38] Nona Tamale, "Adding Fuel to Fire, How IMF Demands for Austerity Will Drive up Inequality Worldwide" (2021) at 16, OXFAM BRIEFING PAPER, OXFAM INTERNATIONAL.

2.3 Review of Colonial Histories, and its Continuities in the IMF and World Bank

The view that there are clear ruptures in time that segregate the world's colonial past from the present, is deeply inaccurate, and is itself a reinforcing factor in the normalization of neo-colonial undertakings. This is of course by design, as colonial epistemologies that shape our perceptions of justice claims are deeply connected with our sense of time, and propositions that seek to establish both historical inequality and its continuing presence in everyday life, are often contested through severing the past, and identifying discrete moments of transition that ultimately result in a neo-liberal linear narrative of history.[39] The IMF exemplifies this phenomenon, as the domination of Egypt, Tunisia, Argentina, and Mexico among many other Third World states that had their economies ravaged, are still subject to the prescriptions set in place by First World actors through IFIs.

These prescriptions are firmly rooted in colonial epistemologies that serve to entrench the First World's hegemony as a whole. The interconnected nature of the First World's power over the Third World is best illustrated through events such as the "offering of Tunisia" by Germany to France, to assuage feelings of public humiliation post France's defeat and subsequent relinquishment of territory (Alsace and Lorraine) to Germany. Another way in which the collective power of the First World was exercised over the Third World, is the creation and utilization of international conventions. Weaponizing debt, as a justification for the use of force in history, on several occasions, the international financial system has historically been complicit in the subjugation of the Global South. For instance, Britain, France, and Spain authorized the use of force, to enforce debt repayments in Mexico.[40]

Implicit in these cases, are a set of colonial norms such as the doctrine of divide and rule, which found themselves embedded in the institutional arrangements that provided both the normative backing and legal precedent required to partition Africa during the Berlin West Africa Conference through international agreements.[41] The

---

[39] This is beafiast evidenced in framings around Black reparations, *See,* Charles P. Henry, "The Politics of Racial Reparations" (2003) at 131–152, Journal of Black Studies, 34(2), Sage Publications.

[40] William H. Wynne, "State Insolvency and Foreign Bondholders: Selected Case Histories of Governmental Foreign Bond Defaults and Debt Readjustments" Vol 2 (1951) at 25, New Haven: Yale University Press.

[41] Matthew Craven, "Between Law and History: The Berlin Conference of 1884–1885 and the Logic of Free Trade" (2015) at 31–32, London Review of International Law.

Memorandum imposed by the Troika in the case of Greece in 1843, articulates precise steps such as the laying off of all civil servants in the national printing office, forest wardens, and most university professors, and the closure of all state health services as a means of ensuring that interest payments could be satisfied.[42] The imposition of austerity measures, and coercive alterations to extant policy frameworks and modes of government organization, in the Third World, and countries such as Portugal, Italy, Ireland, Greece and Spain ensured, is not a discontinuing phenomenon.[43] It is rooted in the deeply unequal relations of the colonial world, that believed the global finance industry was justified (by its very architects) as necessary for its civilizing missions.[44]

To that effect, a perusal of the effects of SAPs on the African Continent reflects similar intrusions on the decisional sovereignty of states. In the case of Tanzania, the health sector has been significantly affected by both the economic crisis, and resultant SAP measures. The share of the health sector in the national budget declined from 7.23 per cent in 1997/89 to 4.62 per cent in 1989/90, creating several issues in terms of intersectoral allocations of resources, and rural healthcare that has been severely deprioritized.[45] Through the imposition of measures such as the abolition of price controls, wage freezes, retrenchment of workers, and a broad-based reduction of government expenditure in social sectors, the ESRs of Tanzanians have been at risk, and this is especially so for vulnerable and disadvantaged communities, such as women and children, and rural populations.[46]

---

[42] Eric Toussaint, "Newly Independent Greece Had an Odious Debt round her Neck" (2016), COMMITTE FOR THE ABOLITION OF ILLEGITIMATE DEBT, available at: https://www.cadtm.org/Newly-Independent-Greece-had-an (accessed on 1st June 2022).

[43] For an excellent review of the implications of Austerity Amidst Debt Restructuring, *see* section 5, Nona Tamale, Debt Restructuring under the G20 Common Framework: "Austerity Again? The Case of Zambia and Chad," AFRICAN JOURNAL OF INTERNATIONAL ECONOMIC LAW.

[44] James Thuo Gathii, "Sovereign Debt as a Mode of Colonial Governance: Past, Present and Future Possibilities, Sovereign Debt Architecture, Suspended, Just Money" (2022), available at: https://just-money.org/about-just-money-page/ (accessed on 13th July, 2022).

[45] For a systematic review of the effects of SAPs on the health sector (and women and children's health in particular), *see* Joe L. P. Lugalla, "The Impact of Structural Adjustment Policies on Women's and Children's Health in Tanzania" (1995) at 47–51, REVIEW OF AFRICAN POLITICAL ECONOMY 22:63, ROUTLEDGE TAYLOR AND FRANCIS GROUP.

[46] *Ibid.; See also,* Hertz, N, "The Debt Threat"(2004), HARPER COLLINS PUBLISHERS.

The IFIs, other development agencies, and the private sector have worked collectively to privatize Kenya's healthcare sector, and this has had devastating consequences for socio-economic minorities who face severe complications finding affordable and accessible healthcare.[47] The profit-oriented incentives of the private sector, deeply undermine the right to health, as less profitable but essential health services stand to neglected.[48] Moreover, the focus of private hospitals is for this reason, likely to be directed towards areas and patients with the most resources.[49]

There is well-documented evidence about the adverse effects of the debt trap and SAPs on the Third World, and the African Continent in particular.[50] To that effect, the deceitfully engineered insistence that neoliberal economic restructuration is effective in generating development carries with it racialized archetypes of the Third World's inability to articulate a vision for its own destiny. Moreover, the production of neoliberal hegemonic discourses has greatly hampered the legitimacy of ESCRs, and helped construct a narrow vision of human rights. The binaries of civil and political rights, and economic and social rights, statist, and neoliberal models of development, and preservation of the debt system (in its current form), and debt repudiation, are themselves reflective of colonial epistemologies. The Western colonial lens tends to structuralize discourse in binary oppositions, that reinforce the narrative that their involvement is justified, leading to the obscuration of critical reflections on policy. More perniciously, these processes are responsible for generating the belief that serious steps towards debt restructuring and institutional reform is neither justified nor effective. The next section shall critically evaluate this proposition.

---

[47] For a comprehensive assessment of gender policies in Uganda, Kenya and Rwanda in the Servicing of Sovereign Debt, *see* Afia Essandoh, "Women and Sovereign in East Africa Debt—A Case Study of Gender Policies in Uganda, Kenya, and Rwanda in Ensuring Gender Equality in the Servicing of Sovereign Debt," African Journal of International Economic Law.

[48] *See* Section 6 of Hakiamii, "Wrong Prescription: The Impact of Privatizing Healthcare in Kenya" (2022), New York Center for Human Rights and Global Justice, Economic and Social Rights Centre, available at https://chrgj.org/kenya-health/.

[49] *Ibid*.

[50] Kentikelenis A, Stubbs T, et al., "Structural Adjustment and Public Spending on Health: Evidence from IMF programs in Low Income Countries" (2015) at 169–176), Soc Sci Med; *See also,* Stubbs T, Kentikelenis A, et al., "The Impact of IMF Conditionality on Government Health Expenditure: A Cross-National Analysis of 16 West African Nations" (2017) at 220–227, Soc Sci Med.

2.4 Institutional Logics Against Progressive Debt Restructuring Processes

There are two sets of arguments levelled against large-scale debt restructuring.[51] Firstly, that endorsing approaches that are aimed at stopping (either temporarily or permanently) private creditors from suing for debt recovery in investor state dispute settlement forums, and national courts, is unjust. And secondly, implied from the unwillingness of IFIs and the First World to undergo serious structural reform, is the view that such measures aren't conducive to development. The ultimately unsuccessful push for the creation of a New International Economic Order, (NIEO), presented one such opportunity to seriously combat this set of arguments, and redesign an international institutional landscape devoid of racial and other inequities.

Emerging from the Non-Aligned Movement, the coalition of newly independent states in the Global South tried to change the rules of the old international economic order and establish an NIEO.[52] They fought for a meaningful conceptualization of self-determination that entailed economic independence, ways to address the balance of payments disequilibrium, and the colonially constituted debt crisis.[53] Legal debates around sovereign debt and its cancellation due to their emergence from a colonial context of subjugation, were an integral aspect of the NIEO movement. To that effect, Special Rapporteur Bedjaoui sought to expand the doctrine of "odious debts"[54] in order to disregard all state debts, unless creditor states could prove that the investment could be dissociated from the colonial context, and that the debt was contracted *after* the expression of need by the colonized populations.

---

[51] For a detailed analysis of the complications and challenges involved in the Sovereign Debt Restructuration Process, see Magalie Masamba, "The Pressing Call for an International Debt Restructuring Framework and the Potential Gains its Creation Will Have for African Countries," Chapter 1 in this book.

[52] Anghie, A, "Imperialism, Sovereignty and the Making of International Law" (2005), CAMBRIDGE: CAMBRIDGE UNIVERSITY PRESS.

[53] This is reflected in the NIEO declaration, United Nations General Assembly, Declaration on the Establishment of a New International Economic Order, A/RES/S-6/3201, Available at: http://www.un-documents.net/s6r3201.htm (accessed on 14th July, 2022).

[54] *Infra* note 86, at 190–192.

Ultimately, the NIEO movement failed to be established, owing to a number of reasons. The inner dynamics of committee work,[55] the contentious international legal landscape (within which there was no agreement within the International Law Commission over whether the jurisdiction of the sub-committee extended to public and private law), and political pressures post the nationalization of Western oil conglomerates, impeded the capacity for genuine norm-generation. Both the moral claim that debt amnesty is unjustified as "one ought to pay their debts," and the material claim regarding its workability to secure development, will be critically reviewed in this section of the chapter.

2.5 *My Moral Claim*

The first thing to note regarding the moral proposition, is that, such an absolutist claim against progressive debt reform is inconsistent even with standard economic theories, let alone, human rights.[56] A core assumption underlying the financial system is that lenders are expected to assume a certain degree of risk while engaging in financial transactions. The view that debt amnesty, or steps to prevent costly lawsuits that have the effect of crippling Third World economies is unjustified, is an unfounded assumption. Historically, banks have enabled incredibly risky transactions, and in the case of Greece, has lent one-hundred-and-twenty per cent of the country's entire annual gross domestic product, to a provisional government that was only just emerging under wartime conditions.[57] Such methods have created devastating institutional design deficits that continue to inhibit state capacity for socio-economic progress.

In fact, the conventional justifications for the imposition of measures such as SAPs, and trade liberalization policies (and its allied negative effects discussed in the previous section) are that they counteract the possibility of commitment-failure

---

[55] Representatives at the ILC had competing incentives to both codify the existing law, and simultaneously perform a legislative function. The empirical work of codifying existing law contradicted their legislative prerogative, given that the rules they identified worked to the advantage of newly independent states.

[56] David Graeber, "Debt: The First 5000 Years," BROOKLYN, NY: MELVILLE HOUSE.

[57] *Supra* note 4, at 52.

given the particular considerations involved in sovereign borrowing (i.e., enforcement issues).[58] The IMF's ability to lend large amounts, and finance the exit of investors seeking high returns in high-risk contexts,[59] perpetuates dynamics of financial dependence, as countries are further incentivized to return to the IMF, or worse yet, private creditors,[60] to enable debt servicing.[61] To that effect, private creditors have played a key role in undermining the sovereignty of several Third World nations.[62] Through (successful)[63] attempts to enforce pari passu clauses, private creditors constrain the nation's ability to service its debts, and simultaneously engage in governance.

---

[58] Marcel Fafchamps, "Sovereign Debt, Structural Adjustment, and Conditionality, Journal of Development Economics" (1996) at 314, 50, ELSEVIER.

[59] "The Impact of The International Monetary Fund: Economic Stability Or Moral Hazard?", Hearing Before the Subcommittee on Monetary Policy and Trade of the Committee On Financial Services, US House of Representatives One Hundred Fourteenth Congress First Session, June 17, 2015, available at: https://www.govinfo.gov/content/pkg/CHRG-114hhrg96996/html/CHRG-114hhrg96996.htm (accessed on 2nd June, 2022).

[60] When debt servicing costs increase, a sub-set of private creditors, namely, vulture funds purchase distressed assets, and worse yet, operate in a "vulture-friendly" global legal framework, *see* section 1.3 Marie Louise F. Aren, "Designing an African Common Position and Strategy on Vulture Fund Litigation," AFRICAN JOURNAL OF INTERNATIONAL ECONOMIC LAW.

[61] Adam Jourdan, Miguel Lo Bianco, "Argentina Faces 1.1 Billion Debt Repayment Deadline as IMF Protests Simmer" (2022), REUTERS, available at https://www.reuters.com/world/americas/argentina-faces-billion-dollar-imf-trip-wire-protests-simmer-2022-01-27/ (accessed on 3rd June 2022); *See also,* Jayati Ghosh, CP Chandrasekhar, "The Roots of Sri Lanka's Debilitating Debt Trap" (2022), THE HINDU, available at: https://www.thehindubusinessline.com/opinion/the-roots-of-sri-lankas-debilitating-debt-trap/article65376335.ece (accessed on 4th June, 2022).

[62] The international landscape of sovereign debt has shifted considerably, and alongside Western IFIs, and private creditors, China has emerged as a key player in sovereign lending. For a comprehensive review of the ways in which the sovereignty and economic health of African states (DRC in particular) has been adversely affected by China, *see* Nciko wa Nciko, "China Have Mercy on the DRC: Is the $509.43 Million Busanga Contract a Barter or an Unsustainable Collateralized Sovereign Debt?", AFRICAN JOURNAL OF INTERNATIONAL ECONOMIC LAW; see also for an extensive review of the specific contractual clauses prescribed by Chinese creditors, Moses Antony Odhiambo, "Legal Risks of Non-Concessional Financing Arising From Chinese Financial Debt," AFRICAN JOURNAL OF INTERNATIONAL ECONOMIC LAW.

[63] Republic of Argentina v NML Capital Ltd, Certiorari to the United States Court of Appeals for the Second Circuit, No. 12-842; *See also,* Supra note 60.

The pari passu clause is a standard clause in public or private international unsecured debt obligations.[64] Typically, the pari passu clause is directed at preventing legal measures which have the effect of preferring one set of creditors over the others, and ensures that there is no discrimination between creditors at a time when the state is unable to pay its dues.[65] There is near consensus that the "rank pari passu" does not imply "pay pari passu".[66] However, in the recent case of *NML v Argentina*, the US Federal District Court and the Second Circuit Court of Appeals, has forbidden Argentina to pay other debts unless it pays NML pro rata.[67] Working in concert, the efforts of private creditors, and IFIs, have crippled both the fiscal resources and decisional sovereignty of Third World nations. In attempt to mitigate risk, nations on the periphery are forced to return to IFIs, and undergo non-democratic neo-colonial institutional shifts in governance and policy structures as a means to survive terrible economic conditions of hardship, that were themselves created as a consequence of colonial subjugation.

In addition to these grounds, there are often compelling human rights perspectives to consider while evaluating the moral claim. At a systems level, it is clear that IFIs have become exemplars of neoliberal hegemony, and have served as a way to entrench First World power, at the cost of the rights of Third World citizens.[68] Taking stock of these challenges against the backdrop of COVID-19, the Human Rights Council, in its resolution 46/8 has recognized the need for reforming the global financial

---

[64] Rodrigo Olivares-Caminal, "The Pari Passu Clause in Sovereign Debt Instruments: Developments in Recent Litigation, in Sovereign Risk: A World Without Risk-Free Assets" at 71, 121–128, BANK FOR INTERNATIONAL SETTLEMENTS, available at https://econpapers.repec.org/bookchap/bisbisbpc/72-23.htm (accessed on 15th July, 2022).

[65] *Encyclopaedia of Banking Law,* (2002).

[66] Mitu Gulati, Kenneth N. Klee, "Sovereign Piracy, The Business Lawyer" (2001) at 56, 635–651; *See also* Lee C. Buchheit, Jeremiah Pam, "The Pari Passu Clause in Sovereign Debt" (2004) at 53, 869, EMORY LAW JOURNAL.

[67] Anna Gelpern, "Contract Hope and Sovereign Redemption" (2013) at 132–149, CAP. MARKETS L. J, 8, available at https://scholarship.law.georgetown.edu/cgi/viewcontent.cgi?article=2324&context=facpub (accessed on 14th July, 2022).

[68] B.S. Chimni, "International Institutions Today: An Imperial Global State in the Making" at 1–5, EUROPEAN JOURNAL OF INTERNATIONAL LAW 15(1).

architecture, to allow nations to respond to the socio-economic repercussions of the pandemic.[69] In fact, the Committee on Economic, Social, and Cultural Rights has even argued that IFIs are bound to comply with human rights that are a part of customary international law, or general principles of international law.[70] Therefore, the view that capital controls and progressive debt restructuration (including repudiation) are unjustified at a principled level of examination, is deeply fallacious. There are plenty of reasons to consider redesigning the international financial architecture more equitably in a manner that is compliant with human rights.

2.6 My Material Claim

Argentina is a good example of the linkage between the suspension of debt, and economic development. Between 2001, and 2005, Argentina's suspension of debt repayments (to the tune of approximately 90 billion dollars) led to sustained development.[71] However, First World states are strongly opposed to such practices, and the IMF's ongoing resistance to serious institutional changes is indicative of the ground reality that it's often-political factors and power consolidation goals that determine what strategies and policies get instrumentalized. It's necessary to situate the responses by Third World states in their proper historical context, as debt repudiation has been an incredibly rare phenomenon.[72]

The material claim against progressive debt reform and institutional reform, is buttressed by the erasure of exogenous explanations of economic crises in the Third World. The debt crisis in the Global South is often directly a product of the Global North's crises. In fact, it's almost always the case that external shocks shape the trajectory of economic crises.[73] A good example of this is the debt crises of Latin American

---

[69] Human Rights Council Res. 46/8, U.N. Doc. A/HRC/RES/46/8 (March 19, 2021).

[70] United Nations Committee on Economic, Social, and Cultural Rights, Public Debt, Austerity Measures and the International Covenant on Economic, Social, and Cultural Rights, New York (2016). *See also*, United Nations General Assembly, Report A/70/274: Extreme Poverty and the Human Rights, New York; 2015: "The organization is a human rights-free zone ... It treats human rights more like an infectious disease than universal values and obligations."

[71] *Supra* note 4 at chapter 1.

[72] A notable exception being Mexico under the mandate of Benito Juarez.

[73] ECLAC 1996, The Economic Experience of the Last Fifteen Years. Latin America and the Caribbean, 1980–1995. Santiago: ECLAC

nations in the 80s, which was in reality, a product of the Federal Reserve's decision to raise interest rates steeply ("Volcker Shock").[74] These observations are often underrepresented in mainstream narratives produced by economic-historical schools of thought,[75] which reinforce neoliberal hegemonic discourses. Resultantly, while the mechanics of the US banking crisis in the 80s is directly responsible for the crisis that afflicted Latin America, it is largely unrecognized as such.[76]

The erasure of such exogenous factors is, both, causally responsible for, and a product of the discriminatory belief that the Third World is accountable for its economic failures. The colonial history of Third World nations struggling to service their debts, and the ensuing violent suppression of independence and national liberation movements has been well documented. It's impossible to disaggregate coloniality from sovereign debt and IFIs, and the genocide of the Paraguayan people is a good example to substantiate this claim.

The state was subjected to a five-year war, and a genocide that eliminated eighty per-cent of its population, for the mere refusal by Paraguay to grant free access to exports from Britain and her allies.[77] The effects of such egregious events have been catastrophic on the Paraguayan consciousness, and on the capacity of the state to heal and progress forward. This has led to the region being overwhelmed by ensuing debt crises constituted through both colonial rule and the practices of neo-colonial IFIs. The increase in total external public debt from 16 billion dollars in 1970 to 442 billion dollars in 2004, helps contextualize the effects of the latter on Paraguay (and the Latin American context as a whole).[78]

---

[74] Jose Ocampo, "The Latin American Debt Crisis in Historical Perspective, Life After Debt" at 12, PALGRAVE MACMILLAN, London, available at https://policydialogue.org/files/publications/The_Latin_American_Debt_Crisis_in_Historical_Perspective_Jos_Antonio_Ocampo.pdf (accessed on 7th June, 2020).

[75] *Supra* note 4; *Supra* note 16 at 5; *See also,* Devlin R., "Debt and Crisis in Latin America: The Supply Side of the Story" (1989), PRINCETON, NJ, PRINCETON UNIVERSITY PRESS.

[76] *Supra* note 64 at 21-22.

[77] Diego Abente, "The War of the Triple Alliance: three explanatory models" (1987), LATIN AMERICAN RESEARCH REVIEW 22(2); *See also* Rosa Luxemburg, "The Accumulation of Capital" (1951), ROUTLEDGE AND KEGAN PAUL LTD, Translated version available at: https://www.marxists.org/archive/luxemburg/1913/accumulation-capital/accumulation.pdf (accessed on 7th June 2022).

[78] *Supra* Note 41 at part 16; See also "The Debt Trap" available at: https://www.cadtm.org/spip.php?page=imprimer&id_article=17553 (accessed on 13th July 2022).

The First World's mainstreaming of narratives that the Third World possesses primitive modes of governance, and lacks the foresight to design institutions and policies, was required to justify their civilizing-colonizing missions—these norms are now firmly entrenched in the normative assumptions of the international system, reflected through the institutional design of modern day IFIs such as the IMF (SAP, resistance to progressive institutional redesign, voting share reform, etc.). And it is precisely this context within which, sets of arguments about, both the alleged amorality and impracticality of debt-amnesty and restructuration arise.

2.7 Extra-Territorial Obligations of First-World Nations to Reform the IMF and World Bank's Institutional Arrangements

In light of the neo-colonial practices and norms that undergird IFIs,[79] it is necessary to consider what principles ought to govern their institutional redesign. The CESCR has, on multiple occasions, articulated a need for IFIs to incorporate human rights norms into their operational practices.[80] There are at least two ways to configure obligations that help in the realization of such a goal. One avenue is to hold the IMF and World Bank directly responsible for the obligations set out in the ICESC. Secondly, First World nations can be made accountable to institutionally redesign the architecture of IFIs in a manner that's conducive to human rights goals. This section of the chapter shall firstly explore the linkages between sovereign debt and ESRs. Secondly, it shall demonstrate that First World nations ought to be held directly accountable for instituting and preserving the application of retrogressive measures, by maintaining the institutional arrangements of IFIs today.

2.8 The Relationship Between Sovereign Debt and Human Rights

Debt repayment places huge stress on Heavily Indebted Poor Countries (HIPC), and crowds out vital investments in health and education.[81] The human rights of the most vulnerable populations are often compromised with increasing poverty, and the

---

[79] Discussed in the previous section.

[80] Francois Gianviti, "Economic, Social and Cultural Rights, and the International Monetary Fund," INTERNATIONAL MONETARY FUND, available at https://www.imf.org/external/np/leg/sem/2002/cdmfl/eng/gianv3.pdf (accessed on; 8th June 2022).

[81] *Supra* Note 12, *See* Cost of Delaying.

creation of budgetary constraints produced through debt servicing requirements.[82] The realization of ESRs, is contingent on social sector spending, directed towards human rights goals. As such, increases in debt repayment reduce the available fiscal space to develop ESRs.[83]

Moreover, the pressure to service debt often induces the institution of austerity programs that pose direct risks to vulnerable households and children.[84] These conditions of hardship have only been exacerbated due to the COVID-19 pandemic, and are responsible for pushing more than 100 million people into extreme poverty.[85] In fact, the situation has reached such dire levels, that Mr. Renato Leao (Chair of the CESCR) urged States to use their voting powers in IFIs to alleviate the financial burden of developing countries through debt relief.[86] Even prior to the pandemic, debt levels were at an all-time high, with the average general government gross debt at about sixty six percent of the GDP. This represents a mammoth twenty-seven per cent increase from 2009 (when it was thirty nine percent of the GDP).[87] Additionally, high debt repayment costs severely reduce the available domestic revenue, to finance social-sector spending (through the budget), and emergency measures.[88]

---

[82] *Ibid.*

[83] In 2019, Angola spent approximately 57 per cent of its annual budget on debt servicing, *see* "World Bank International Debt Statistics, 2021," available at: https://www.worldbank.org/en/programs/debt-statistics/ids/products (accessed on 5th June 2022).

[84] *Supra* note 64 at 1.

[85] World Bank, "Debt Service Suspension Initiative," WORLD BANK BRIEF MARCH 10, 2022, available at https://www.worldbank.org/en/topic/debt/brief/covid-19-debt-service-suspension-initiative (accessed on: 3rd June 2022) (While the debt service suspension initiative produced a suspension of 12.9 billion dollars, it is important to note that only one private creditor participated in the initiative on comparable terms).

[86] OHCHR, Human Rights Treaties Branch, Compilation of Statements by Human Rights Treaty Bodies in the Context of COVID-19, Office of the High Commissioner of Human Rights, Geneva, September 2020, pp. 54, available at https://www.ohchr.org/sites/default/files/Documents/HRBodies/TB/COVID19/External_TB_statements_COVID19.pdf (accessed on 4th June, 2022).

[87] Supra note 72 at 6, and Figure 2 that compiles the general government gross debt in ESA countries, from 2002-2019, sourced from: IMF, World Economic Outlook Database, World Economic and Financial Sur*veys, 20*21, available at https://www.imf.org/en/Publications/WEO/weo-database/2021/April (accessed on: 4th June, 2022).

[88] For an exhaustive review of the composition of Sovereign Debt in Africa, *see* Section 1, Ian Murithii, "The Challenge of Securitization of Public Assets in Loan Contracts and Indentures: What is the Way Forward?", AFRICAN JOURNAL OF INTERNATIONAL ECONOMIC LAW.

Debt servicing as a percentage of revenue has risen from seven per cent in 2010, to twenty-two per cent in 2019, and perhaps more distressing for the Third World, total debt service costs grew at a faster rate than government revenue, in the period between 2010–2019.[89]

The IMF and World Bank's operations (specifically, SAPs) tend to produce deeply negative effects on health equity, food safety, and the financial safety of vulnerable populations such as rural communities.[90] In fact, the spread of market-oriented policies made possible through IFIs has tended to be a strong driver of health inequity.[91] A concern that's only liable to be amplified as a result of the COVID-19 pandemic.[92] Given the wide range of socio-economic concerns that stand to be affected adversely by budgetary allocations that deprioritize social-sector spending, it is clear that ESRs are implicated by the actions of the IMF and World Bank.

In order to understand why human rights considerations have been disaggregated from the issue of sovereign debt, it's necessary to explore the latter's conceptualization in law (specifically, the law governing the succession of debts). Alexander Nahum Sack, whose work (on succession of sovereign debt, and illegitimate, or odious debt) has become the starting point of inquiry for modern rules that govern the issue of debt today, showed how the interests of borrowing nations were subordinated to the interests of private creditors. This hierarchization remains embedded in the institutional arrangements of today. Moreover, it was of little concern to Sack whether the Government was democratic or dictatorial, and the mere presence of a regular government exercising power within the state's territory, was sufficient for debts to transfer to the newly instituted regime. This shifted the scope of discussion

---

[89] *Ibid.*, see p. 22–24.

[90] J. Barry Riddell, "Things Fall Apart Again: Structural Adjustment Programmes in Sub-Saharan Africa" (1992) at 66, THE JOURNAL OF MODERN AFRICAN STUDIES, 30(1); *See* Michael Watts, "Silent Violence: food, famine and peasantry in Northern Nigeria" (1983) at footnote 35, BERKELEY.

[91] Timon Forster, et al., "Globalization and health equity: The Impact of Structural Adjustment Programs on Developing Countries, Social Science & Medicine" at 267, ELSEVIER.

[92] Akinyi J. Eurallyah, "COVID-19 and Balance of Payments Crisis in Developing Countries: Balancing Trade, Sovereign Debt, And Development in Africa's Post-Pandemic Era" at section 2.2.

from considerations of the form of government being transacted with, to questions of the propriety of its use-cases, and of creditor complicity.[93]

These assessments also typically reinforce the extant international system, and authors subscribing to such positions, often quite expressly articulate this view that the preservation of institutional arrangements is a crucial object of their normative frameworks. The O'Connell-Bedjaoui debate on the *universal succession vs clean slate theory,* is a good example of this,[94] and brings to bear the precise sort of dynamics that produced a de-prioritization of human rights concerns. Bedjaoui believed (in line with the decolonization movement) that the political liberation of peoples must be consummated through their economic independence.[95] O'Connell contrastingly believed that settlements ought to be devised in a manner that causes minimal disruption of the world's economic system.[96] He goes onto elaborate in his treatise on state succession, that lenders (predominantly in the First World), maybe affected by a system that truly emancipates the economic agency of Third World states.[97] His work

---

[93] Sarah Ludington, Mitu Gulati, Alfred Brophy, "Applied Legal History: Demystifying the Doctrine of Odious Debts" (2010) at 247–281, THEORETICAL INQUIRIES IN LAW, 11(1); *See also* for a robust discussion of Sack's view, and the effects of diverting the government's foreign exchange reserves to debt service payments, Mitu Gulati, Ugo Panizza, Maduro Bonds, "Sovereign Debt Diplomacies: Decolonization and Sovereign Debt: A Quagmire, Rethinking Sovereign Debt From Colonial Empires to Hegemony" (2021), OXFORD UNIVERSITY PRESS.

[934] Michael Waibel, "Sovereign Debt Diplomacies: Decolonization and Sovereign Debt: A Quagmire, Rethinking Sovereign Debt From Colonial Empires to Hegemony" (2015) at 215, OXFORD UNIVERSITY PRESS.

[95] International Law Commission, Report of the International Law Commission on the Work of its Twenty-ninth Session (UN Doc. A/32/10). New York: General Assembly Official Records. (1977a) at 106; *See also,* United Nations, Summary Record of the Special Committee on Principles of International Law Concerning Friendly Relations and Co-Operation Among States, UN Doc. A/AC. 125/SR.43, New York: General Assembly Official Records at 7; *See also,* Judge Abdulqawi A. Yusuf, Keynote Address 70th Anniversary of the International Law Commission, available at https://legal.un.org/ilc/sessions/70/pdfs/english/ILC_70th_anniversary-KeyNoteAddress-ICJ%20President(5Jul18).pdf (accessed on 11th July, 2022).

[96] O'Connell, "Recent Problems of State Succession in Relation to New States" (1970) at 148,THE HAGUE ACADEMY OF INTERNATIONAL LAW (ed), Collected Courses of the Hague Academy of International Law, Leiden: Brill.

[97] *Ibid.* at 149.

is replete with paternalistic, racial analogies that seek to compare the conditions of Third World states as they underwent decolonization, to a child (i.e., Third World) born into a society (First World) and is subjected to it by virtue of the order of being in which it is integrated.[98]

2.9 First World Accountability—Preservation of Institutional Arrangements within the IMF and World Bank

Despite strong reasons to hold First World states responsible for the relations of inequality that they manufacture, between them and the Third World, (mediated through IFIs) there is much resistance due to the colonial assumption of methodological nationalism that undergirds the international system.[99] The previous sections definitively establish the myriad ways in which the neocolonial norms and practices of the IMF and World Bank, violate the ESRs of Third World citizens. In a deeply globalized world, where policy decisions and information flows emanating from developed countries have massive ramifications on the rights of Third World citizens, it is necessary to consider alternative pathways to holding state actors accountable for the direct-transboundary effects of their conduct.[100]

Extraterritoriality refers to the competence of a state to make, apply, and enforce rules of conduct in respect of persons, property or events beyond its territory.[101] Establishing extra-territorial jurisdiction in law, is a means to such an end. The ICCPR specifically constraints the application of the treaty on a territorial basis. Comparatively,

---

[98] He argued that, "in a highly complex international society, the need for continuity and stability is more necessary than ever"; *See* O'Connell, "The Role of International Law" (1970) at 49–65, S. HOFFMAN (ED), CONDITIONS OF WORLD ORDER, BOSTON: HOUGHTON MIFFLIN.

[99] Overwhelming support for the belief that the nation-state is the perfect category for organizing social life, *see* Sassen S, "Analytic Borderlands: Race, Gender, and Representation in the New City, In Representing the City: Ethnicity, Capital, and Culture in the Twenty First Century Metropolis" at 183–202, ed. AD KING, NEW ORK: NY UNIV: PRESS.

[100] Obiora C. Okafor, Report of the Independent Expert on Human Rights and International Solidarity, A/RES/76/167

[101] Menno T Kamminga, Extraterritoriality, *Max Planck Encyclopaedia of Public International Law,* available at https://opil.ouplaw.com/view/10.1093/law:epil/9780199231690/law-9780199231690-e1040 (accessed on 15th July).

the argument for extra-territoriality is much stronger in the case of the ICESCR than even the ICCPR, given that there is no specific constraining on the grounds of jurisdiction and territory while laying out the scope and application of the treaty.[102]

Additionally, the Preamble of the ICESCR references Art. 55 and 56 of the UN Charter, i.e., *"to promote universal respect for, and observance of, human rights and freedoms."*[103] The formulation of Art. 2(1) makes it clear that the international community is possessed of the duty to cooperate in the realization of ESCRs. Moreover, the obligation to respect (not to undertake retrogressive measures that actively violate the infringement of Covenant rights) has been interpreted extra-territorially by the CESCR in General Comment No. 24.[104] Keeping in line with such assessments, the CESCR has specified that states may not deliberately take retrogressive measures that hinder the realization of ESCRs, in General Comment No. 3.[105] When First World states choose to preserve institutional configurations by refusing to work towards structural reform (i.e., progressive debt restructuration and vote-share democratization), they continue to disempower the rights of Third World states.

Another important factor to consider, is that the CESCR has recognized the particular circumstances surrounding the pandemic and has more generally recognized the extra-territorial nature of the right to health. Although the CESCR has recognized the extra-territorial obligations of developed states to avoid limiting exports of medical equipment, and the role of international cooperation (through COVAX) to reduce vaccine distribution inequities, it falls short of recognizing the obligation to structurally reform IFIs, and merely suggests differential mechanisms of debt relief. The General Comment on the right to health, even stipulates that, "States Parties should refrain at all times from imposing embargoes or similar measures restricting

---

[102] Art. 2(1) of the ICESCR.

[103] For a comprehensive review of the ways in which the UN is itself a site of transformation for the sovereign debt architecture, *see* Kevin Mbithi, "Supervising Sovereign Debt Restructuring Through The United Nations," AFRICAN JOURNAL OF INTERNATIONAL ECONOMIC LAW.

[104] ICESCR General comment No. 24 (2017) on State obligations under the International Covenant on Economic, Social and Cultural Rights in the context of business activities, E/C.12/GC/24, (10 August 2017) ¶ 26.

[105] ICESCR General Comment No. 3, The Nature of States Parties' Obligations Art. 2, Para 1, of the Covenant, E/1991/23, Committee on Economic, Social, and Cultural Rights.

the supply of another state with adequate medicines and medical equipment."[106] Insofar as the CESCR holds that measures restricting the supply of medicines, are violative of the right to health, debt amnesty ought to be a right, as debt servicing costs adversely affect the realization of the right to health. And connectedly, First World States who maintain such institutional arrangements ought to be obligated to reform such structures, in a manner that is consistent with the duty to prevent.

International and regional courts have validated these positions, by describing the general character of legal obligations, and the conditions in which they accrue onto state parties. To that effect, the Inter-American Court in *Velasquez Rodriguez v Honduras,* clarified that the state could be held in violation of its duty to prevent such violations from occurring *even in the absence of a causally attributable link* that verifies the state's commissioning of the violation.[107] Given that the Committee has also recognized in the same vein, that debt relief mechanisms ought to be incorporated while addressing the pandemic, it is necessary to consider the different ways in which the international debt system is perpetuating conditions of economic hardship that hinder the ability of Third World states to realize their ESCR goals. Therefore, it is perhaps necessary to consider the ways in which IFIs hamper the realization of ESRs by Third World states, as direct violations of the right to health (given the COVID-19 pandemic), and other allied socio-economic rights that are implicated. To that effect, it's crucial to hold the First World states directly accountable for creating and maintaining an institutional environment (the IMF and World Bank) that facilitates such rights violations.

Concluding Remarks

The human rights system has been fairly responsive to novel contexts that call for reinterpretations which innovatively utilize strategic linkages between different rights regimes. For instance, sexual orientation and gender identity rights cleverly applied

---

[106] ICESCR General Comment No. 14: The right to highest attainable standard of health (art. 12), 4 July 2000, E/C.12/2000/4; 8 IHRR 1 (2001), *see* para 41.

[107] Velásquez Rodríguez Case, Inter-Am.Ct.H.R. (Ser. C) No. 4 (1988), Inter-American Court of Human Rights (IACrtHR), 29 July 1988, available at: https://www.refworld.org/cases,IACRTHR,40279a9e4.html (accessed on 3rd June 2022).

CPR protections, and helped herald global recognition that conversion therapy is a form of torture (Convention Against Torture),[108] and that the death penalty for homosexuality, was itself patently arbitrary and unreasonable, and a violation of the ICCPR.[109] Similarly, the right to water now finds itself within the confines of the ICESCR, despite it not being mentioned through the entirety of the Covenant's text.[110] Sovereign Debt as a colonially constituted category and its allied negative effects (e.g., debt servicing, SAPs), and the constraints it places on social-sector spending, collectively amplify extant inequities in the international political order. It is clear now more than ever that institutional redesign is of categorical import, when Third World nations are stressed to meet debt repayments while simultaneously navigating a global pandemic.

The colonial character of IFIs that helped establish the global financial architecture within which colonial-extractive epistemologies were ossified into legal regimes, is itself a reason to consider investigating novel ways to recognize the rights of Third World citizens. Their historical treatment has helped obtain a political identity that entails a relegated status-designation, which has resulted in reduced economic agency.[111] The self-determination project in that sense, is incomplete given the undemocratic nature in which nations have been forced to reorient their governance structures, and the deeply racialized engagement of First World states (who possess disproportionately more voting power) that place the most vulnerable populations

---

[108] UN Independent Expert on Protection Against Violence and Discrimination Based on Sexual Orientation and Gender Identity, Report on Conversion Therapy, UN Office of the Independent Expert, A/HRC/44/53, 1 May 2020 available at https://www.ohchr.org/en/calls-for-input/reports/2020/report-conversion-therapy (accessed on 4th June 2022).

[109] UN Office of the High Commissioner for Human Rights, Born Free and Equal: Sexual Orientation and Gender Identity in International Human Rights Law, HR/PUB/12/06, September 2012, UN OHCHR, available at https://www.refworld.org/docid/5065a43f2.html (accessed on 3rd June 2022).

[110] Committee on Economic, Social, and Cultural Rights, Substantive Issues Arising in the Implementation of the International Covenant on Economic, Social, and Cultural Rights, General Comment No. 15, UN CESCR, E/C.12/2002/11, 20th January 2003 available at https://www2.ohchr.org/english/issues/water/docs/CESCR_GC_15.pdf (accessed on 5th June 2022).

[111] For a consideration of how this applies to the coloniality of migration, *see* Prof. Achiume's claims concerning the E. Tendayi Achiume, Migration as Decolonization, STANFORD LAW REVIEW, 71. 1509, *See* p. 1552.

within the Third World in an all-consuming debt trap that inhibits them from realizing the ESRs of Third World citizens.

Recognizing the extra-territorial obligations of First World nations that preserve unequal institutional arrangements, is crucial in three broad respects. It is firstly a step in the direction of long-awaited structural reform that addresses inequities in the current financial system. Secondly, this interpretation that imputes extra-territorial obligations onto First World states moves the conversation from the specific to the general. This is in part a result of the fact that the underlying and immediate factors that explain the deprivation and breach of ESCRs, are more accurately described, i.e., that the rights-violation is causally attributed to the specific conduct of First World actors. It is also due to the establishment of a novel legal base to hold such actors accountable.

In doing so, it addresses the core issue, which is, that the IMF and World Bank, in many ways encapsulate extractive neo-colonial epistemologies that underlie the normative frameworks internalized by the debt system. Thirdly, extra-territorial obligations move the jurisprudential goal post closer to a broader universalized mandate of rights-recognitions (that the UDHR envisioned). The inclusion of ESCRs into mainstream discussions of the rights of citizens, is both principally and practically a response to neoliberal hegemonic discourses, that were responsible for the hierarchization of the human rights system. By securing the economic agency of Third World citizens, these strategies provide the gateway for meaningful and complete decolonization.

Index

A

African Continental Free Trade Area (AfCFTA)   46, 47, 73
African Development Bank (AfDB)   xix, 45, 61, 90, 92, 107, 270
African Sovereign Debt Forum (ASDF)   xv, 45
Angola Model   272
Arbitration Agreements   112, 113, 117, 120, 125
Austerity measures   xii, xviii, xxii, 43, 154, 157, 158, 159, 160, 163, 165, 166, 178, 310, 312

B

Balance-of-payment (BOP)   xviii, xix, 62, 187, 240, 314
Brady Bonds   41, 56, 89, 90
Bretton Woods Conference   197, 202

C

Chad   xviii, xxii, 29, 32, 44, 86, 153, 154, 155, 156, 159, 160, 161, 162, 262, 270, 276
Champerty, doctrine of   59, 60, 80, 95, 99, 100
Collateralized Future Receipt (CFR) Arrangements   263, 266, 267
Collective action clauses (CACs)   xvi, 63, 64, 95, 100, 108, 120
Coloniality   319
Common African Position (CAP)   xvi, 53, 71, 72, 73, 76, 77
Common Framework for Debt Treatments beyond the DSSI (The Common Framework)   xii, xv, xxii, 32, 33, 34, 44, 66, 153, 154, 155, 156, 157, 160, 161, 162, 166, 276
Credit Ratings   54, 91, 246, 271, 274

D

Debt amnesty   315, 326

Debt contracts 55, 57, 59, 63, 97, 110, 275
Debt Relief Act (DRA) 68, 98
Debt Relief for a Green and Inclusive Recovery (DRGIR) xv, 37, 39, 48
Debt Service Suspension Initiative (DSSI)
 xv, 31, 62, 153, 155, 176, 276
Debt servicing xviii, 154, 155, 162, 182, 206, 207, 217, 219, 220, 222, 236, 238, 240, 248, 258, 303, 316, 321, 322, 326, 327
Debt Sustainability xi, xv, xvii, xviii, xxii, 32, 45, 46, 47, 61, 62, 65, 77, 87, 111, 120, 128, 154, 157, 162, 163, 164, 165, 175, 211, 217, 218, 219, 236, 269, 273, 274, 276
Debt sustainability assessments (DSA) xxii, 128, 274
DOVE Fund (Debts of Vulnerable Economies Fund) xv, 37, 38, 39, 48, 107

E

Emergency circumstance clauses 82
Equitable treatment of creditors xiii, 67, 111, 127
Ethiopia 28, 29, 32, 44, 53, 86, 90, 153, 228, 257
Exit Consents and Amendments xvi, 63, 95, 103, 108

F

Fiscal Agency Agreements (FAA) 104, 105
Fiscal consolidation xii, 157, 160, 162, 175
Foreign Direct Investment (FDI) 137, 170

G

General Agreement on Tariff and Trade (GATT) xviii, 169, 184, 186, 187, 188, 189. 190, 191, 193, 194, 195

H

Holdout creditors 52, 54, 59, 69, 98, 100, 102, 103, 104, 111, 119, 133, 138, 152
Human rights impact assessment 47, 48

I

Intercreditor competition 120, 121
International Bank for Reconstruction and Development (IBRD) 197, 203
International commercial arbitration 112, 114, 134, 138
International Court of Justice 215
International Development Association (IDA) 203
International financial institutions (IFIs) xiii, xxi, 36, 158, 277, 302

Investment treaty arbitration   110, 112, 113, 114, 115, 117, 136

K
Kenyan High Court   209
Kenyan SGR project   263, 264, 267, 272, 275

M
Marketable Collateralized Instrument   260, 261
Model Pari Passu Clauses   xvi, 108
Mozambique Tuna Bond scandal   123

N
Natural Disaster Clauses   xvi, 95, 100, 105, 106
Neoliberalism   308, 309
New International Economic Order (NIEO)   314, 315
Non-Commodity Related Assets   259, 263, 278
Non-Marketable Collateralized Instrument   260, 261

O
Odious debt   210, 302, 314, 322

P
Pari-passu clause   81, 95, 104, 108, 316, 317
Paris Club Creditors   65, 256

R
Reform of debt restructuring architecture   xvi, 27, 74, 159,
Regional integration   46, 75
Resource Backed Loans (RBLs)   259, 260, 261, 262, 263, 268, 269, 270, 271, 273, 274, 276
Right to development   81, 82

S
South Africa   33, 49, 125, 170, 197, 210, 222, 223, 228, 238, 246, 248
Sovereign debt default   57, 61, 132, 135
Sovereign Debt Restructuring Mechanism (SDRM)   xii, xv, xxii, 40, 62, 87, 95, 96, 97, 107, 155, 159
Special and Differential Treatment (SDT)   xix, 189, 192, 193, 194, 195
Special drawing rights (SDR)   178, 181, 246
State Owned Enterprises (SOEs)   161, 262
Structural reform   xi, xxi, 36, 304, 305, 314, 325, 328
Sudan   29, 30, 86, 197, 262
Sustainable development goals (SDGs)   xxii, 71, 162

T
Third World Approach to International Law (TWAIL)   xix, xxi, 88, 198, 199, 200, 201, 305

Trusteeship   63

U

Uganda   29, 90, 264, 266, 273, 274, 293

UNCTAD (United Nations Conference on Trade and Development)   xii, xviii, xix, 33, 35, 66, 132, 165, 204, 214, 215, 217, 219, 220

United Nations Committee on Economic, Social and Cultural Rights (CESCR)   304, 318,

United Nations General Assembly (UNGA)   96, 212

V

Vulture Fund   xvi, xvii, 49, 50, 51, 52, 54, 55, 57, 59, 60, 61, 79, 87-95, 97-107, 115, 117, 119, 120, 138

W

World Trade Organization (WTO)   xviii, 169, 184-195, 308

Z

Zambia   xv, xviii, xxii, 28, 29, 30, 44, 50, 68, 86, 94, 128, 153, 154, 156, 159, 160, 161, 162, 195, 234, 235, 236, 239, 248, 257, 262, 269, 290

Zimbabwe   30, 86, 264, 273

Afronomicslaw.Org Editors

James Thuo Gathii is the Wing-Tat Lee Chair of International Law at Loyola University Chicago School of Law, and the 2022-23 William H. Neukom Fellows Research Chair in Diversity and Law American Bar Foundation

Olabisi D. Akinkugbe is the Viscount Bennett Professor of Law and Associate Professor (as of July 1) at the Schulich School of Law, Dalhousie University. He is also co-editor-in-chief of the African Journal of International Economic Law; and International Decision section editor, American Journal of International Law.

Titilayo Adebola is a Lecturer in Law at the University of Aberdeen, Associate Director of its Center for Commercial Law and President of the African International Economic Law Network.

Ohio Omiunu, Reader/Associate Professor in Law Kent Law School, University of Kent, Canterbury.